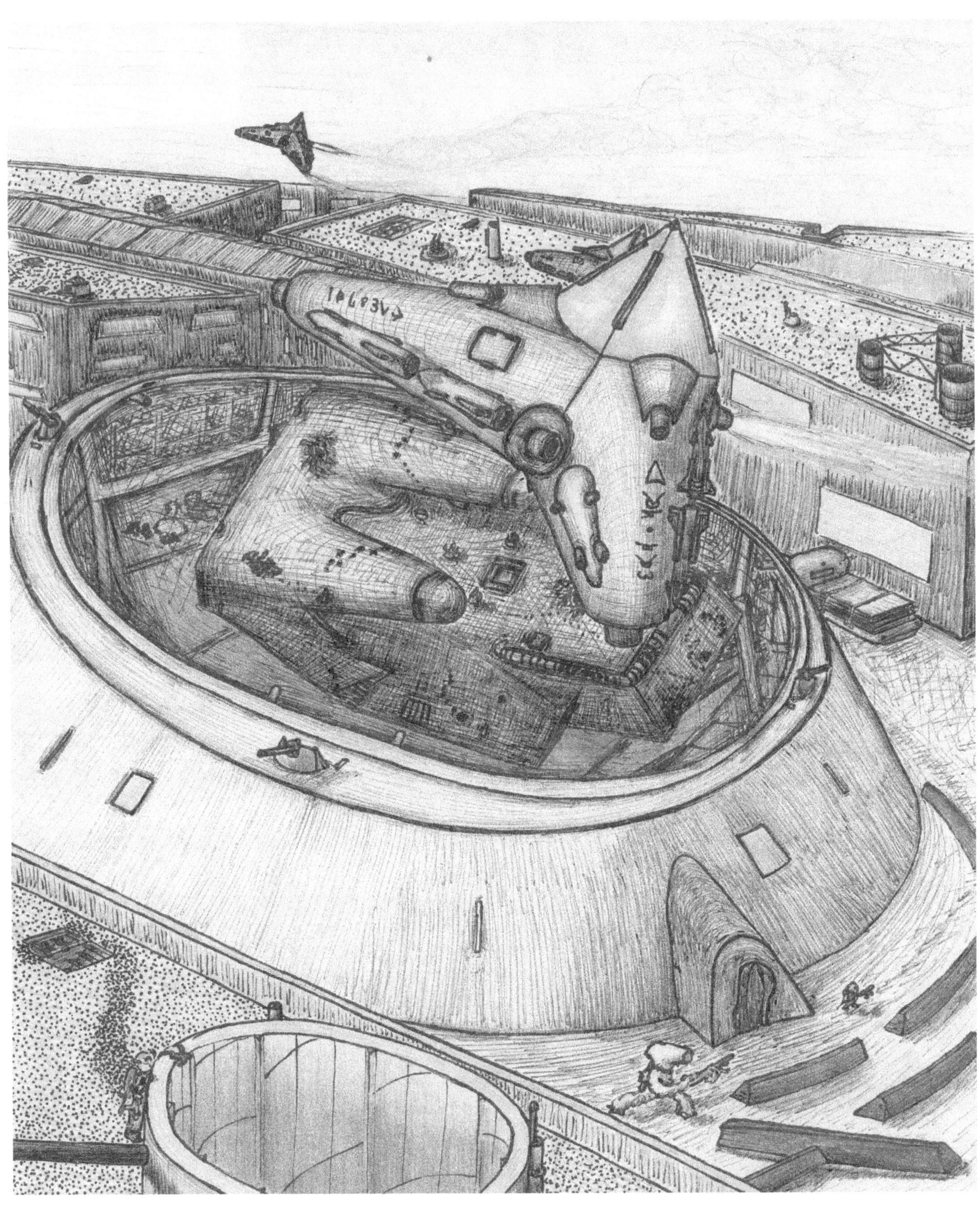

In Need of Repairs

LONE SOLDIER APPENDIX

SCHEMATICS VOLUME II:
CONSOLIDATION TO THE YOUNG CONFEDERATION

by Reliĉ Kimah

a Pleiades Publications imprint

ACKNOWLEDGEMENTS

All the schematics included here, and related sketches not printed, are my work. I spent considerable time developing the science behind mechanisms and background for these fictional vehicles and facilities, and while I have no skill with three-dimensional programs outclassing my drawing, I can say my designs are as original and realistic as the genre allows.

That said, I cannot claim all the credit for the designs and inspirations. Many of these ships began as Lego constructions of my friends'. Tangents detailed here are partially or entirely wrought from their minds, and included in my stories with their gracious permission. They have given me ideas I could never have had alone, which have enriched my story arc infinitely. I am grateful for their effort, their creativity, and their consultation—even if their ships and such resisted my efforts to line up.

Table of Contents

se non è vero, è ben trovato

Preface

What follow are my musings for schematics I have drawn to date with the corresponding schematics. Some have been simulated in the three-dimensional modeling system as well as going through stages of development in concept and on paper (to say nothing of the few requiring more than one final version before presented as seen here). There is a spoiler alert for some of these, so be warned.

None of these schematics are really necessary to further the *Lone Soldier* story arc, but they provide some material for new ideas or help me to remember the old ones. If one is interested, they give some reasoning into ships and constructions of the story arc, as well as the fictional races who built them. Most of the ships and other vehicles were built of Legos by close friends or myself. Once on paper they were modified slightly by will or simple Human error, but I tried to capture the essence of one's intended function and systems.

Upon (relative) completion of the schematics list, I attributed a symbol to each. Each is part of the standardized codified symbology for all recognized craft classification. There are thirty-three overall categories: fourteen are further designed as short- or long- range, and a list of four specific symbols exist for facilities, ground-based if not necessarily on a planet.

Seoreh Ybedäm Confederation Codified
Symbols Denoting Recognized Constructs

Terrestrial Designations

Aircraft

	fighter, short-range
	fighter, long-range
	bomber, short-range
	bomber, long-range
	nautical ship (military) short-range
	nautical ship (military) long-range
	nautical ship (civilian) short-range
	nautical ship (civilian) long-range

Facilities

	manufacture
	habitation
	mixed
	defense

Other

Mining Units	
	labor unit
	habitation
	mixed
Satellites	
	energy
	sensor
	communications
	habitation
	defense
Weapons	
	short-range
	long-range

Seoreh Ybedäm Confederation Codified
Symbols Denoting Recognized Constructs

Spacecraft

Symbol	Construct	Symbol	Construct
	fighter, short-range		capital ship (mixed)
	fighter, long-range		communications ship
	bomber, short-range		energy ship
	bomber, long-range		messenger, short-range
	transport (goods) short-range		messenger, long-range
	transport (goods) long-range		scout
	transport (beings) short-range		private commercial transport
	transport (beings) long-range		exploration craft, short-range
	transport (mixed) short-range		exploration craft, long-range
	transport (mixed) long-range		ramship, short-range
	supply ship short-range		ramship, long-range
	supply ship long-range		escape unit
	frigate		special functions assembly
	capital warship		

# Set 20:
Unremitting

An earlier grand design, the *Unremitting* was the Kvhingleyemlit's attempt to crush the Resistance and subdue rivals with one massive, powerful ship. When I first saw it, I immediately wanted it as a cargo vessel, but I needed first to sketch it out as an attack craft. For *Lone Soldier* space in this time, it is massive. It took an alliance of Resistance and related groups to force this ship into an atmosphere, where it is less maneuverable, and pummel it until the ship was destroyed. Given this, and the fact its very existence helped resisting groups unite against the parasite, the Kvhingleyemlit did not order another dreadnaught.

Even while being built, the Shipbuilders considered the escape pods a bit ridiculous. But the parasite thought officers should be able to fire at their enemy… and if they could command from where they could flee at a moment's notice, why not?

The nascent Resistance front briefly made a frightening campaign on the Gaepvihn that reminiscent of the war's opening years. When this campaign ceased, serious talk began about a unified central Gaepvihnyemlit. It was this unified parasite command which could best destroy the Resistance and threatened to do so prior to the conclusion of the coeval *Lone Soldier* novella.

Gluk Incuis-class dreadnaught B5C-1 Unremitting

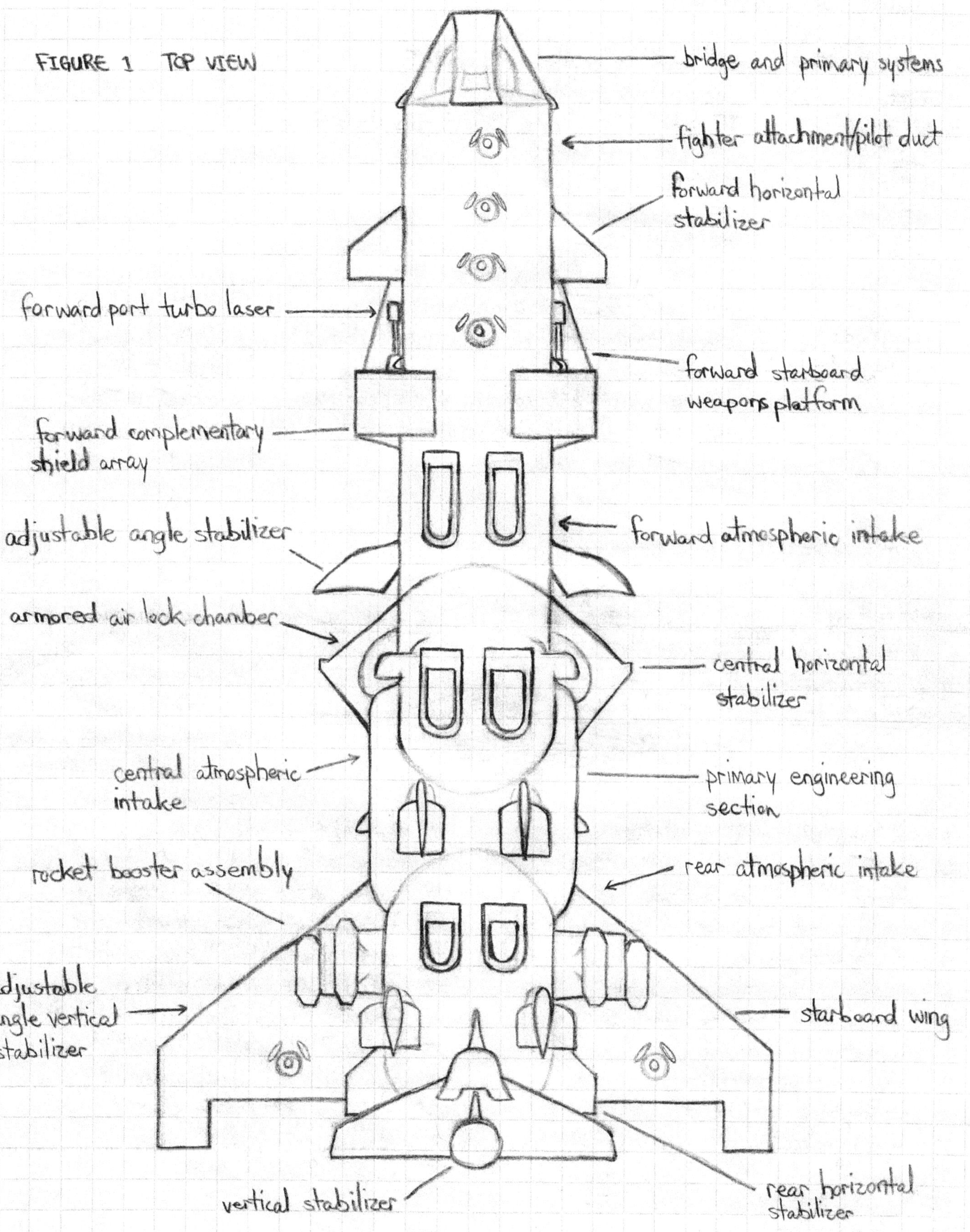

Gluk B5C-1 *Unremitting*

CLASSIFICATION: battle-worthy capital ship grade 5
TYPE: Incuis-class dreadnaught
CREW: 12 total (3 officers, 3 enlisted, six fighter pilots)
LENGTH: 314 standard feet
WIDTH: 204 standard feet
HEIGHT: 99 standard feet
BEAM: 24 standard feet
MASS: 181,890 standard mass units
ARMOR: reinforced steetonicarb and pyroceramite hull, 4gen EM shields
ENGINES: six electromagnetic reciprocating turbines (two anti-gravitational)
ARMAMENT: two forward turbo laser cannon, two forward missile tubes, two tri-barrel laser cannon, four rear missile and rocket batteries, two external personnel weapons stations, EM countermeasures, nine pod laser cannons

CUTAWAY: FORWARD WEAPONS PLATFORM

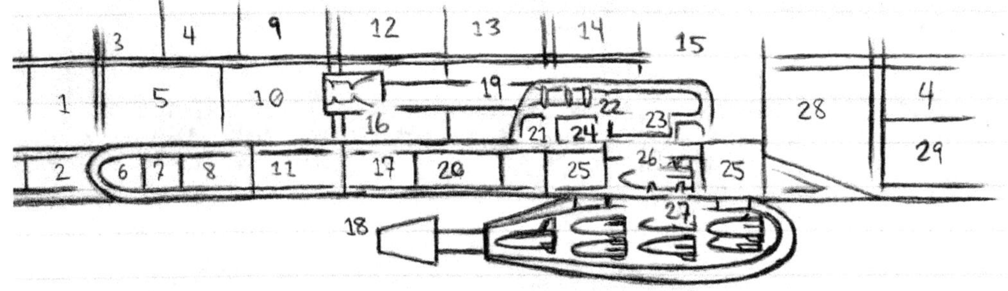

1 auxiliary pilot duct regulator
2 escape pod monitoring computer
3 internal frame construction
4 shield distributor capacitor array
5 atmosphere tank
6 weapons targeting computer
7 propulsion-targeting interface
8 navigation-communications interface
9 life support computer
10 atmosphere scrubber
11 time equalization field generator
12 memory computer systems
13 communications encoding computer

14 power regulation interface
15 forward complementary shield array
16 turbo laser cannon beam emitter
17 sensor array
18 forward missile tube
19 turbo laser cannon beam disbursal tube
20 turbo laser power regulator
21 turbo laser angle adjuster
22 turbo laser cannon beam generator
23 turbo laser cannon battery
24 forward missile loading mechanism battery
25 forward missile loading mechanism servo
26 forward missile loading mechanism
27 forward port missile battery
28 stored water tank
29 engine capacitor array

Gluk Incuis-class dreadnaught B5C-1 *Unremitting*

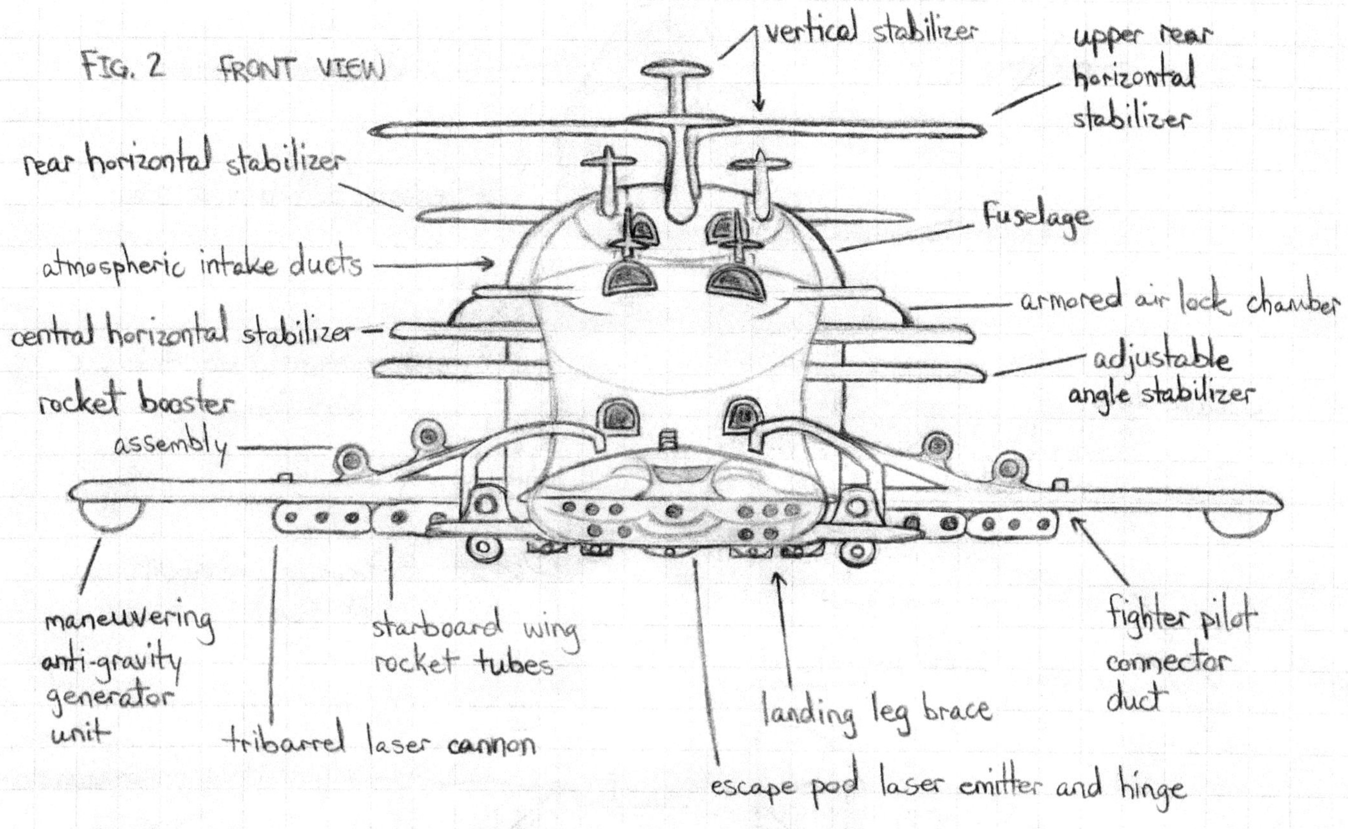

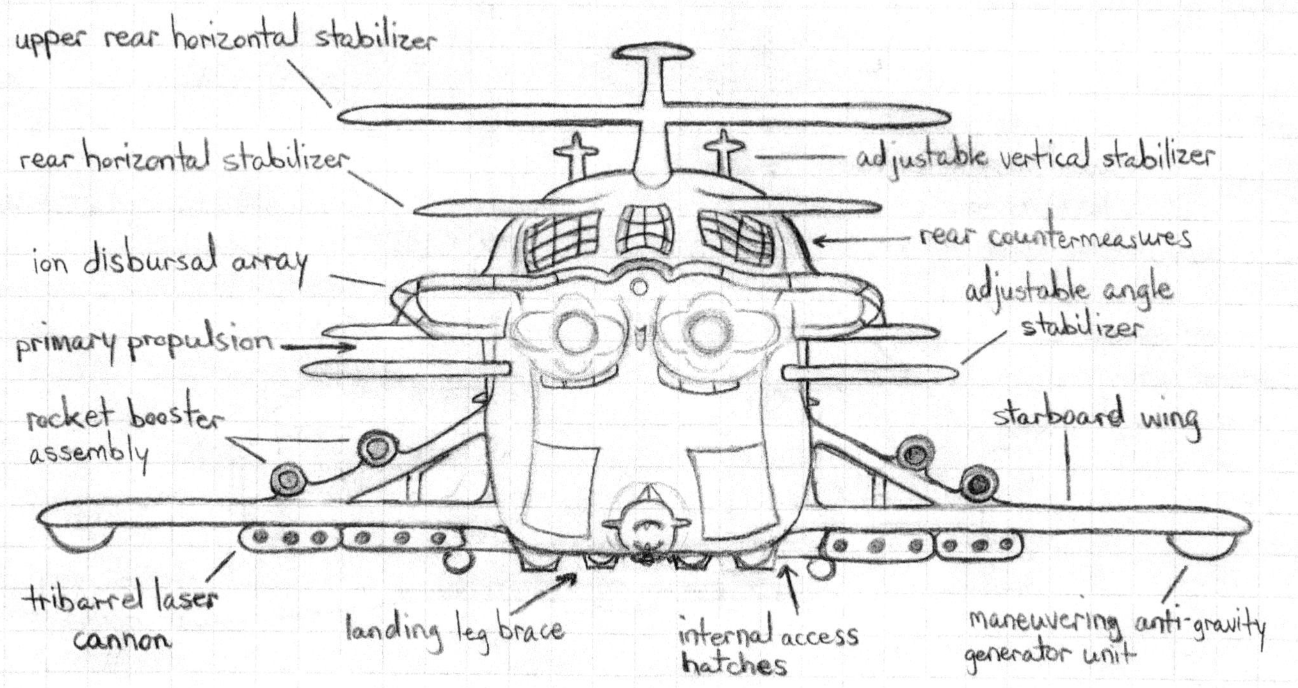

Gluk Incuis-class dreadnaught B5C-1 *Unremitting*

FIG. 4   BOTTOM VIEW

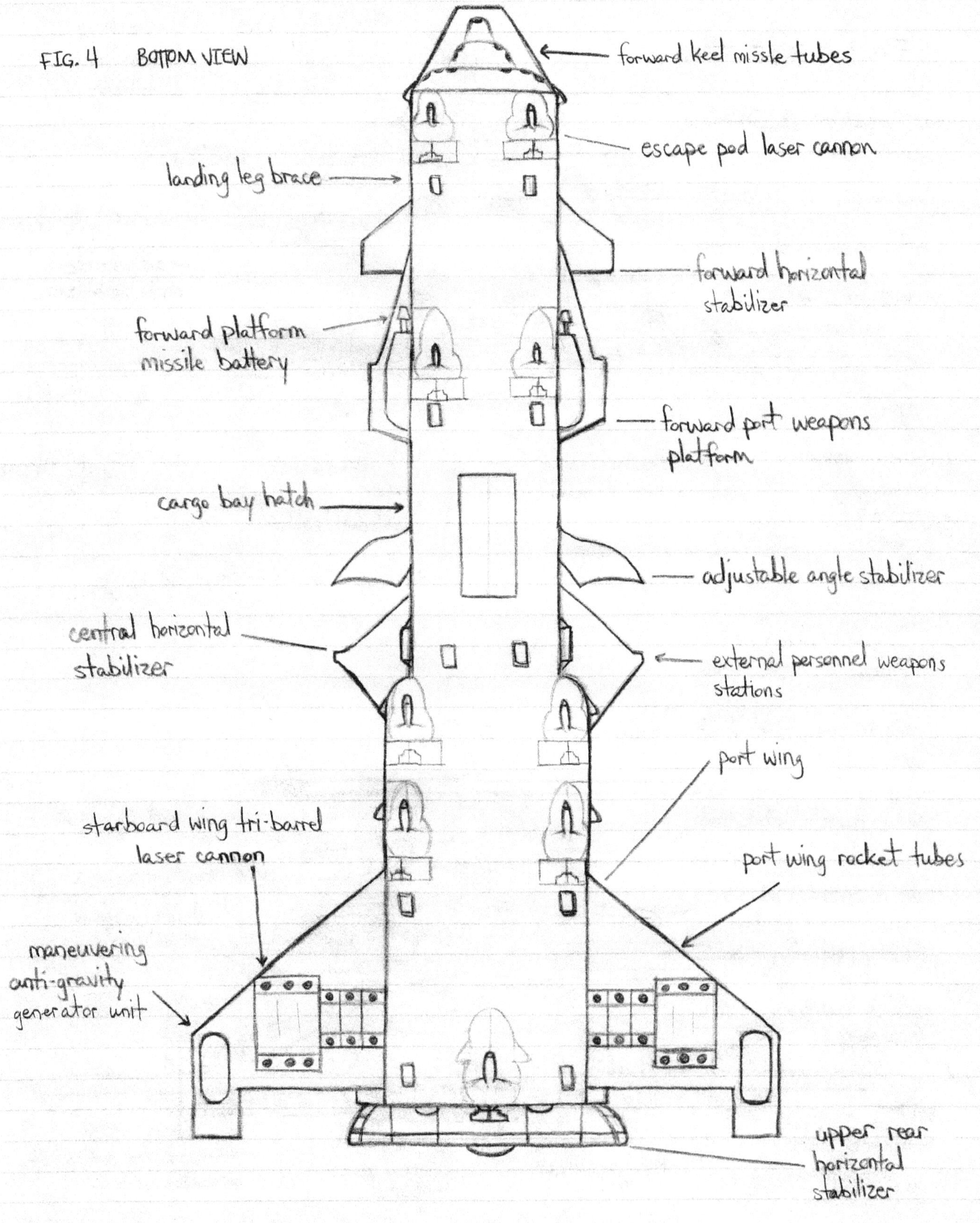

Gluk Incuis-class dreadnaught B5C-1 Unremitting

FIG. 5 SIDE VIEW

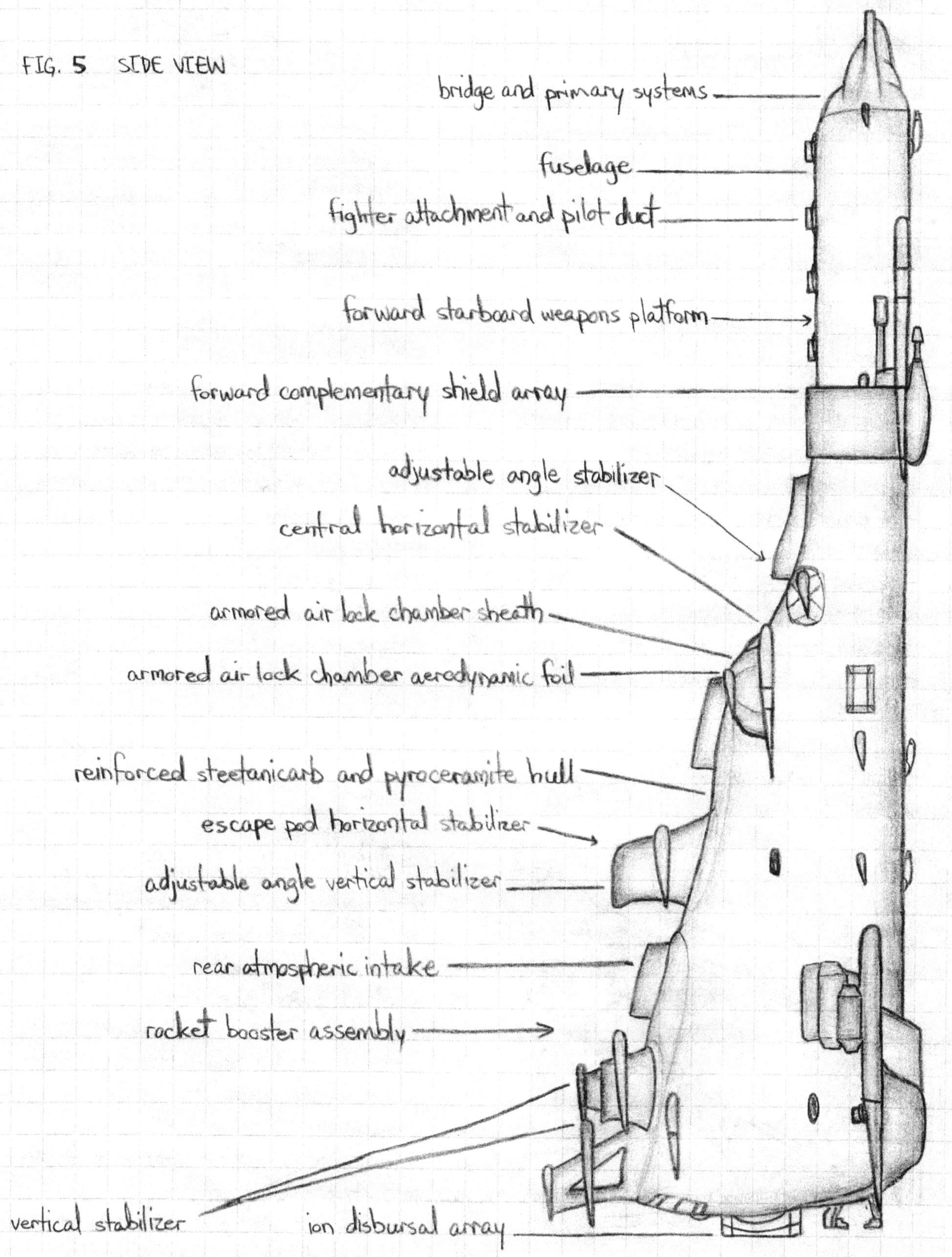

CUTAWAY: FIGHTER ATTACHMENT AND PILOT DUCT

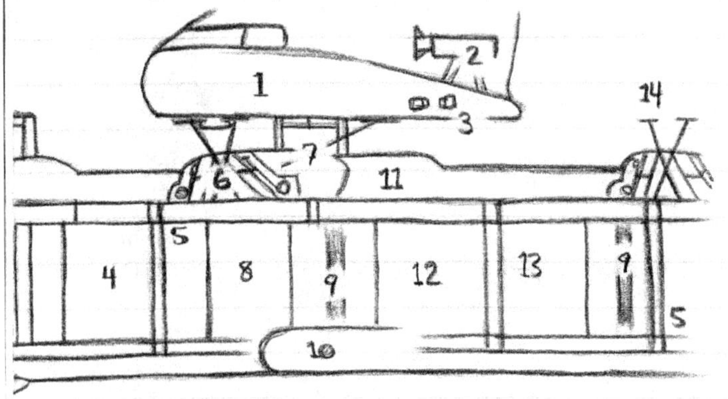

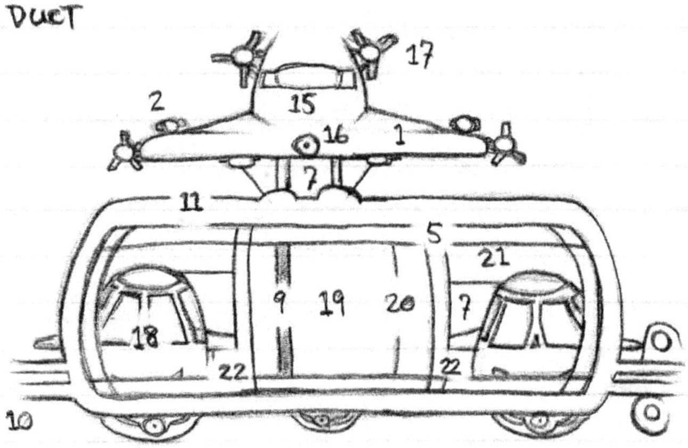

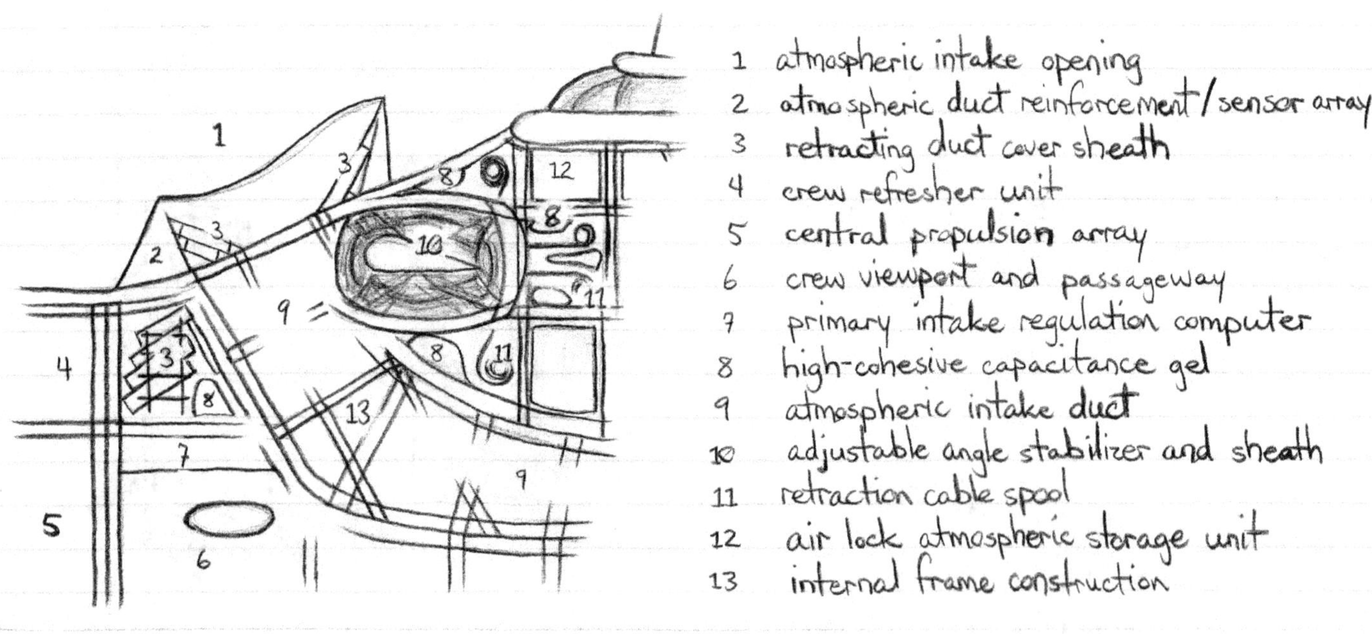

1. Biv model 2.4 fighter wing
2. model 2.4 fighter adjustable laser
3. space intercept missile attachment clamps
4. water purification equipment
5. internal frame construction
6. fighter attachment rods extenders
7. access duct
8. fire surpression system
9. ascention pipe fixture
10. forward horizontal stabilizer
11. reinforced outer hull and 4gen shields
12. artificial gravity generator
13. reserve shield array battery
14. magnetized fighter attachment rods
15. model 2.4 fighter cockpit viewscreen
16. model 2.4 fighter fixed offensive laser
17. model 2.4 fighter space intercept missile
18. escape pod
19. crew passageway
20. computer bank
21. atmosphere scrubber
22. escape pod separation computer and battery

CUTAWAY: ATMOSPHERIC INTAKE DUCT AND ADJUSTABLE ANGLE STABILIZER

1. atmospheric intake opening
2. atmospheric duct reinforcement / sensor array
3. retracting duct cover sheath
4. crew refresher unit
5. central propulsion array
6. crew viewport and passageway
7. primary intake regulation computer
8. high-cohesive capacitance gel
9. atmospheric intake duct
10. adjustable angle stabilizer and sheath
11. retraction cable spool
12. air lock atmospheric storage unit
13. internal frame construction

Gluk *Incuis*-class dreadnaught B5C-1 *Unremitting*

CUTAWAY: REAR CREW SECTION

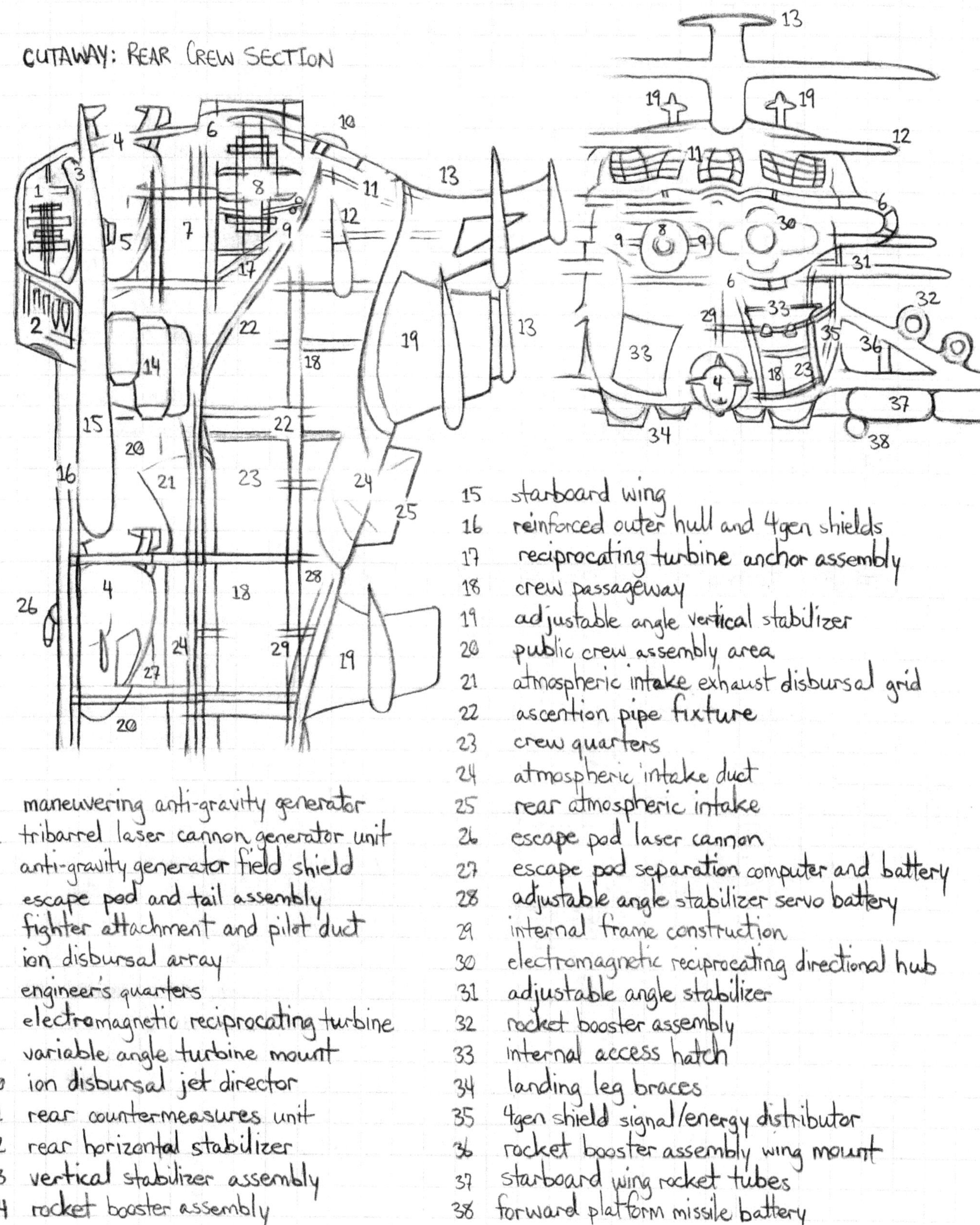

1   maneuvering anti-gravity generator
2   tribarrel laser cannon generator unit
3   anti-gravity generator field shield
4   escape pod and tail assembly
5   fighter attachment and pilot duct
6   ion disbursal array
7   engineer's quarters
8   electromagnetic reciprocating turbine
9   variable angle turbine mount
10 ion disbursal jet director
11 rear countermeasures unit
12 rear horizontal stabilizer
13 vertical stabilizer assembly
14 rocket booster assembly

15 starboard wing
16 reinforced outer hull and 4gen shields
17 reciprocating turbine anchor assembly
18 crew passageway
19 adjustable angle vertical stabilizer
20 public crew assembly area
21 atmospheric intake exhaust disbursal grid
22 ascension pipe fixture
23 crew quarters
24 atmospheric intake duct
25 rear atmospheric intake
26 escape pod laser cannon
27 escape pod separation computer and battery
28 adjustable angle stabilizer servo battery
29 internal frame construction
30 electromagnetic reciprocating directional hub
31 adjustable angle stabilizer
32 rocket booster assembly
33 internal access hatch
34 landing leg braces
35 4gen shield signal/energy distributor
36 rocket booster assembly wing mount
37 starboard wing rocket tubes
38 forward platform missile battery

Gluk *Incuis*-class dreadnaught B5C-1 *Unremitting*

CUTAWAY: ARMORED AIRLOCK CHAMBER

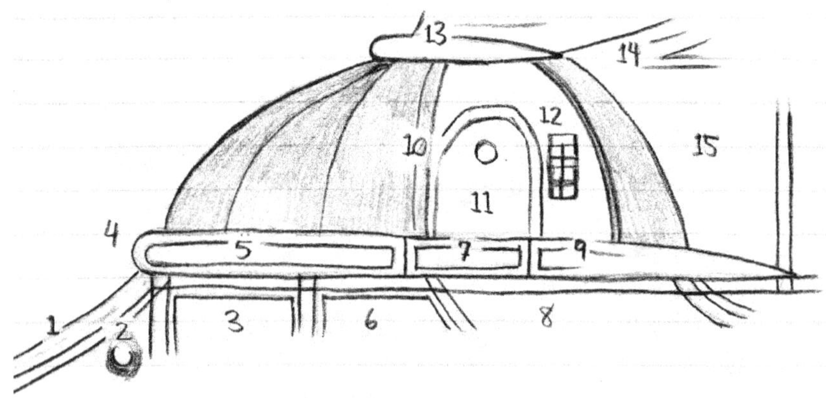

1 4gen shields
2 retraction cable spool
3 air lock atmospheric storage unit
4 central horizontal stabilizer
5 armored airlock chamber battery
6 atmospheric scrubber
7 sensor array
8 atmospheric intake duct
9 armored airlock chamber capacitor

10 armored airlock housing sheath
11 airlock access doorway
12 airlock access security panel

13 armored airlock chamber aerodynamic foil
14 reinforced outer hull
15 crew passageway

CUTAWAY: BRIDGE AND PRIMARY SYSTEMS

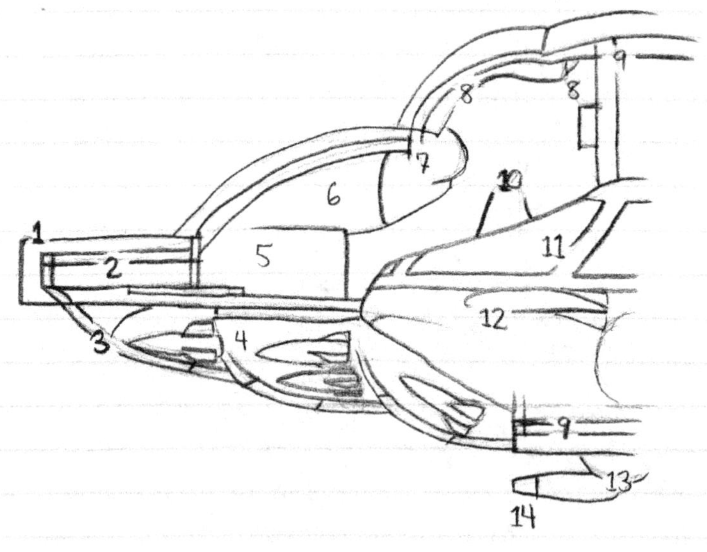

1 4gen shields
2 forward sensor array
3 forward keel missle bay and master weapons computer
4 offensive missiles
5 master interface computer
6 navigation computer
7 pilot control interface
8 pilot datascreen assembly
9 internal frame construction
10 pilot recline unit
11 First Officer communications and weapons module / executive escape pod two
12 escape pod horizontal stabilizer
13 escape pod targeting hinge housing
14 escape pod laser cannon

Gluk *Incuis*-class dreadnaught B5C-1 *Unremitting*
Escape pod assembly

FIGURE 1   B5C-1E v1 PROFILE VIEW

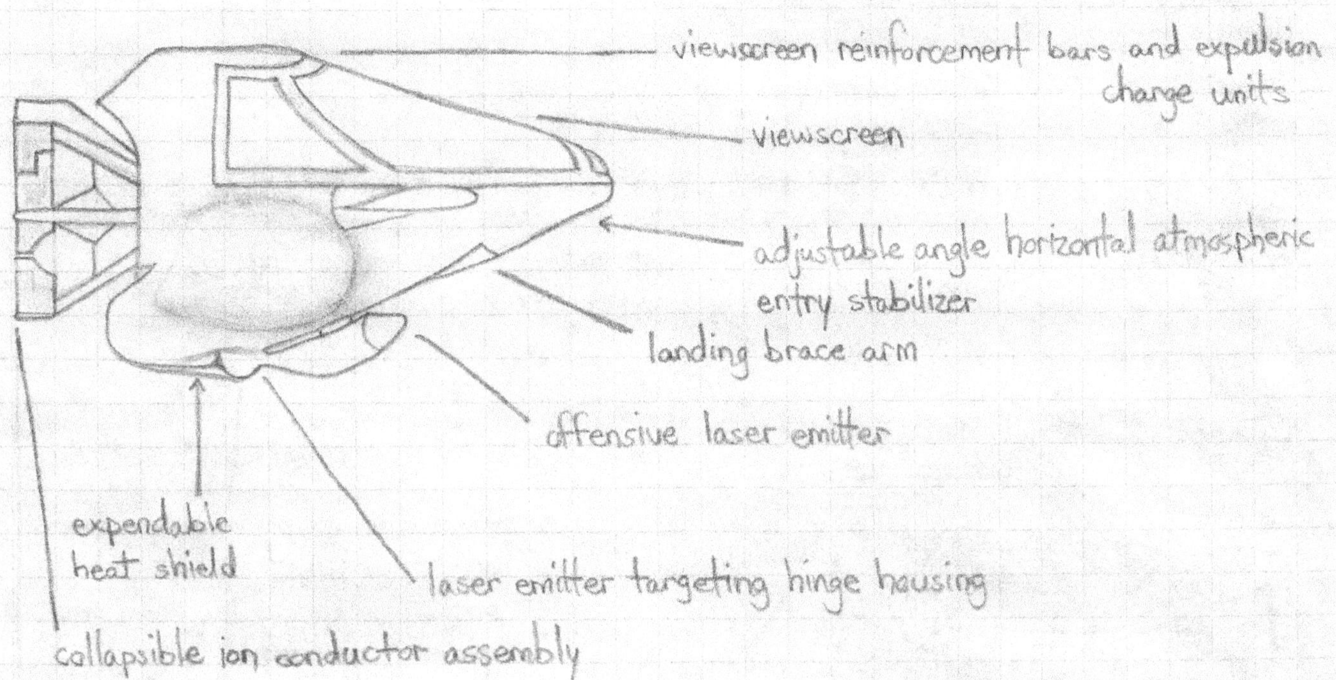

FIG. 2   B5C-1E v2 FRONT VIEW

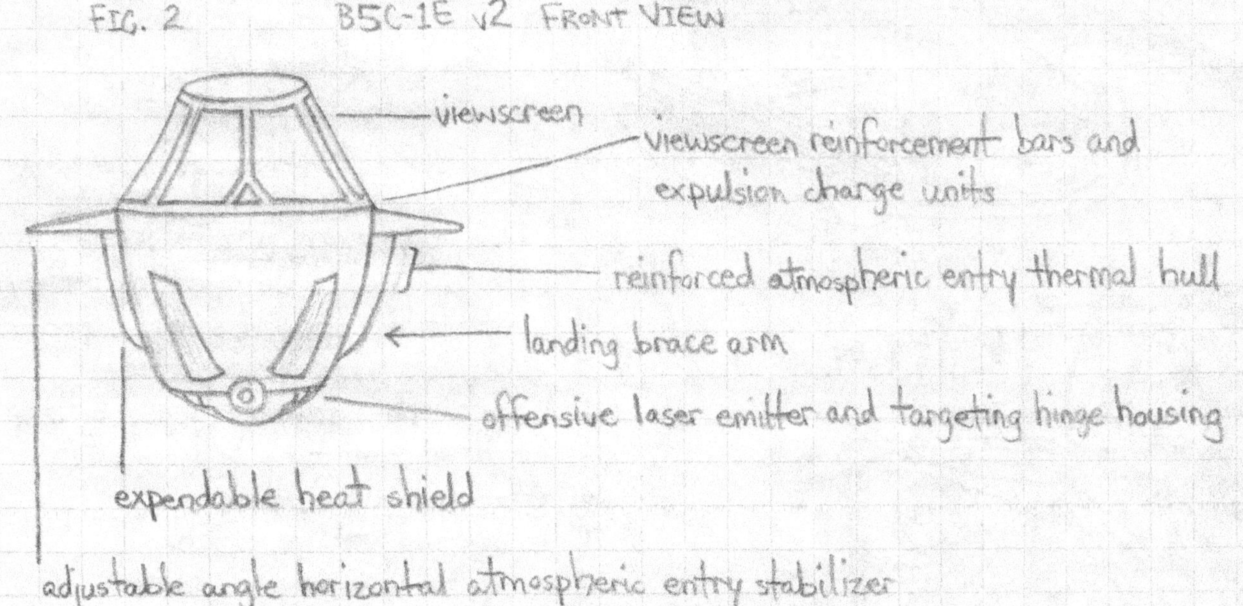

13

B5C-1 *Unremitting* escape pod

CLASSIFICATION:	crew withdrawal unit
TYPE:	multi-passenger limited-range capsule
CREW:	up to three passengers per pod
LENGTH:	3.65 m (12 feet)
WIDTH:	2.7 m (9 ft)
HEIGHT:	1.8 m (6 ft)
MASS:	1,740 kg (3836 lbs_f)
ARMOR:	pyroceramite-coated steetanicarb alloy and thermal insulator gloss
ENGINES:	one high-density ion drive, maximum speed 297 km/hr. (185 mph)
ARMAMENT:	one medium-power laser emitter, 4800 Nm or 1200 j/s
RANGE:	0.000142313 light-years (1,346,380,836 km/836,009,592 miles)

CUTAWAY: B5C-1E v1 PROPULSION MODULE

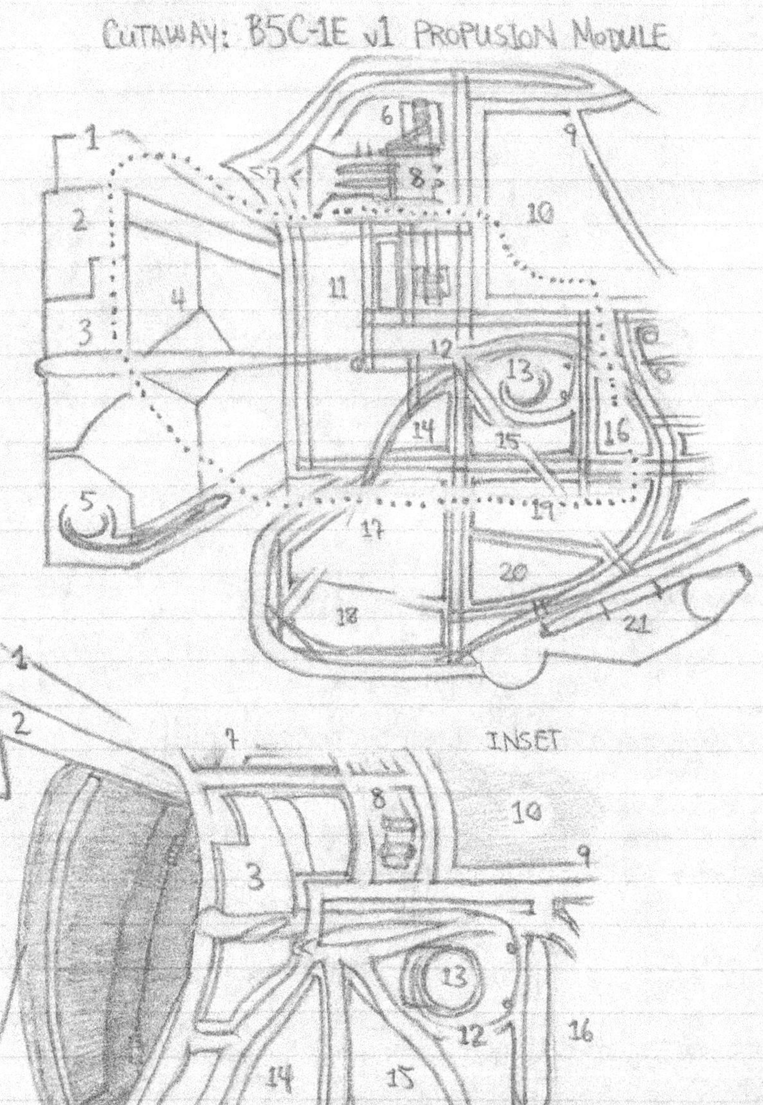

1 fixed atmospheric entry stabilizer
2 ion drive exhaust conductor
3 retractable atmospheric entry stabilizer ion conductor arm
4 ion drive conductor and support cables
5 fixed stabilizer support cable spool/battery
6 high density ion fuel tank
7 high density ion drive nozzle
8 ion drive positioning mechanism and spool chamber
9 viewscreen reinforcement bars
10 viewscreen
11 retractable ion conductor housing
12 conductor arm retraction cable
13 retraction cable spool and battery
14 retractable stabilizer servo capacitor
15 collapsible wing servo battery
16 horizontal entry stabilizer servo battery
17 ion drive fuel tank and computer
18 offensive laser battery
19 escape pod atmospere tank
20 collapsible wing servo computer
21 offensive laser emitter

Gluk Incuis-class dreadnaught BSC-1   Unremitting
Escape pod assembly

FIG. 3   BSC-1E v3   TOP VIEW

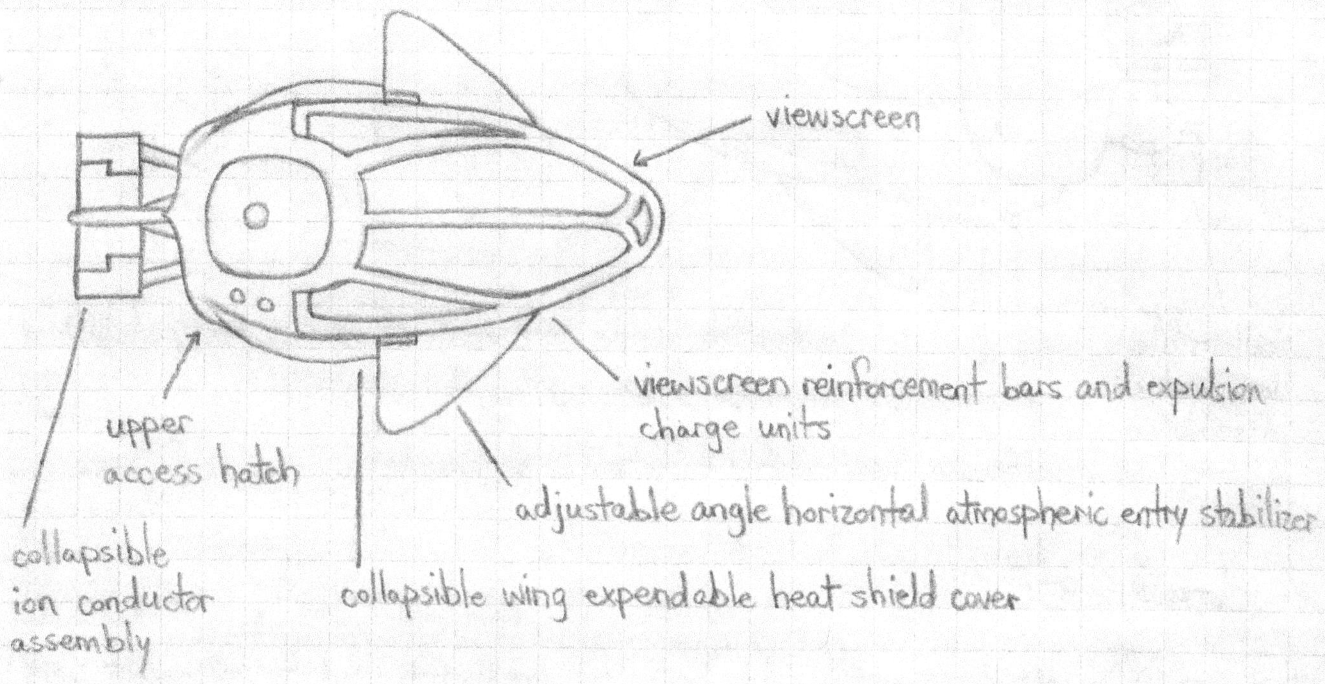

FIG. 4   BSC-1E v1   REAR VIEW

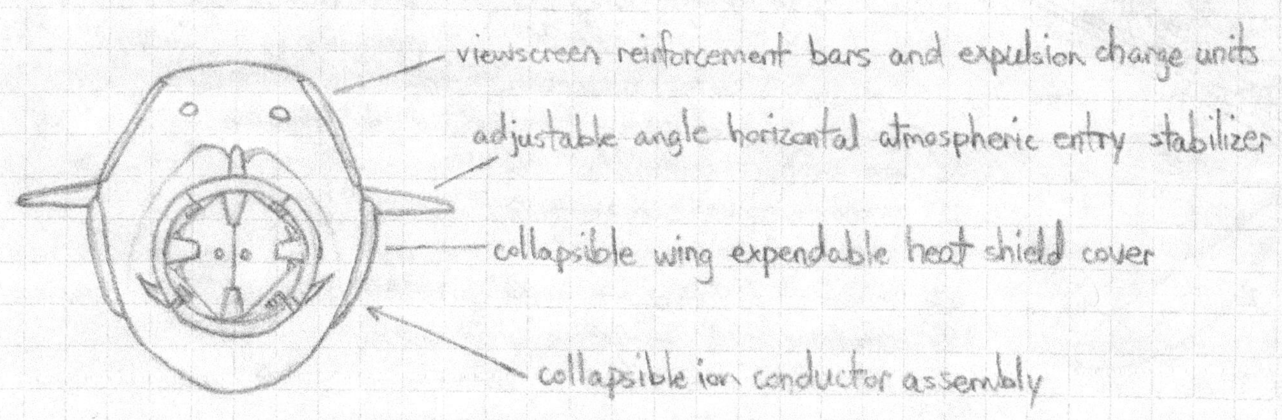

15

FIG. 5   B5C-1E v2   BOTTOM VIEW

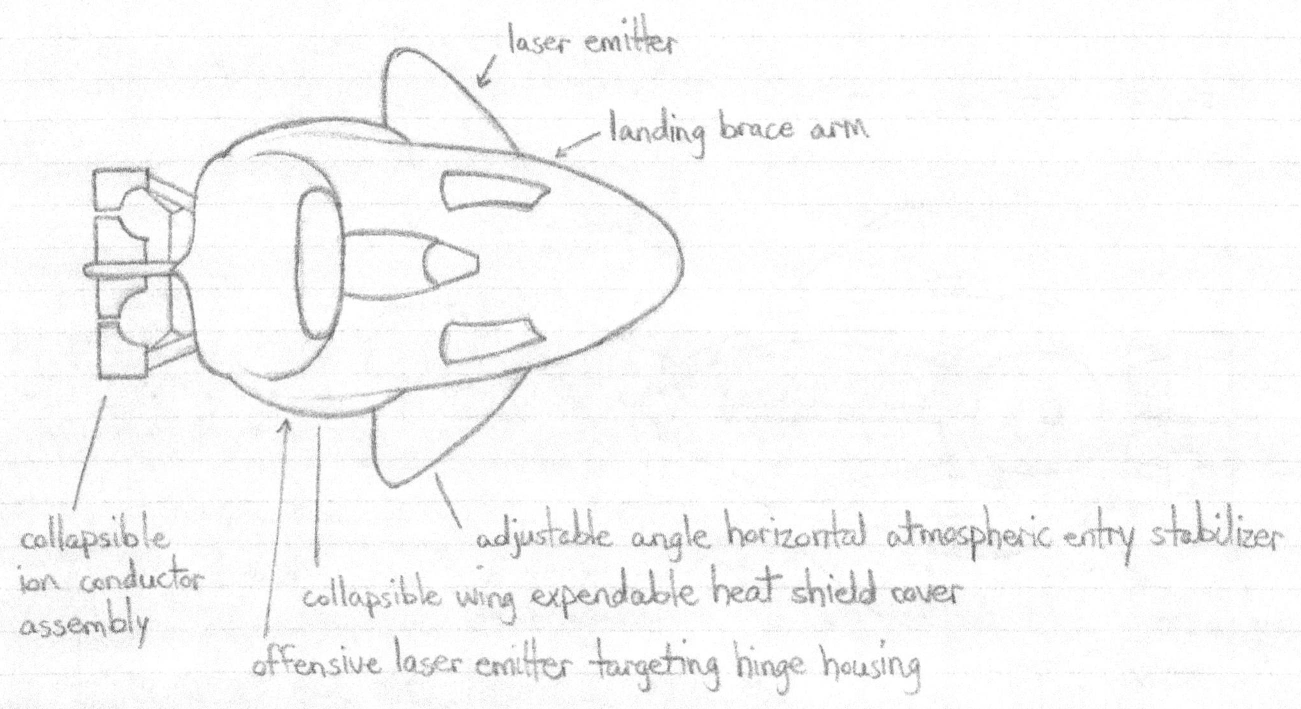

CUTAWAY: B5C-1E v3 FORE

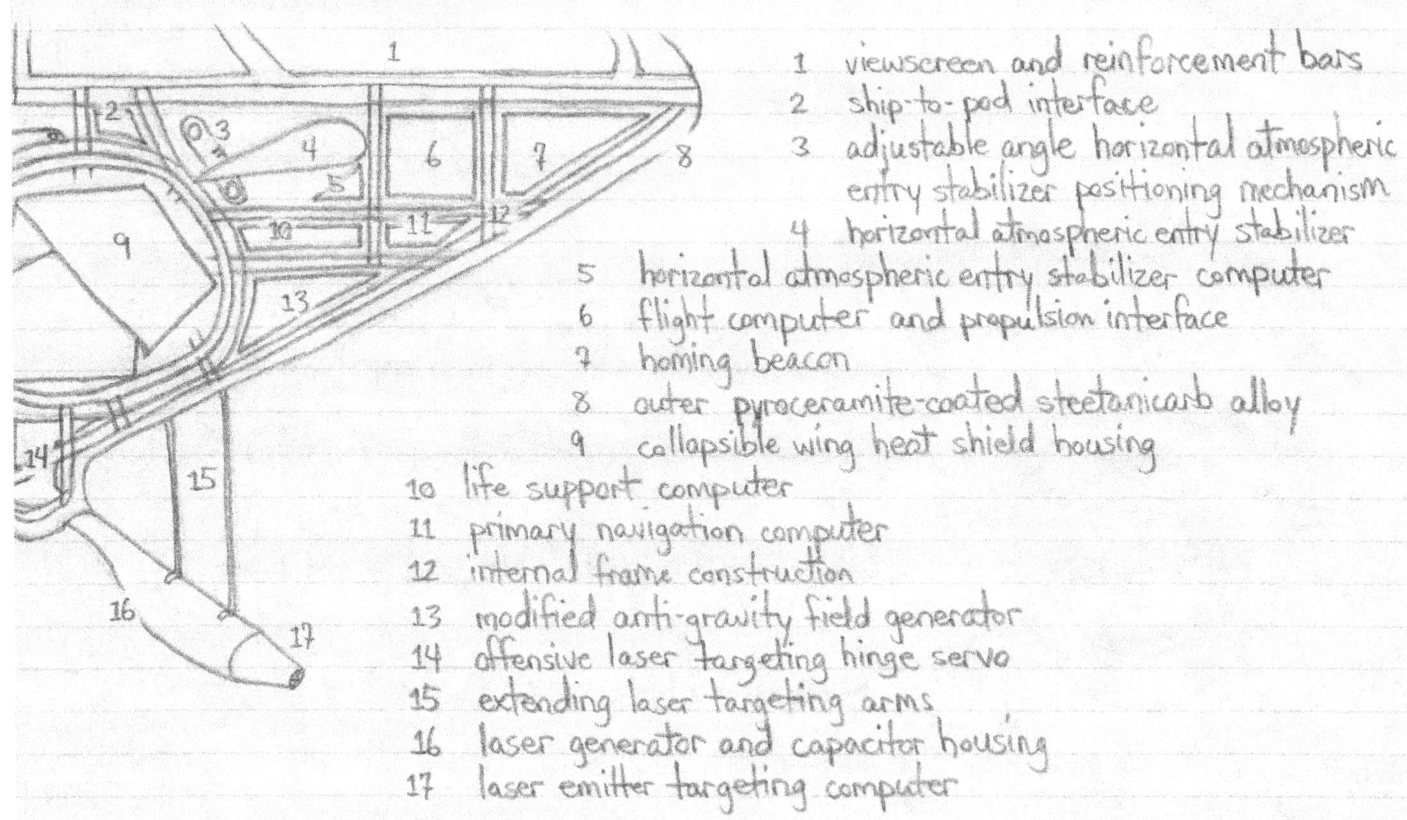

1 viewscreen and reinforcement bars
2 ship-to-pod interface
3 adjustable angle horizontal atmospheric entry stabilizer positioning mechanism
4 horizontal atmospheric entry stabilizer
5 horizontal atmospheric entry stabilizer computer
6 flight computer and propulsion interface
7 homing beacon
8 outer pyroceramite-coated steetanicarb alloy
9 collapsible wing heat shield housing
10 life support computer
11 primary navigation computer
12 internal frame construction
13 modified anti-gravity field generator
14 offensive laser targeting hinge servo
15 extending laser targeting arms
16 laser generator and capacitor housing
17 laser emitter targeting computer

16

Set 21:
Derytram

This ship is based on the dreadnaught *Unremitting*, the Kvhingleyemlit's attempt to obliterate enemies and competitors with a single vessel. When I first saw it, I immediately wanted it as a transport ship. For *Lone Soldier* space in this time, it is massive. Though this cargo vessel proved too much for later generations, the *Derytram* became the staple design for large transports in the following generations. It is the same class as the *Unremitting*, which is a jab at the parasite the Gaepvihn never really understood.

Gluk Incuis-class frigate C4B-1 Derytram

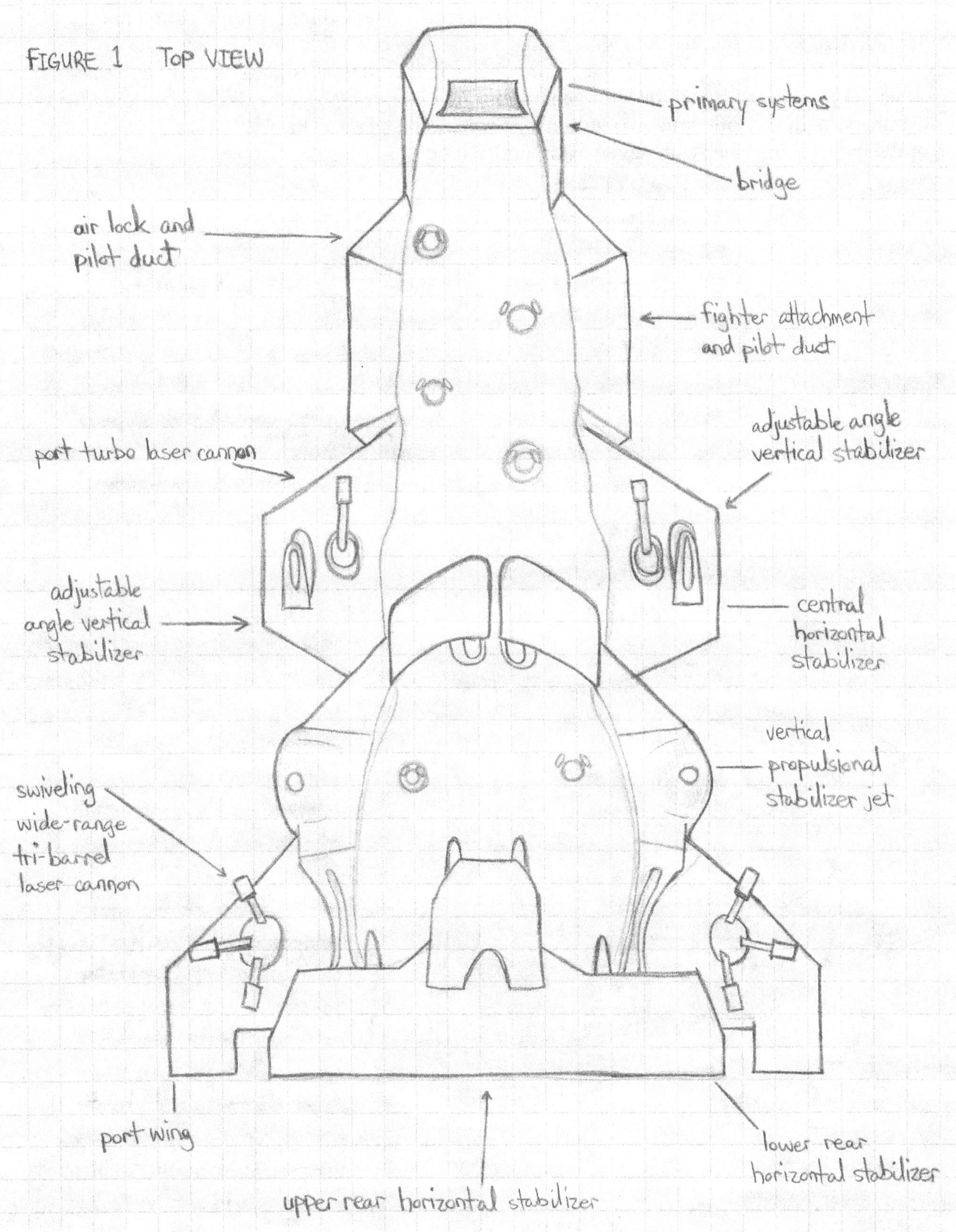

Gluk C4B-1 *Derytram*

CLASSIFICATION: battle-worthy cargo ship grade 4
TYPE: Incuis-class frigate
CREW: 16 total (8 officers, 3 enlisted, five fighter pilots)
LENGTH: 325 standard feet
WIDTH: 46 standard feet
HEIGHT: 73 standard feet
BEAM: 62 standard feet
MASS: 202,826 standard mass units empty (6,180 mass unit capacity)
ARMOR: reinforced steetanicarb and pyroceramite hull, 4gen EM shields
ENGINES: eight electromagnetic reciprocating turbines (two anti-gravitational)
ARMAMENT: two central swivel-mounted turbo laser cannon, two forward missile pods, two central swivel-mounted guided missile pods, two swivel-mounted wide-range tribarrel laser cannon, two rear missile pods, four unguided rocket stabilizer-mounted pods

CUTAWAY: PRIMARY SYSTEMS AND BRIDGE

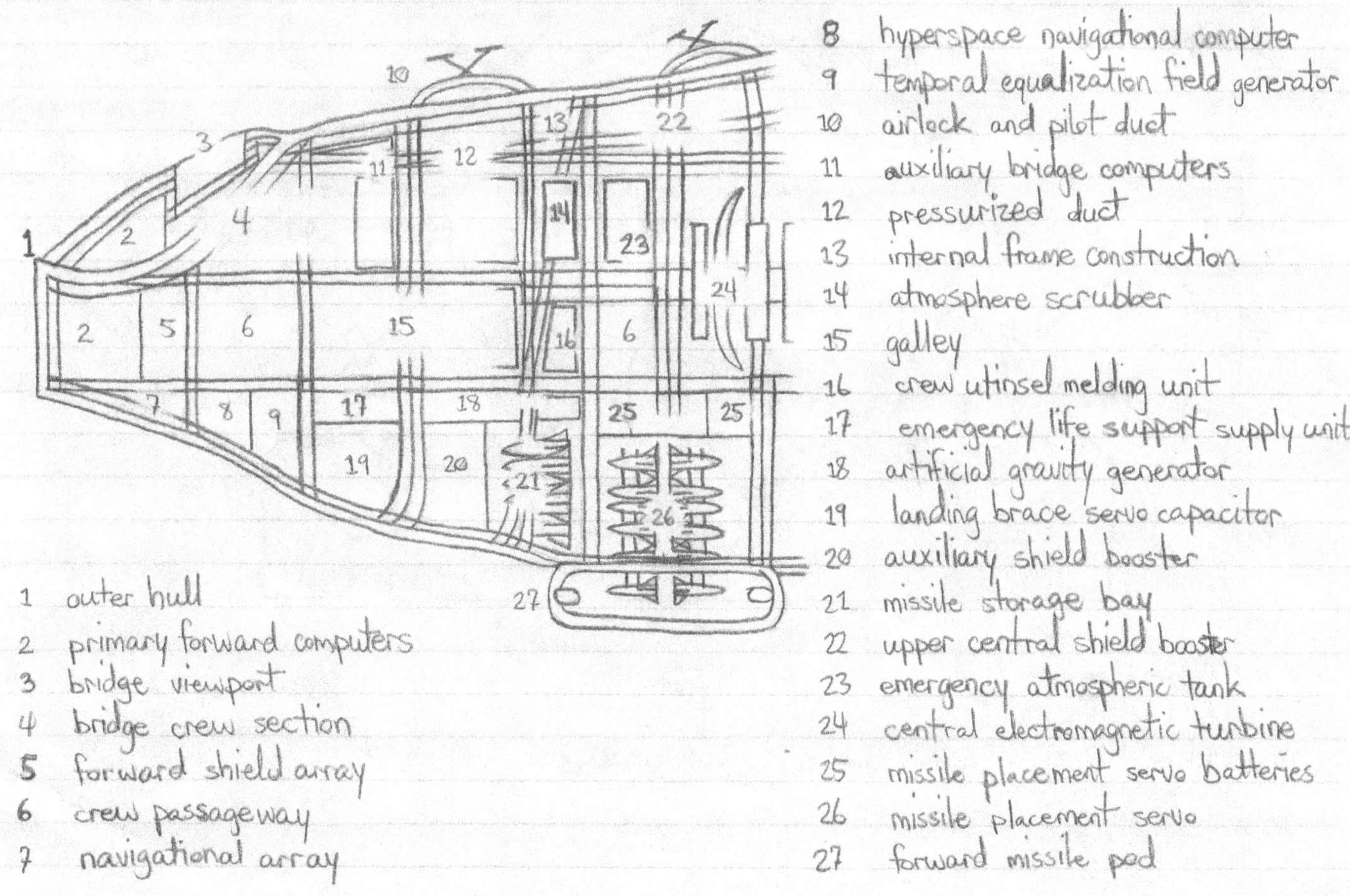

1 outer hull
2 primary forward computers
3 bridge viewport
4 bridge crew section
5 forward shield array
6 crew passageway
7 navigational array

8 hyperspace navigational computer
9 temporal equalization field generator
10 airlock and pilot duct
11 auxiliary bridge computers
12 pressurized duct
13 internal frame construction
14 atmosphere scrubber
15 galley
16 crew utinsel melding unit
17 emergency life support supply unit
18 artificial gravity generator
19 landing brace servo capacitor
20 auxiliary shield booster
21 missile storage bay
22 upper central shield booster
23 emergency atmospheric tank
24 central electromagnetic turbine
25 missile placement servo batteries
26 missile placement servo
27 forward missile pod

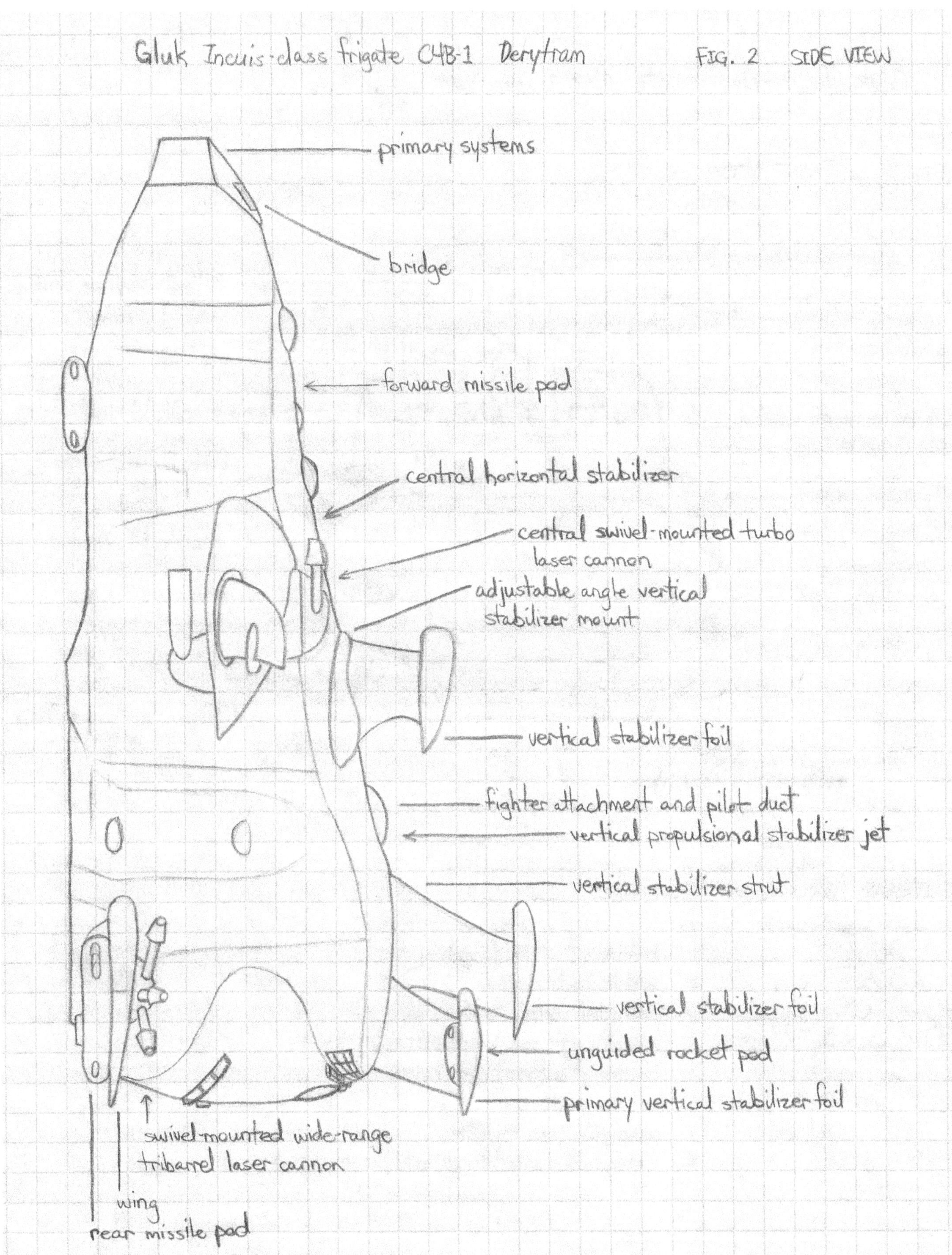

primary systems
bridge
forward missile pod
central horizontal stabilizer
central swivel-mounted turbo laser cannon
adjustable angle vertical stabilizer mount
vertical stabilizer foil
fighter attachment and pilot duct
vertical propulsional stabilizer jet
vertical stabilizer strut
vertical stabilizer foil
unguided rocket pod
primary vertical stabilizer foil
swivel-mounted wide-range tribarrel laser cannon
wing
rear missile pod

20

Gluk Incuis-class frigate C4B-1 Derytram

FIG. 3   FRONT VIEW

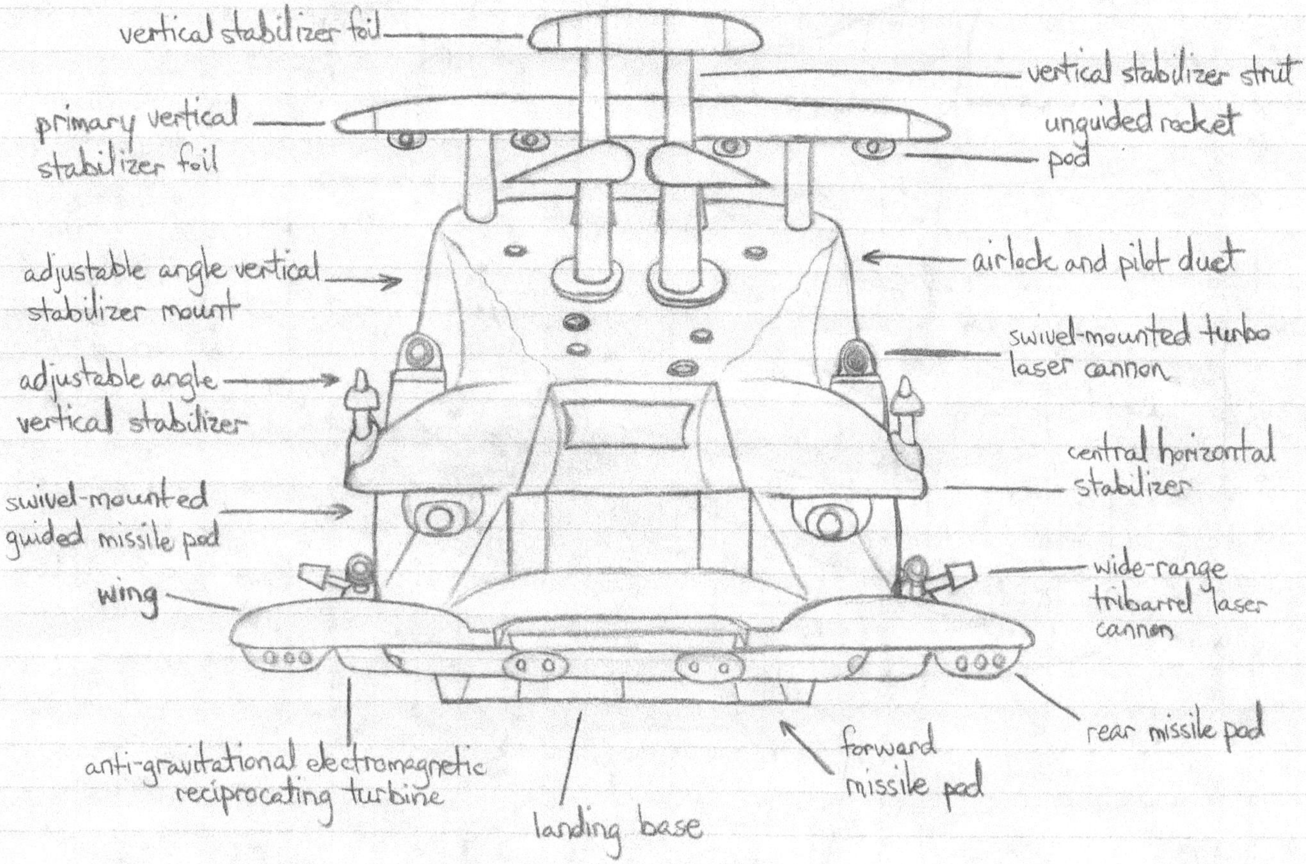

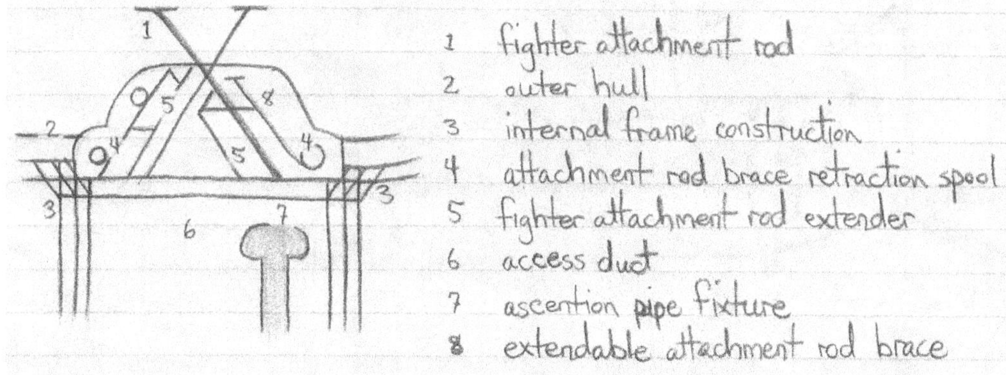

CUTAWAY: AIRLOCK AND PILOT DUCT

1   fighter attachment rod
2   outer hull
3   internal frame construction
4   attachment rod brace retraction spool
5   fighter attachment rod extender
6   access duct
7   ascention pipe fixture
8   extendable attachment rod brace

21

Gluk Incuis-class frigate C4B-1 Derytram

FIG. 4 BOTTOM VIEW

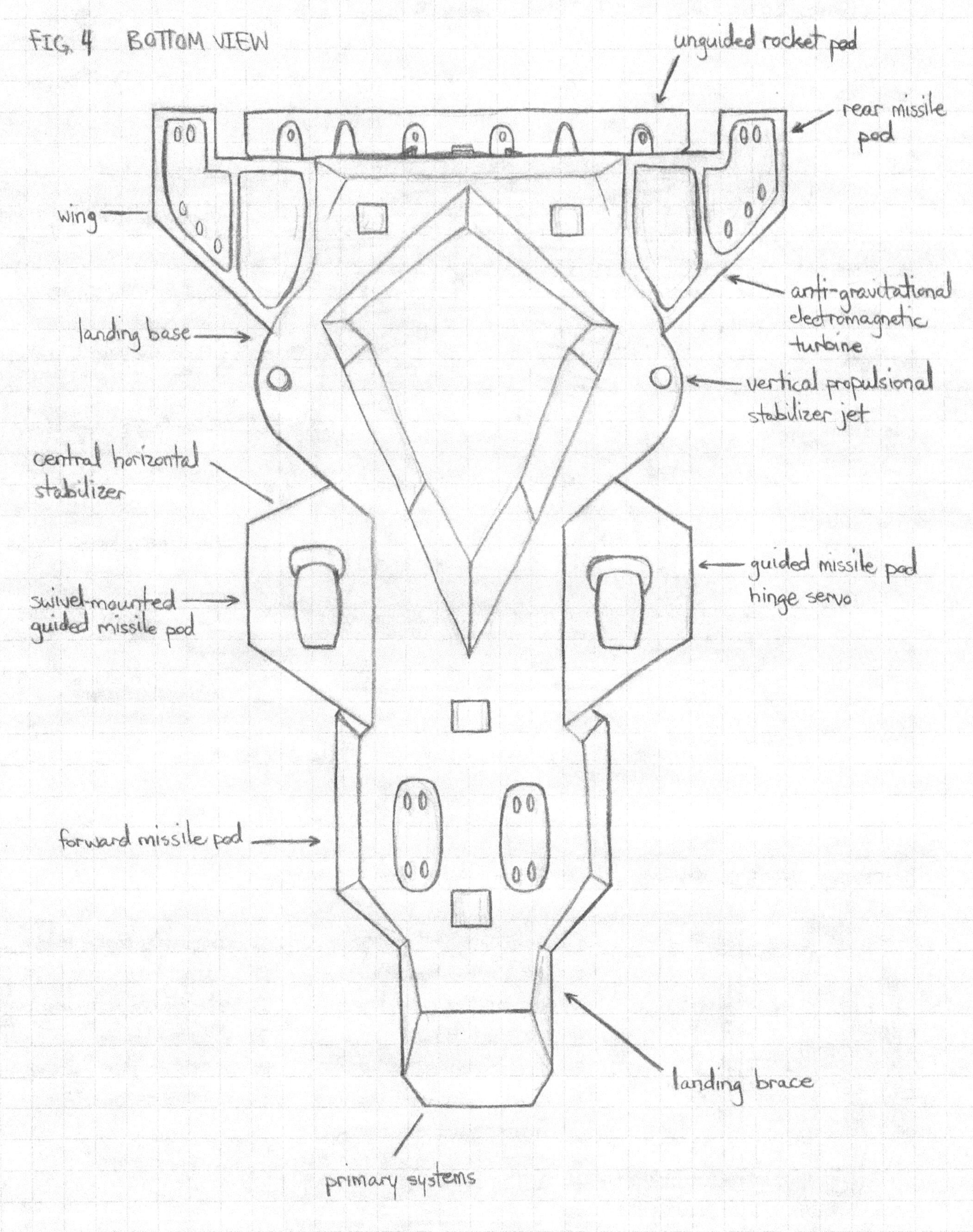

22

Gluk Incuis-class frigate C4B-1 Derytram

FIG. 5   REAR VIEW

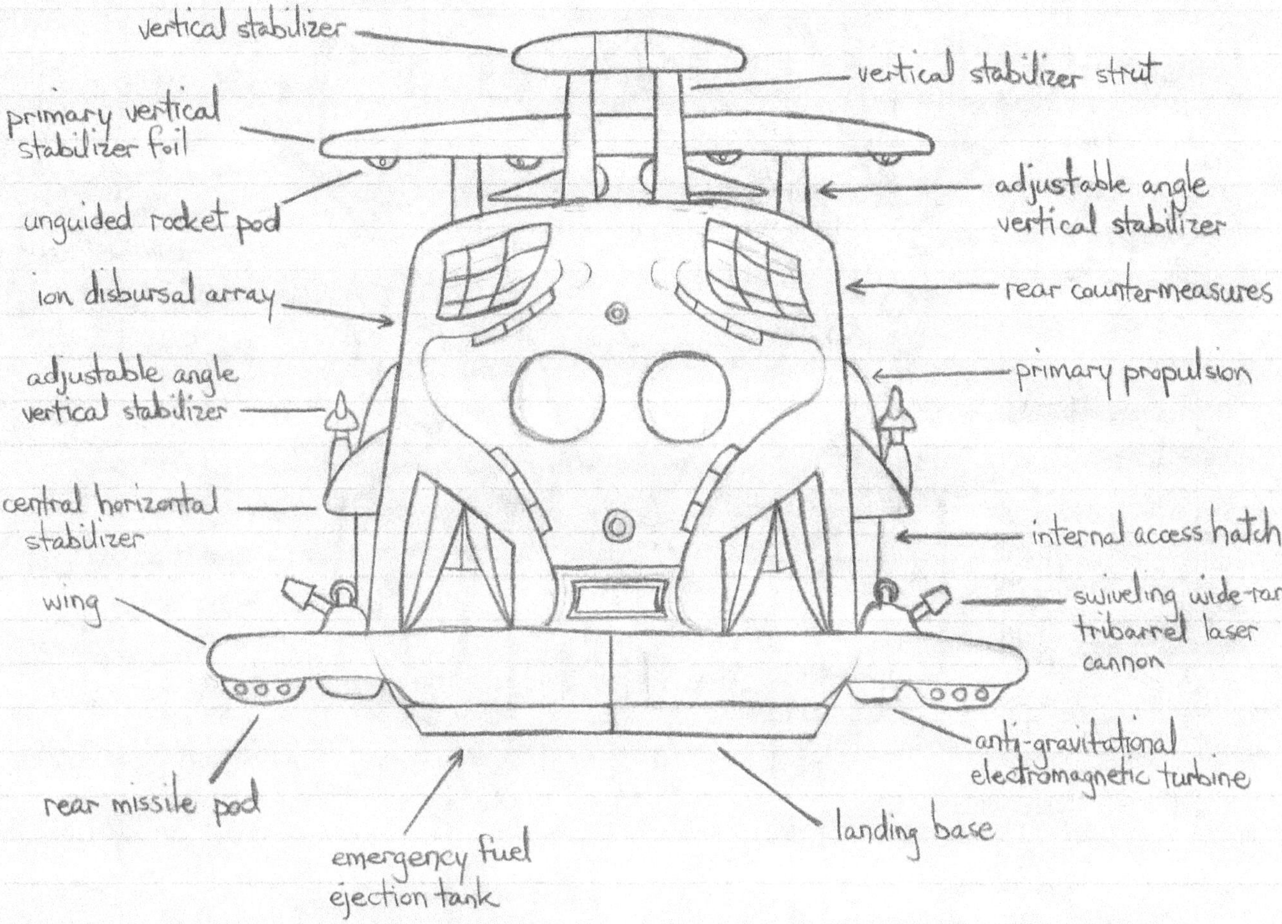

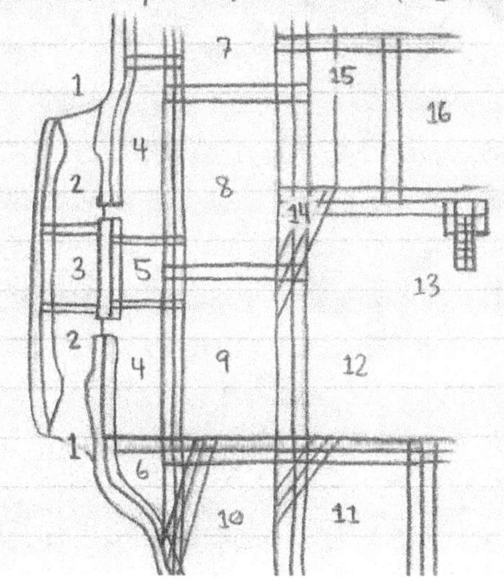

CUTAWAY: VERTICAL PROPULSIONAL STABILIZER JET

1 directional jet nozzle
2 jet combustion chamber
3 jet ignition initializer
4 jet fuel tank
5 directional jet regulator
6 navigational-jet interface
7 fighter pilot quarters
8 upper crew access passage
9 spare parts storage chamber
10 lower crew access passage
11 specialty cargo hold
12 cargo bay
13 retractable cargo bay brace
14 internal frame construction
15 ascention pipe fixture
16 engineer's quarters

CUTAWAY: CENTRAL CREW SECTION

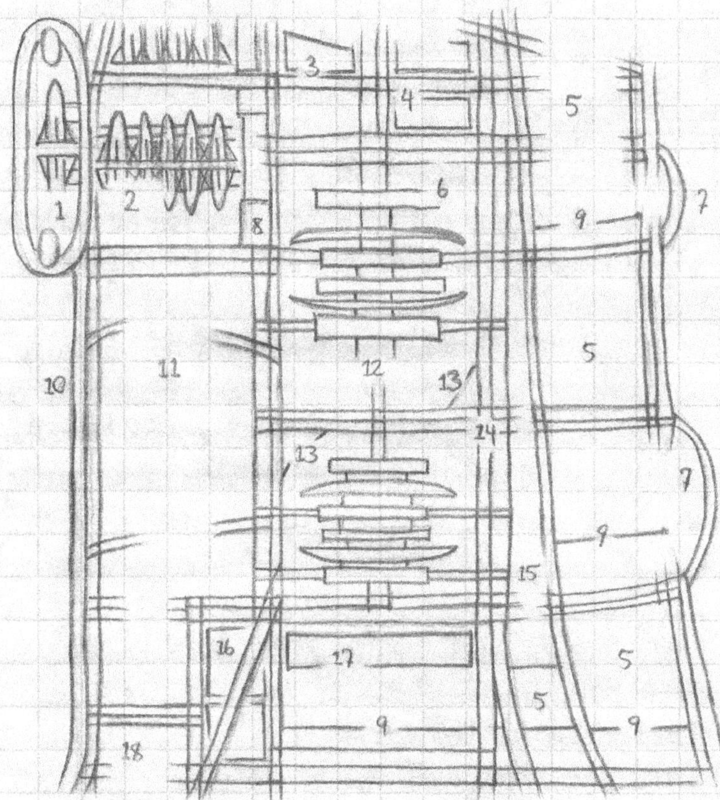

1 forward missile pod
2 servo-placed missile battery
3 crew utinsel melding unit
4 emergency atmospheric tank
5 crew passageway
6 electromagnetic reciprocating turbine
7 airlock and pilot duct
8 missile placement servo batteries
9 ascention pipe fixture
10 outer hull
11 central cargo bay
12 reciprocating turbine rotation shaft
13 engine maintenance computer
14 internal frame construction
15 artificial gravity array
16 atmospheric pressurizer
17 engine surge capacitor
18 atmospheric storage tank

CUTAWAY: CENTRAL HORIZONTAL STABILIZER

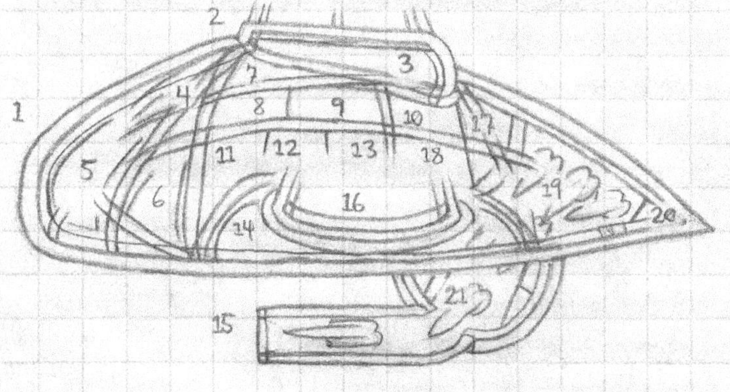

7 turbo laser surge capacitor
8 turbo laser capacitor
9 turbo laser generator
10 navigational-targeting interface
11 auxiliary sensor array
12 maintenance access passageway
13 adjustable angle stabilizer servo housing
14 adjustable angle stabilizer regulator
15 missile tube
16 adjustable angle vertical stabilizer
17 master missile computer
18 adjustable angle vertical stabilizer battery
19 missile storage unit
20 missile positioning system
21 missile positioning system battery

1 outer hull
2 swivel-mounted turbo laser cannon
3 swivel battery
4 internal frame construction
5 laser cannon battery
6 targeting sensor array

Gluk: *Incuis-class frigate* CHB-1 *Derytram*

CUTAWAY: ADJUSTABLE ANGLE VERTICAL STABILIZER ASSEMBLY

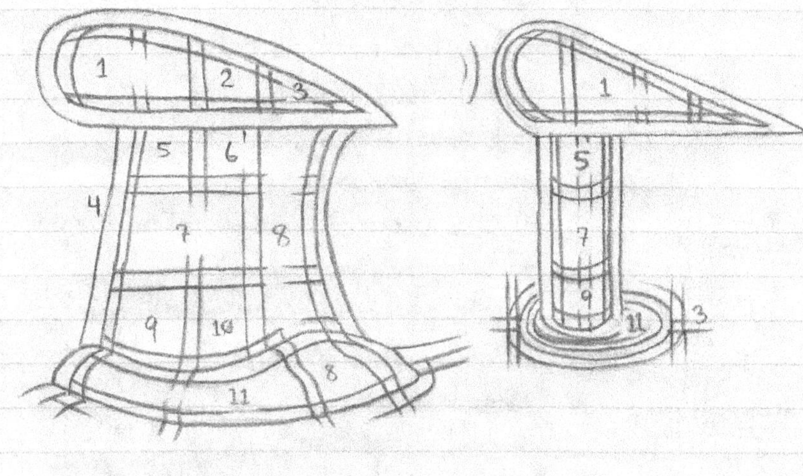

1 auxiliary shield array
2 auxiliary communications array
3 internal frame construction
4 outer hull
5 adjustable angle stabilizer auxiliary capacitor
6 angle adjustment master computer
7 sensor array
8 crew access passageway
9 adjustable angle stabilizer servo battery
10 adjustable angle stabilizer servo capacitor
11 adjustable angle stabilizer servo housing

CUTAWAY: TRI-BARREL LASER CANNON

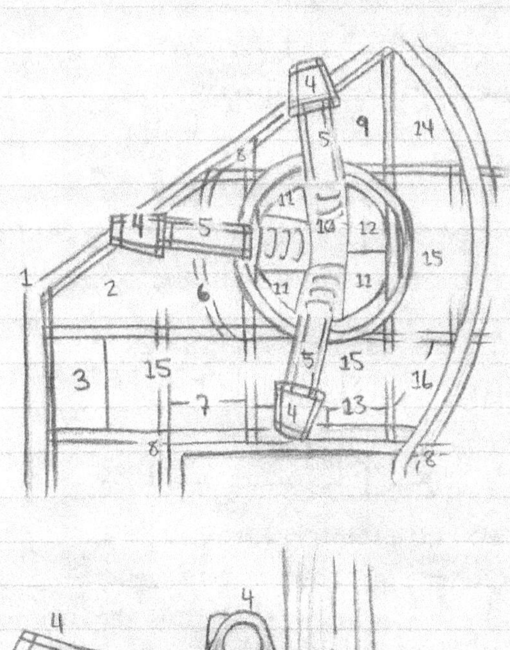

1 outer hull
2 stored pressurized liquid tank
3 laser cannon spare parts storage unit
4 laser cannon beam emitter
5 laser cannon beam disbursal tube
6 laser cannon swivel and angle adjustor servo battery
7 emergency supplies
8 internal frame construction
9 laser cannon battery
10 laser cannon beam generator and power distributor
11 laser cannon capacitor
12 laser cannon targeting computer
13 sensor array
14 laser cannon surge capacitor
15 crew access passageway
16 atmospheric pressurizer
17 stored pressurized atmosphere tank
18 cargo bay internal access hatch housing
19 laser cannon angle adjuster servo
20 shield booster assembly

Gluk *Incuis*-class frigate C4B-1 *Derytram*

CUTAWAY: REAR CREW SECTION

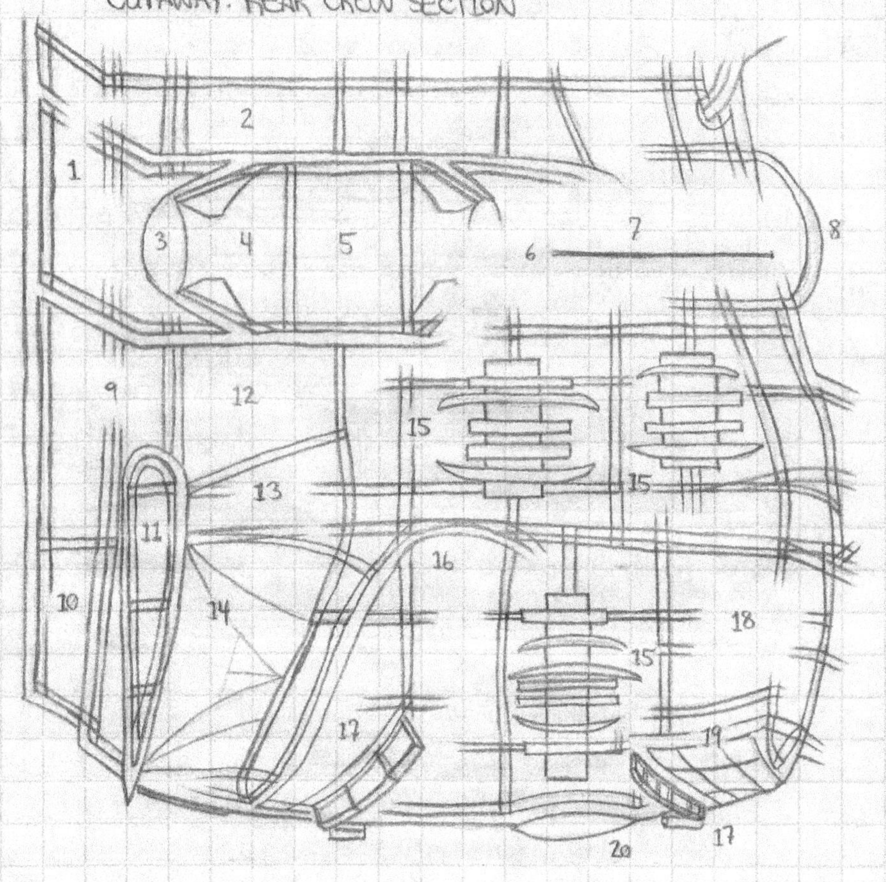

1 lower crew access passage
2 spare parts storage chamber
3 directional jet nozzle
4 jet combustion chamber
5 jet ignition initializer
6 ascention pipe fixture
7 crew passageway
8 airlock and pilot duct
9 stored pressurized fluid tank
10 specialty cargo hold
11 port wing
12 cargo bay
13 cargo bay internal access hatch housing
14 cargo bay internal access hatch
15 electromagnetic reciprocating turbine
16 engine capacitor
17 ion disbursal array
18 fighter pilot quarters
19 rear countermeasures unit
20 electromagnetic reciprocating turbine directional hub

CUTAWAY: REAR VERTICAL STABILIZER ASSEMBLIES

1 vertical stabilizer foil
2 auxiliary shield array
3 atmospheric pressurizer
4 atmosphere scrubber
5 auxiliary maintenance
6 crew access passageway
7 fighter spare parts unit
8 pressurized crew water storage
9 primary vertical stabilizer rocket battery
10 rocket placement servo
11 unguided rocket pod
12 rocket positioning system
13 stored pressurized fluid tank
14 fighter pilot quarters

Gluk *Incuis*-class frigate C4B-1 *Derytram*

CUTAWAY: SEPARABLE CARGO BAY

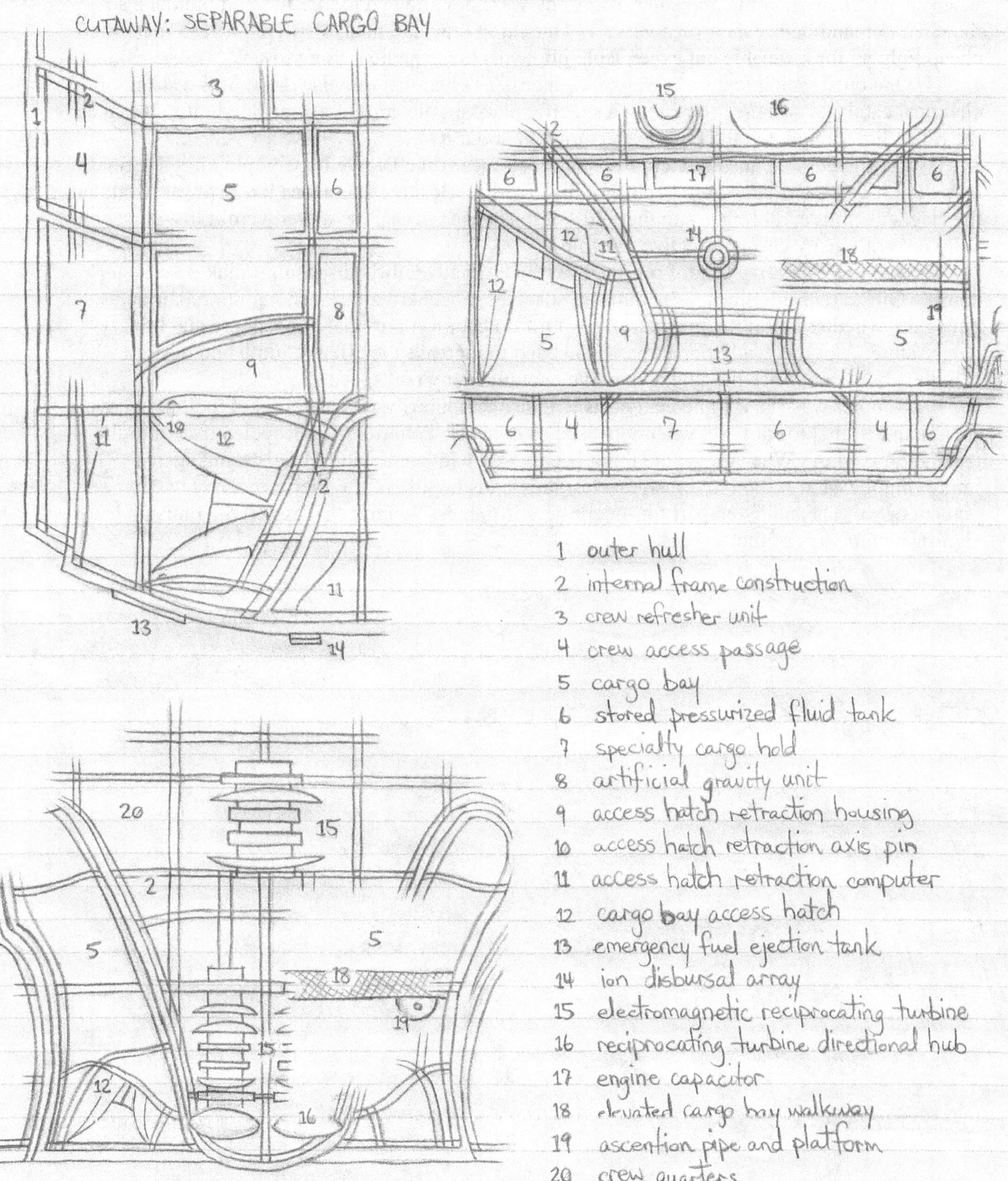

1 outer hull
2 internal frame construction
3 crew refresher unit
4 crew access passage
5 cargo bay
6 stored pressurized fluid tank
7 specialty cargo hold
8 artificial gravity unit
9 access hatch retraction housing
10 access hatch retraction axis pin
11 access hatch retraction computer
12 cargo bay access hatch
13 emergency fuel ejection tank
14 ion disbursal array
15 electromagnetic reciprocating turbine
16 reciprocating turbine directional hub
17 engine capacitor
18 elevated cargo bay walkway
19 ascention pipe and platform
20 crew quarters

Set 22:
Hsghedyemlit war craft

The Hsghedyemlit and the Iwuaryemlit never allied with the central Gaepvihnyemlit, when such a chain of command emerged. They were not allowed to hire the Shipbuilders, so they had to manufacture their own vessels. One thing they had many of were Ojif, so making cheap fighters for a capable but expendable pilot was the expedient thing to do.

One outstanding feature of the 2.6 fighter is its chemical impulse drive: it is a string of chemical catalysts designed to react in a specific place on the craft at a controlled rate. It makes the ride a little rough, but the Ojif don't complain about it.

I designed the ramship later. I consider it a means the Braulé may employ in their final battle but it needs a precursor to balance it historically. Besides, there was likely a war to subdue the Hsghedyemlit and bring it into the fold—if this was the case, the united yemlit lost somehow. Why not with many cheap, effective ramships?

Due to the relative lack of resources at the Hsghedyemlit's disposal, it makes sense to employ Ojif in reusable ships. The ramship survives most hard attacks enough to repair and send out again, whether or not the pilot survives. Ojif do better in minimal atmosphere and low temperature. Not much additional mass is needed to increase the effect of collision besides what is in the nose cone, since the ship is massive enough at any real speed.

Another way the Hs-ghed cut costs is to use temporarily-recycled rocket fuel; they have a set amount of fuel to start, but when it is used as much as a quarter of it is cycled back into the tank and mixed in. When the whole thing is enriched with some kind of bolstering agent improving the catalyzation in thrust nozzles, it extends the life of the fuel overall by twenty percent or so. The annoying part for the masters is the loss when it strikes and the ramship loses significant amounts of fuel to hard vacuum.

Hsghedyemlit v2.6 Ojif fighter

FIGURE 1 TOP VIEW

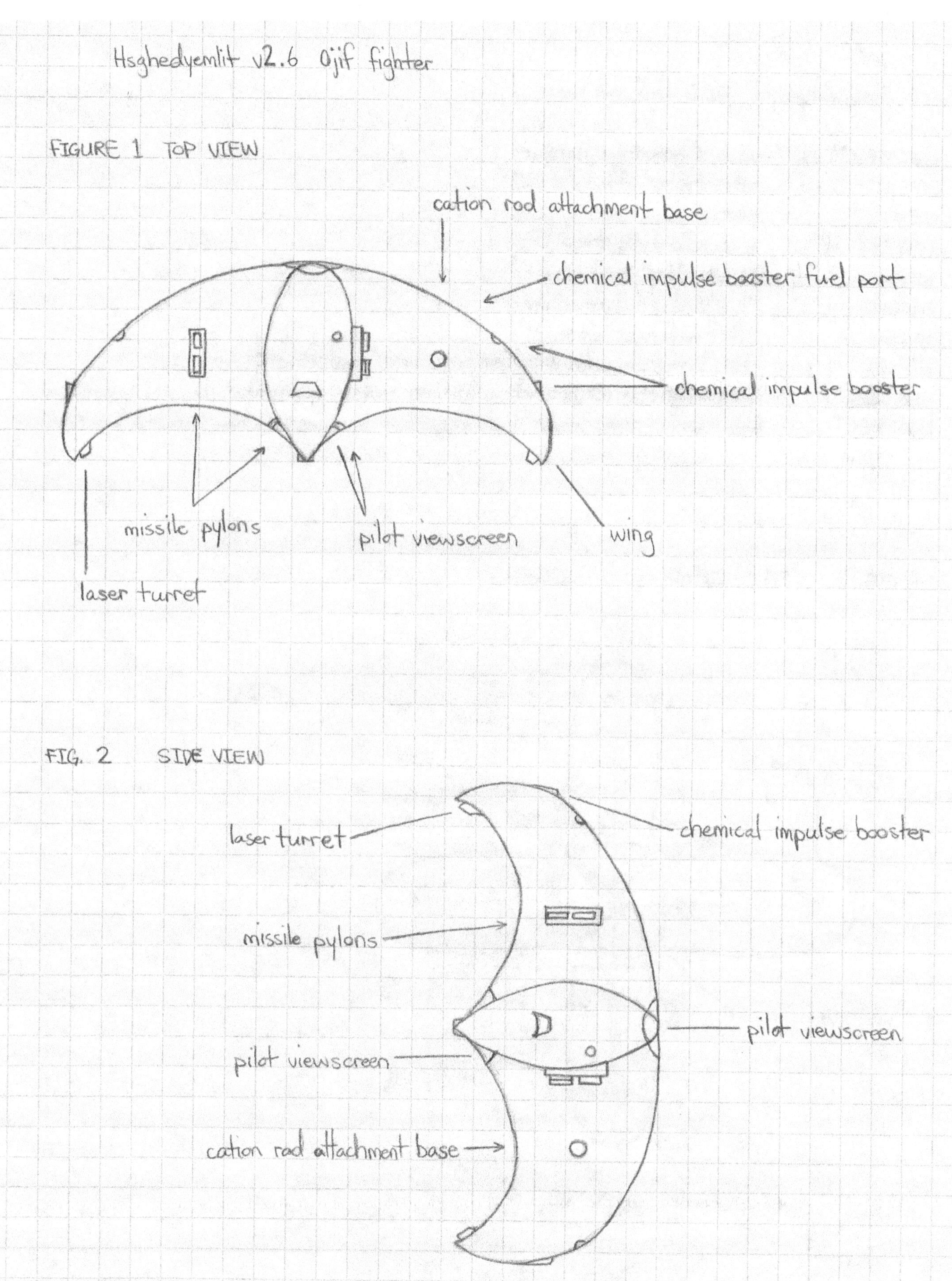

Hsghedyemlit v2.6 Ojif fighter

CLASSIFICATION: v2.6 short-range fighter
TYPE: interstellar attack vessel
CREW: pilot
LENGTH: 6 standard Hs-ghed lengths
WIDTH: 14 standard Hs-ghed lengths
HEIGHT: 14 standard Hs-ghed lengths
MASS: 2,984 micromass units
ARMOR: steealumicarb with pyroceramite poxy encasement
ENGINE: electromagnetic reciprocating turbine pulse generator, chemical booster
ARMAMENT: four sëp-âr-sïnc laser turrets, four missiles or two guided bombs

FIG. 3   FRONT VIEW

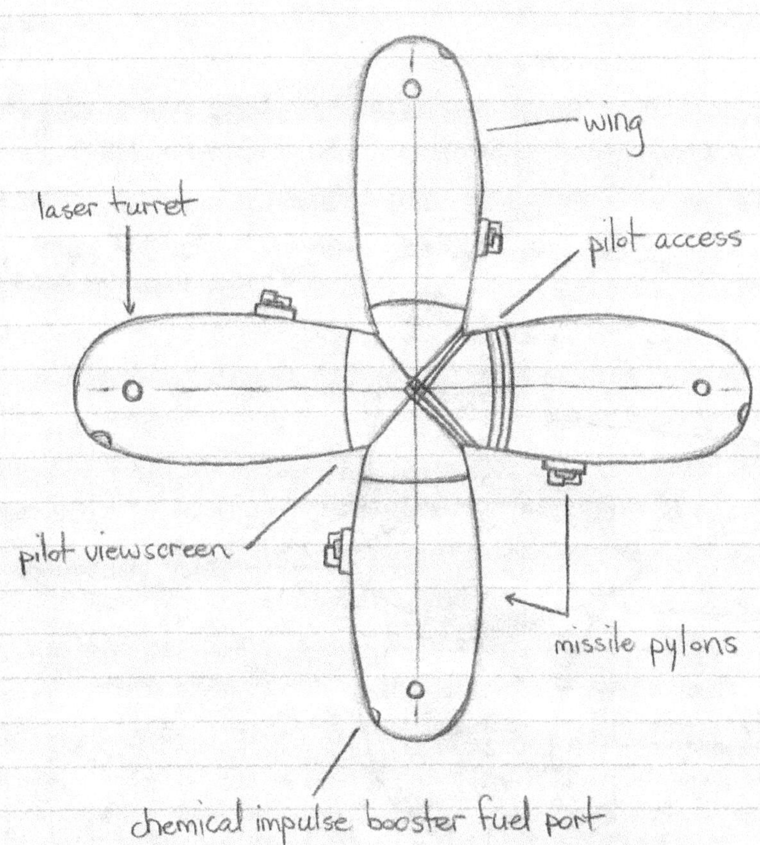

Hsghedyemlit v2.6 ojif fighter

FIG. 4   REAR VIEW

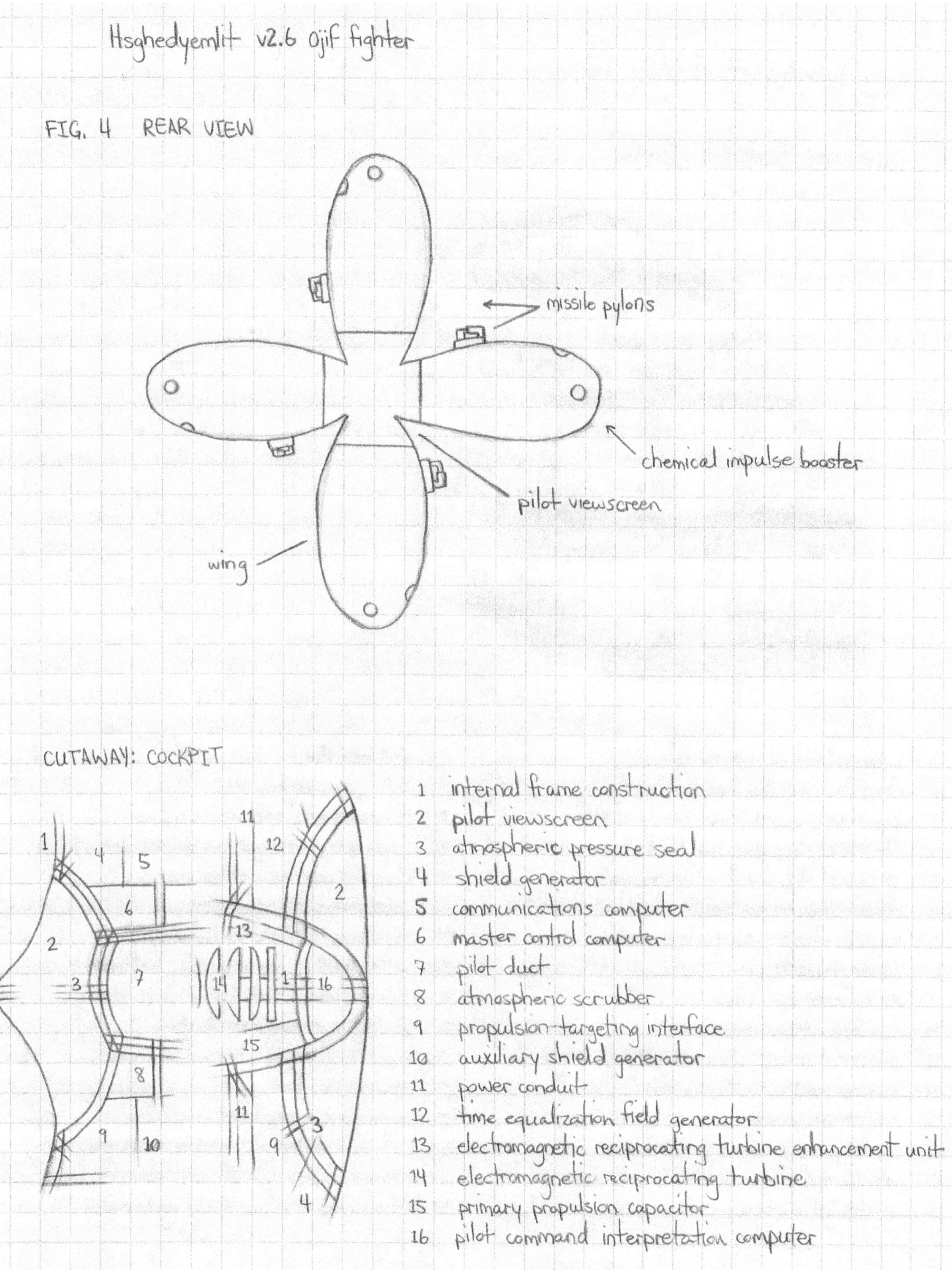

31

Hsghedyemlit v2.6 Ojif fighter

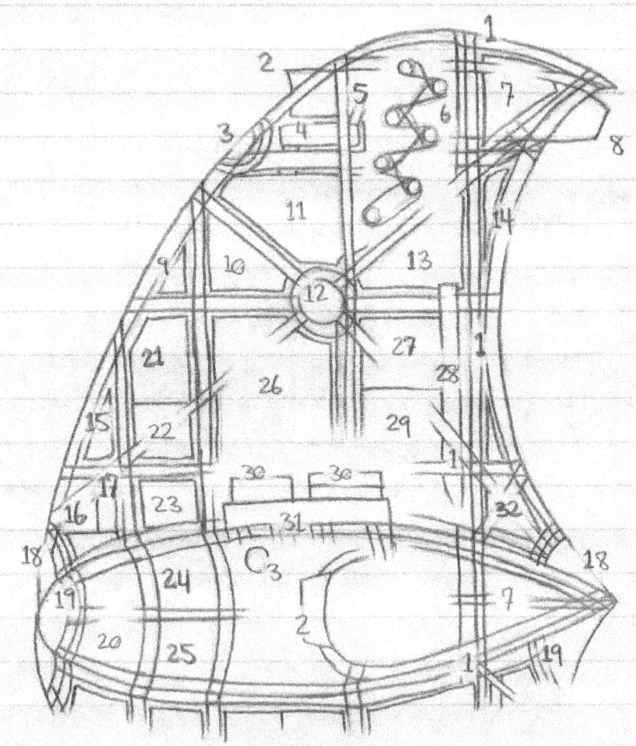

1	internal frame construction	17	sensor array
2	chemical impulse booster nozzle	18	pilot viewscreen
3	chemical impulse booster fuel port	19	atmospheric pressure seal
4	chemical impulse booster fuel pressurizer	20	auxiliary navigations sensor array
5	chemical impulse booster regulator	21	hyperspace field generator
6	chemical impulse booster catalyst fuse	22	communications array
7	synchronizing computer	23	reserve atmospheric tank
8	laser turret	24	emergency life support battery
9	targeting computer	25	shield distributor array
10	anion-cation ammeter	26	surge capacitor assembly
11	impulse booster chemical storage tank	27	auxiliary shield generator
12	cation rod attachment base	28	power conduit
13	anion generator	29	primary navigations computer
14	identify friend-or-foe transmitter	30	missile pylon attachment clamp
15	electromagnetic countermeasures unit	31	missile pylon attachment clamp base
16	shield generator	32	time equalization field generator

Hsghedyemlit v1.7 Ojif Ramship

FIGURE 1 SIDE VIEW

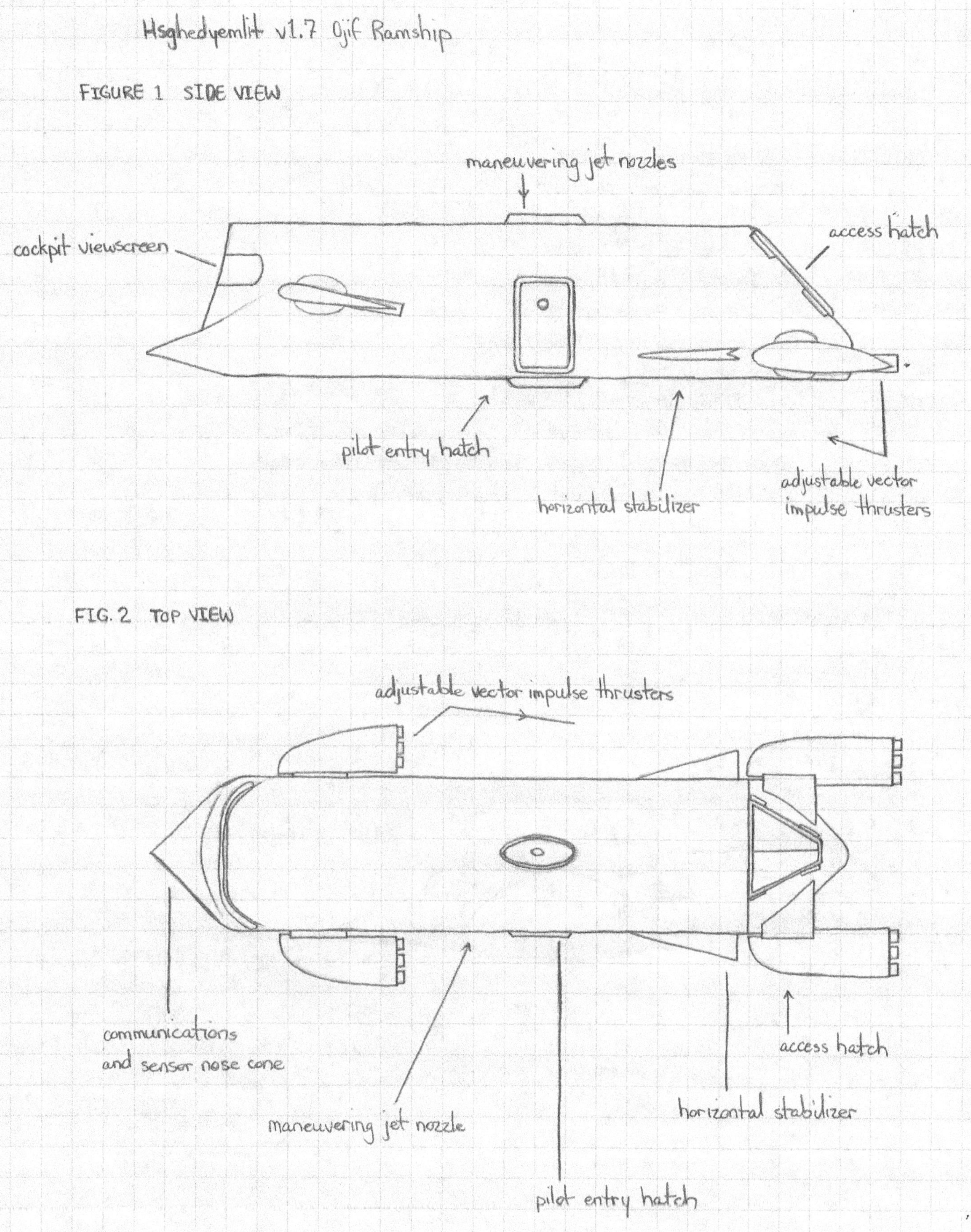

FIG. 2 TOP VIEW

Hsghedyemlit v1.7 Ojif Ramship

CLASSIFICATION: v1.7 short-range ramship
TYPE: interplanetary collision craft
CREW: two (ojif pilot and remote controller specialist)
LENGTH: 16 standard Hs-ghed lenghts
WIDTH: 6.5 standard Hs-ghed lengths
HEIGHT: 4.2 standard Hs-ghed lengths
MASS: 1,789 micromass units (fully fueled)
ARMOR: silicaluminum hull
ENGINE: chemical thrust impulse assembly
ARMAMENT: capacity for 1,200 micromass units of ordinance or payload
SPEED: 5,400 standard Hs-ghed plain lengths per hour (maximum)
RANGE: 2,000 standard Hs-ghed plain lengths (effective)

FIG. 3   FRONT VIEW

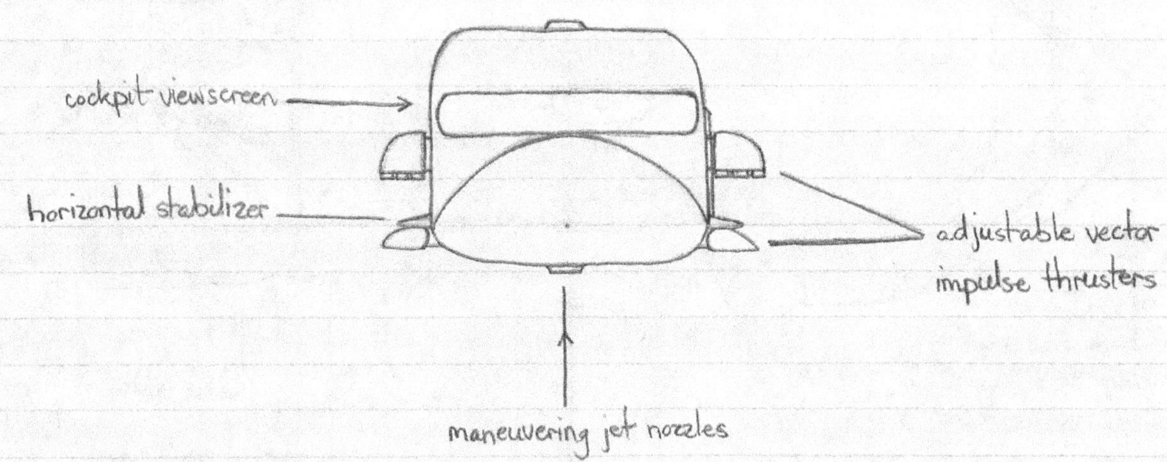

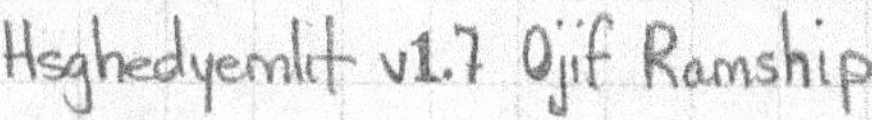

Hsghedyemlit v1.7 Ojif Ramship

FIG. 4   REAR VIEW

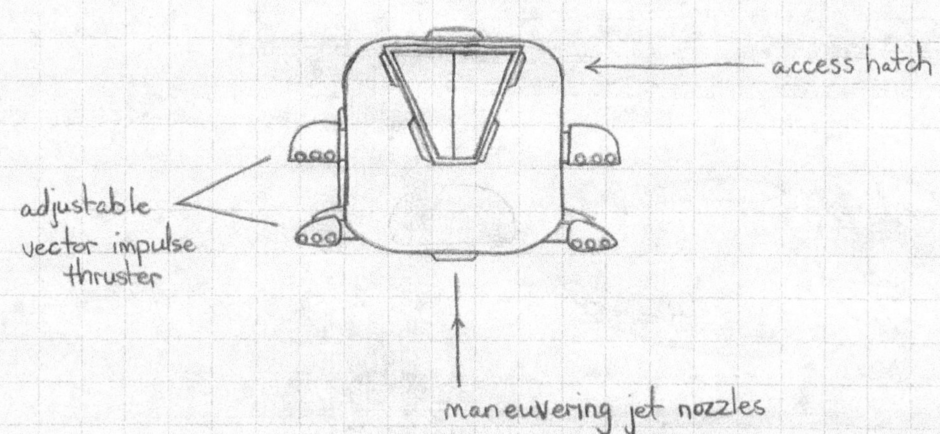

CUTAWAY: INTERIOR SECTIONS

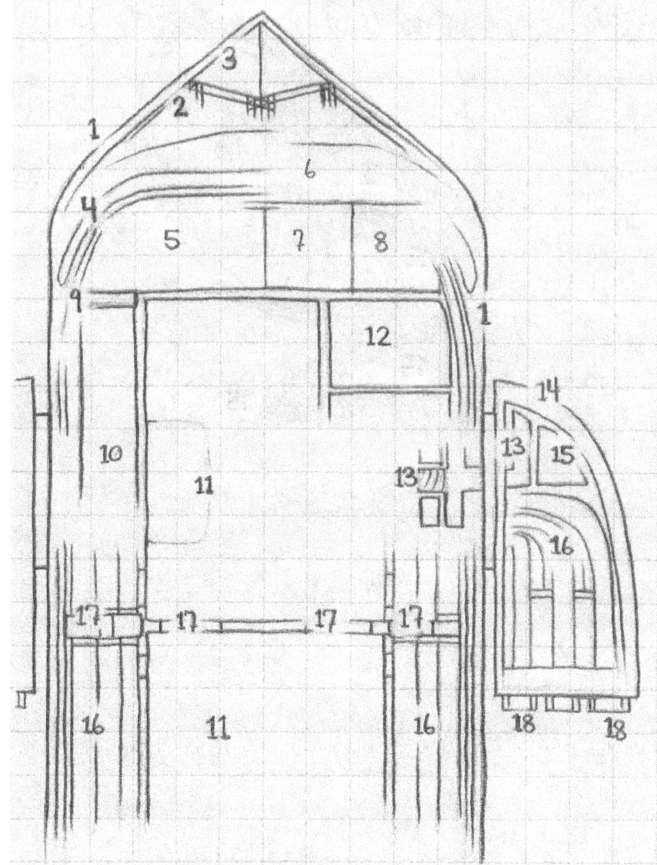

1 outer hull
2 internal frame construction
3 hardened collision tip
4 cockpit viewscreen
5 cockpit
6 atmospheric storage tank
7 atmospheric scrubber
8 thermal generator
9 pressure hull
10 pilot passageway
11 compartmentalized fuel tank
12 primary battery unit
13 adjustable vector impulse thruster directional rod
14 adjustable vector impulse thruster plane
15 spatial sensor
16 impulse thruster fuel conduit
17 impulse fuel conduit pressure regulator
18 impulse fuel thruster nozzle

Hsghedyemlit v1.7 Ojif Ramship

CUTAWAY: FUEL TANK ASSEMBLY

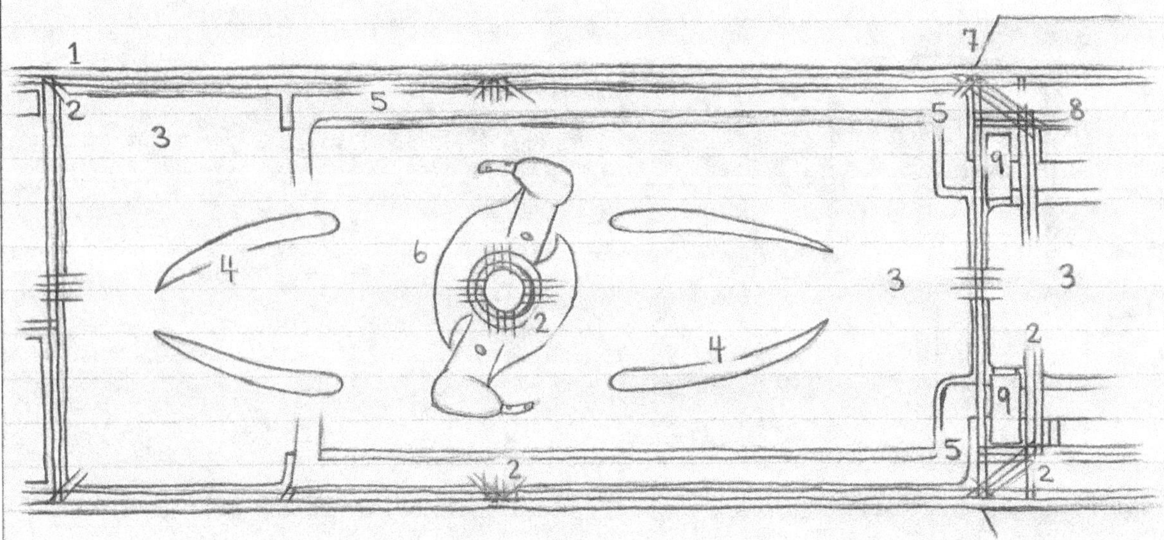

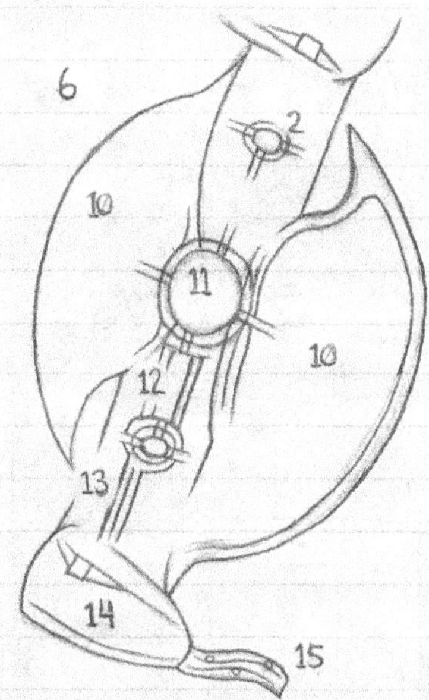

1   outer hull
2   internal frame construction
3   compartmentalized fuel tank
4   fuel circulation plane
5   impulse thruster fuel conduit
6   fuel enrichment assembly
7   maneuvering jet nozzle exhaust
8   maneuvering jet nozzle
9   impulse fuel conduit pressure regulator
10 fuel enrichment additive tank
11 fuel enrichment assembly rotation rod
12 fuel enrichment additive pressure release valve
13 fuel enrichment additive conduit
14 fuel induction chamber
15 fuel enrichment additive disbursal sleeve

 Set 23:
Shadrach

    This vessel, the last ship design found in my oldest drawings began with another case of unintentional symbolism. As it happens, though, the coincidence works perfectly for the story. I randomly decided the species this should belong to was a Suu-Cares race (or Detalernu, depending on the timeframe and one's own sensitivity). It was deemed one of the Suu-Niv, known to themselves as the Ibleb. This is the religious one with Christian facets, though I never expected them to actually be used. They are firmly against the pagan Nee-kelian gods. Species One likely used their initial ship design to develop the iconic double-helix craft it is later known for.

    Shadrach and *Azaria* are names relating to the three Hebrew brothers cast into the furnace, a famous Biblical story in the first chapters of Daniel. I happened to be reading about it before this set of schematics was started. If that makes Species 001 a tyrannical Babylonian king or not, I can't be sure.

Shadrach
FIGURE 1   TOP VIEW
antigravity generator
connector duct
generator sphere
viewport
pressurized compartments
fuel sphere
defensive rocket battery
chemical thrust pod

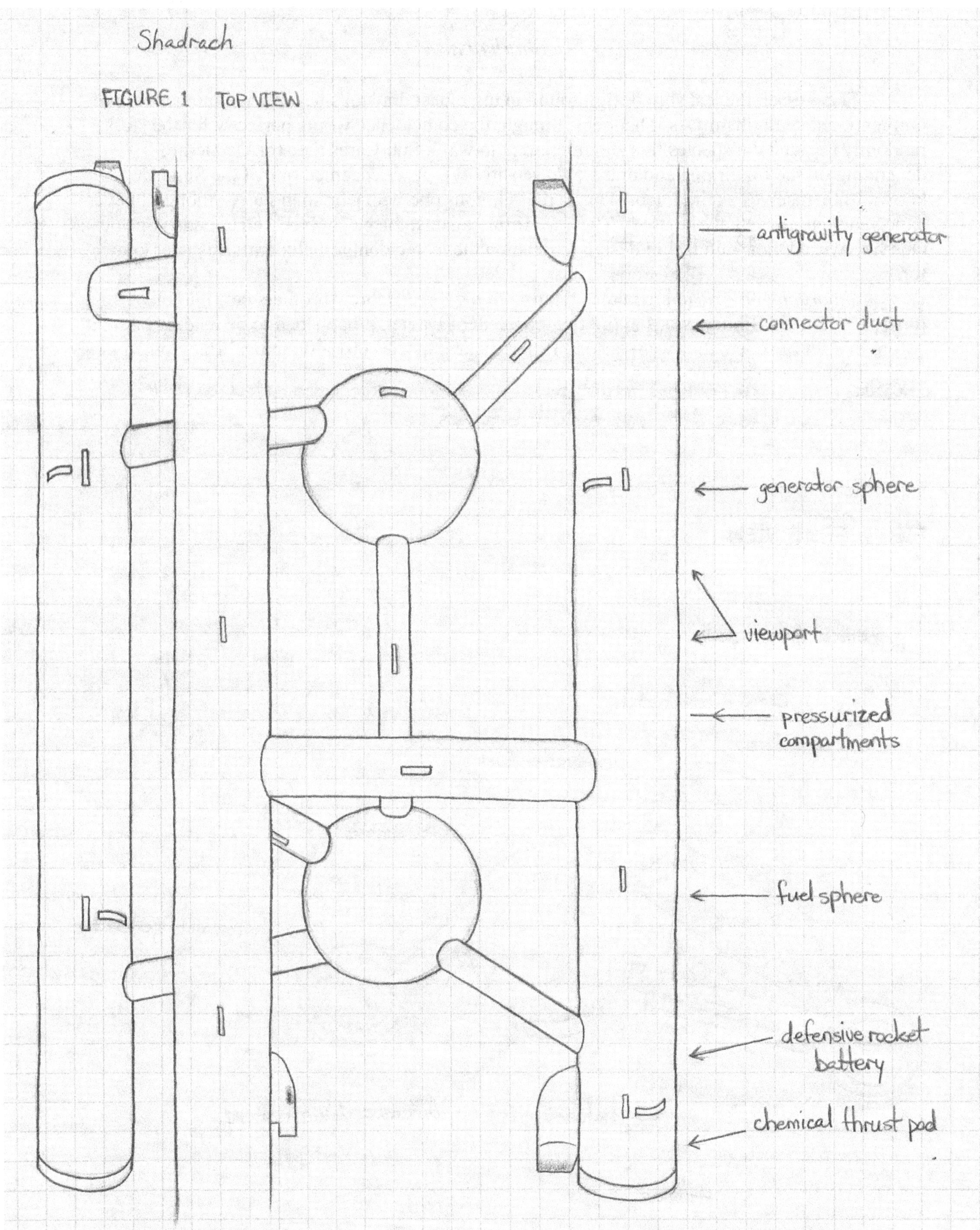

Shadrach

CLASSIFICATION: Azaria-class passenger ferry
TYPE: Suu-Niv cargo vessel
CREW: twelve (4 officers, 8 enlisted) (capacity for 28 sentients)
LENGTH: 72 Nikel units
WIDTH: 6.7 Nikel units
HEIGHT: 4.2 Nikel units
MASS: 58.36 Nikel temple masses (5,836 Nikel pane masses)
ARMOR: aluminum-reinforced steetanicarb
ENGINES: six chemical thrust pods, fission generator, coordinated ion drive
ARMAMENT: four defensive rocket batteries

FIG. 2 FRONT VIEW

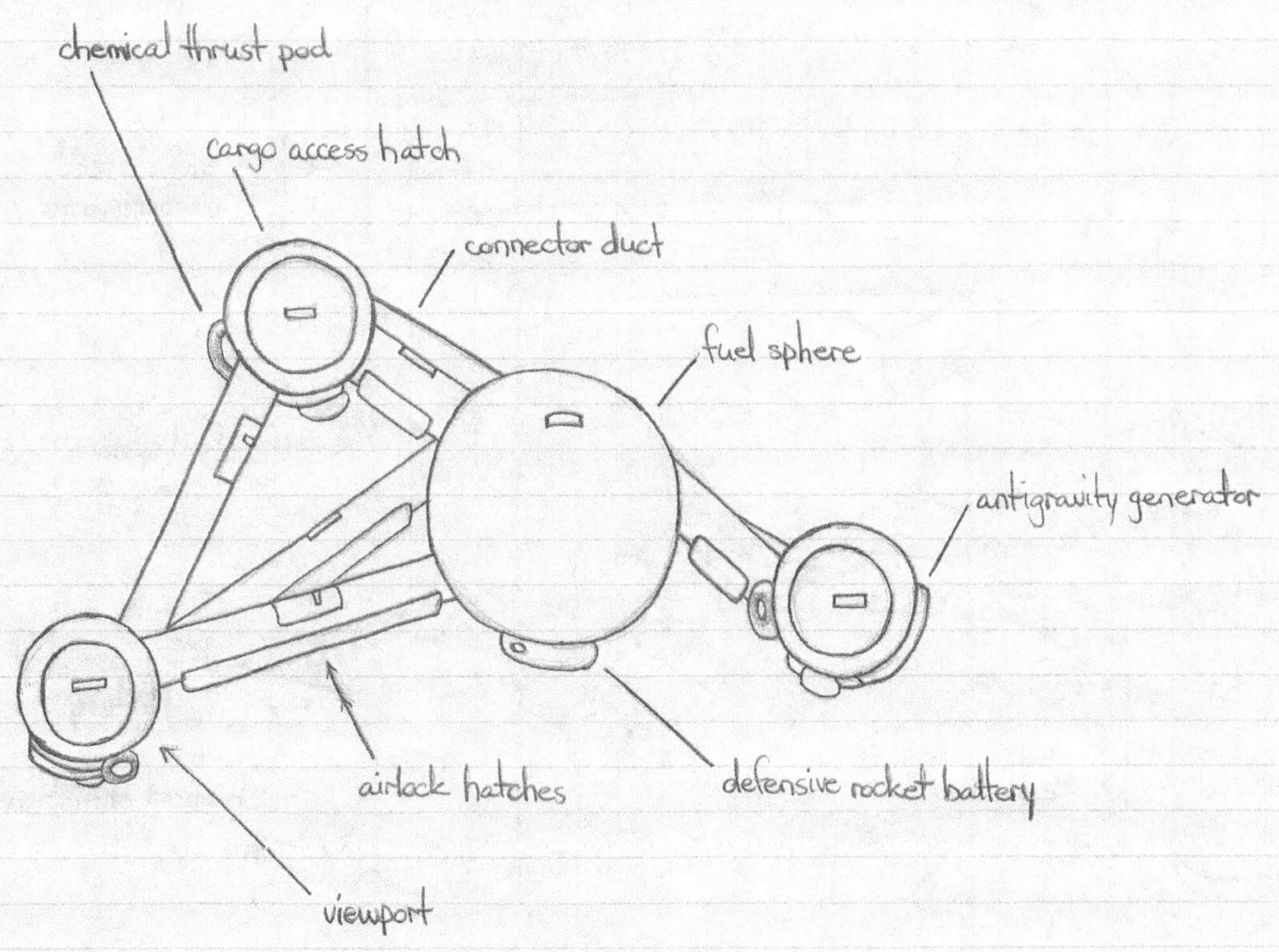

Shadrach

FIG. 3   BOTTOM VIEW

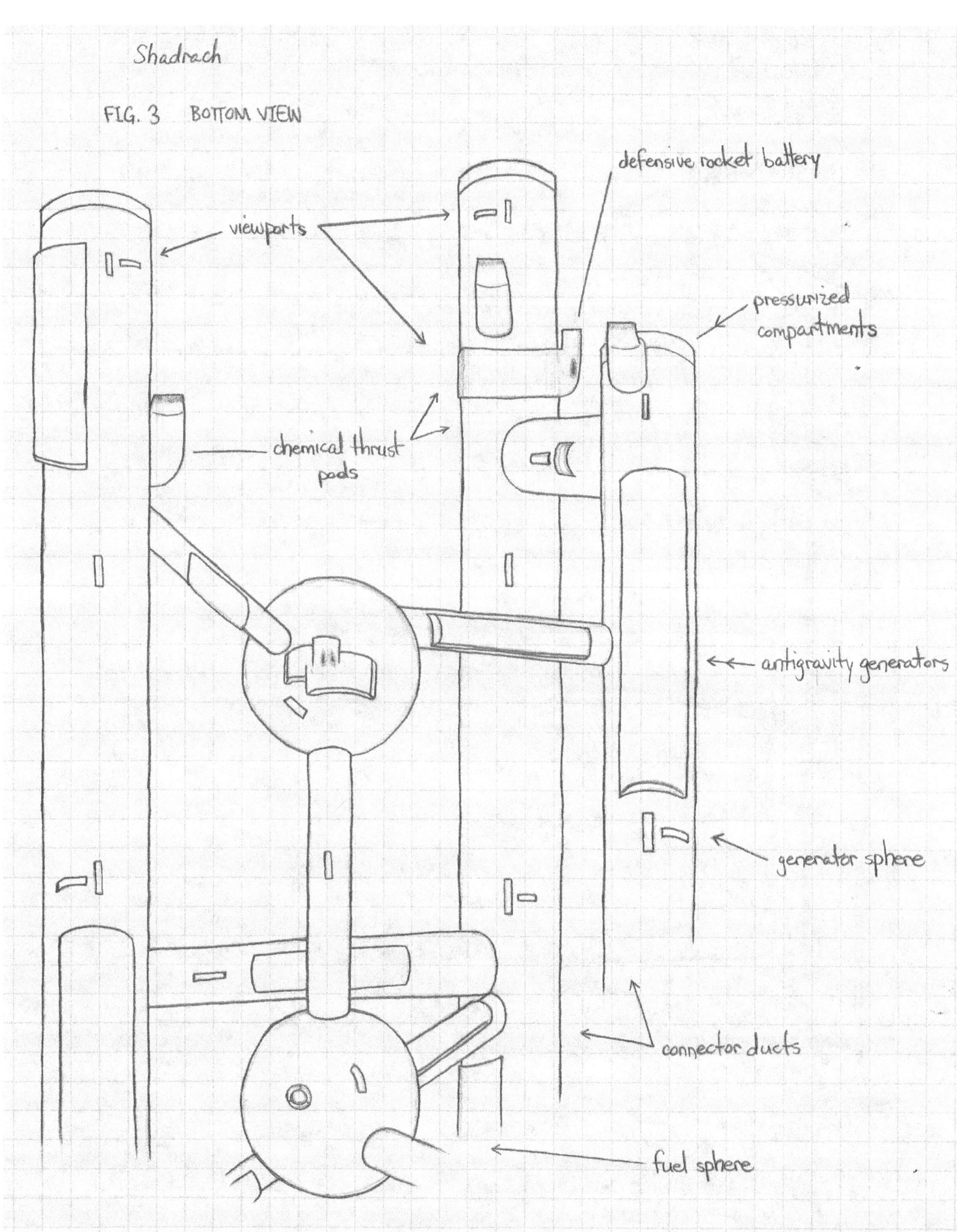

Shadrach

FIG. 4   SIDE VIEW

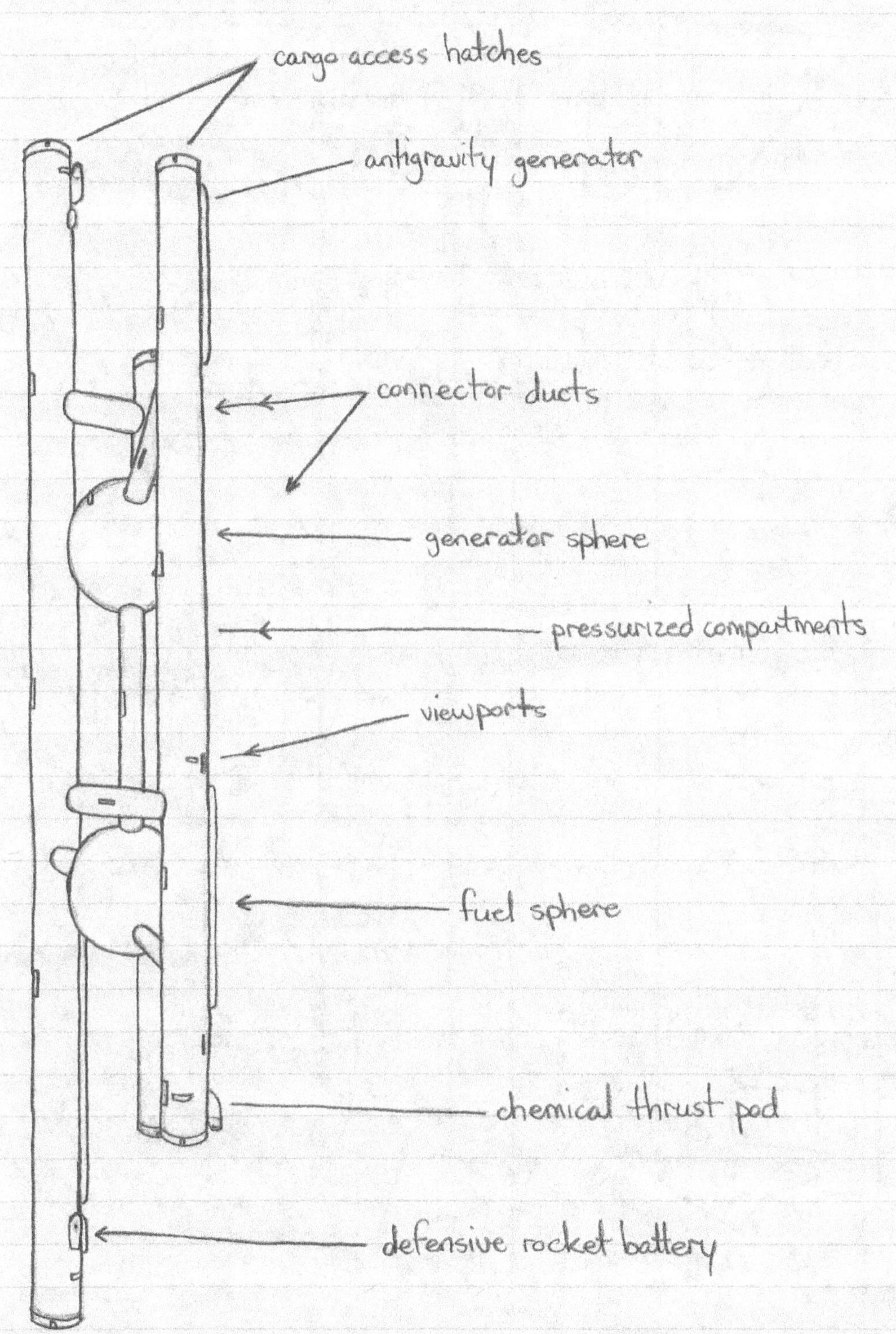

Shadrach

CUTAWAY: PRESSURIZED COMPARTMENT

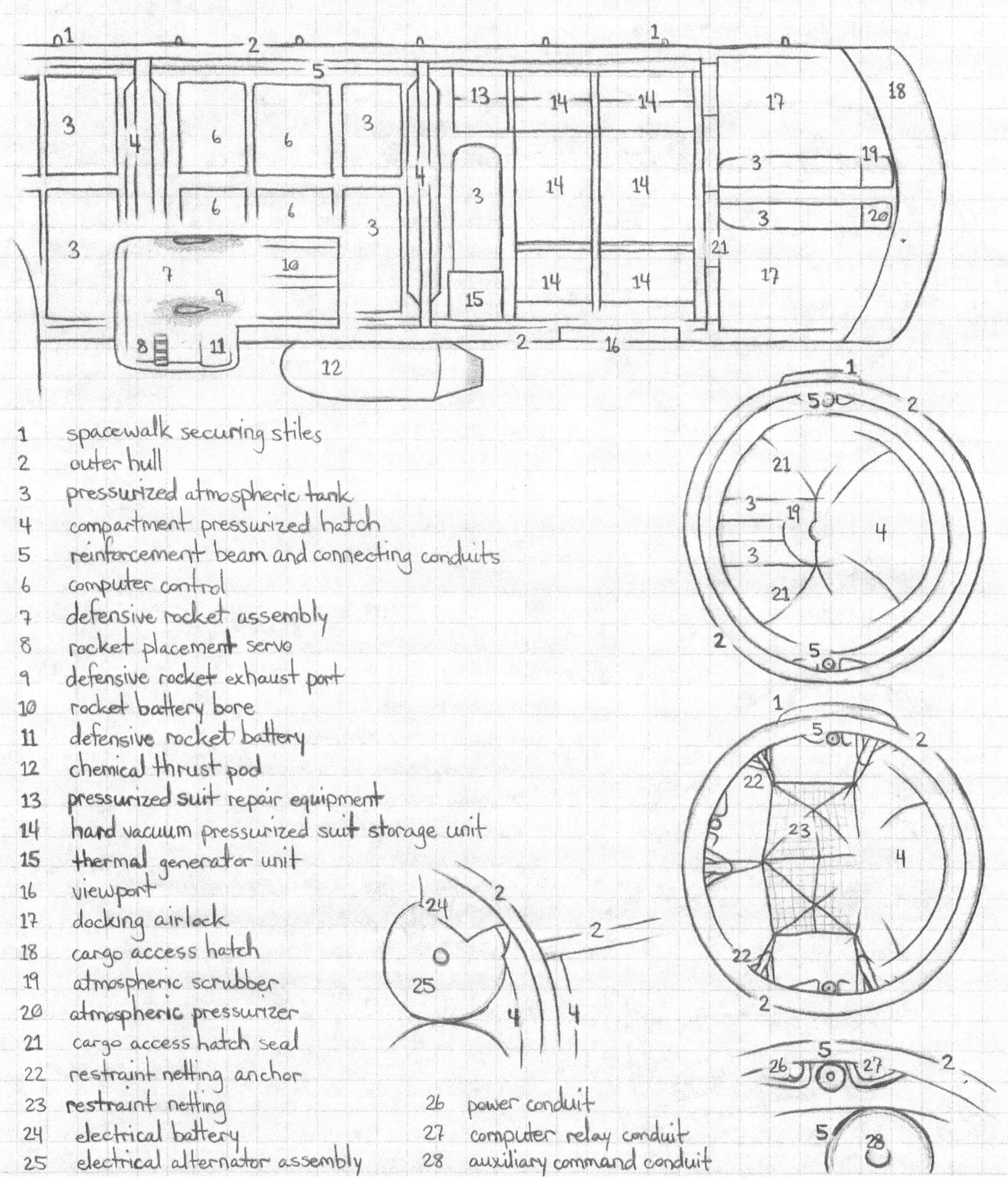

1 spacewalk securing stiles
2 outer hull
3 pressurized atmospheric tank
4 compartment pressurized hatch
5 reinforcement beam and connecting conduits
6 computer control
7 defensive rocket assembly
8 rocket placement servo
9 defensive rocket exhaust port
10 rocket battery bore
11 defensive rocket battery
12 chemical thrust pod
13 pressurized suit repair equipment
14 hard vacuum pressurized suit storage unit
15 thermal generator unit
16 viewport
17 docking airlock
18 cargo access hatch
19 atmospheric scrubber
20 atmospheric pressurizer
21 cargo access hatch seal
22 restraint netting anchor
23 restraint netting
24 electrical battery
25 electrical alternator assembly
26 power conduit
27 computer relay conduit
28 auxiliary command conduit

42

Shadrach

CUTAWAY: GENERATOR SPHERE

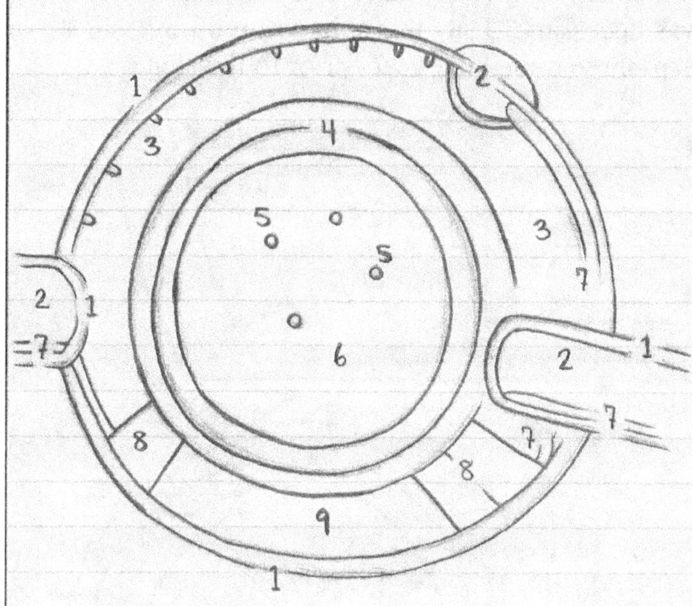

1 outer hull
2 connector duct
3 crew passage
4 electrothermal converter
5 fission generator fuel rod
6 fission generator chamber
7 electrical conduit
8 electrical transformer
9 electrothermal capacitor

CUTAWAY: FUEL SPHERE

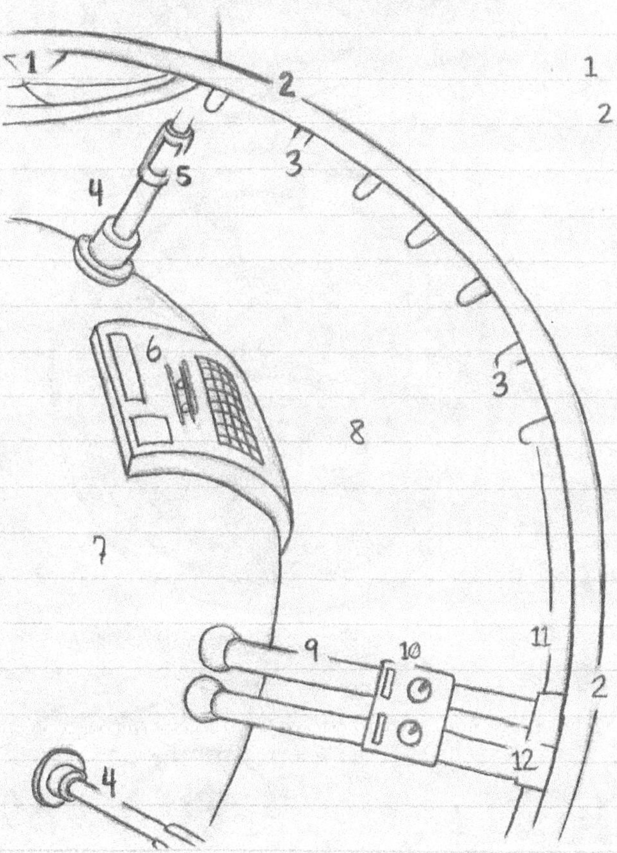

1 connector duct pressure hatch
2 outer hull
3 crew securing stiles
4 fuel tank reinforcement brace
5 fuel tank brace reinforcement sensor
6 primary fuel disbursal control nexus
7 stored chemical thrust fuel tank
8 crew access duct
9 chemical thrust distribution conduit
10 fuel conduit auxiliary control nexus
11 pressurized chemical thrust fuel conduit
12 chemical thrust fuel line pressure regulator

Set 24:
Viands Nidor

It occurred to me, all sentients need food. This ship is specifically designed for transporting edible material. While looking up good words in the *Flip Dictionary*, which is merely the best thesaurus EVER MADE, I found many convenient and funny candidate words to apply. Thus, no clever wordplay or reverse spelling was necessary. I say this ship was built by someone other than Species 096, but for the united Gaepvihnyemlit some years prior to the siege of Lynop.

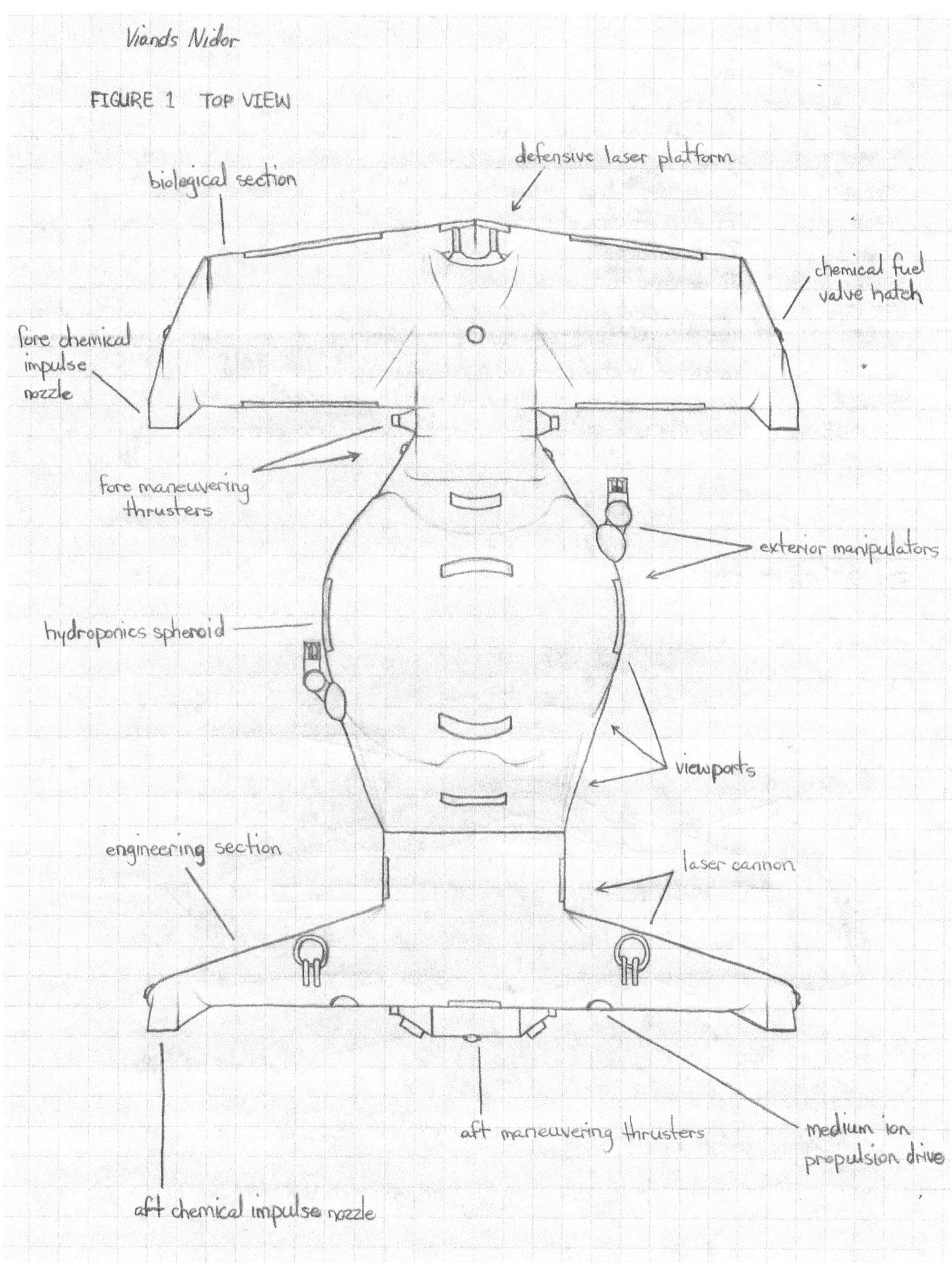

Viands Nidor
FIGURE 1   TOP VIEW
biological section
defensive laser platform
chemical fuel valve hatch
fore chemical impulse nozzle
fore maneuvering thrusters
exterior manipulators
hydroponics spheroid
viewports
engineering section
laser cannon
aft maneuvering thrusters
medium ion propulsion drive
aft chemical impulse nozzle

Viands Nider

CLASSIFICATION: Gastronomical class 3 transport, Ort-class
TYPE: heavy yemlit food transport
CREW: 14 (five officers, nine enlisted)
LENGTH: 28 standard feet
WIDTH: 22 standard feet
HEIGHT: 10.3 standard feet
MASS: 185,000 standard mass units (fully loaded)
ARMOR: reinforced steetanicarb and pyroceramite hull, 4gen shields
ENGINES: heavy chemical impulse thruster, medium ion propulsion drive
ARMAMENT: defensive laser platform, two swivel-mounted laser cannon

FIG. 2   FRONT VIEW

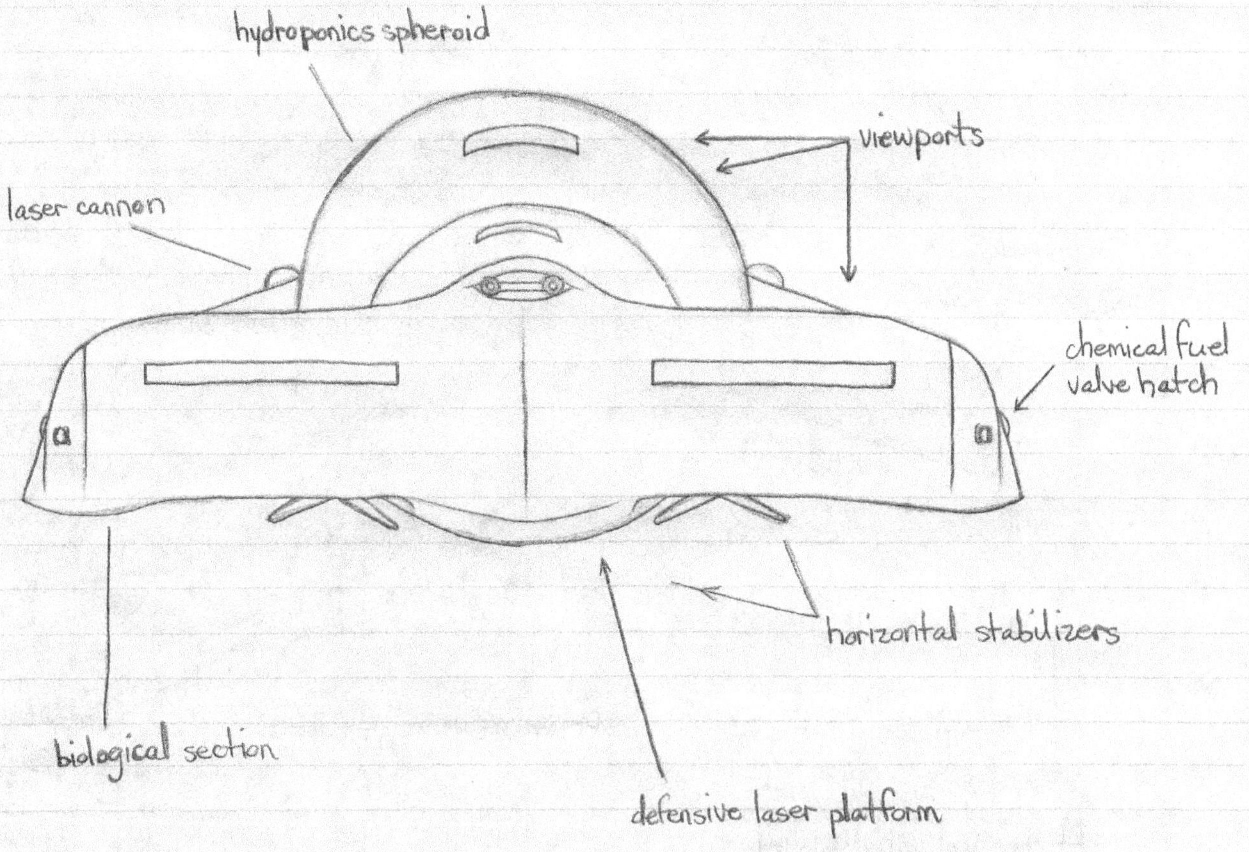

Viands Nidor
FIG. 3 SIDE VIEW
defensive laser platform
biological section
fore maneuvering thrusters
viewports
exterior manipulator
hydroponics spheroid
laser cannon
engineering section
aft chemical impulse nozzle
aft maneuvering thrusters

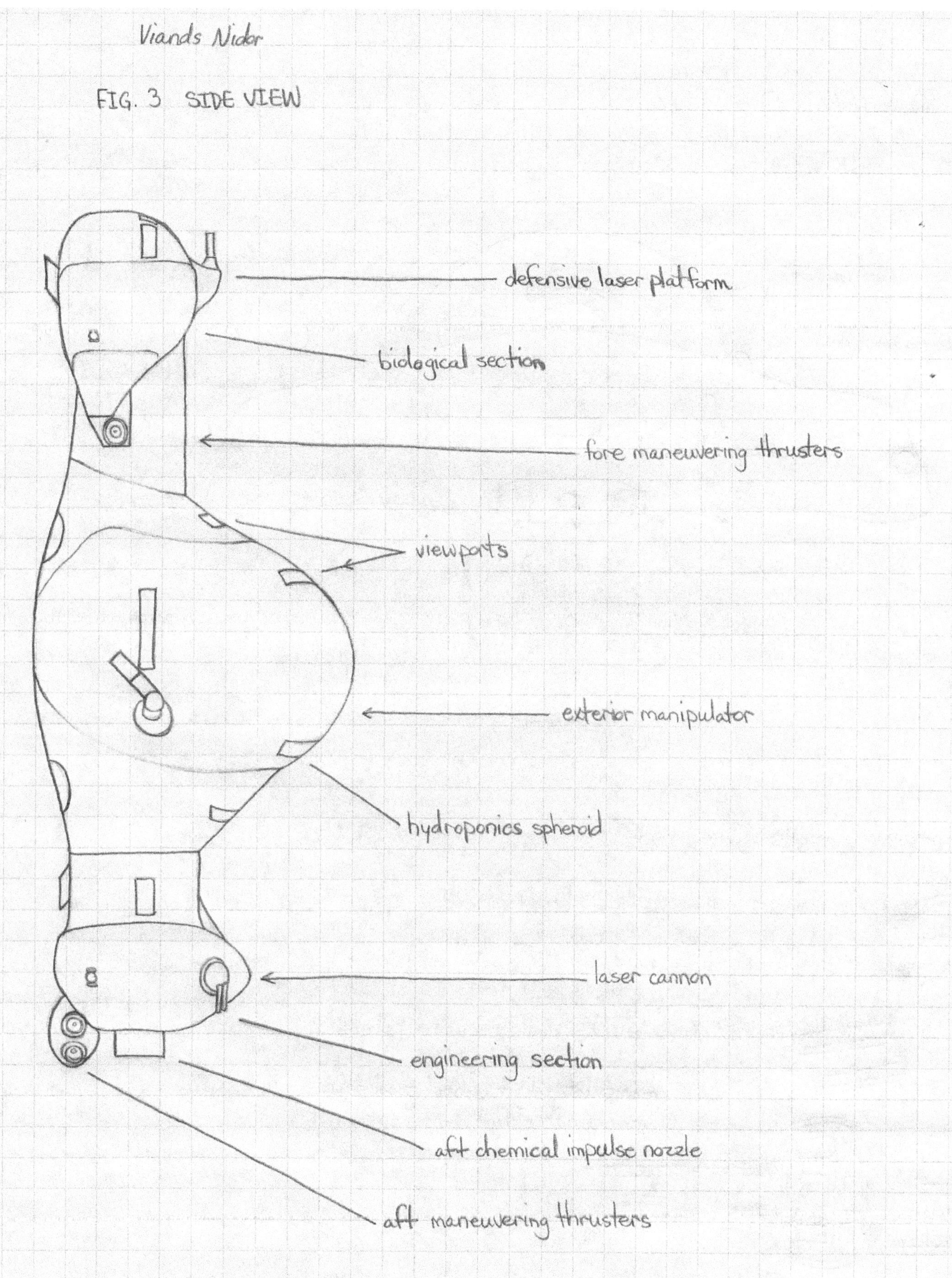

FIG. 4   REAR VIEW

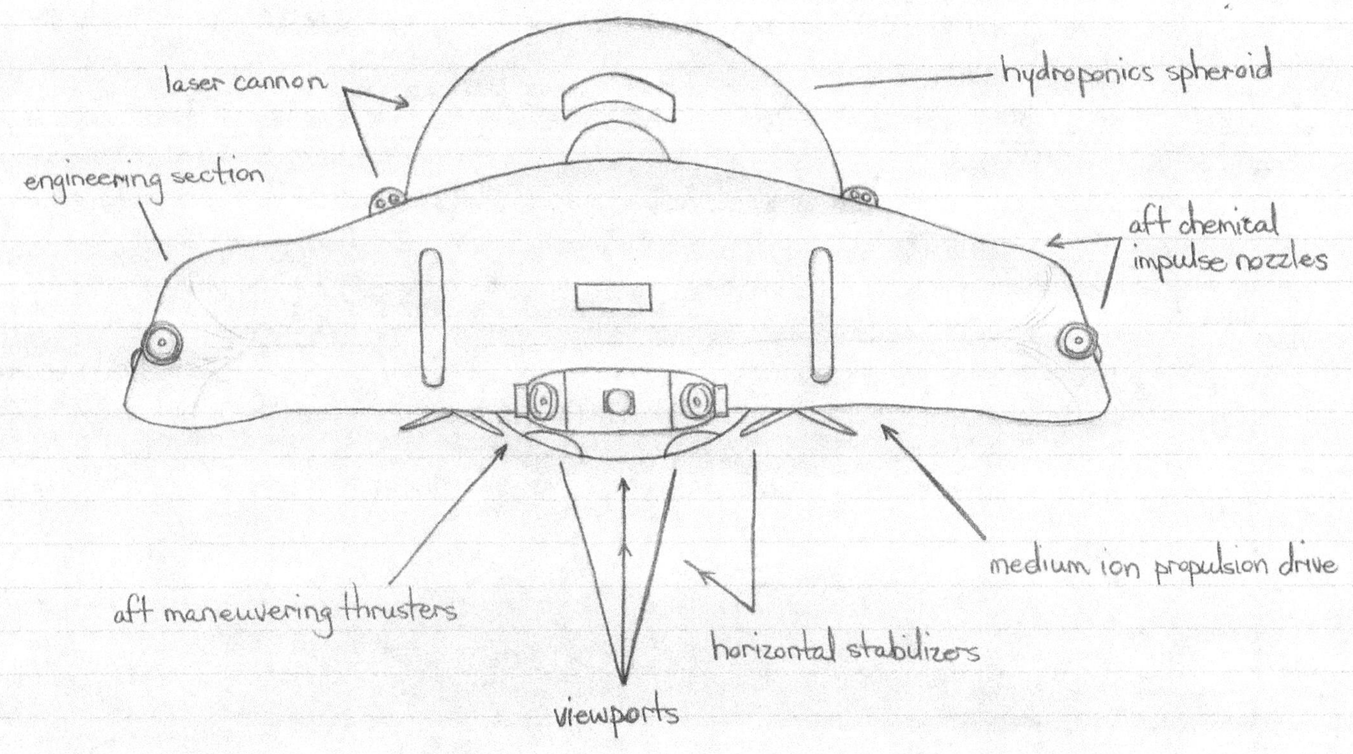

CUTAWAY: EXTERIOR MANIPULATORS

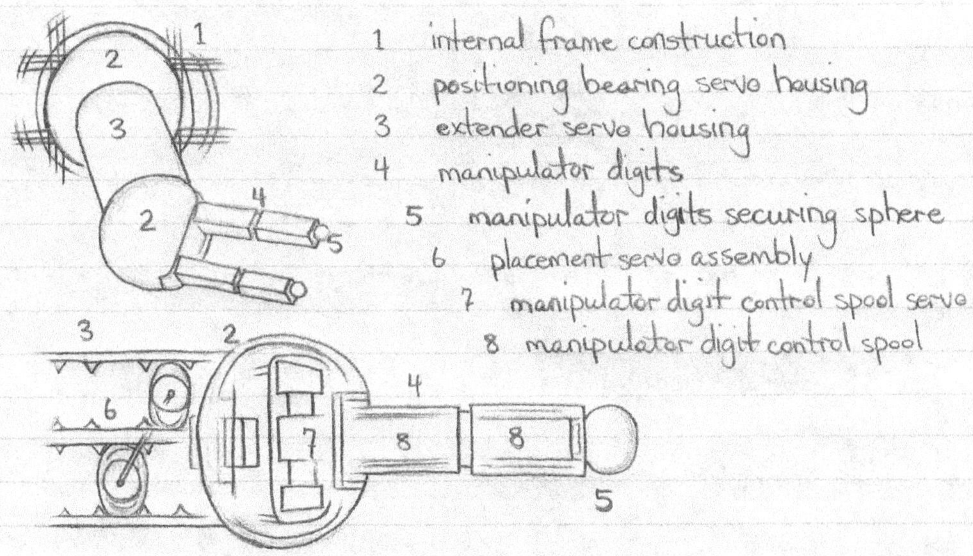

1   internal frame construction
2   positioning bearing servo housing
3   extender servo housing
4   manipulator digits
5   manipulator digits securing sphere
6   placement servo assembly
7   manipulator digit control spool servo
8   manipulator digit control spool

48

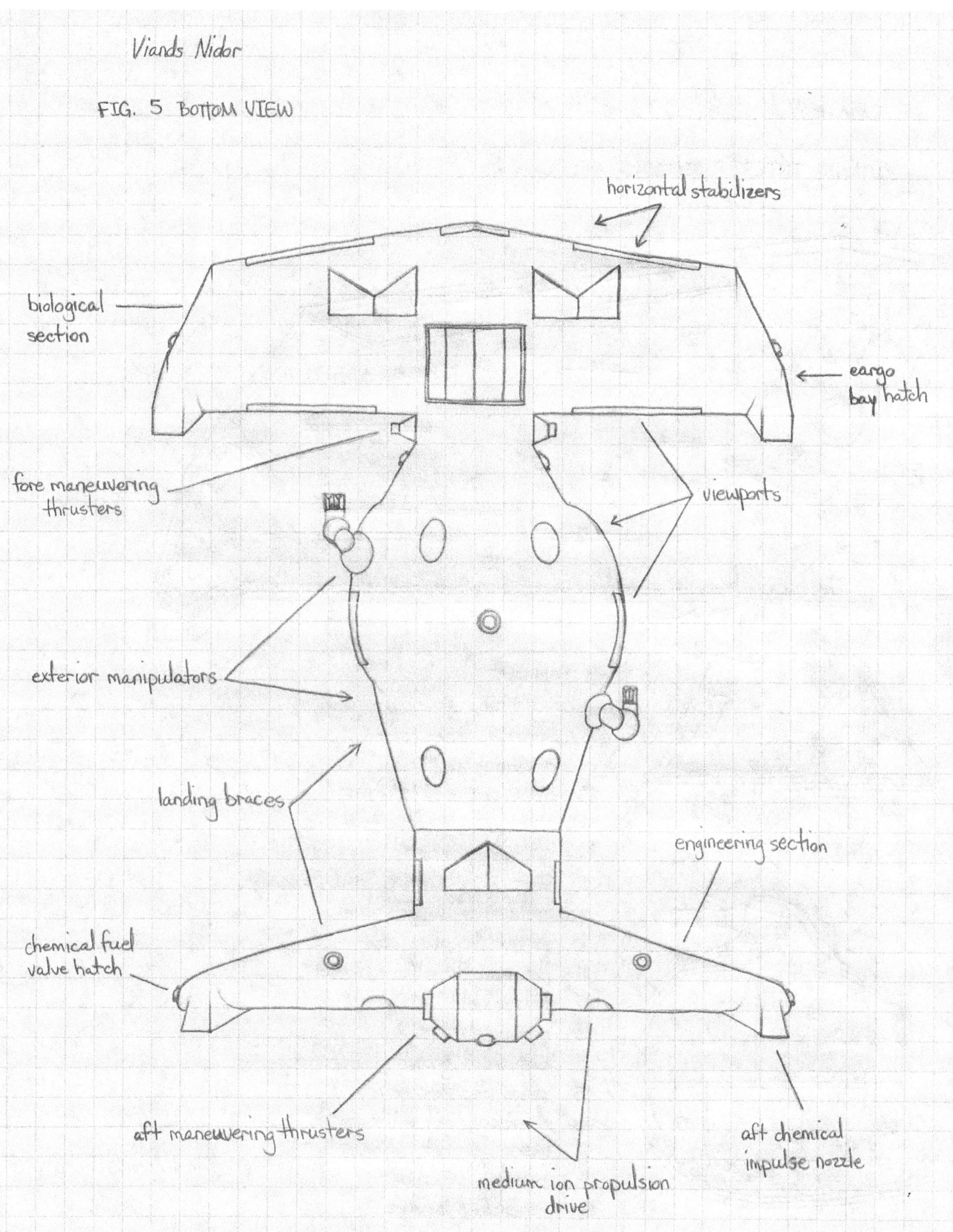

Viands Nidor
FIG. 5 BOTTOM VIEW
horizontal stabilizers
biological section
cargo bay hatch
fore maneuvering thrusters
viewports
exterior manipulators
landing braces
engineering section
chemical fuel valve hatch
aft maneuvering thrusters
medium ion propulsion drive
aft chemical impulse nozzle

CUTAWAY: INTERIOR BIOLOGICAL SECTION

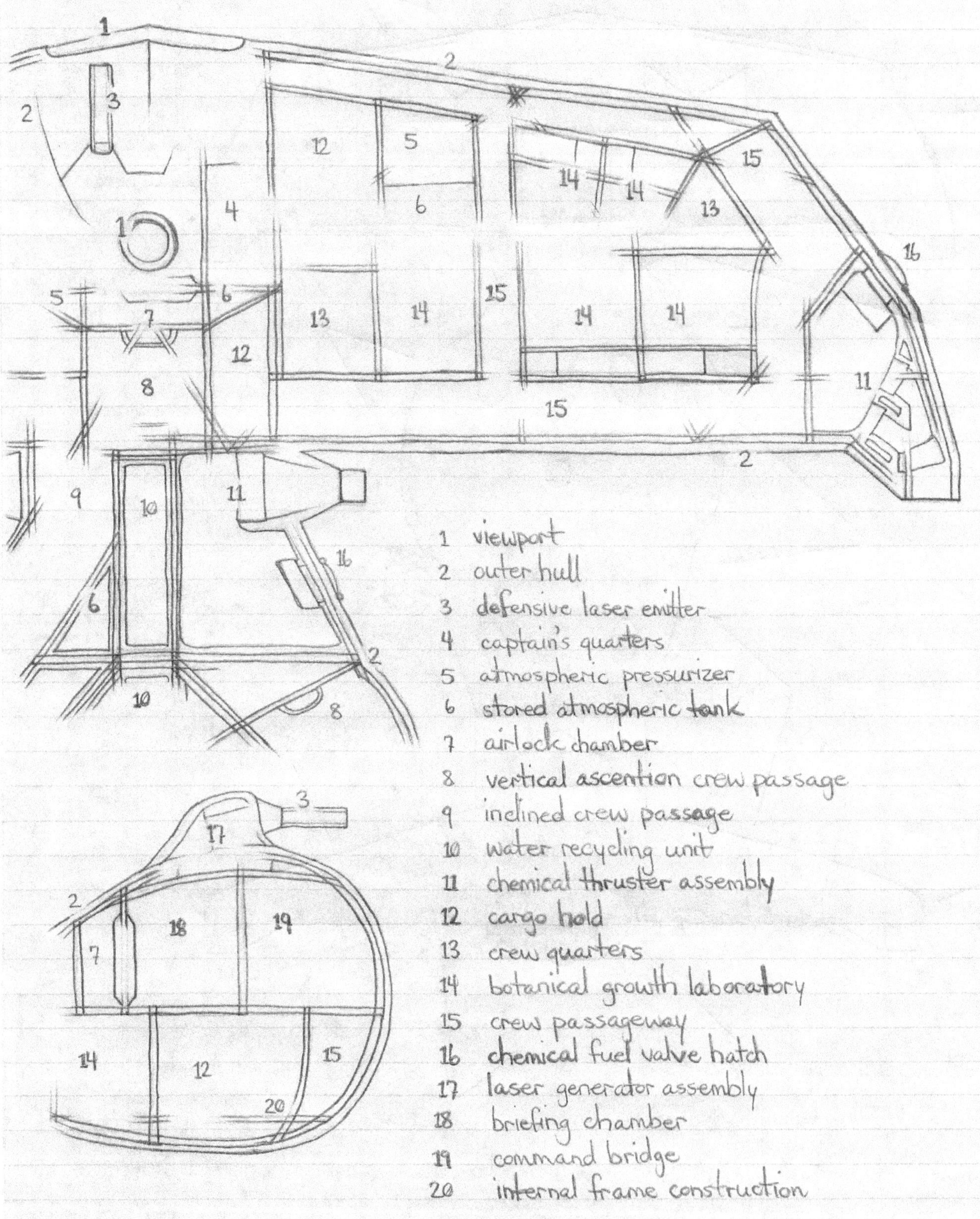

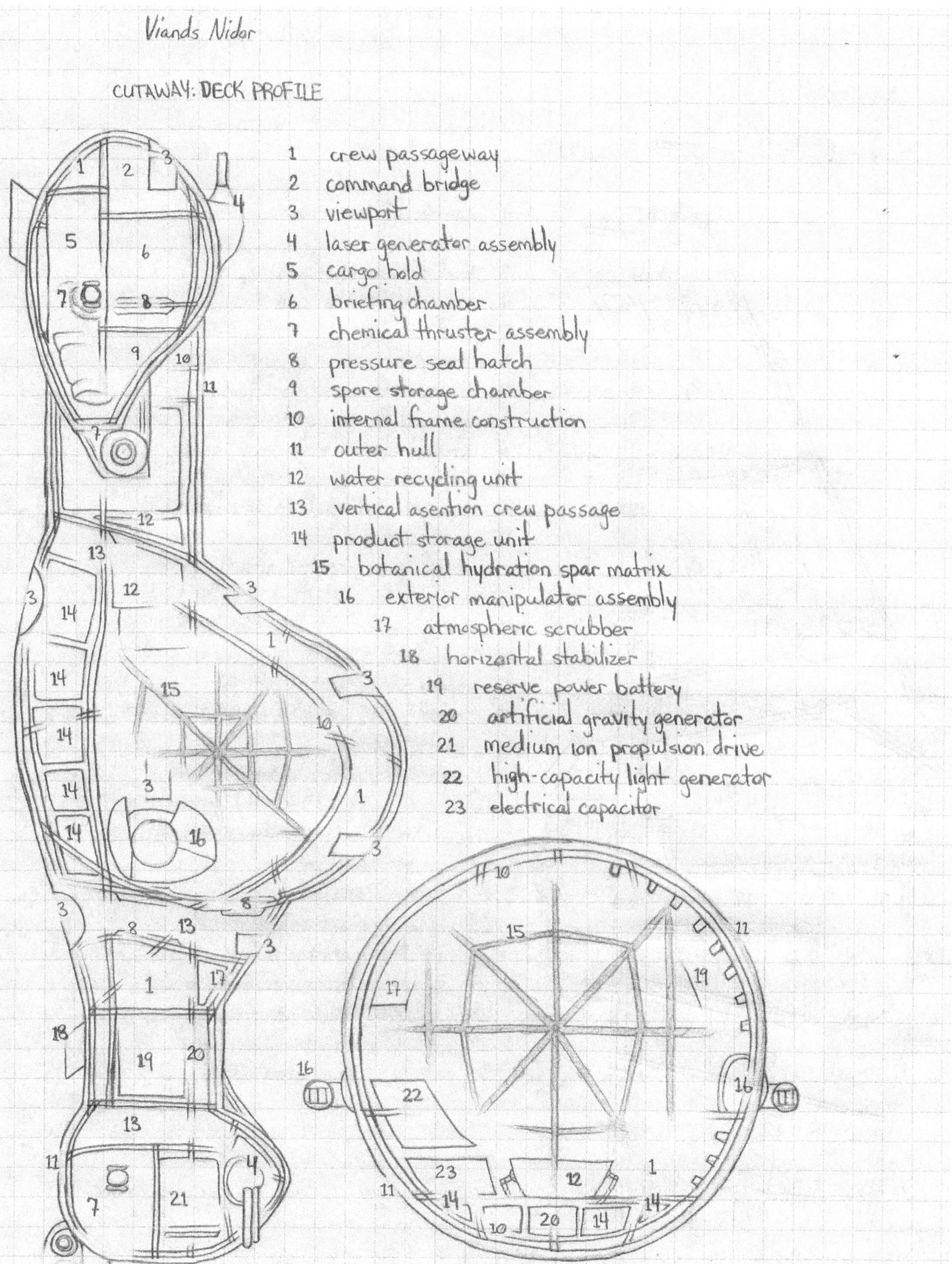

51

CUTAWAY: INTERIOR ENGINEER SECTION

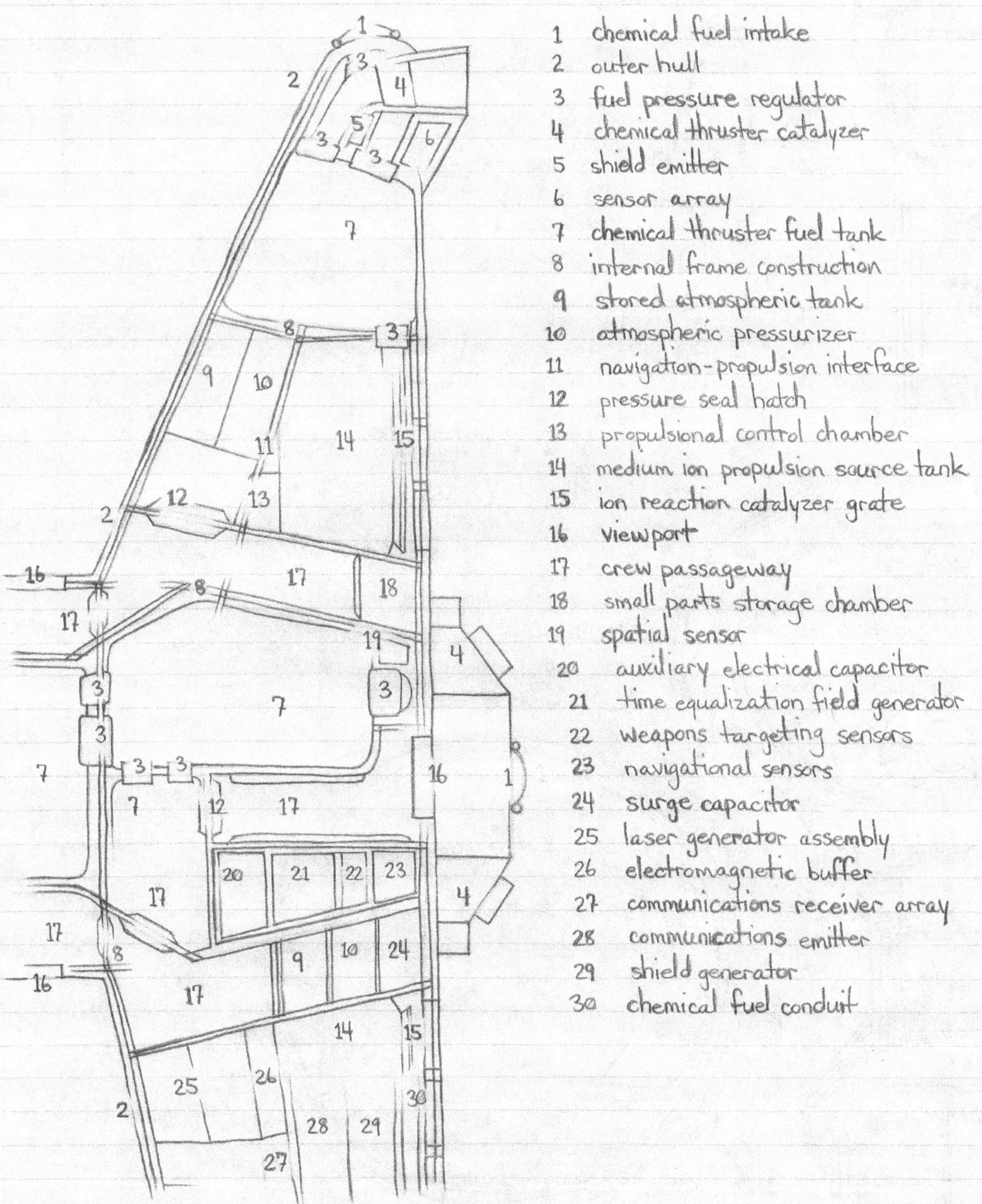

1 chemical fuel intake
2 outer hull
3 fuel pressure regulator
4 chemical thruster catalyzer
5 shield emitter
6 sensor array
7 chemical thruster fuel tank
8 internal frame construction
9 stored atmospheric tank
10 atmospheric pressurizer
11 navigation-propulsion interface
12 pressure seal hatch
13 propulsional control chamber
14 medium ion propulsion source tank
15 ion reaction catalyzer grate
16 viewport
17 crew passageway
18 small parts storage chamber
19 spatial sensor
20 auxiliary electrical capacitor
21 time equalization field generator
22 weapons targeting sensors
23 navigational sensors
24 surge capacitor
25 laser generator assembly
26 electromagnetic buffer
27 communications receiver array
28 communications emitter
29 shield generator
30 chemical fuel conduit

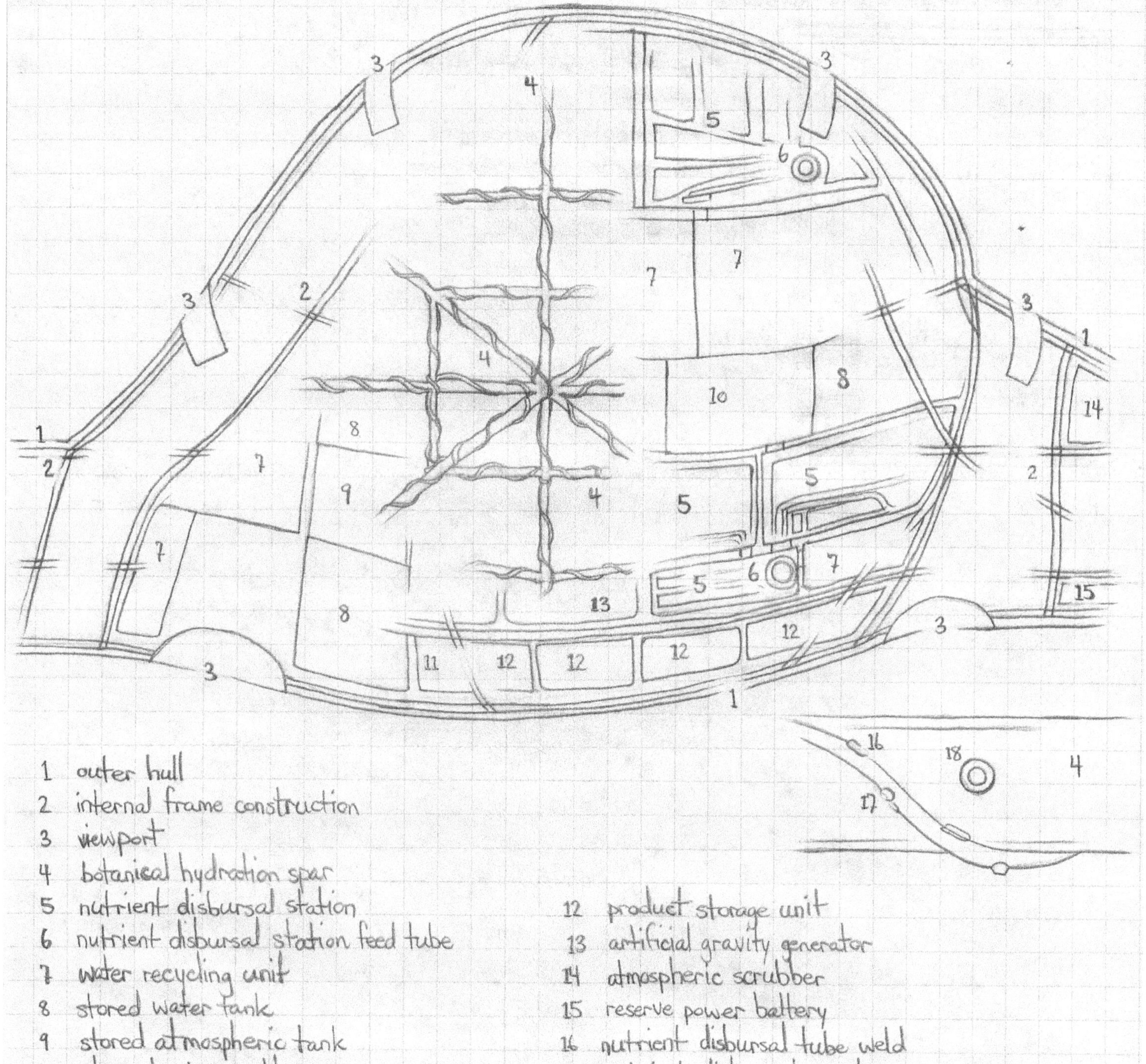

1 outer hull
2 internal frame construction
3 viewport
4 botanical hydration spar
5 nutrient disbursal station
6 nutrient disbursal station feed tube
7 water recycling unit
8 stored water tank
9 stored atmospheric tank
10 atmospheric scrubber
11 thermal generator
12 product storage unit
13 artificial gravity generator
14 atmospheric scrubber
15 reserve power battery
16 nutrient disbursal tube weld
17 nutrient disbursal nozzle
18 air pressure valve

53

CUTAWAY: MEDIUM ION PROPULSION DRIVE

1   internal frame construction
2   outer hull
3   ion propulsion source tank
4   ion reaction catalyzer grate
5   ion funneler
6   ion directional grate
7   chemical fuel conduit

Set 25:
Undaunted-class fighter-bomber

This later form of the *Ambitious*-class vehicle, used alternatively as a fighter and a bomber, was used extensively against the conquests of the Kvhingleyemlit. Many of the *Undaunted*-class fighters and freighters were stolen by Lynopte in their flight after subjugation, as one may read in *Lone Soldier*. The heavy transport was an original design meant to cope well with atmosphere, notwithstanding its reverse resemblance to other science fiction arcs wherein humans have settled on three worlds over its long, generally forgotten history…

FIGURE 1   TOP VIEW

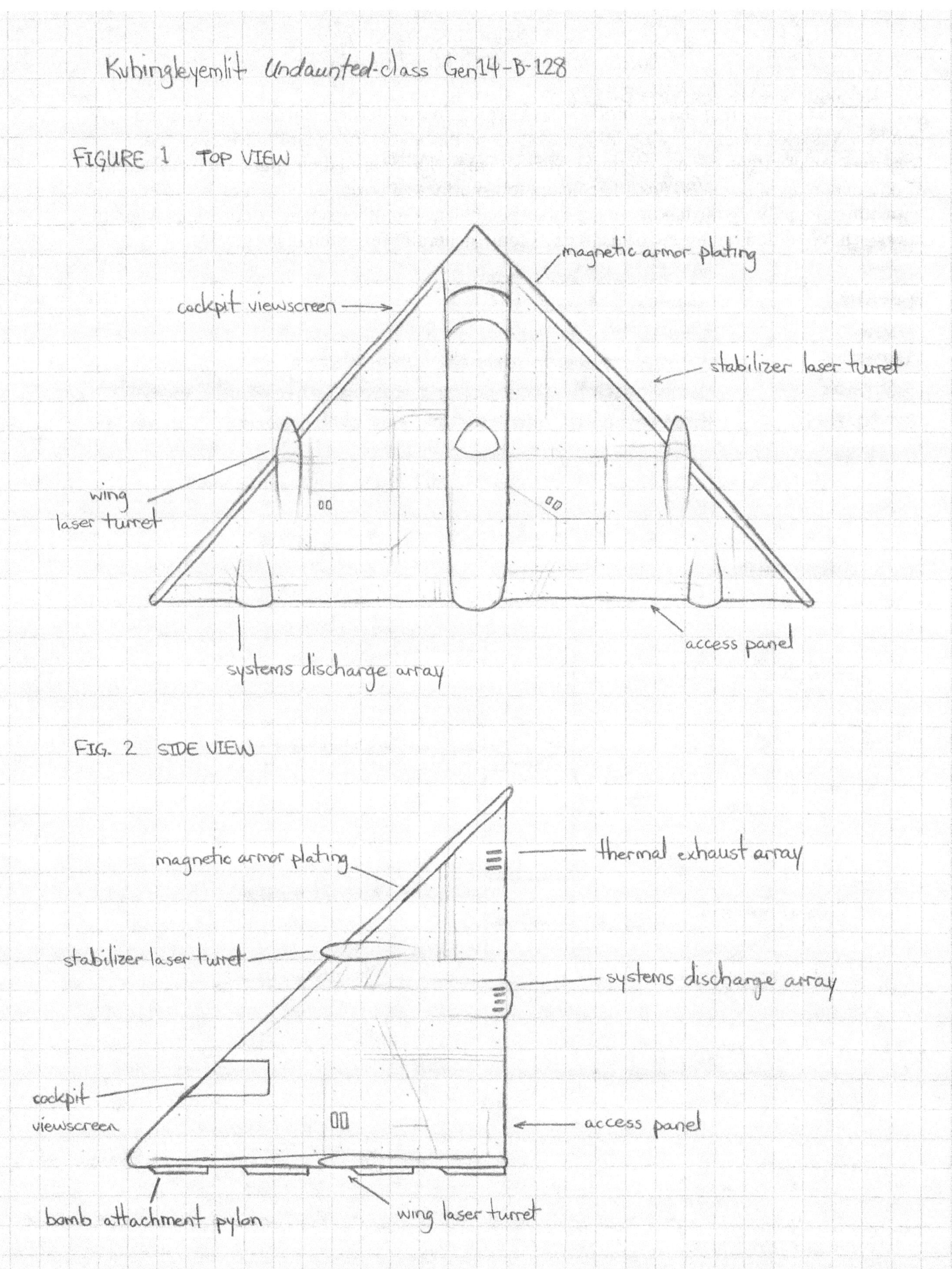

FIG. 2   SIDE VIEW

Kvhingleyemlit Gen14-B-128

CLASSIFICATION:	generation 14 short-range fighter
TYPE:	Undaunted-class attack bomber
CREW:	pilot
LENGTH:	14 standard body lengths
WIDTH:	28 standard body lengths
HEIGHT:	14 standard body lengths
MASS:	9,446 kg (20,824 lbs$_f$)
ARMOR:	steetanicarb with magnetic armor plating
ENGINES:	electromagnetic reciprocating turbine, anti-gravity generator
ARMAMENT:	three offensive laser turrets, four bomb capacity

FIG. 3   FRONT VIEW

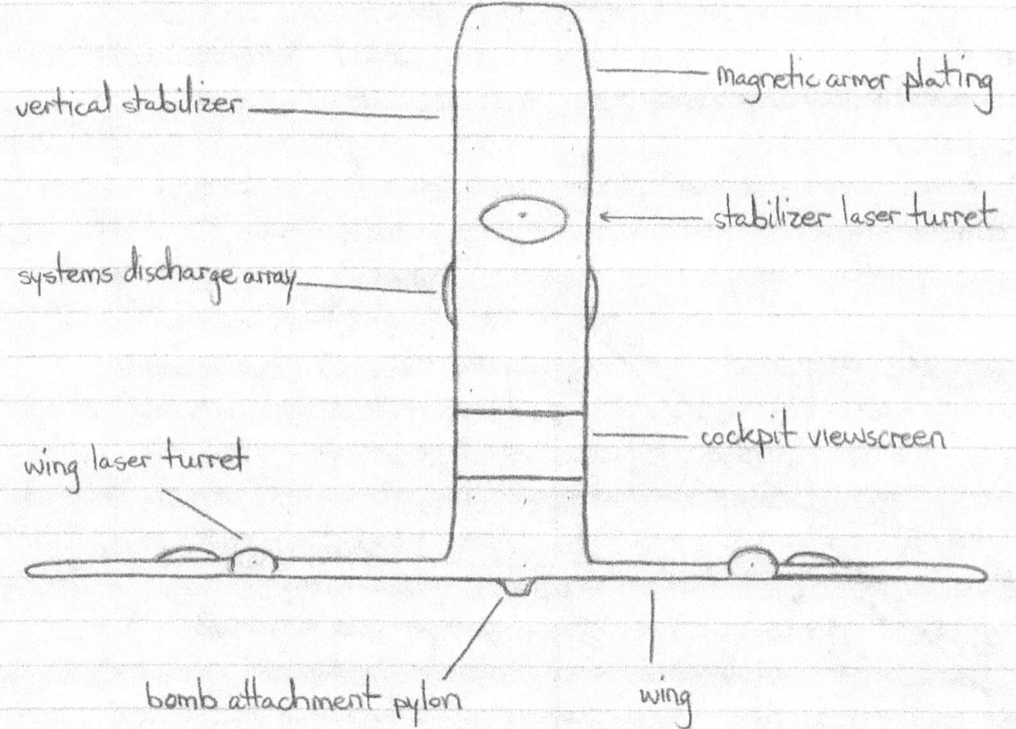

Kvhingleyemlit Undaunted-class Gen 24-B-128

CUTAWAY: INTERIOR VERTICAL STABILIZER SYSTEMS

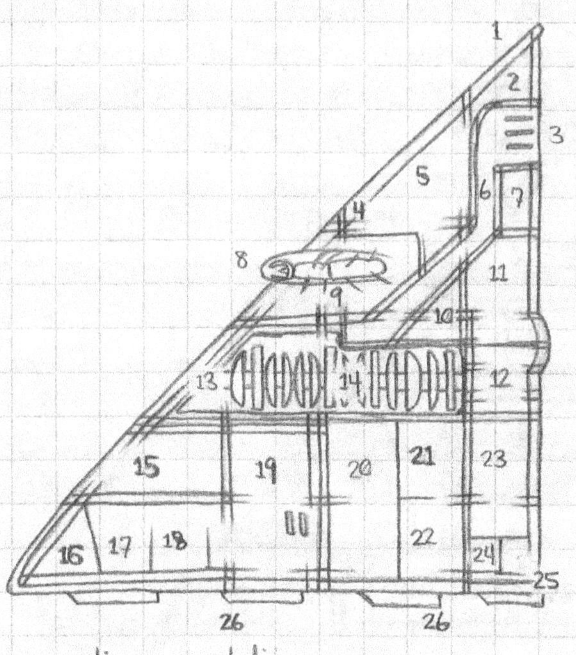

6 thermal exhaust duct
7 rear sensor array
8 offensive laser turret emitter
9 laser capacitor cell
10 hyperspace navigational computer
11 rear shield generator
12 rear shield array
13 electromagnetic buffer
14 electromagnetic reciprocating turbine
15 cockpit viewscreen
16 master control computer
17 atmospheric pressure regulator
18 atmospheric scrubber
19 pilot access hatch
20 anti-gravity generator
21 primary memory computer
22 emergency supplies compartment
23 weapons computer
24 navigation-weapon interface
25 emergency beacon
26 bomb attachment pylons

1 magnetic armor plating
2 life support computer
3 thermal exhaust array
4 internal frame construction
5 hyperspace field generator

CUTAWAY: SYSTEMS DISCHARGE ARRAY

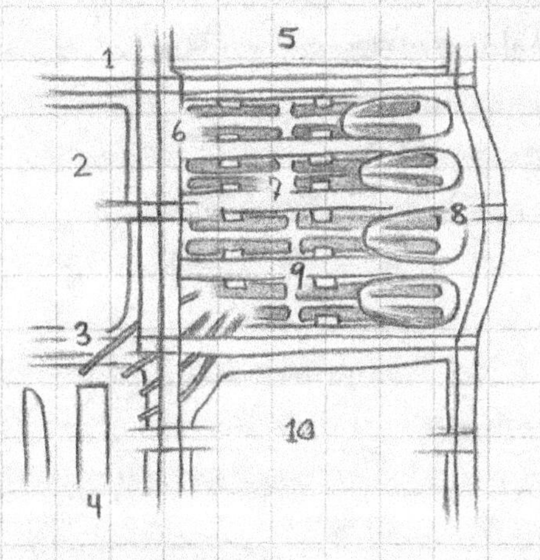

1 internal frame construction
2 hyperspace navigational computer
3 electromagnetic surplus energy conduit
4 electromagnetic deionizing disc
5 rear shield generator
6 electrical capacitor rod
7 capacitor rod release control ammeter
8 capacitor rod release port
9 capacitor rod securing clamp
10 rear shield array

Kuhingleyemlit Undaunted-class Gen 14-B-128

CUTAWAY: INTERIOR WING SYSTEMS

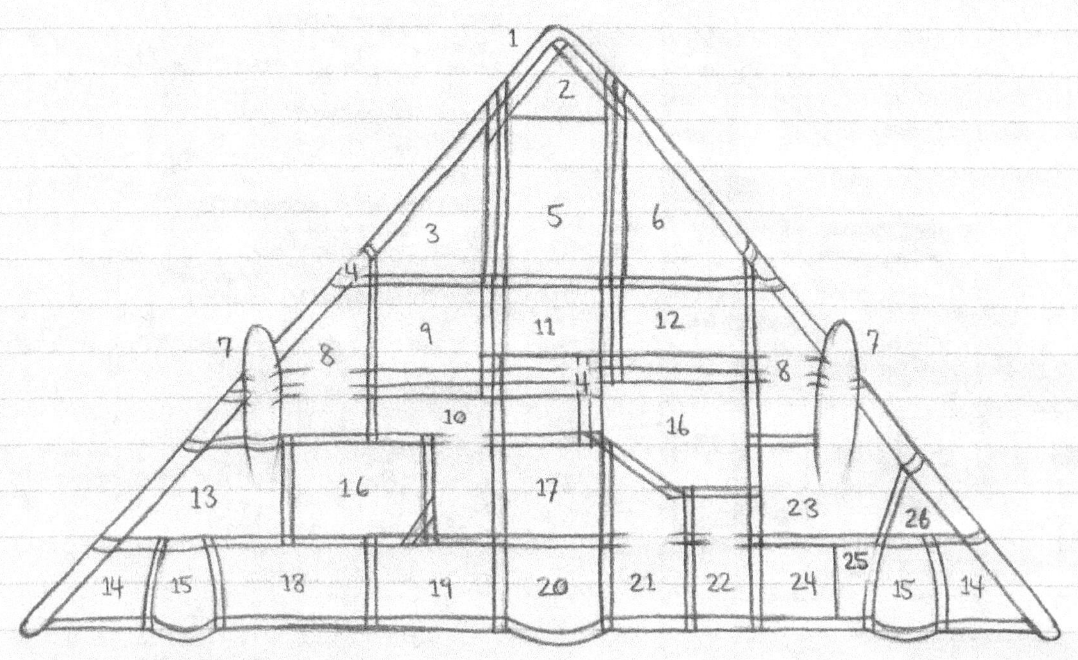

1	magnetic armor plating	14	navigational sensors
2	master control computer	15	systems discharge array
3	anti-gravity generator	16	pilot access hatch
4	internal frame construction	17	auxiliary memory computer
5	forward shield array	18	multiple system capacitor
6	communications computer	19	emergency battery
7	offensive laser turret emitter	20	targeting computer
8	laser capacitor cell	21	time equalization field generator
9	electromagnetic surge capacitor	22	rear sensor array
10	anti-gravity disbursal unit	23	starboard shield array
11	communications array	24	navigational array
12	pilot atmospheric tank	25	targeting computer
13	port shield array	26	bomb control computer interface

Set 26:
Undaunted-class freighter

Many of the *Undaunted*-class ships were stolen by Lynopte in their homeworld's invasion, including one flown away by Doug Laisault and Dale Lewison. This heavy transport is certainly larger than others, though not famous for it except when modified to have greater storage capacity. When this is done, it is less aerodynamic, but it works well enough for most races.

Kuhingleyemlit *Undaunted-class* Gen9-D-39

FIGURE 1   TOP VIEW

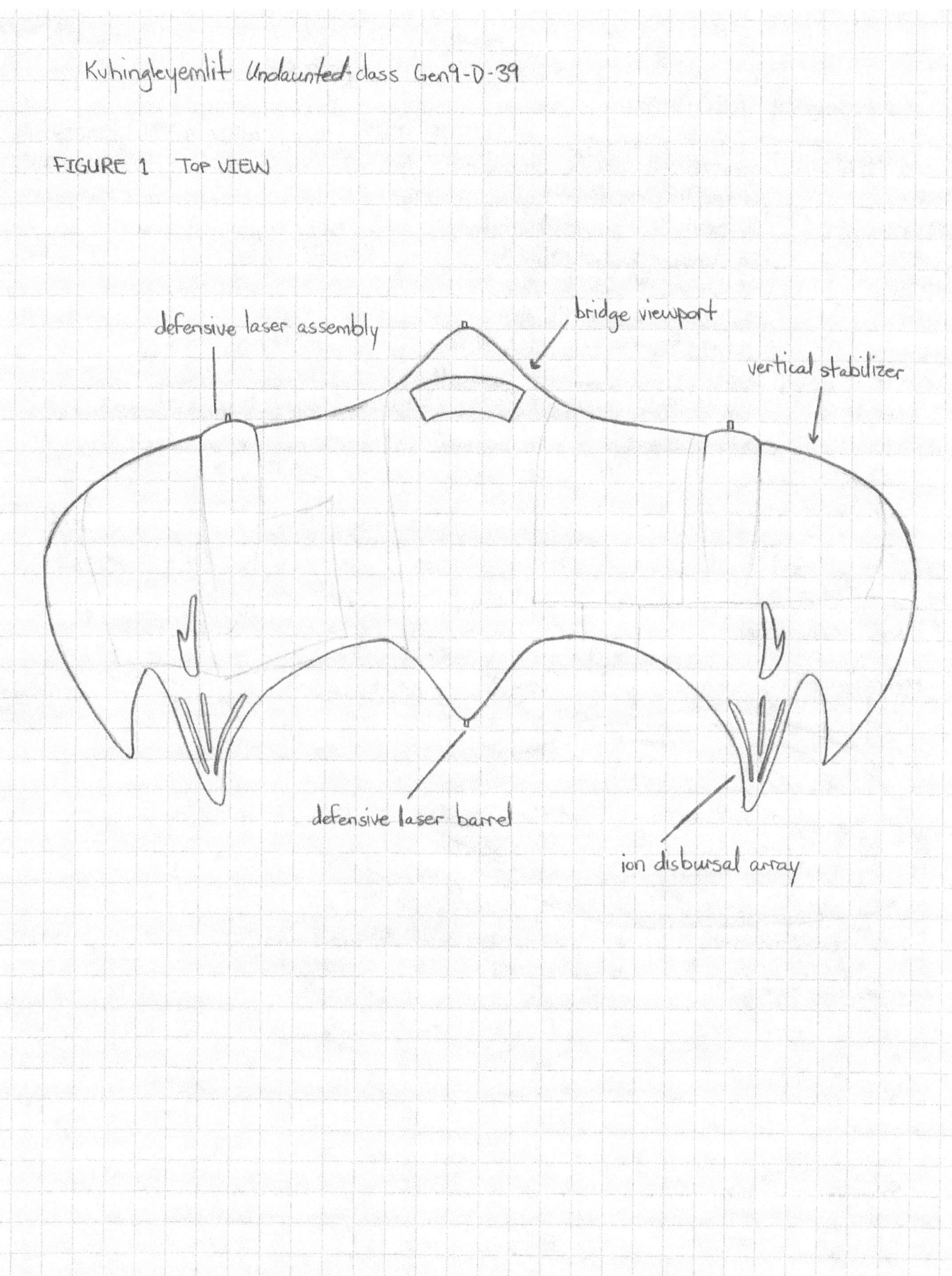

Kuhingleyemlit Gen9-D-39

CLASSIFICATION: generation 9 heavy transport
TYPE: Undaunted-class freighter
CREW: 12 total (4 officers, 9 enlisted)
LENGTH: 26 standard body lengths
WIDTH: 49 standard body lengths
HEIGHT: 20 standard body lengths
MASS: 161,135 kg (355,242 lbs$_f$)
ARMOR: pyroceramite-reinforced steetanicarb, magnetic armor plating
ENGINES: two electromagnetic reciprocating turbines, three anti-gravity generators
ARMAMENT: four anti-projectile laser batteries, anti-missile countermeasures

FIG. 2   SIDE VIEW

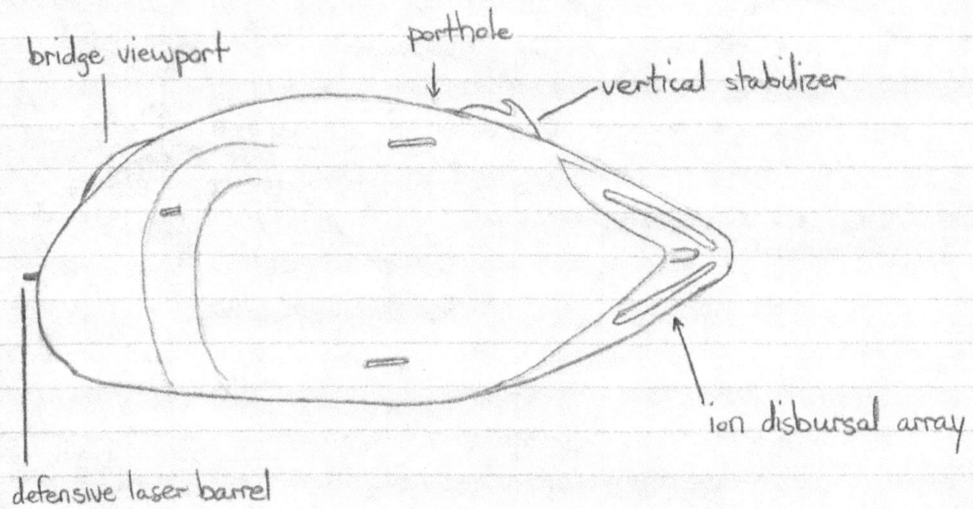

Kvhingleyemlit *Undaunted*-class Gen9-D-39

FIG. 3   FRONT VIEW

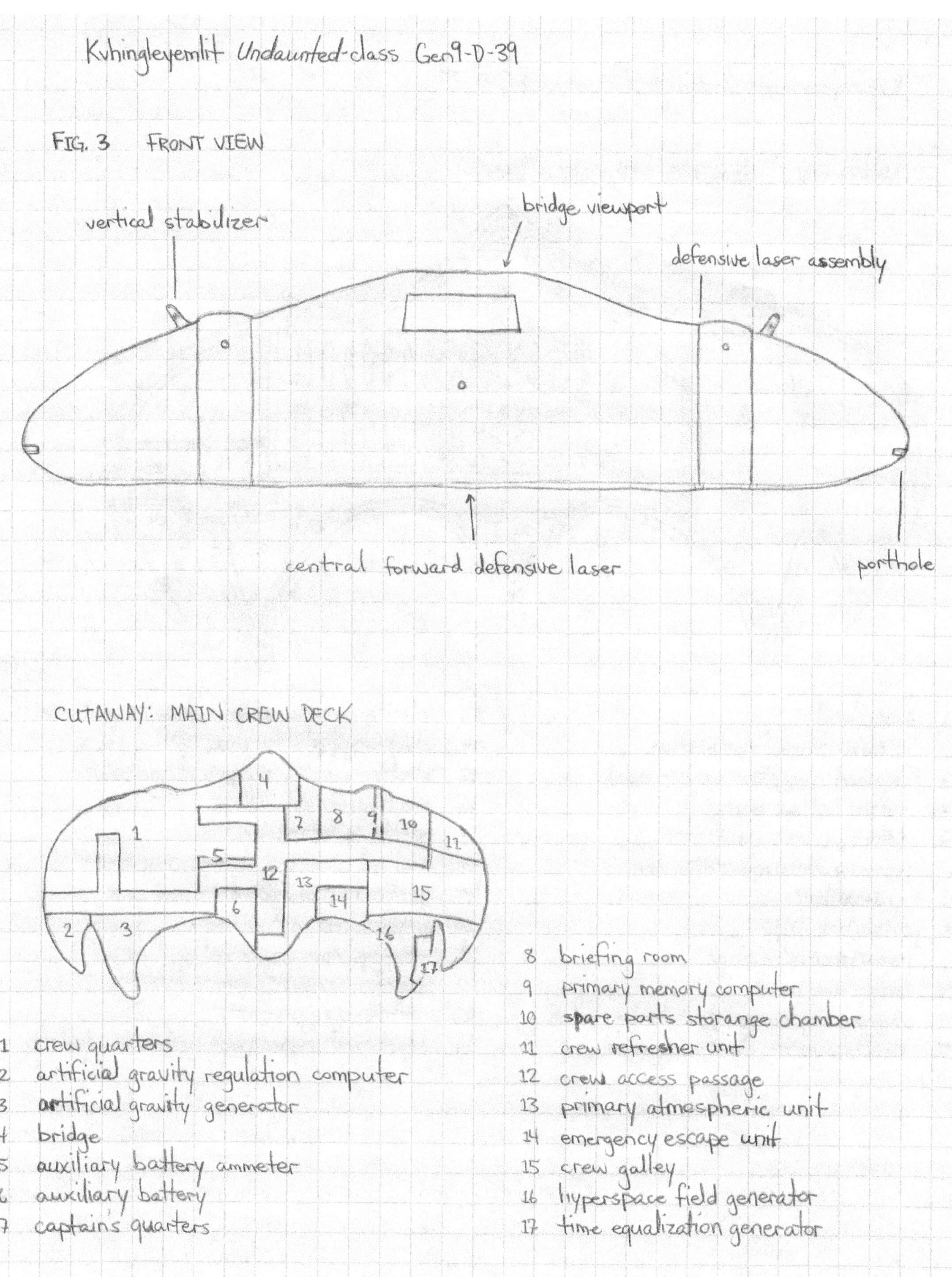

1 crew quarters
2 artificial gravity regulation computer
3 artificial gravity generator
4 bridge
5 auxiliary battery ammeter
6 auxiliary battery
7 captain's quarters
8 briefing room
9 primary memory computer
10 spare parts storange chamber
11 crew refresher unit
12 crew access passage
13 primary atmospheric unit
14 emergency escape unit
15 crew galley
16 hyperspace field generator
17 time equalization generator

Kuhingleyemlit *Undaunted*-class Gen9-D-39

CUTAWAY: ENGINEERING AND CARGO DECKS

1	outer hull	13	electromagnetic reciprocating turbine assembly
2	internal frame construction	14	electromagnetic turbine axle
3	forward navigation sensor bank	15	electromagnetic reciprocating turbine
4	defensive laser barrel	16	electromagnetic buffer
5	defensive laser generator	17	guest quarters
6	primary communications site	18	vertical ascention control computer
7	medical bay	19	vertical crew ascention passage
8	cargo bay deck	20	pressurized water tank
9	crew access passage	21	energy capacitance gel
10	cargo bay hatch	22	countermeasures compartment
11	engineering computer and maintenance	23	aft shield generator
12	electromagnetic deionizing disc	24	starboard hyperspace generator regulator

# Set 27:
Brômb Lplãs

Before the *Rot-des* culture of the Nee-kelian, the Crilex were trading partners with the Trel-Nipon. Their ships were small and often attacked by large predators while landed on their homeworld, so they adopted the thorny design to deter such attacks. This design carried over when the Nee-kelian enslaved the Crilex and gave them the name Suu-Lost. The design remained, because it was convenient for the Nee-kelian. It was seen in the main port by the Resistance envoy party just prior to the Nee-kelian's second campaign on the parasite.

The second campaign was a dismal failure for technical and strategic miscalculation, but more *Egetna*-Trel class ships would have changed that. They use the same neutron particle cannon as the coeval Nee-kelian arsenal, but the thorns reduce time required to recharge and dissipate excess particles and energy. This was one factor in the Gaepvihn's victory.

After the Gaepvihn followed Species One to their home system and effectively destroyed their role as overlords, the Crilex reclaimed their culture and became a respectable power in themselves. They kept the original thorn design.

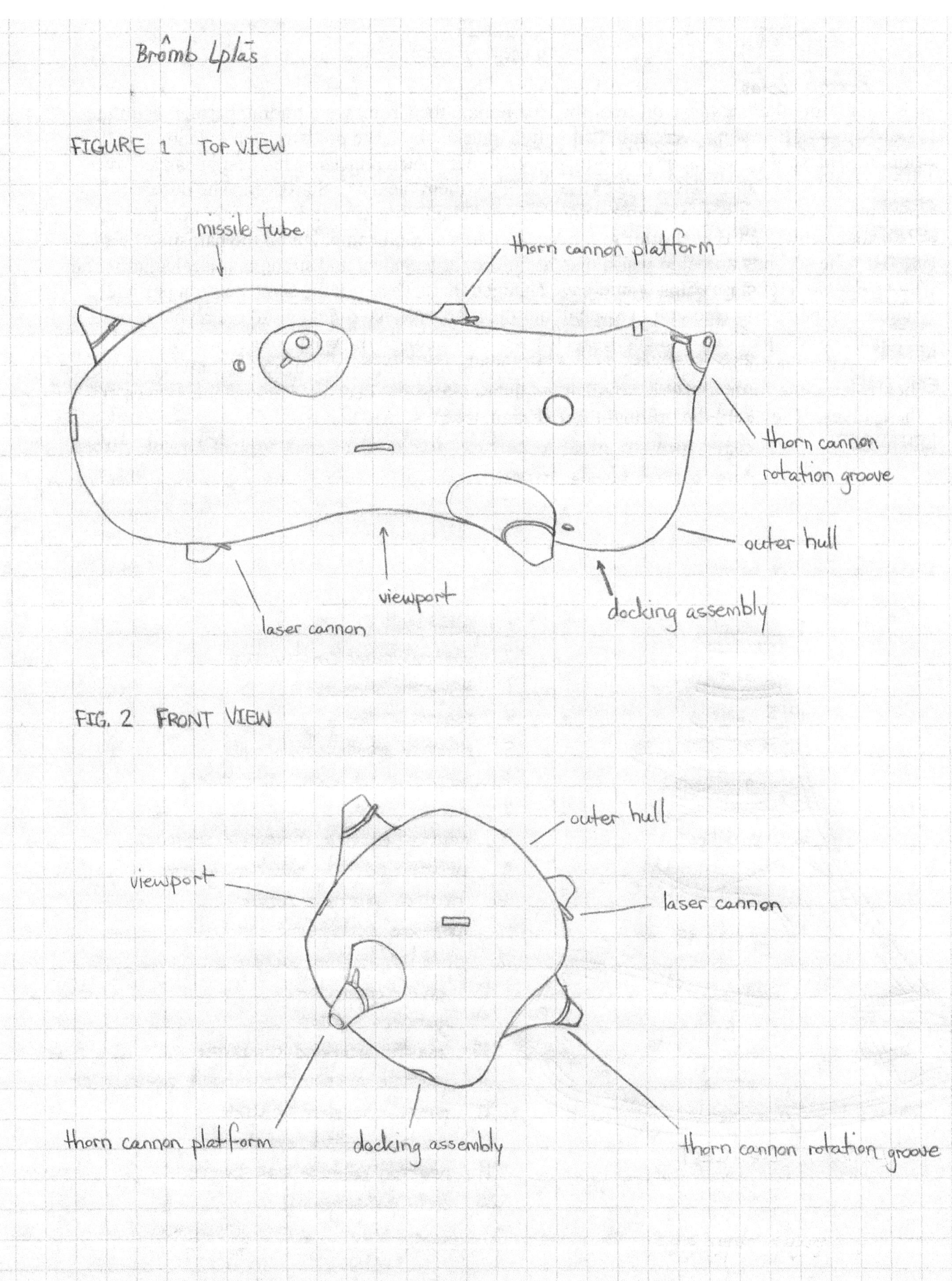

Brômb Lplǎs
FIGURE 1   TOP VIEW
missile tube
thorn cannon platform
thorn cannon rotation groove
outer hull
docking assembly
viewport
laser cannon
FIG. 2   FRONT VIEW
outer hull
laser cannon
viewport
thorn cannon platform
docking assembly
thorn cannon rotation groove

Brômb Lplás

CLASSIFICATION: Crilex *Egetna-Trel* cargo ship
TYPE: armored transport vessel
CREW: seventeen (10 officers, 7 enlisted)
LENGTH: 14 Nikel units
WIDTH: 5.3 Nikel units
HEIGHT: 5.1 Nikel units
MASS: 37.44 Nikel temple masses (3,744 Nikel pane masses)
ARMOR: pyroceramite- and aluminum- reinforced steetanicarb
ENGINES: one heavy electromagnetic reciprocating turbine, one fission-powered
                 artificial gravity generator matrix
ARMAMENT: eight medium neutron particle accelerators, six unguided missile tubes,
                 two guided missile tubes

CUTAWAY: THORN CANNON

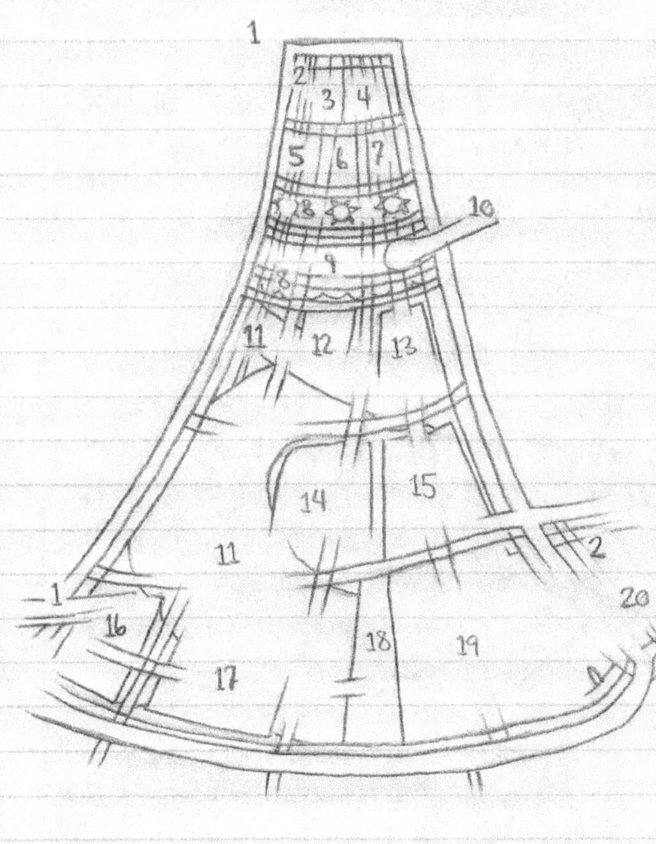

1   outer hull
2   internal frame construction
3   targeting sensors
4   spatial sensor
5   rotation servo battery
6   propulsion-weapons interface
7   sensor array
8   neutron particle movement servo
9   neutron particle rotation groove
10 neutron particle nozzle
11 particle accelerator conduit
12 shield distributor array
13 shield capacitor
14 gunners' station
15 master weapons computer
16 particle accelerator conduit pressurizer
17 particle decelerator unit
18 neutron particle accelerator
19 neutron particle raw source
20 crew passageway

Brâmb Ļplás

CUTAWAY: INTERIOR SYSTEMS

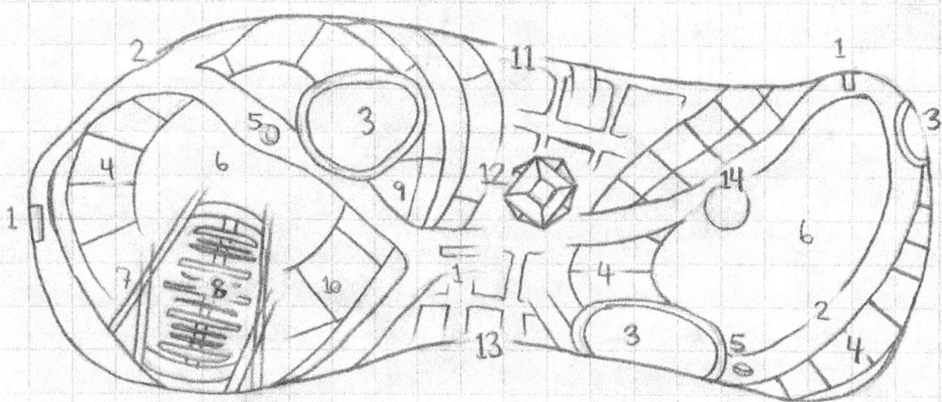

1	viewport	8	electromagnetic reciprocating turbine
2	crew passageway	9	sustenance storage
3	thorn cannon mounting	10	officer's quarters
4	compartmentalized cargo hold	11	neutron particle raw source
5	missile tube hatch	12	fission reaction chamber
6	cargo bay	13	fissionable fuel storage units
7	internal frame construction	14	cargo bay airlock

CUTAWAY: ARTIFICIAL GRAVITY ARRAY

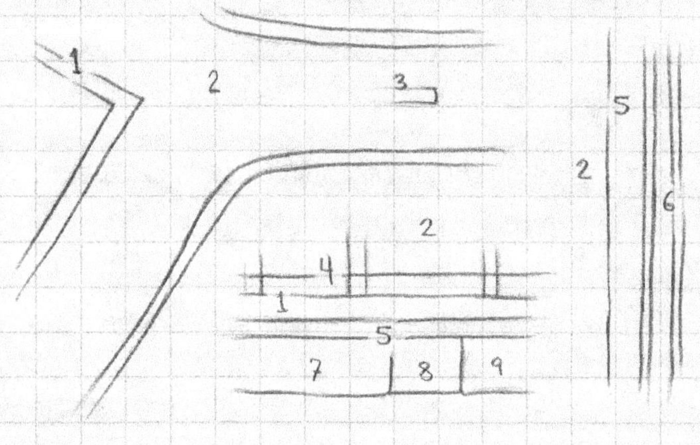

1	pressurized crew conduit
2	crew passageway
3	viewport
4	internal frame construction
5	artificial gravity generator
6	power relay conduit
7	atmospheric storage tank
8	crew passageway atmospheric pressurizer
9	atmospheric scrubber

Brômb Lplás

CUTAWAY: CARGO BAY

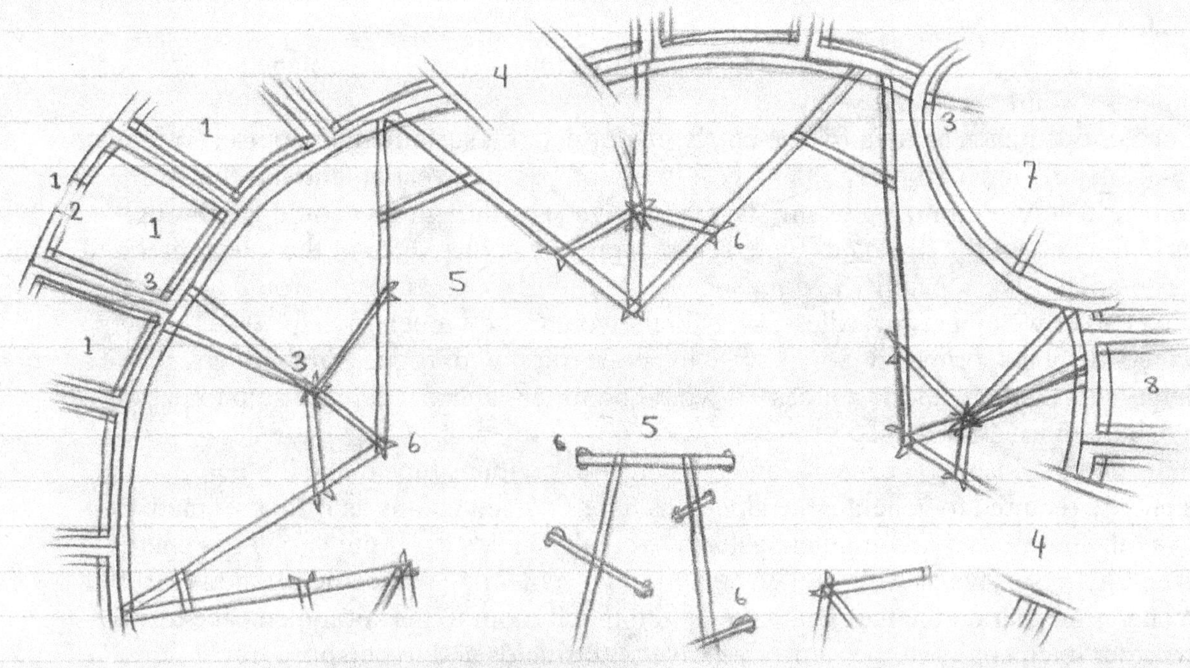

1   compartmentalized cargo hold
2   compartmentalized cargo hold access hatch
3   internal frame construction
4   crew passageway
5   cargo securing frame
6   cargo securing clamp
7   thorn cannon mount
8   sustenance storage

Set 28:
Av1.2 Auf Bolt Interceptor

The concept for this space-based interceptor was "borrowed" from the Ori motherships in MGM's *Stargate: SG1*. I like the idea of the energy source for a vessel being physically *outside* it. Though it is not the case here—the energy produced is more for the generation of electromagnetic shielding—the center hole design remains. The shape is actually inspired more by the warships at the very end of *History of the World: Part I*, where (as Mel Brooks said) they belonged to "Jews in space!"

I think it's funny, maybe because it's an alliterative thing to say. Interplanetary Stars of David would be so weird to see. Anyway…

The center opening is an area for the catalyzing effect of a sustained EM pulse. With the interceptor and friendly units properly shielded, it is a good passive weapon and has the convenient side effect of minimizing enemy laser effectiveness (though few could get through the shielding). Because of the generator type, sensors must be at the edges of the interceptor and the vessel has no defensive capability in atmosphere. Truthfully, the Auf Bolt would not necessarily maneuver well there regardless, so a shield wouldn't do much to help. The builders were Resistance members, primarily Small Wise in cooperation with rogue Shipbuilders, to access the latter's technology and resources. It would be for a planetary defense ship to patrol Idumzt space, but not used for long.

Both its poor atmospheric capacity and its danger to civilian ships make it a liability, and because the energy required to generate the shields is not as advantageous as it first seemed. It does take away the necessity for computer systems to create shields, so if the vessel has energy to run it has energy to survive as well, if the enemy has no remaining projectile weapons. But the energy generation gear on the Auf Bolt take up too much room to permit hyperspace travel systems, and other interceptors of the same size have both shields and hyperspace travel capacity. They can also be broken down and repaired with much less technical expertise.

In order to lighten the craft, thus making room for more fuel occupied by energy production units, the hull is partially wrought by use of serine, a crystalline serum derived from silk gum. With this applied it was similar to the Rloe Hox ships, but far inferior, and though the process was discontinued it led to a better refinement of ballistics resin in common usage later.

Av1.2 Auf Bolt Interceptor

FIGURE 1   TOP VIEW

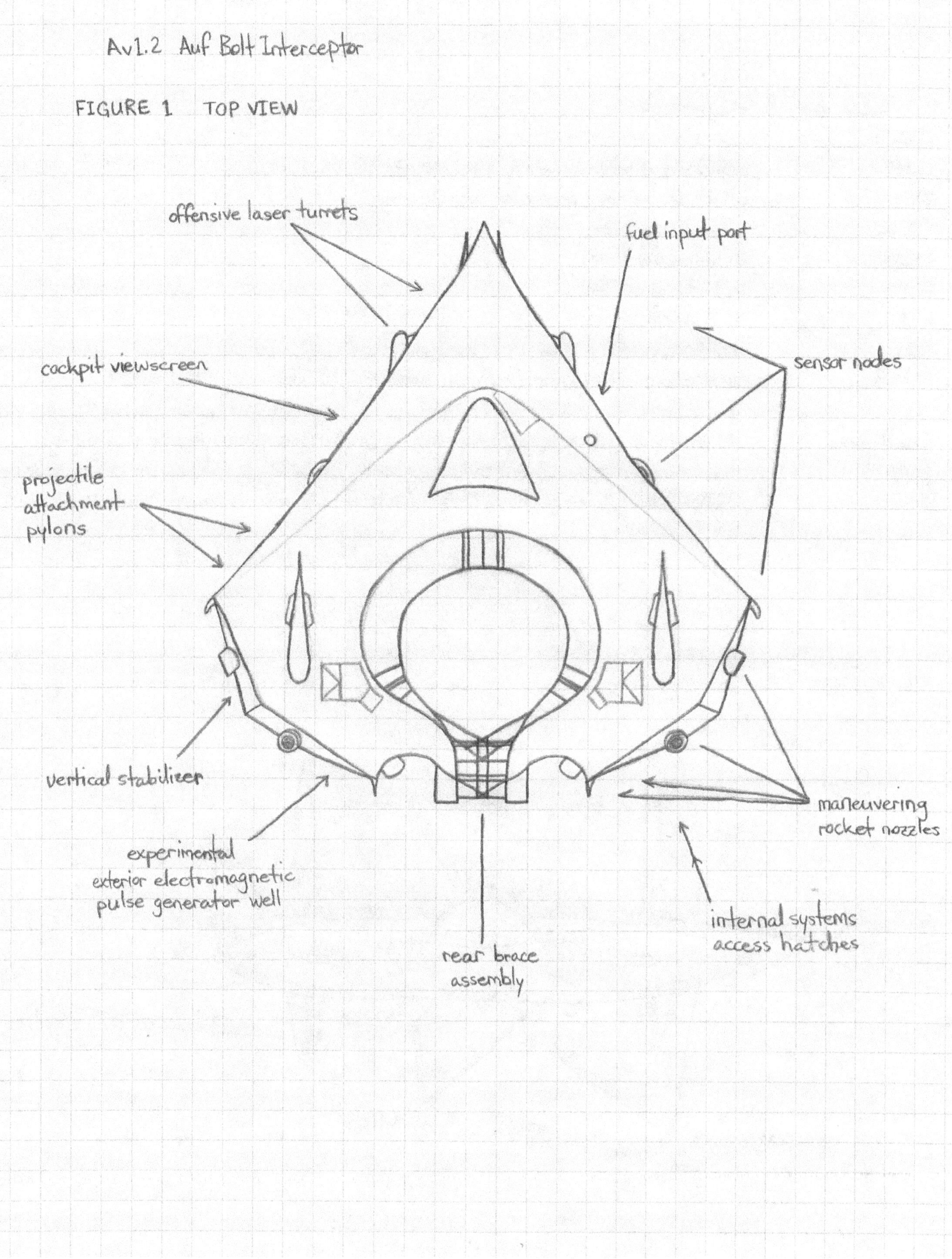

Av1.2 Auf Bolt Interceptor

CLASSIFICATION: experimental interplanetary interceptor
TYPE: prototype exterior generator attack craft
CREW: pilot
LENGTH: 8 standard feet
WIDTH: 7.9 standard feet
HEIGHT: 4.2 standard feet
MASS: 11,740 standard mass units (without fuel)
ARMOR: serine-enhanced steelan alloy, experimental exterior electromagnetic
pulse generator (EEMP g2.0)
ENGINES: electromagnetic reciprocating turbine circuit, maneuvering rocket assembly
ARMAMENT: two forward offensive laser cannon, capacity for twelve projectiles and critical pulse emission
RANGE: 0.00000 0007 light-years (64,373 kilometers / 40,000 standard miles) maximum
on propulsion

FIG. 2 FRONT VIEW

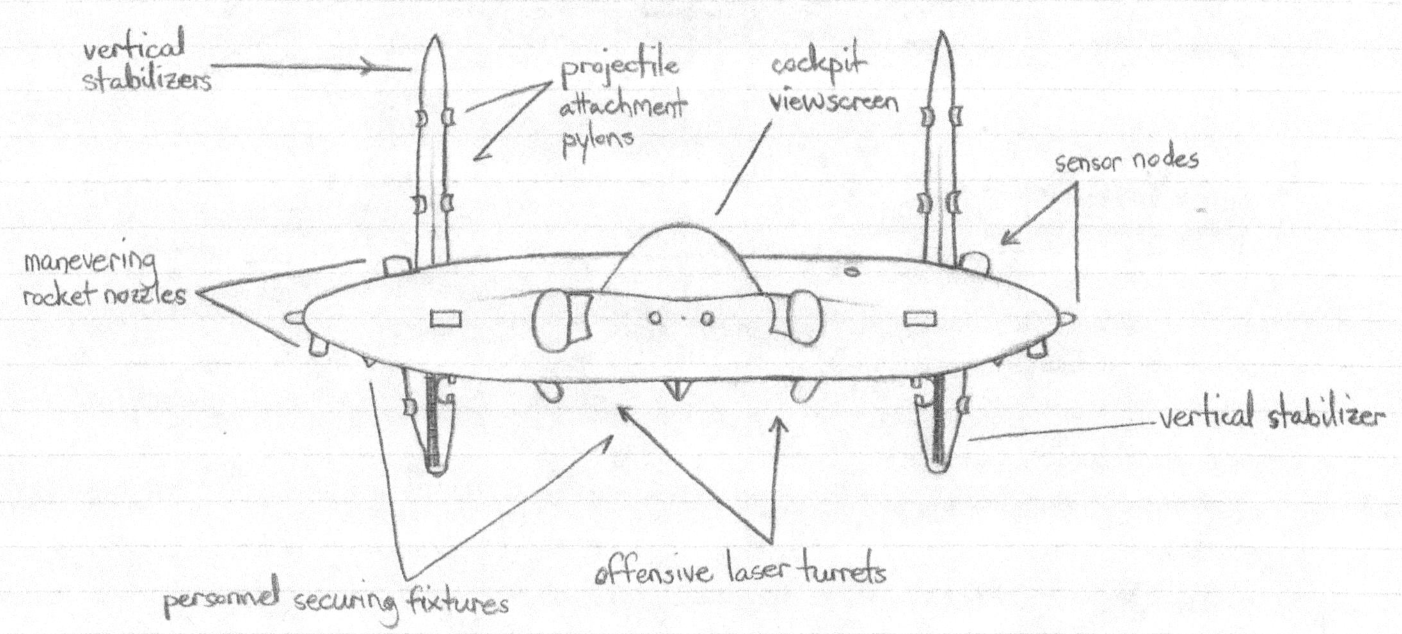

Av1.2 Auf Bolt Interceptor

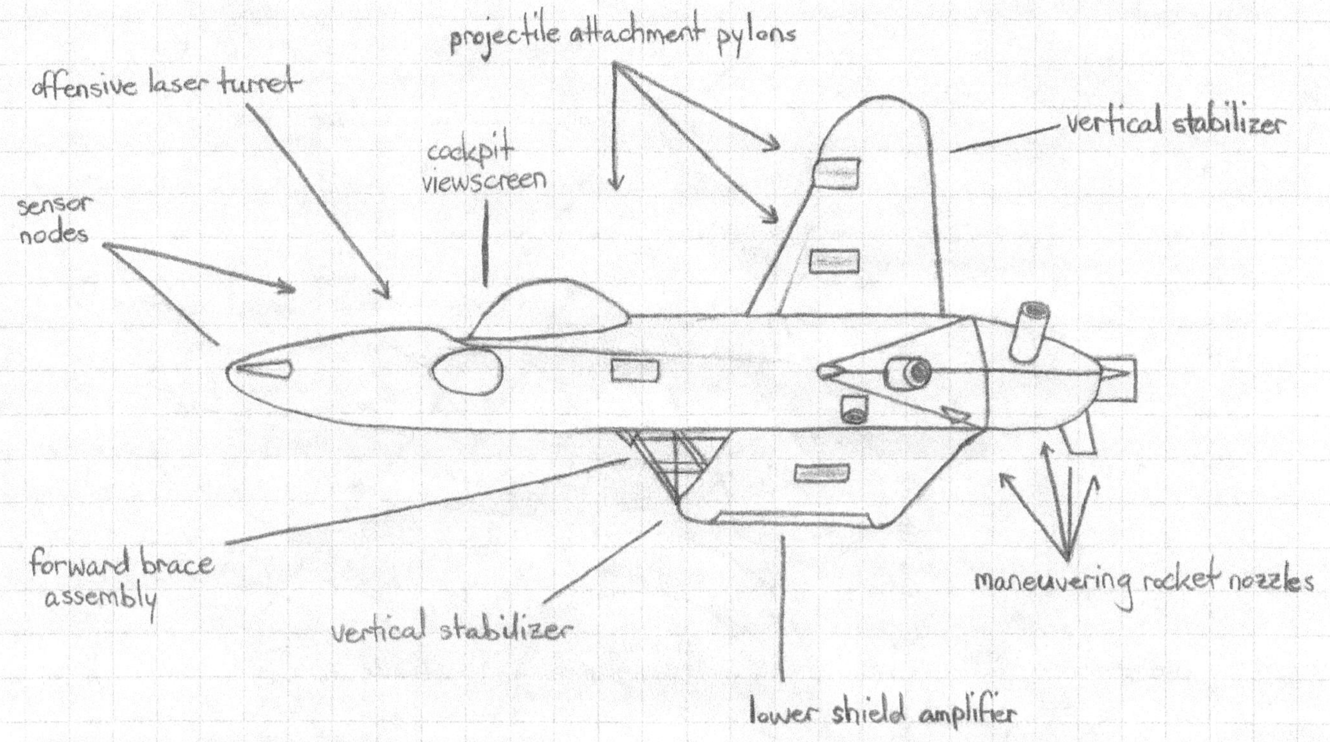

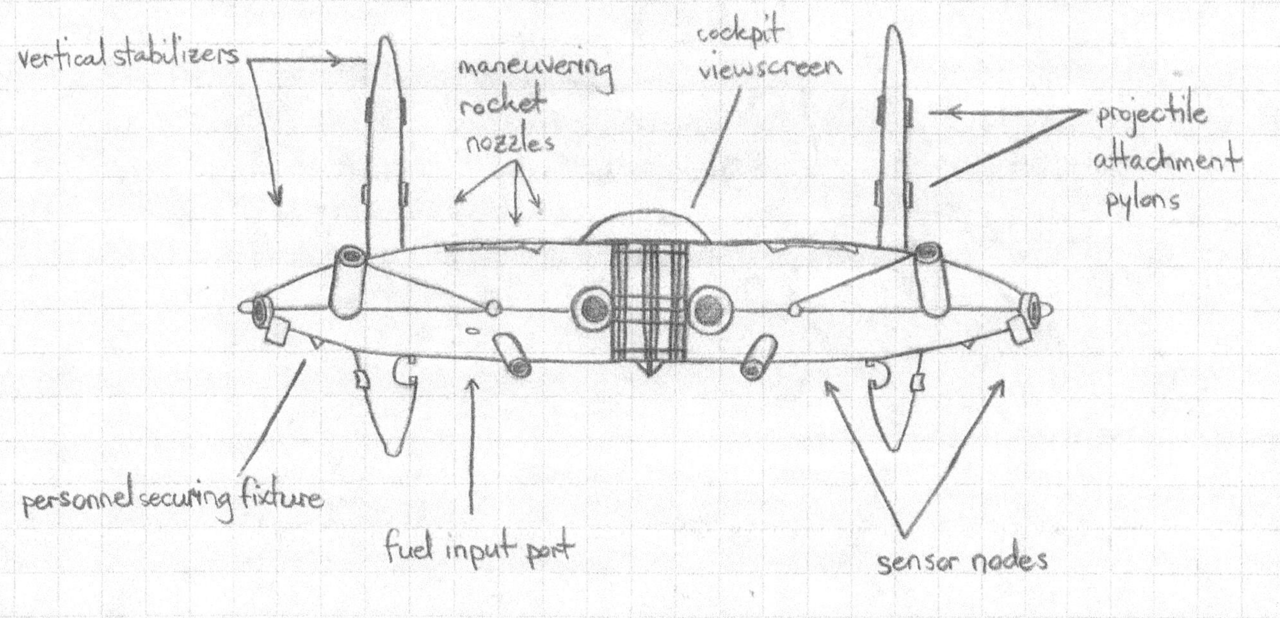

Av1.2 Auf Bolt Interceptor

FIG. 5 BOTTOM VIEW

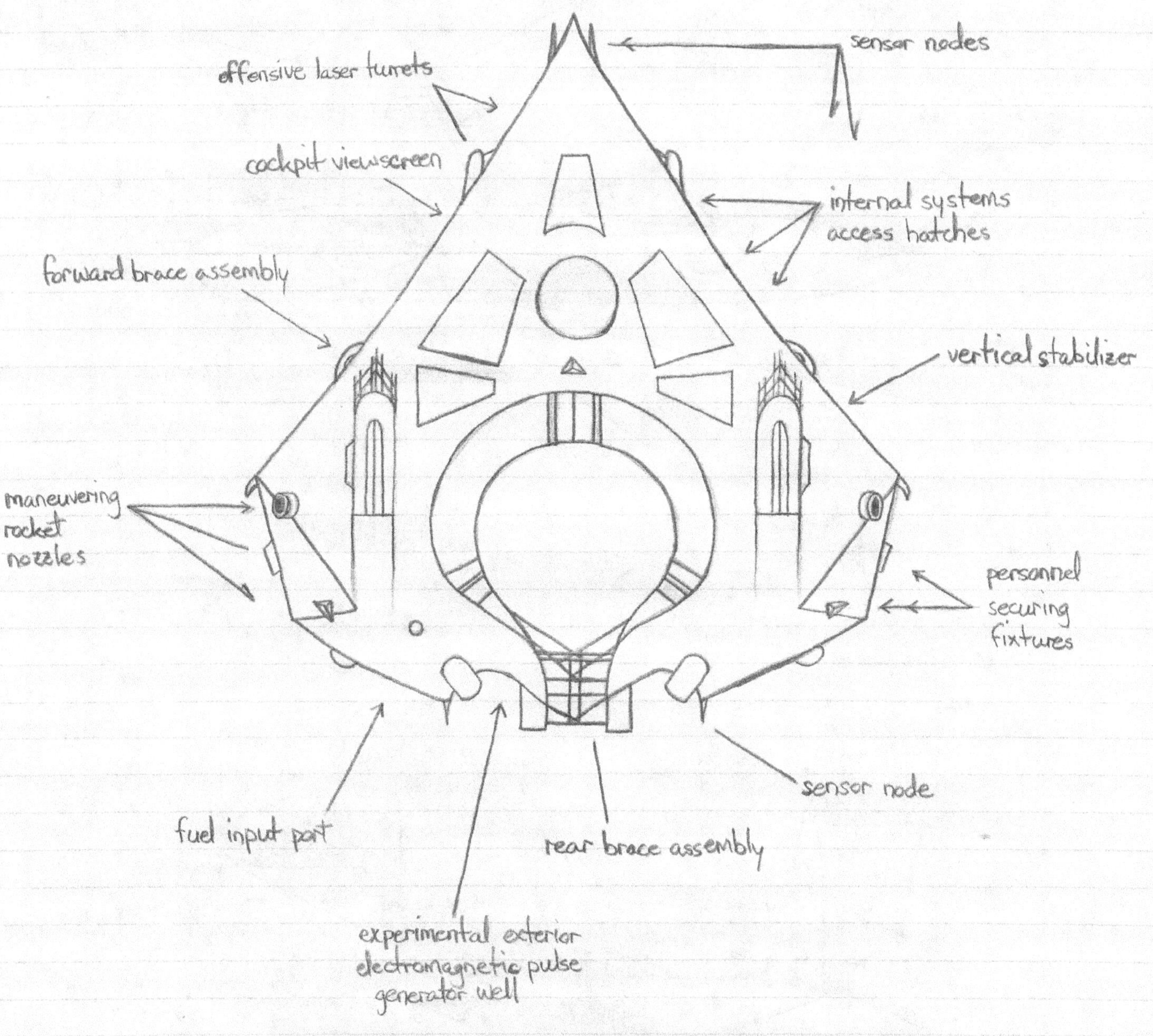

Av1.2 Auf Bolt Interceptor

CUTAWAY: INTERIOR SYSTEMS

1 sensor receiver
2 communications emitter
3 weapons targeting computer
4 offensive laser emitter assembly
5 offensive laser emitter battery
6 offensive laser emitter capacitor
7 communications relay system
8 offensive laser emitter housing
9 outer hull
10 offensive laser generator casing
11 weapons-propulsion interface
12 emergency systems capacitor
13 homing beacon
14 emergency supplies compartment
15 internal frame construction
16 cockpit viewscreen
17 pilot atmospheric storage tank
18 propulsion-fuel interface
19 navigational sensor
20 communications interference unit
21 sensor analyzer computer
22 electromagnetic shielding apparatus
23 electrical surge capacitor
24 projectile attachment pylon
25 vertical stabilizer
26 electromagnetic reciprocating turbine chamber
27 electrochemical catalyst storage tank
28 chemical rocket fuel tank
29 chemical rocket fuel conduit pressure regulator
30 shielded primary systems housing
31 chemical rocket fuel conduit
32 electrochemical catalyst amplification and modulation assembly
33 electrochemical catalyst regulator
34 electromagnetic reciprocating turbine
35 retractable electrostatic discharge conductors
36 electrochemical catalyst subatomic particle regulator chamber

Av1.2 Auf Bolt Interceptor

CUTAWAY: ELECTROMAGNETIC PULSE GENERATOR

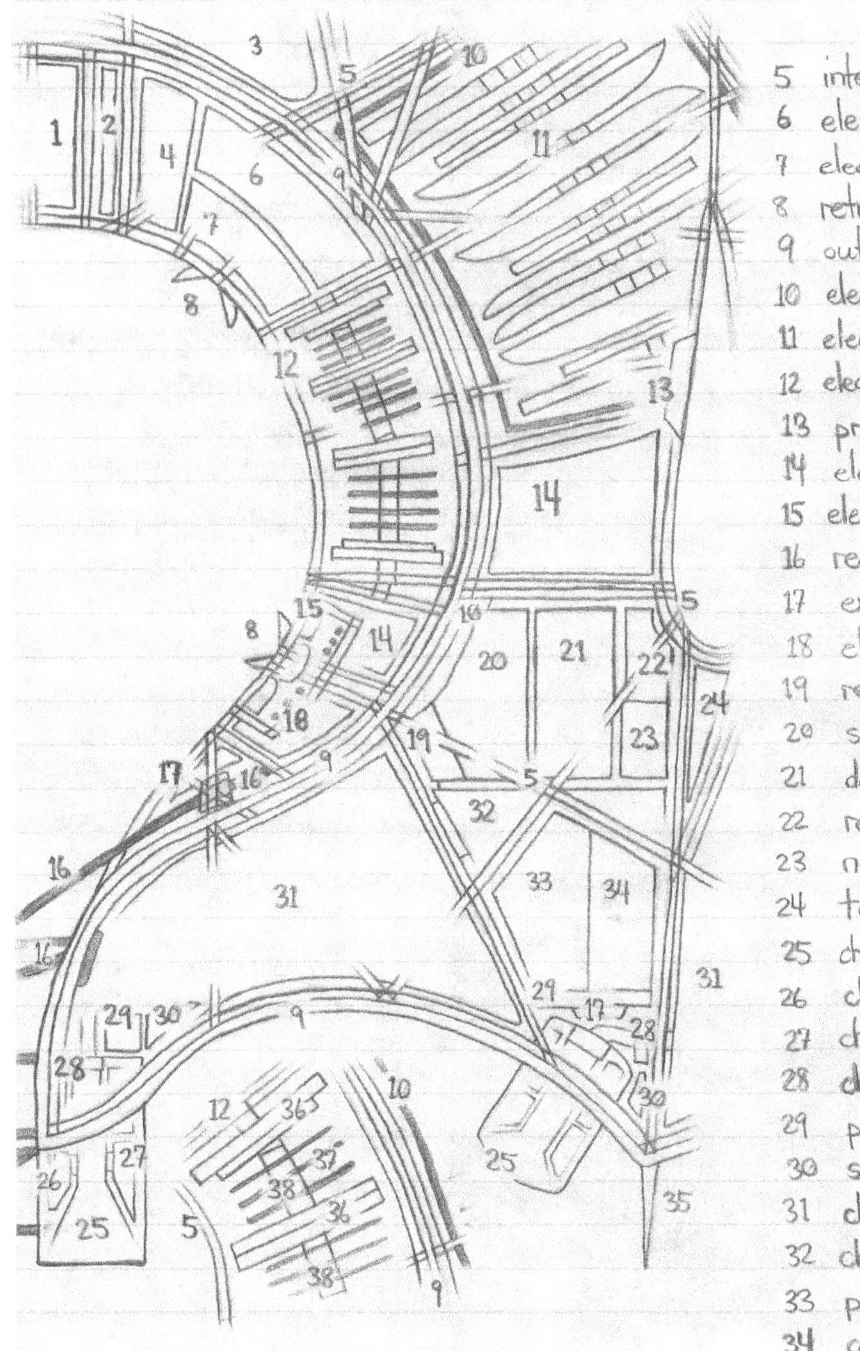

5 internal frame construction
6 electrostatic discharge auxiliary battery
7 electrostatic discharge capacitor
8 retractable electrostatic discharge conductors
9 outer hull
10 electromagnetic shielding apparatus
11 electromagnetic reciprocating turbine
12 electrochemical catalyst subatomic particle regulator chamber
13 projectile attachment pylon
14 electrical surge capacitor
15 electrostatic discharge conductor retraction sheath
16 rear brace assembly rod
17 exterior discharge initializer node
18 electrostatic discharge revolving conductors
19 replacement revolving conductors
20 spare electrochemical catalyst storage tank
21 decoy storage compartment
22 reserve power battery
23 navigational sensor bank
24 targeting computer
25 chemical rocket nozzle
26 chemical rocket ignition suppression unit
27 chemical rocket ignition unit
28 chemical rocket fuel conduit pressure regulator
29 propulsion-weapons interface
30 spatial sensor
31 chemical rocket fuel tank
32 chemical rocket emergency fuel reserve
33 primary power capacitor
34 communications array
35 sensor receiver
36 neutrino net disc
37 subatomic particle flywheel
38 subatomic particle flywheel anchor rod

1 electrochemical catalyst regulator
2 electrochemical particle discriminator
3 shielded primary systems housing
4 electrochemical circuit amplification unit

Set 29:
Krash'regit

Ah, yes, the *Krash'regit*. This was the cargo ship used by the party in a *Lone Soldier* role-playing session and it SHOULD HAVE BEEN DESTROYED… sigh.

This vessel was borrowed from the Eht fo from their facility by the mercenary Ijihuil, often known as the IJ. Its *Spokcalb* detachment flew the heavy transport ship out of the Eht Aux System immediately after damaged from a battle against the parasite was repaired. It had a big, round hole right through the cargo bay floor. The *Spokcalb* party was not thrilled to see this.

It was the mission of the party in "Quantum Recoup" to find missing Lynopte weapons, hopefully in time for the *Lone Soldier* novella's conclusion. The *Krash'regit* features a hidden tribarrel laser cannon below the main communications array. In escaping a parasite research facility in the Eno Nebula, this array had to be torn off in atmospheric flight under fire from many defense vessels. By the time the broken ship was returned to the Eht fo, it had endured two aborted hyperspace jumps and a life support failure. But the party STILL survived, even if the Epjio's bugs entrapped in the cargo bay did not last long enough for the Corinth Panther's character to enjoy them.

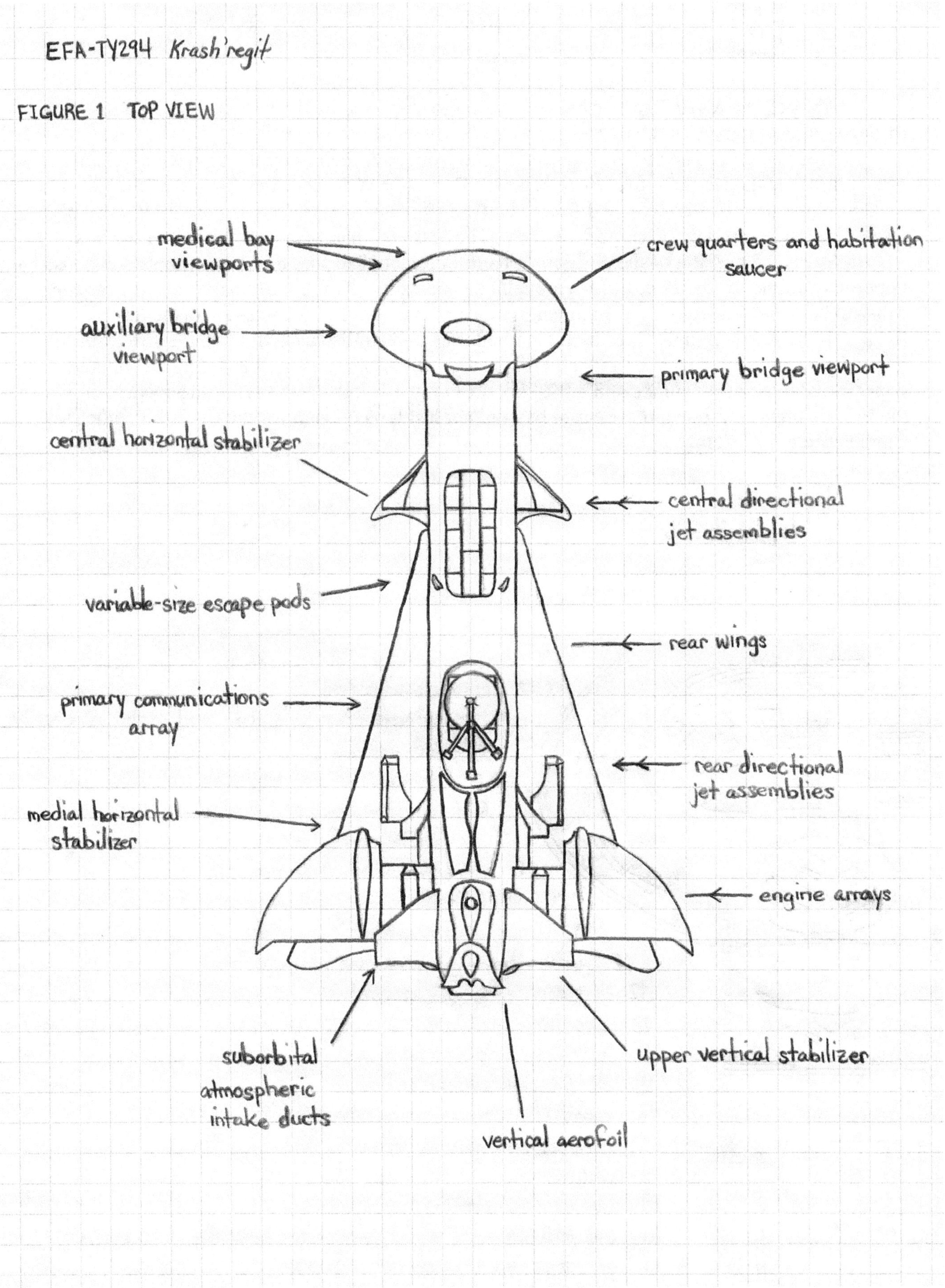

EFA-TY294 Krash'regit

FIGURE 1   TOP VIEW

medical bay viewports

crew quarters and habitation saucer

auxiliary bridge viewport

primary bridge viewport

central horizontal stabilizer

central directional jet assemblies

variable-size escape pods

rear wings

primary communications array

rear directional jet assemblies

medial horizontal stabilizer

engine arrays

suborbital atmospheric intake ducts

upper vertical stabilizer

vertical aerofoil

EFA-TY294 *Krash'regit*

CLASSIFICATION: Eht fo heavy transport, Yvaeh-class
TYPE: modified Species 061 cargo vessel
CREW: 9 (seven officers, two enlisted)
LENGTH: 78 standard Ijihuil feet
WIDTH: 65 standard IJ feet
HEIGHT: 34 standard IJ feet
MASS: 107 standard IJ mass units
ARMOR: average steetanicarb hull
ENGINES: two electromagnetic reciprocating turbines, chemical thrust assembly
ARMAMENT: two electromagnetic countermeasures pods, tribarrel laser cannon,
                reserve offensive missile pods

CUTAWAY: HABITATION SAUCER

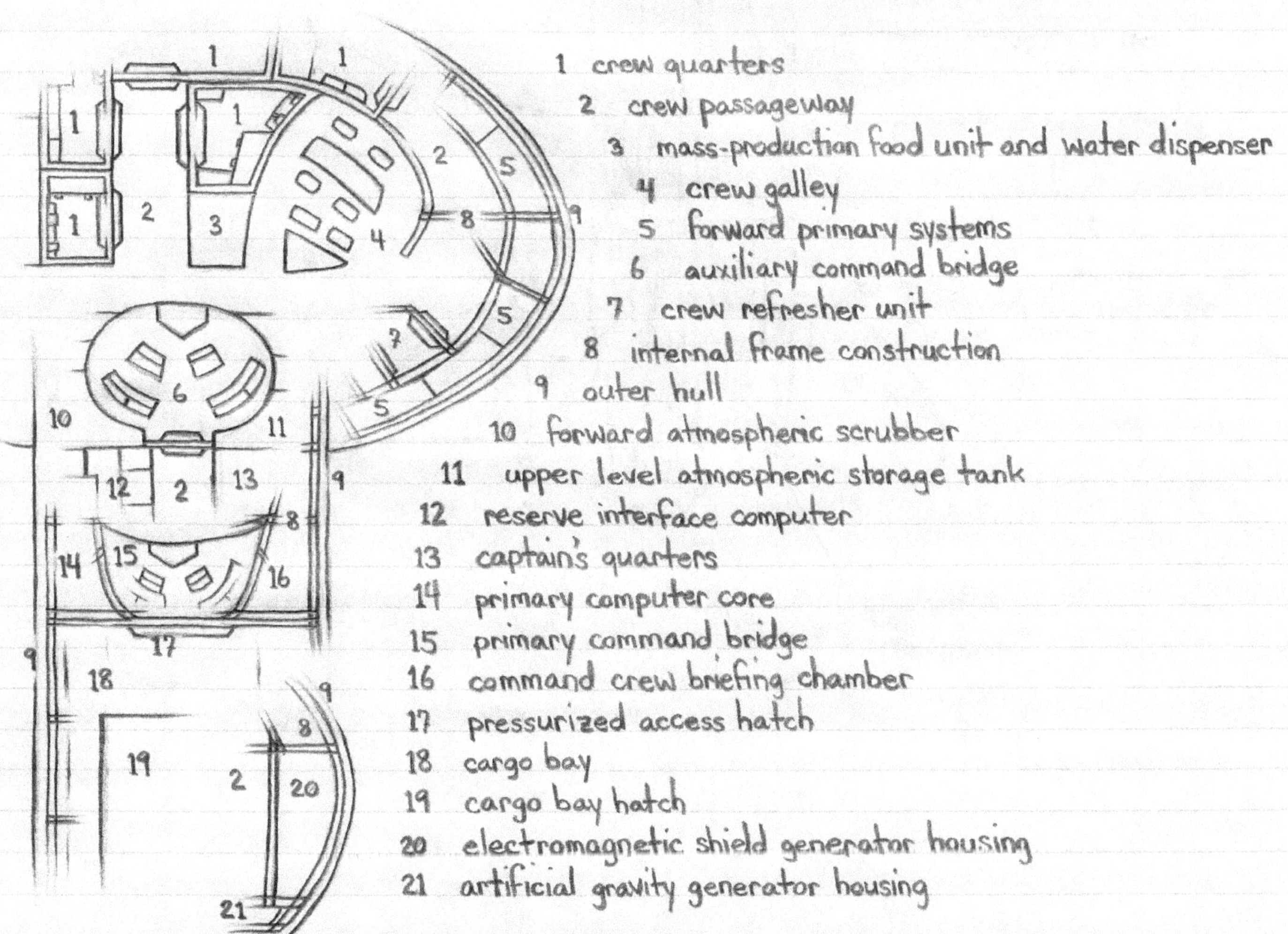

1 crew quarters
2 crew passageway
3 mass-production food unit and water dispenser
4 crew galley
5 forward primary systems
6 auxiliary command bridge
7 crew refresher unit
8 internal frame construction
9 outer hull
10 forward atmospheric scrubber
11 upper level atmospheric storage tank
12 reserve interface computer
13 captain's quarters
14 primary computer core
15 primary command bridge
16 command crew briefing chamber
17 pressurized access hatch
18 cargo bay
19 cargo bay hatch
20 electromagnetic shield generator housing
21 artificial gravity generator housing

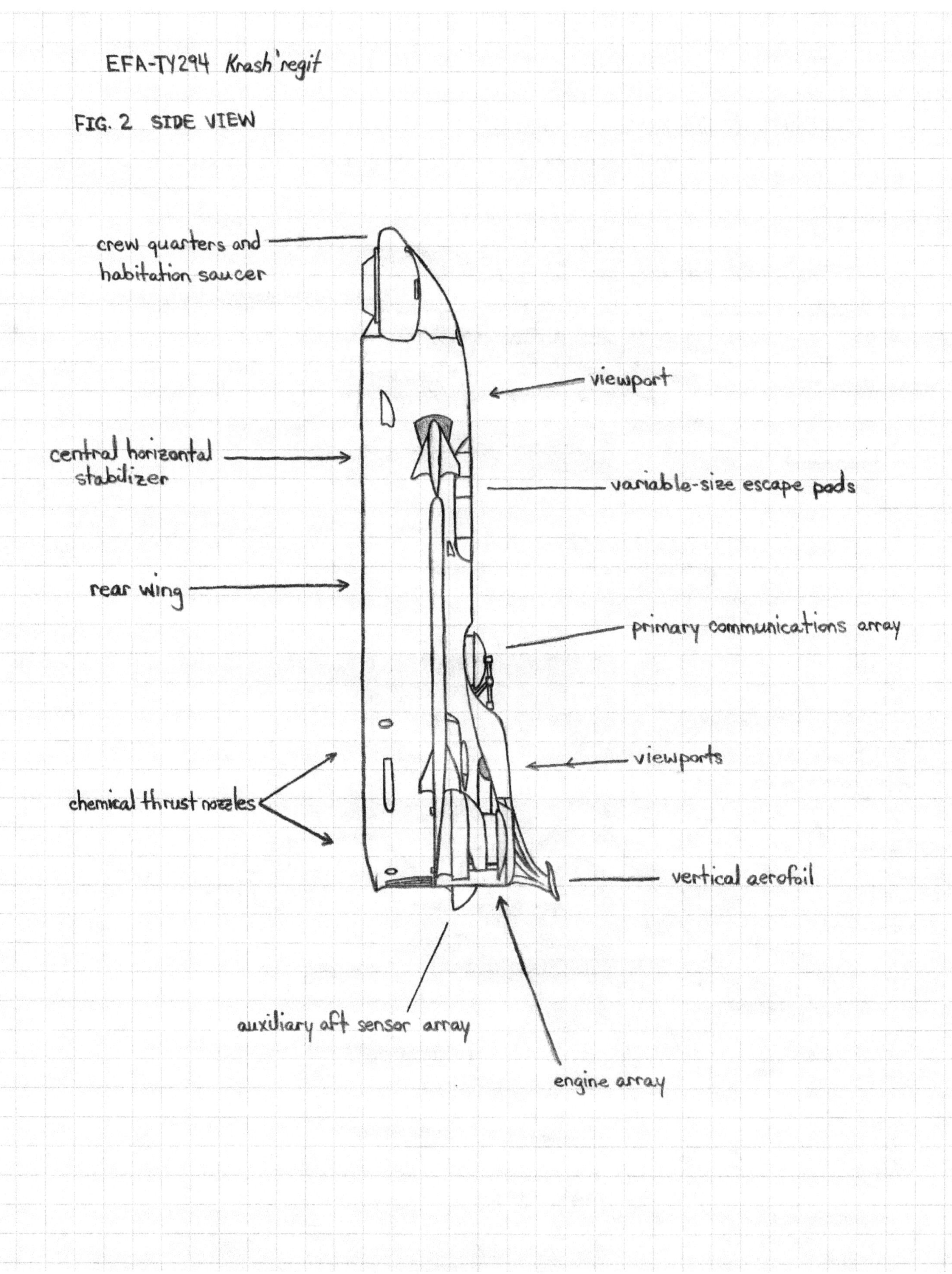

EFA-TY294 Krash'regit
FIG. 2 SIDE VIEW
crew quarters and habitation saucer
central horizontal stabilizer
rear wing
chemical thrust nozzles
viewport
variable-size escape pods
primary communications array
viewports
vertical aerofoil
auxiliary aft sensor array
engine array

EFA-TY294 *Krash'regit*

FIG. 3   FRONT VIEW

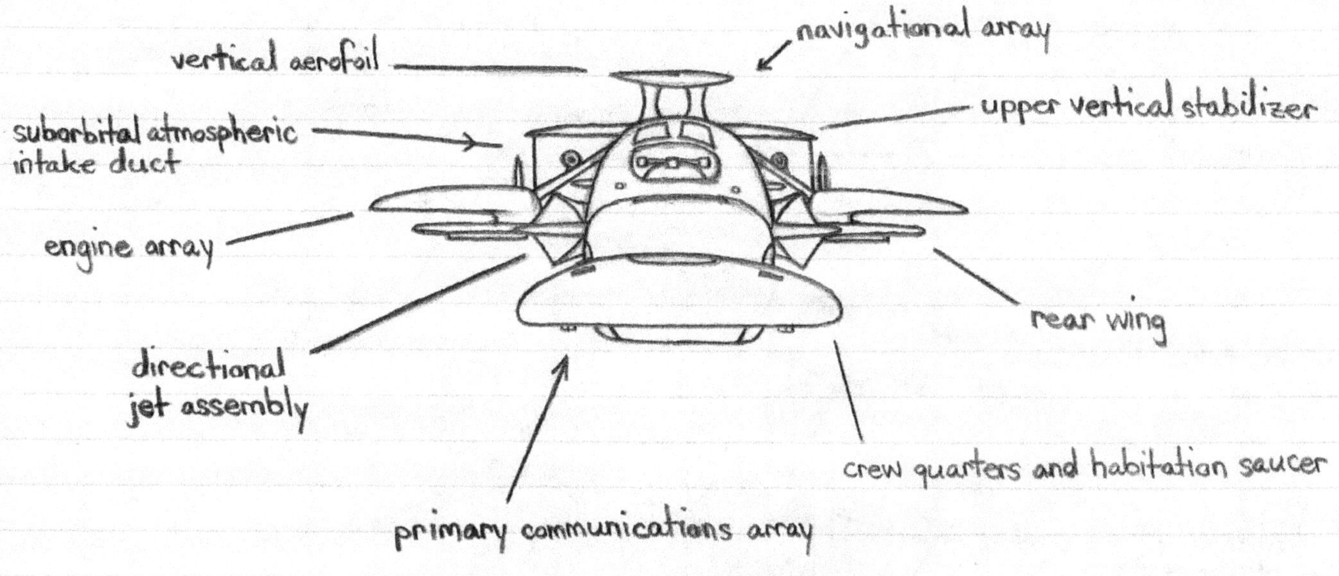

FIG. 4   REAR VIEW

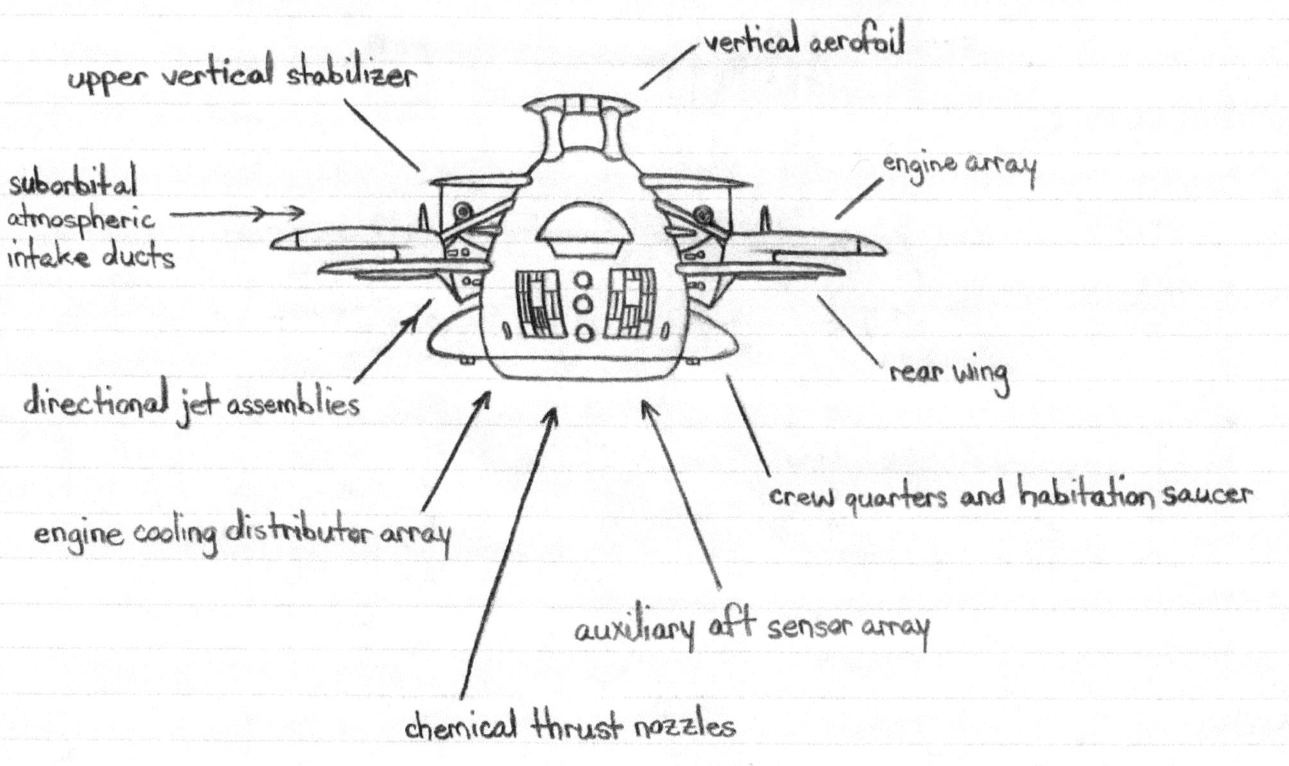

EFA-TY294 *Krash'regit*

FIG. 5   BOTTOM VIEW

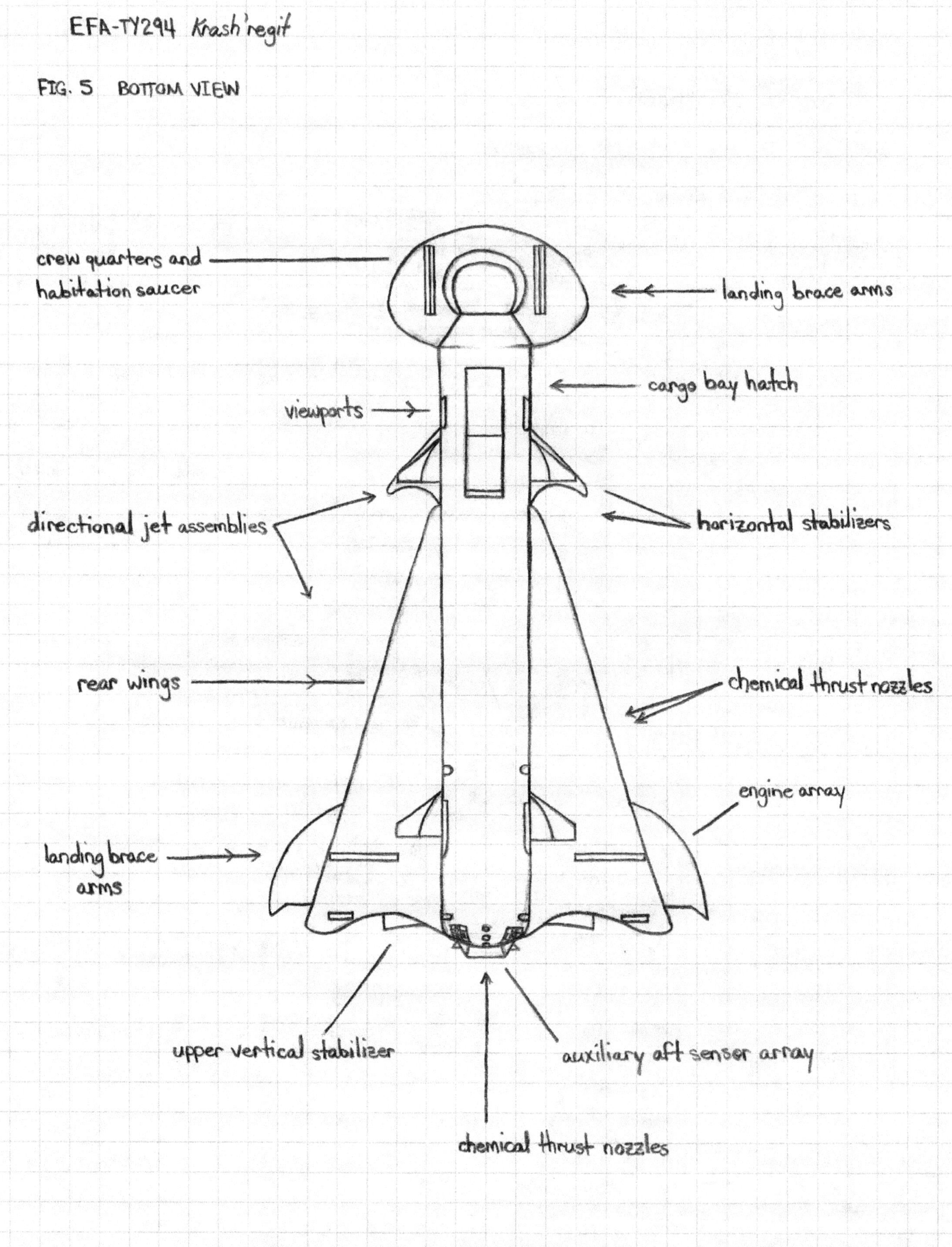

EFA-TY294 *Krash'regit*

CUTAWAY: CENTRAL INTERIOR COMPARTMENTS

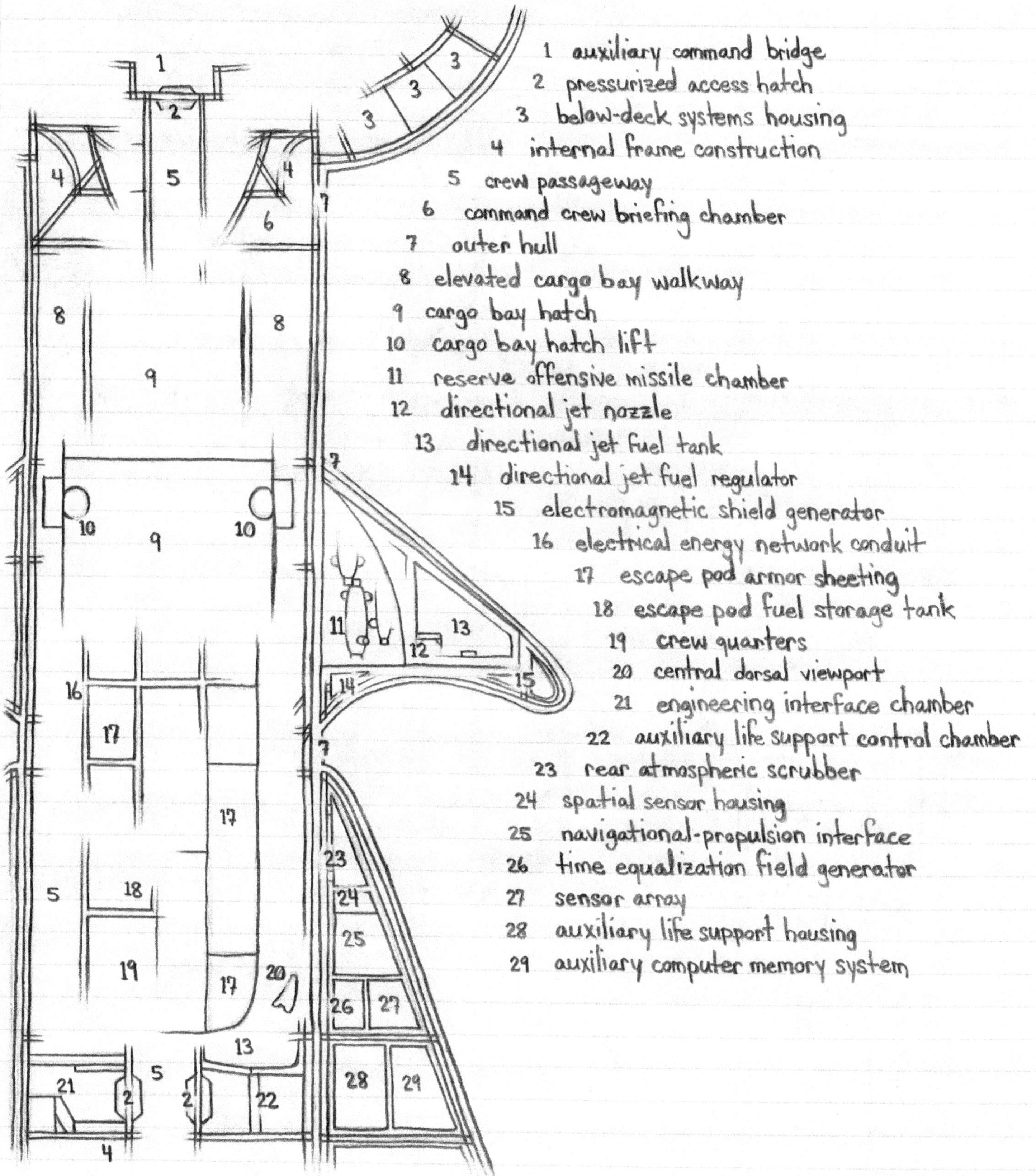

EFA-TY294 *Krash'regit*

CUTAWAY: AFT INTERIOR SECTIONS

1. retracting arm lift servo
2. vertical aerofoil
3. weapons targeting sensor housing
4. spatial sensor
5. shield distributor array
6. electromagnetic reciprocating turbine
7. internal frame construction
8. communications interface
9. navigational sensor array
10. hyperspace generator housing
11. electromagnetic shield generator
12. engineering crew access passage
13. artificial gravity generator
14. electrical capacitor
15. electrical battery
16. chemical thrust fuel tank
17. wing attachment construction
18. engine cooling distributor array
19. chemical thrust nozzle

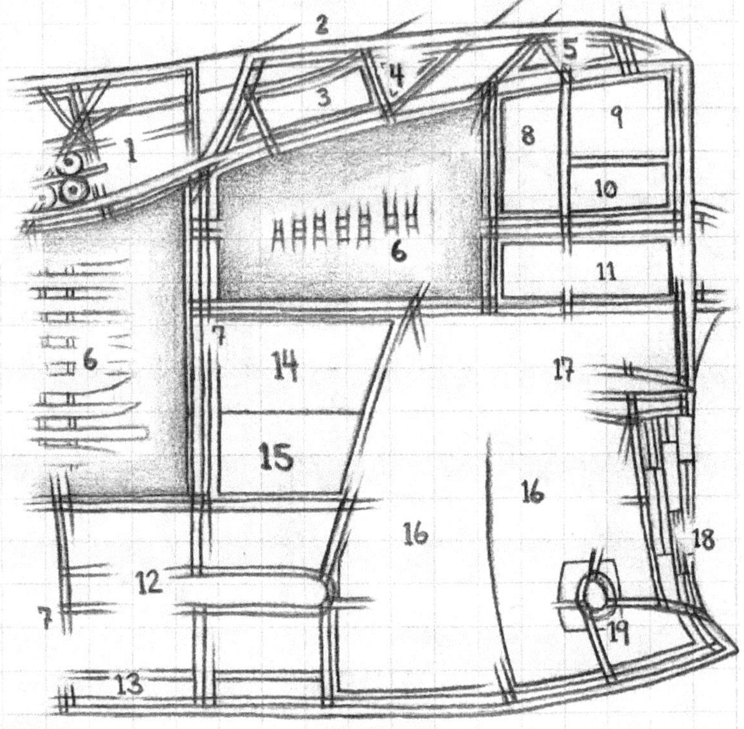

CUTAWAY: HATCH LIFTS

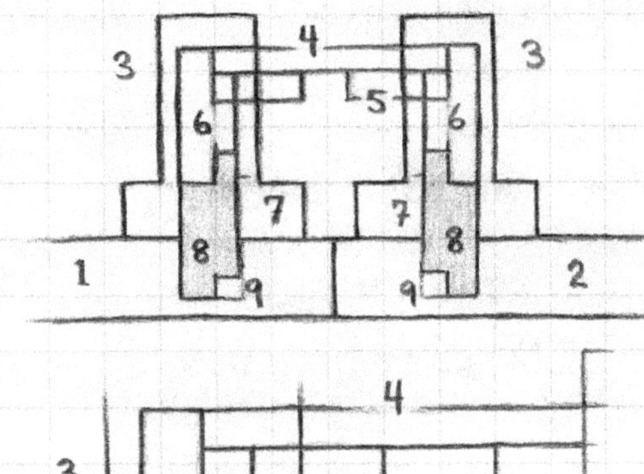

1. hatch deck
2. ship hull deck
3. hatch lift servo
4. variable height lowering arm
5. lowering bracket and arm brace
6. lowering brackets
7. lowering braces sleeve
8. variable angle lowering bracket sheath
9. pressure integrity sensor

84

EFA-TY294 *Krash'regit*

CUTAWAY: COMMUNICATIONS ASSEMBLY

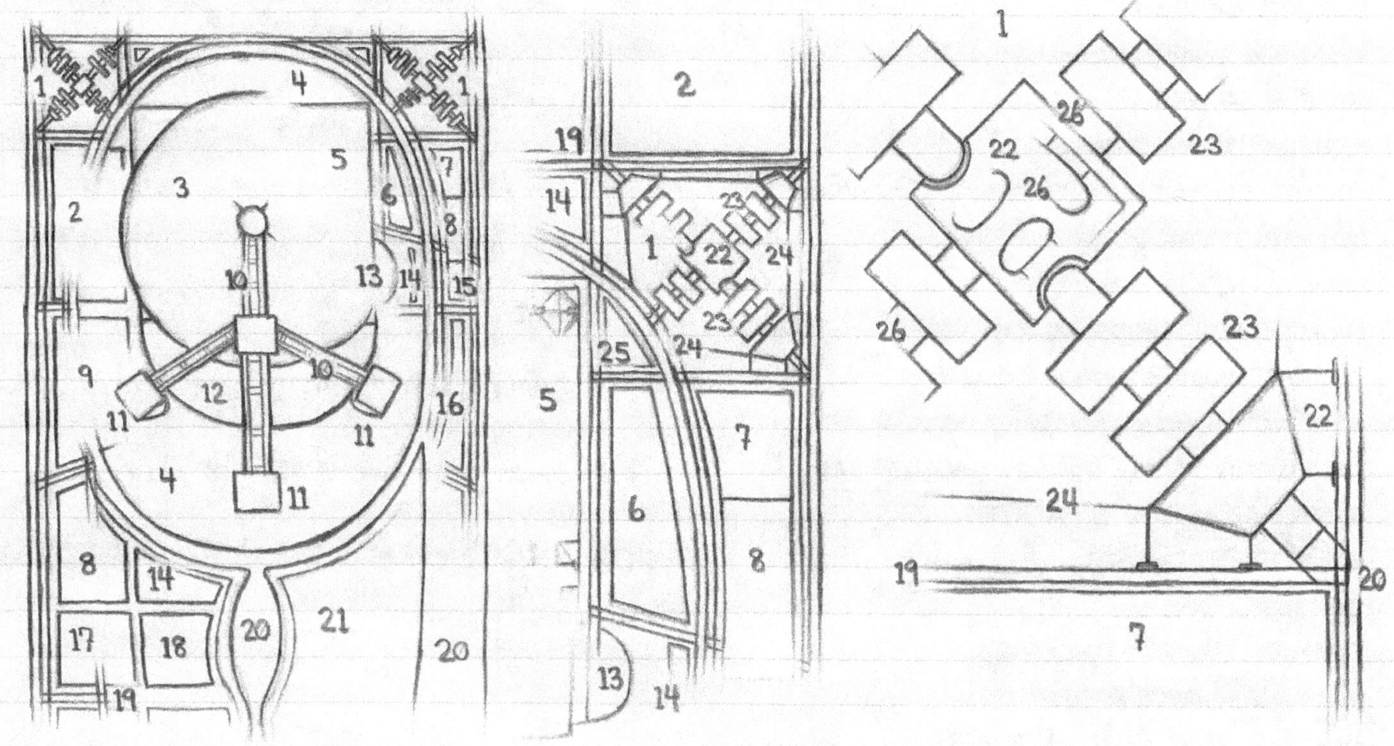

1	communications array servo motor
2	atmospheric storage tank
3	retractable communications array
4	primary interface capacitor basin
5	tribarrel laser cannon
6	electromagnetic shield distributor node
7	targeting computer
8	sensor array
9	water recycling system housing
10	communications array retracting arm
11	retracting arms and servo housing
12	general purpose reserve battery
13	tribarrel laser cannon swivel servo
14	control computer
15	temporal equalization field emission amplifier
16	life support relay computer
17	communications receiver encoding systems
18	navigational sensor array
19	internal frame construction
20	outer hull
21	primary shield generator
22	servo motor gyrator socket assembly
23	servo motor reinforcement capacitor
24	nitrogen silicate reinforcement cable
25	servo motor reserve capacitor
26	internal silicate graphite rotation rod

EFA-TY294 *Krash'regit*

CUTAWAY: ENGINE ARRAY

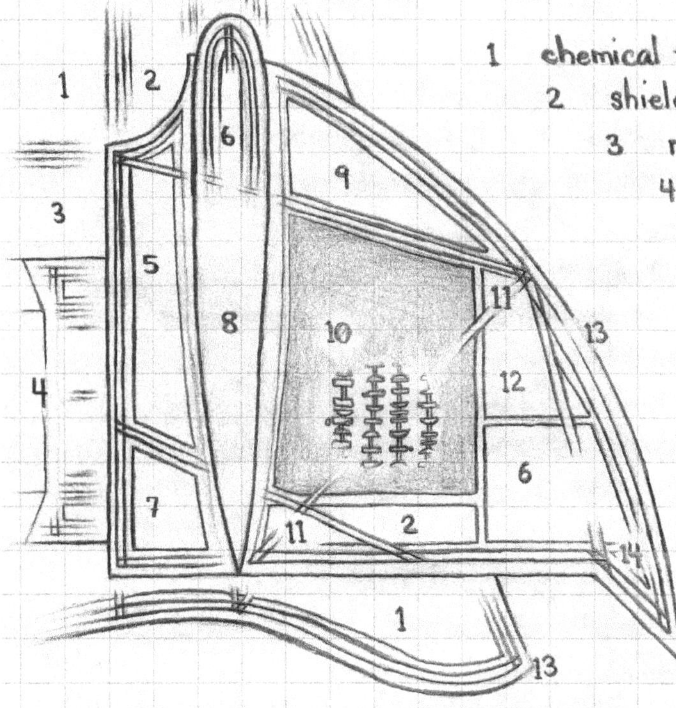

1 chemical thrust fuel tank
2 shield generator
3 navigational-propulsional interface
4 suborbital atmospheric intake assembly
5 sensor array housing
6 electrical capacitor
7 hyperspace field generator
8 engine array vertical stabilizer
9 electrical surge capacitor
10 reserve electromagnetic reciprocating turbine
11 internal frame construction
12 temporal equalization field generator
13 outer hull
14 spatial sensor

CUTAWAY: LANDING BRACE ARM

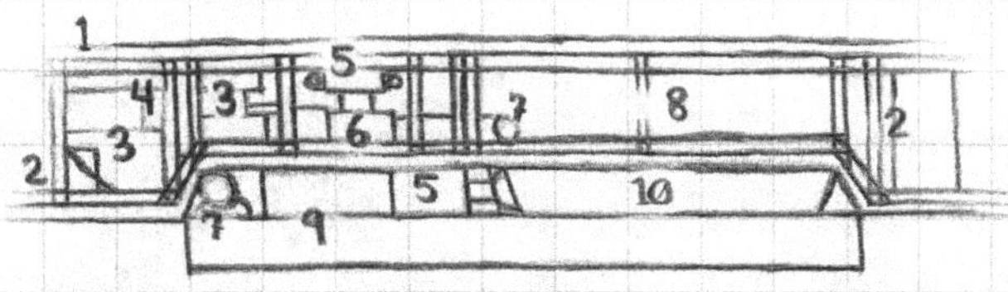

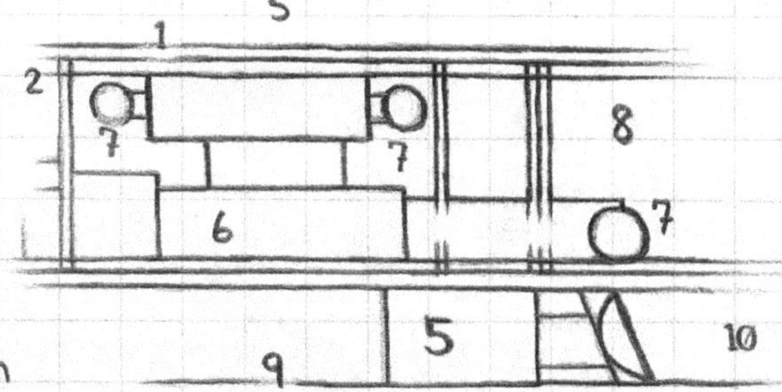

1 outer hull
2 internal frame construction
3 hydraulic landing brace arm reinforcement mechanism
4 landing brace arm control computer
5 positioning extender placement servo assembly
6 crosspiece support beam positioning extender
7 servo adjustment gear
8 crosspiece support beam positioning extender cavity
9 landing brace arm
10 landing brace arm crosspiece support beam

EFA-TY294 *Krash'regit*

CUTAWAY: REAR WING SUPERSTRUCTURE

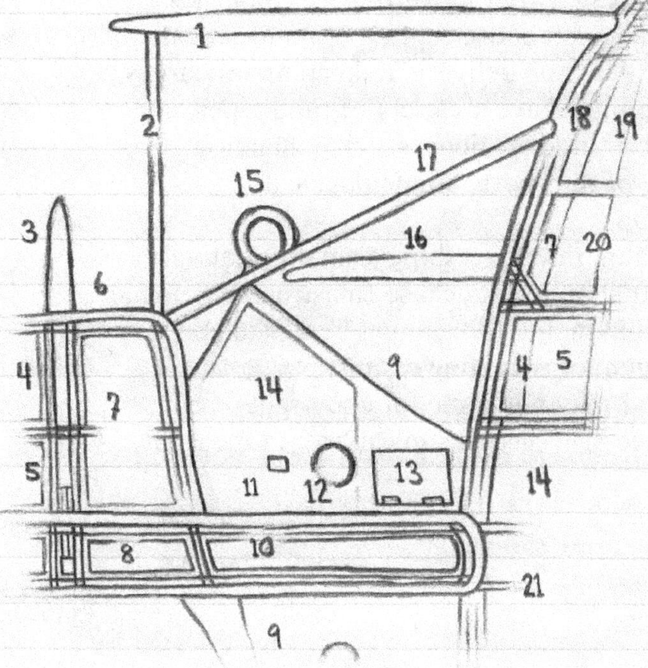

1 upper horizontal stabilizer
2 upper horizontal stabilizer support strut
3 engine array vertical stabilizer

4 electromagnetic shield generator
5 artificial gravity generator
6 engine array
7 hyperspace generator housing
8 temporal equalization field generator
9 directional jet assembly
10 electrical capacitor
11 directional jet assembly refueling port
12 directional jet nozzle
13 offensive missile exit hatch
14 chemical thrust fuel tank
15 suborbital atmospheric intake duct
16 medial horizontal stabilizer
17 atmospheric intake duct mounting platform
18 navigational sensor array
19 atmospheric pressure regulator
20 atmospheric storage tank
21 internal frame construction

Set 30:
Slaver 11

The Dercix are the most unsavory slavers in *Lone Soldier* space. Their raider escort vessel is itself a transport for several captured slaves, harvested after the *Slaver 11* ambushes a potential target and causes enough damage for its occupants to choose capture or painful death. It has quite complex systems for different atmosphere and poison delivery, to keep their charges breathing but alternately awake or asleep. This ship also must have a variety of food types and guards, who are less concerned with who or how many captured sentients survive than how much they get for them. Ojif are preferred for their ease of transport, simple physical requirements, and the unintelligent ones never try to escape.

This is one ship equipped with an actual kinetic gun, rare for a ship so small (relatively). Not many weapons are needed in this space shooting actual bullets, to cause catastrophic damage to a ship's structural integrity. Such a weapon is more convincing for sentient beings to endure slavery, when faced with death by exposure to hard vacuum or accepting chains.

The name of this ship is an homage to a story arc I may not name for copyright reasons, but I can say it involves a bounty hunter. (It could be read as a second *slave* maker in the right font.)

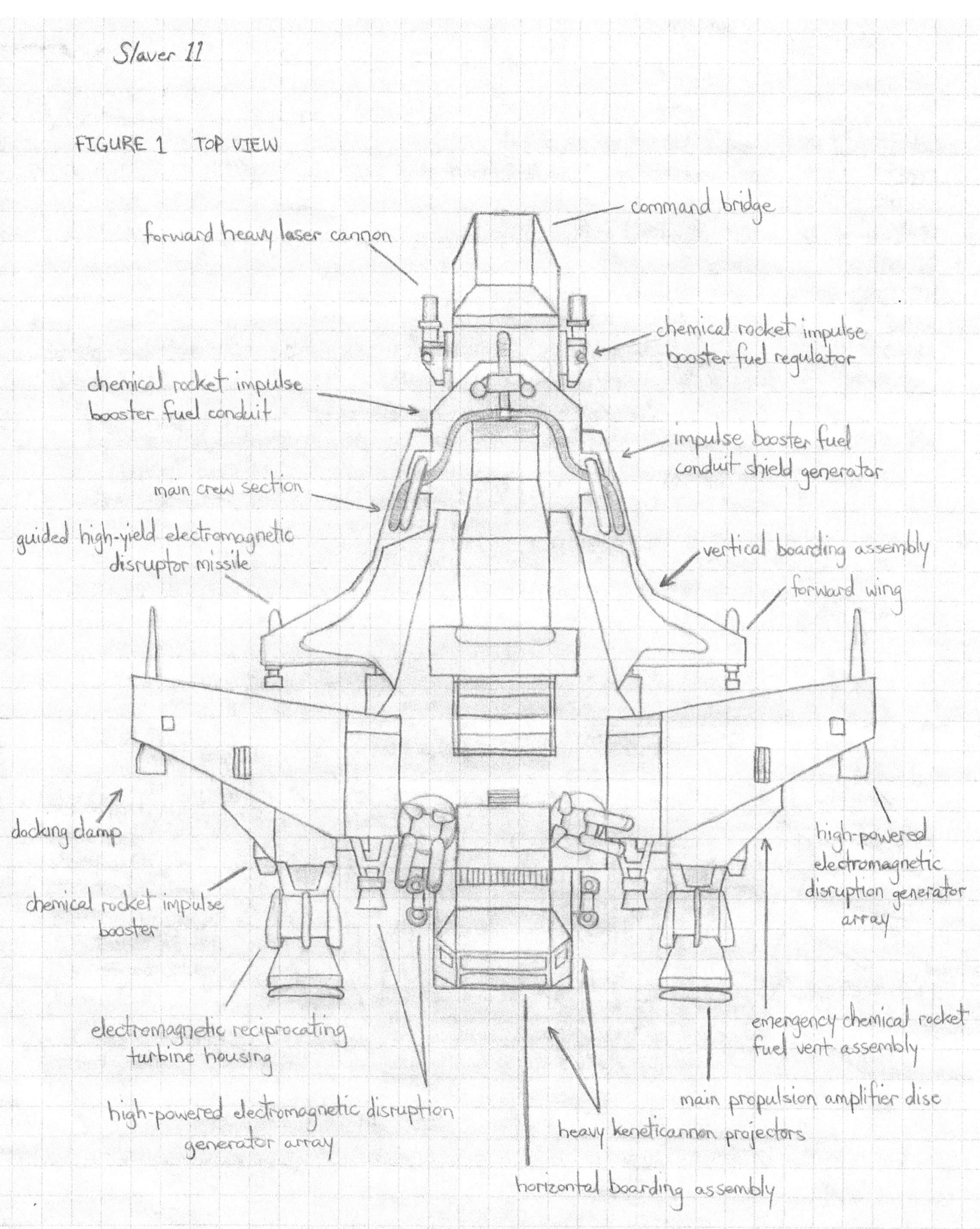

89

Slaver 11

CLASSIFICATION: Dercix raider escort vessel
TYPE: armored slave siezure/transport ship
CREW: 22 (four officers, eighteen enlisted or impressed) (capacity for 40 prisoners)
LENGTH: 13.1 standard feet
WIDTH: 11 standard feet
HEIGHT: 4.8 standard feet
MASS: 24,300 standard mass units
ARMOR: reinforced steetanicarb with thermal insulator gloss and magnetic armor plating
ENGINES: two electromagnetic reciprocating turbines, four chemical rocket impulse boosters, emergency chemical escape booster
ARMAMENT: two swivel-mounted heavy keneticannon projectors, eight high-powered electromagnetic disruption generator arrays, two forward heavy laser cannon, two guided high-yield electromagnetic disruptor missiles

FIG. 2 FRONT VIEW

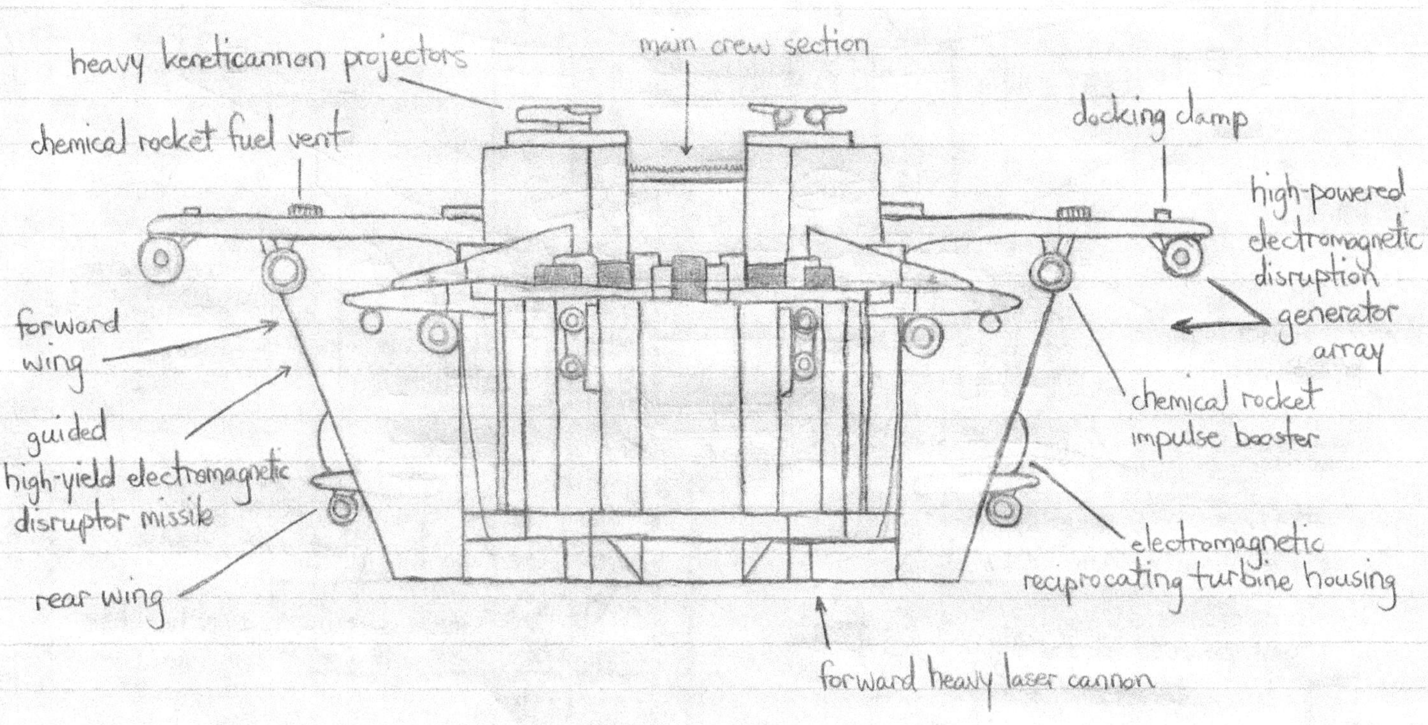

FIG. 3   SIDE VIEW

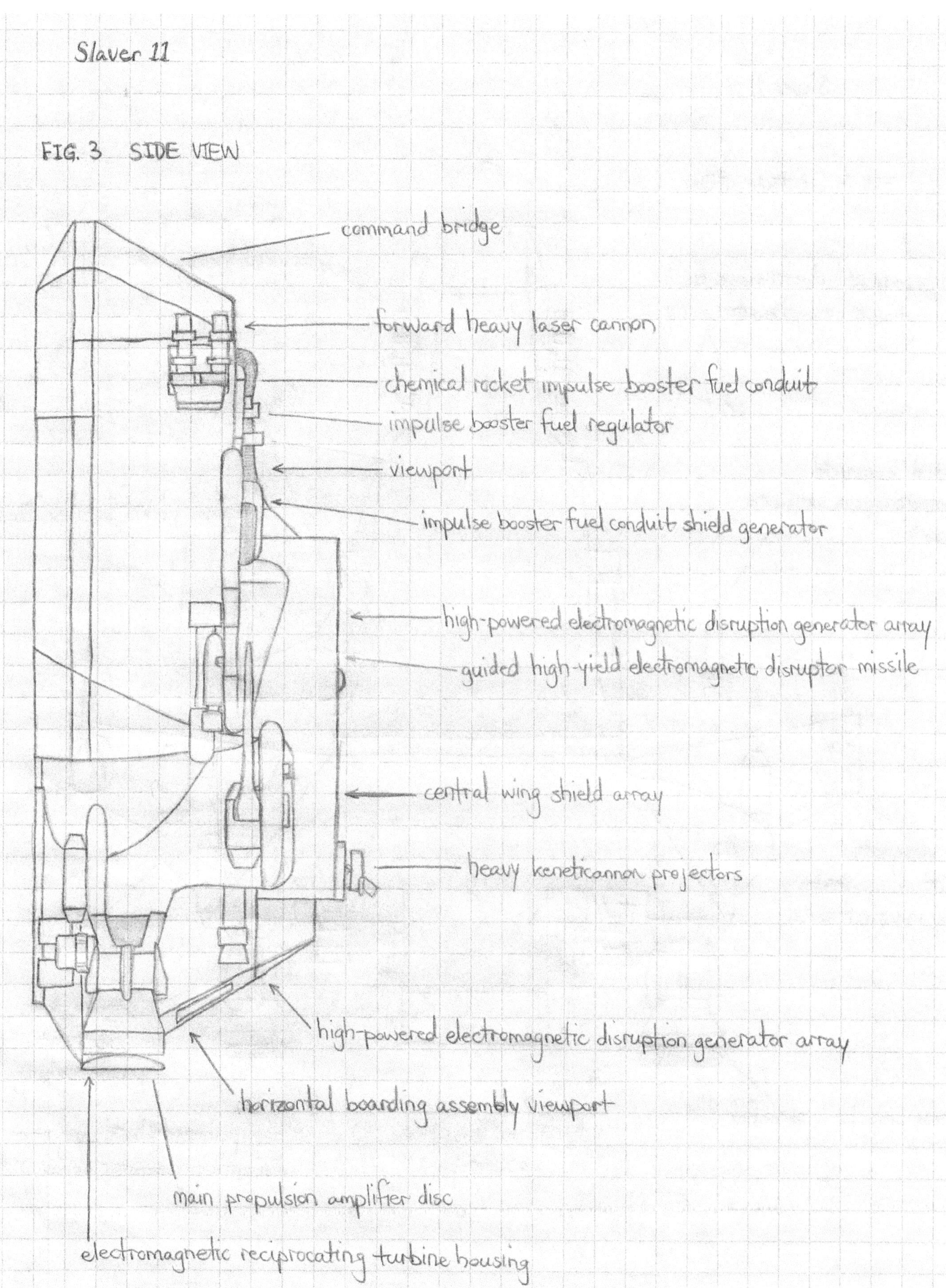

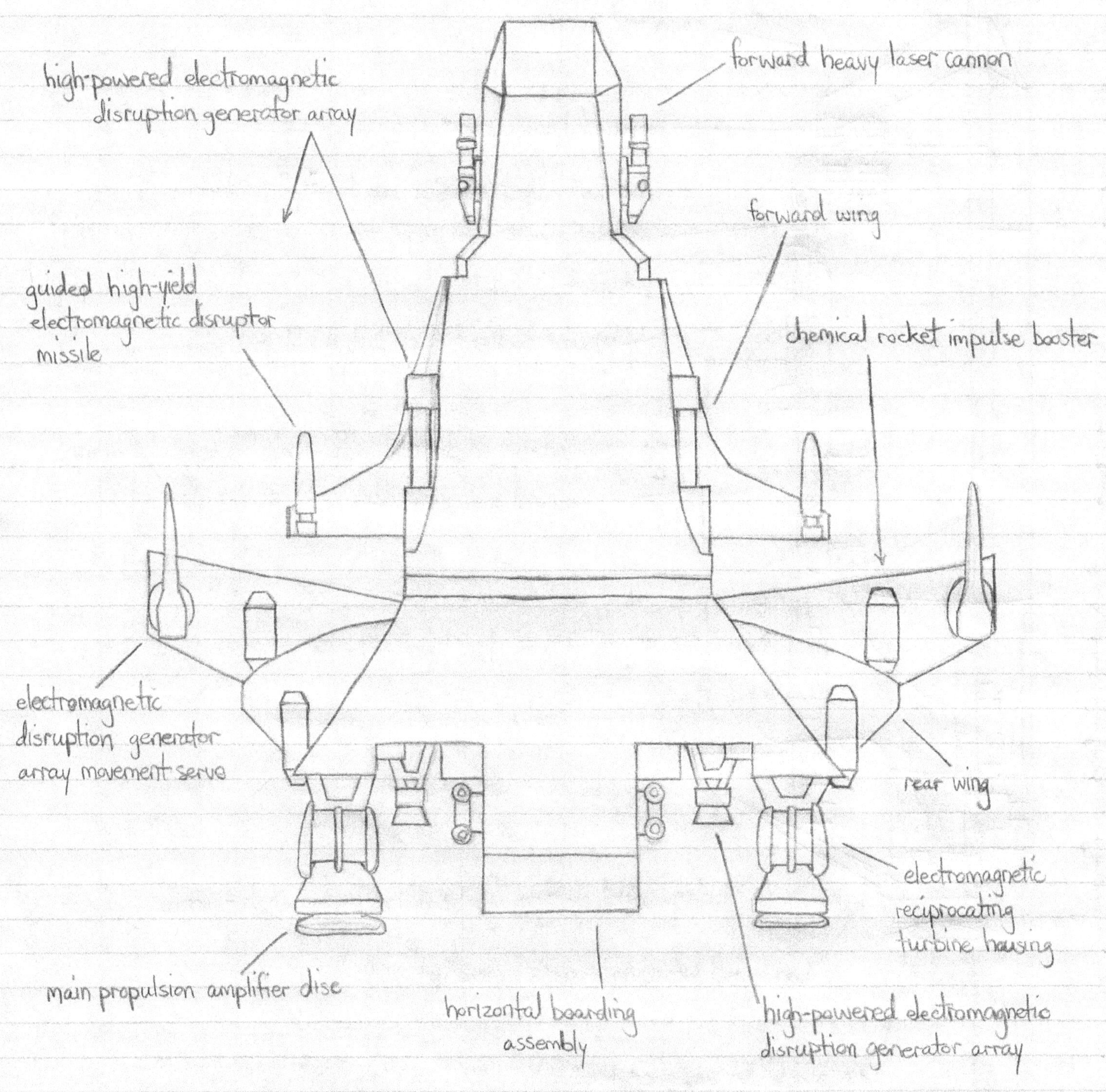

Slaver 11

FIG. 4   BOTTOM VIEW

high-powered electromagnetic
disruption generator array

forward heavy laser cannon

forward wing

guided high-yield
electromagnetic disruptor
missile

chemical rocket impulse booster

electromagnetic
disruption generator
array movement servo

rear wing

main propulsion amplifier disc

horizontal boarding
assembly

high-powered electromagnetic
disruption generator array

electromagnetic
reciprocating
turbine housing

Slaver 11

FIG. 5   REAR VIEW

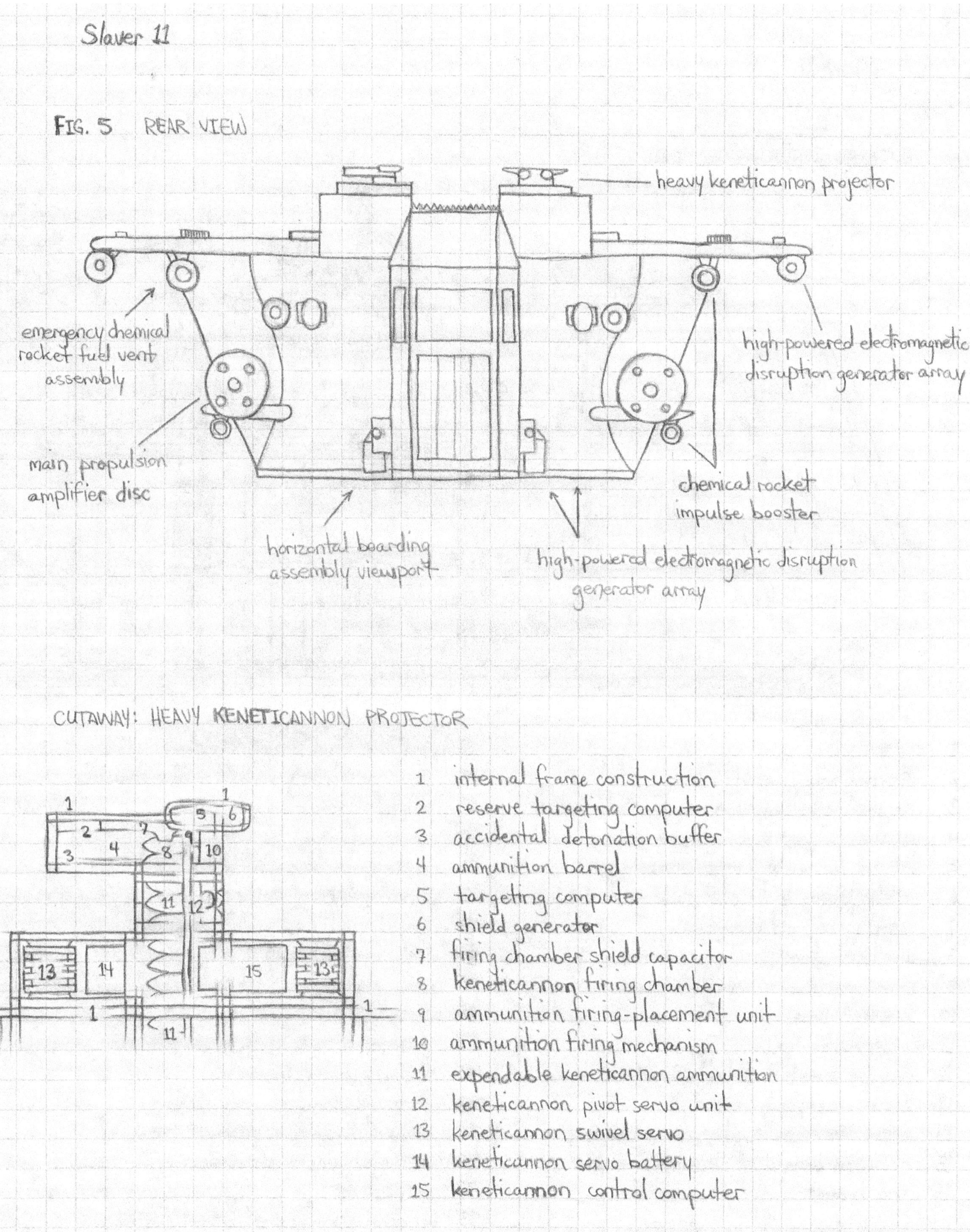

CUTAWAY: HEAVY **KENETICANNON** PROJECTOR

1 internal frame construction
2 reserve targeting computer
3 accidental detonation buffer
4 ammunition barrel
5 targeting computer
6 shield generator
7 firing chamber shield capacitor
8 keneticannon firing chamber
9 ammunition firing-placement unit
10 ammunition firing mechanism
11 expendable keneticannon ammunition
12 keneticannon pivot servo unit
13 keneticannon swivel servo
14 keneticannon servo battery
15 keneticannon control computer

Slaver 11

CUTAWAY: INTERIOR SECTIONS

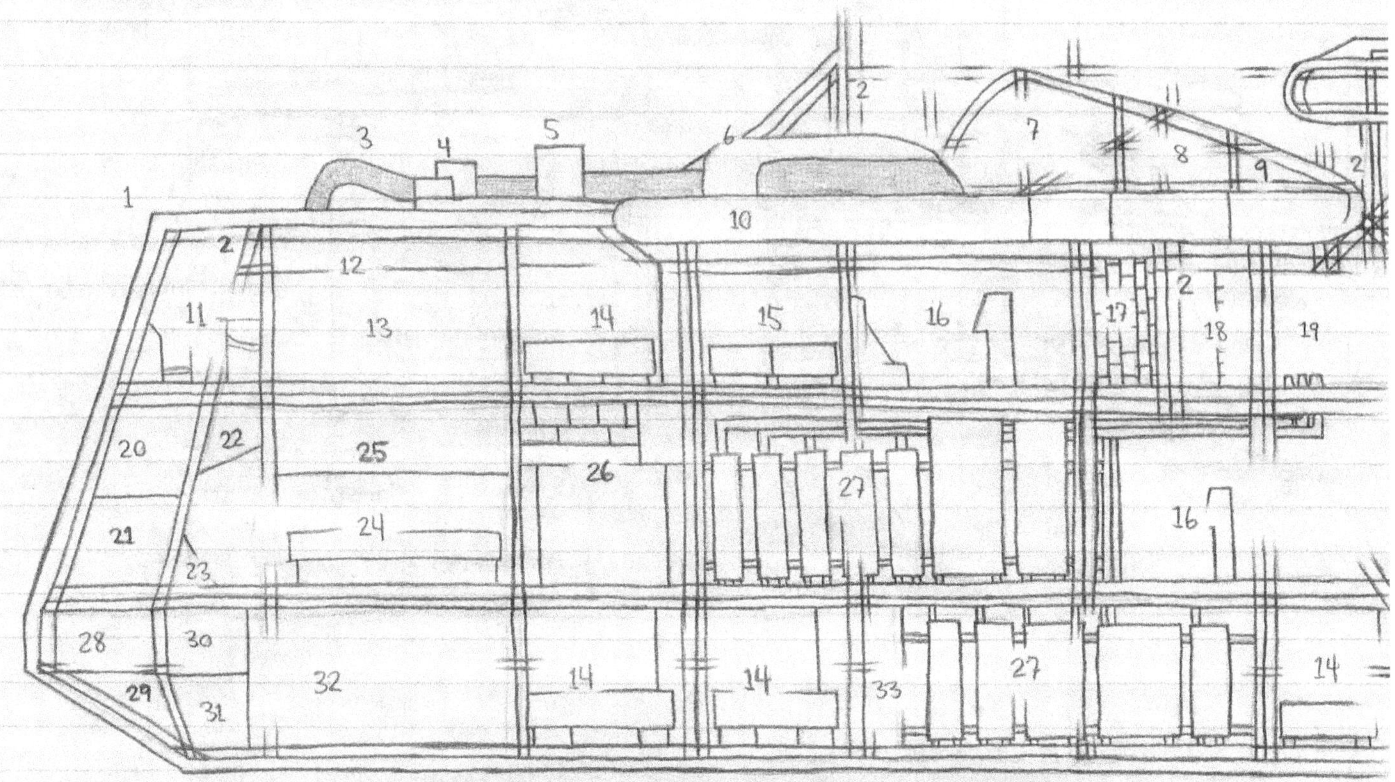

1	outer hull	17	prisoner food storage chamber
2	internal frame construction	18	prisoner feeding and refresher chamber
3	chemical rocket impulse booster fuel conduit	19	prisoner detention cell
4	impulse booster fuel regulator	20	communications array
5	impulse booster fuel reserve regulator	21	hyperspace navigational computer
6	impulse booster fuel conduit shield generator	22	primary memory computer
7	hyperspace field generator	23	life support maintenance computer
8	auxiliary atmospheric pressurizer	24	crew medical bay
9	shield distributor array	25	crew atmospheric storage tank
10	forward wing	26	crew galley
11	command bridge	27	prisoner atmospheric storage tanks
12	impulse booster control computer	28	forward shield generator
13	crew access passageway	29	forward sensor array
14	crew quarters	30	crew atmospheric pressure regulator
15	security personnel sleeping chamber	31	artificial gravity generator
16	security station	32	cargo hold
		33	prisoner atmosphere control systems

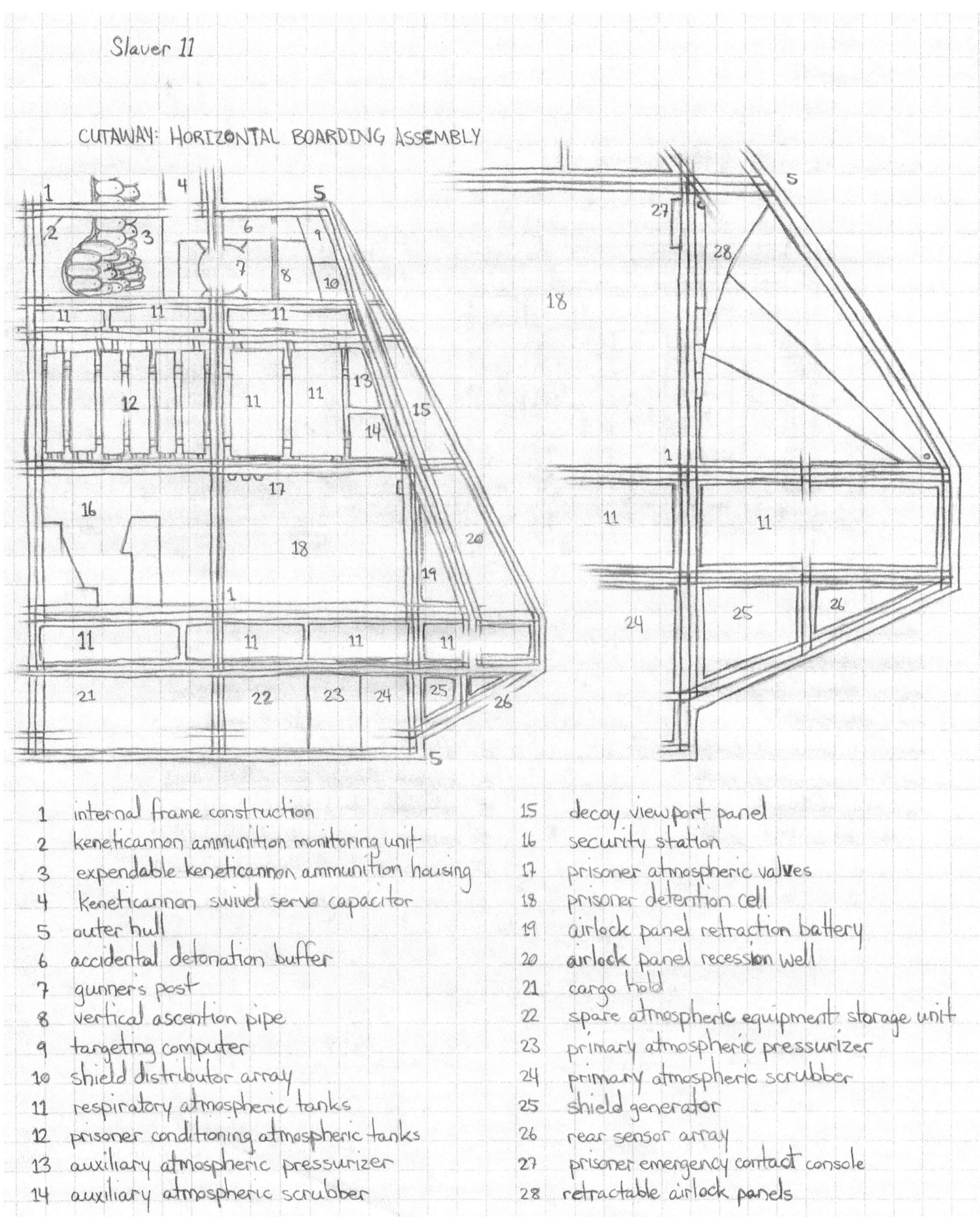

1	internal frame construction	15	decoy viewport panel
2	keneticannon ammunition monitoring unit	16	security station
3	expendable keneticannon ammunition housing	17	prisoner atmospheric valves
4	keneticannon swivel servo capacitor	18	prisoner detention cell
5	outer hull	19	airlock panel retraction battery
6	accidental detonation buffer	20	airlock panel recession well
7	gunner's post	21	cargo hold
8	vertical ascention pipe	22	spare atmospheric equipment storage unit
9	targeting computer	23	primary atmospheric pressurizer
10	shield distributor array	24	primary atmospheric scrubber
11	respiratory atmospheric tanks	25	shield generator
12	prisoner conditioning atmospheric tanks	26	rear sensor array
13	auxiliary atmospheric pressurizer	27	prisoner emergency contact console
14	auxiliary atmospheric scrubber	28	retractable airlock panels

CUTAWAY: PRISONER DETENTION SYSTEMS

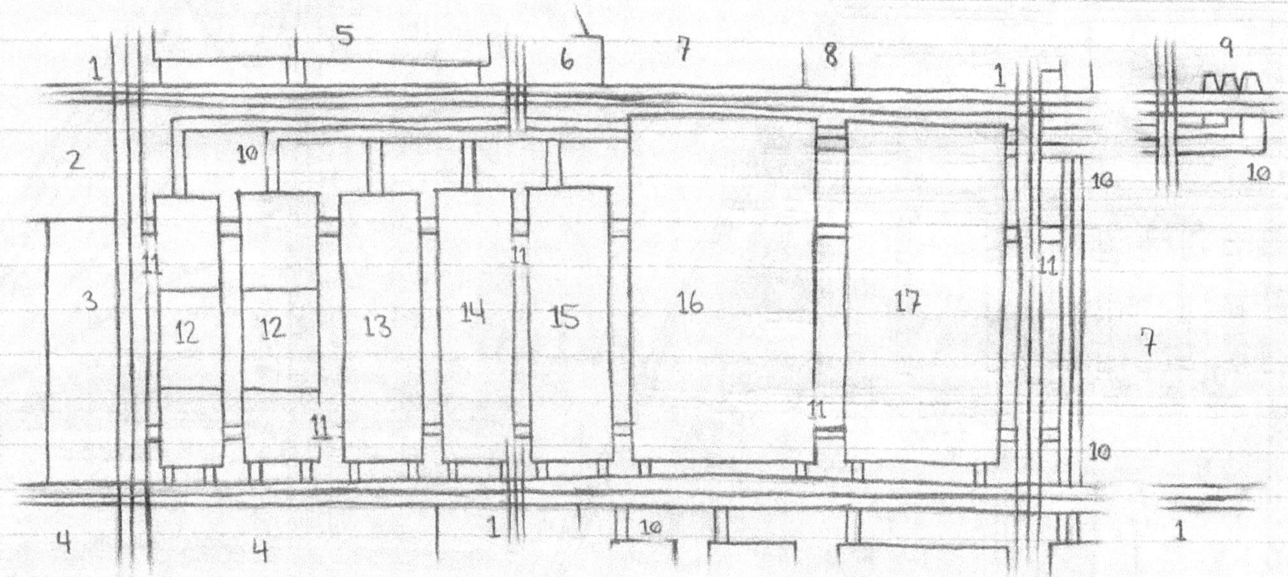

1	internal frame construction	9	prisoner atmospheric valves
2	galley utensil recycler	10	atmospheric transmission tube
3	galley utensil dispenser	11	atmospheric tank securing brace
4	crew quarters	12	hydrogen atmospheric tank
5	security personnel sleeping unit	13	argon atmospheric tank
6	security personnel seat	14	carbon dioxide atmospheric tank
7	security station	15	nitrogen atmospheric tank
8	reinforced control panel	16	oxygen blend atmospheric tank
		17	ammonia blend atmospheric tank

# Set 31:
Dircens Rirosaw Ktikinpratg

This could be the most famous ship in Confederation or Detalernu space. The *K-tin* began as a Dex Hox troop transport, very long ago as ships go. The Dex Hox (and consequently, the *Dir Riro*) make few new ships when they have parts and means to repair those on hand. Even if the restoration and repair of old ships is exhaustive, it is preferred to scrapping a tested and trusted vessel in favor of a new one. **Below follows a spoiler, so be warned.**

This vessel was built with assistance from the Small Wise. True to form, survived the Gaepvihn assault on the Hoxian home system and served in the war until First Siege, when the young *Dir Riro* fled local space and eventually found the Adreg races. Before this flight, the troop transport was converted to a biome ship to help preserve water and grow food. Great Leader Nopalés didn't expect to find friendly alien races or compatible sustenance quickly.

Over hundreds of years, the *K-tin* changed from an aerodynamic biome ship near its original construction to a sphere—as well as one of the most powerful, and largest, ships in home space. I needed to work out the evolutionary forms of this ship to construct the inner sections appropriately. Each renovation changed the outer appearance and took away from the original form, so it is hardly recognizable as the same ship it started as. This is the only integral *Dircens Rirosaw* ship to be so altered, even though most are maintained for centuries.

Once the *K-tin* ship reached a certain size, its crew understood it would never be an atmosphere-capable craft again if allowed to keep growing, so all such efforts were redirected to effectively maximizing use of a spheroid shape. As of the time it arrived in Eeomet Glar space, it hadn't made atmospheric entry in more than three hundreds years. Besides housing more than one thousand separate biomes for study and growth, the *Ktikinpratg* has the capacity to recharge a dozen capital ships simultaneously, if necessary. It also has more complexity and depth of sections than I feel up to drawing on paper, so I try to work such things into a story.

Dircens Rirosaw Ktikinpratg
FIGURE 1 PROFILE VIEW
utility access
access hatches
chemical rocket
impulse thrust
exhaust nozzles
escape pod
armor sheaths
weapons stations
ion impulse
nozzles
impulse fuel
intake nozzles
communications network

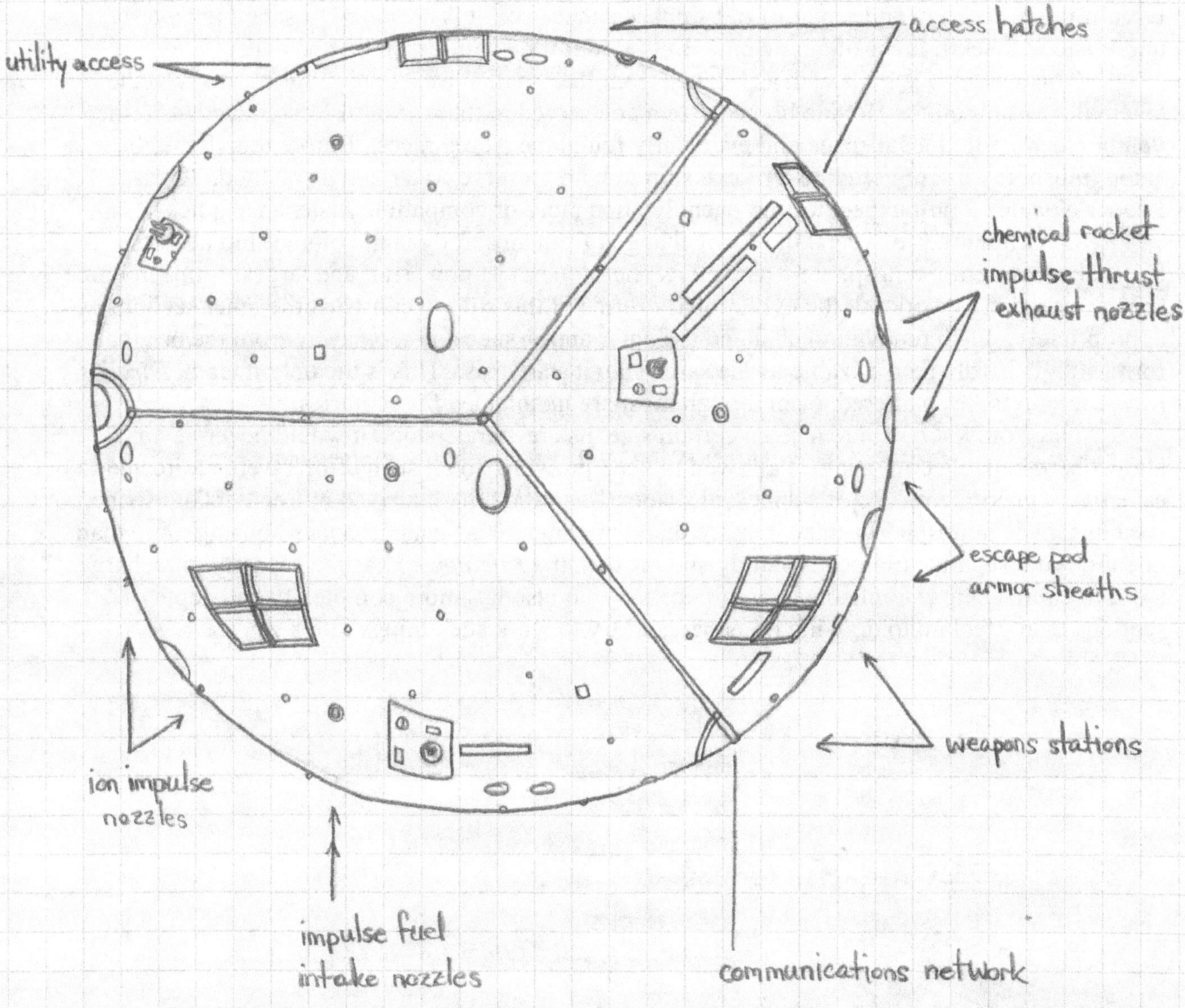

Dircens Rirosaw *Ktikinpratg*

CLASSIFICATION: biome ship
TYPE: modified troop transport
CREW: 332 (thirty-eight officers, two hundreds ninety-four enlisted)
LENGTH: 465 standard feet
WIDTH: 465 standard feet
HEIGHT: 465 standard feet
MASS: 746,050 standard mass units
ARMOR: carbon-reinforced silicasteel hull with electromagnetic shielding
ENGINES: chemical rocket thrust assembly, ion thrust assembly, hyperspace
               macrogenerator assembly, seven elecromagnetic reciprocating helices
ARMAMENT: six quadbarrel laser platforms with missile tubes, two electromagnetic
               countermeasures pods, defensive electromagnetic net system
IMPLEMENTS: sphere radius communication network, ship recharging ports, exterior
               docking conduits, six auxiliary electromagnetic reciprocating turbines

CUTAWAY: INTERIOR SECTIONS

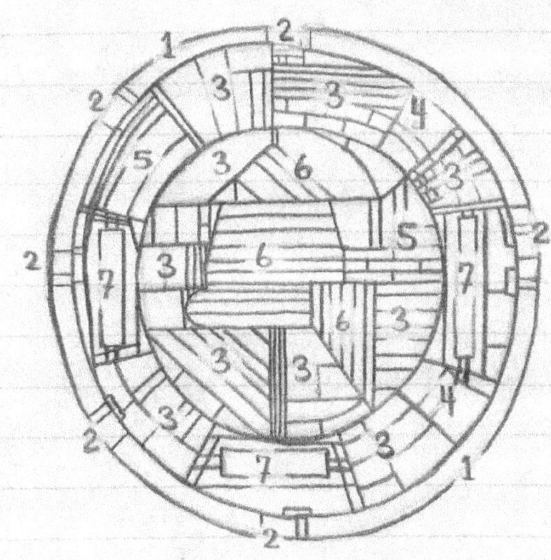

1 buffer hull
2 chemical rocket thrust assembly
3 biome decks
4 exterior access facilities
5 reserve crew areas
6 crew decks
7 electromagnetic reciprocating helix housing

CUTAWAY: AVIAN HEMISPHERE

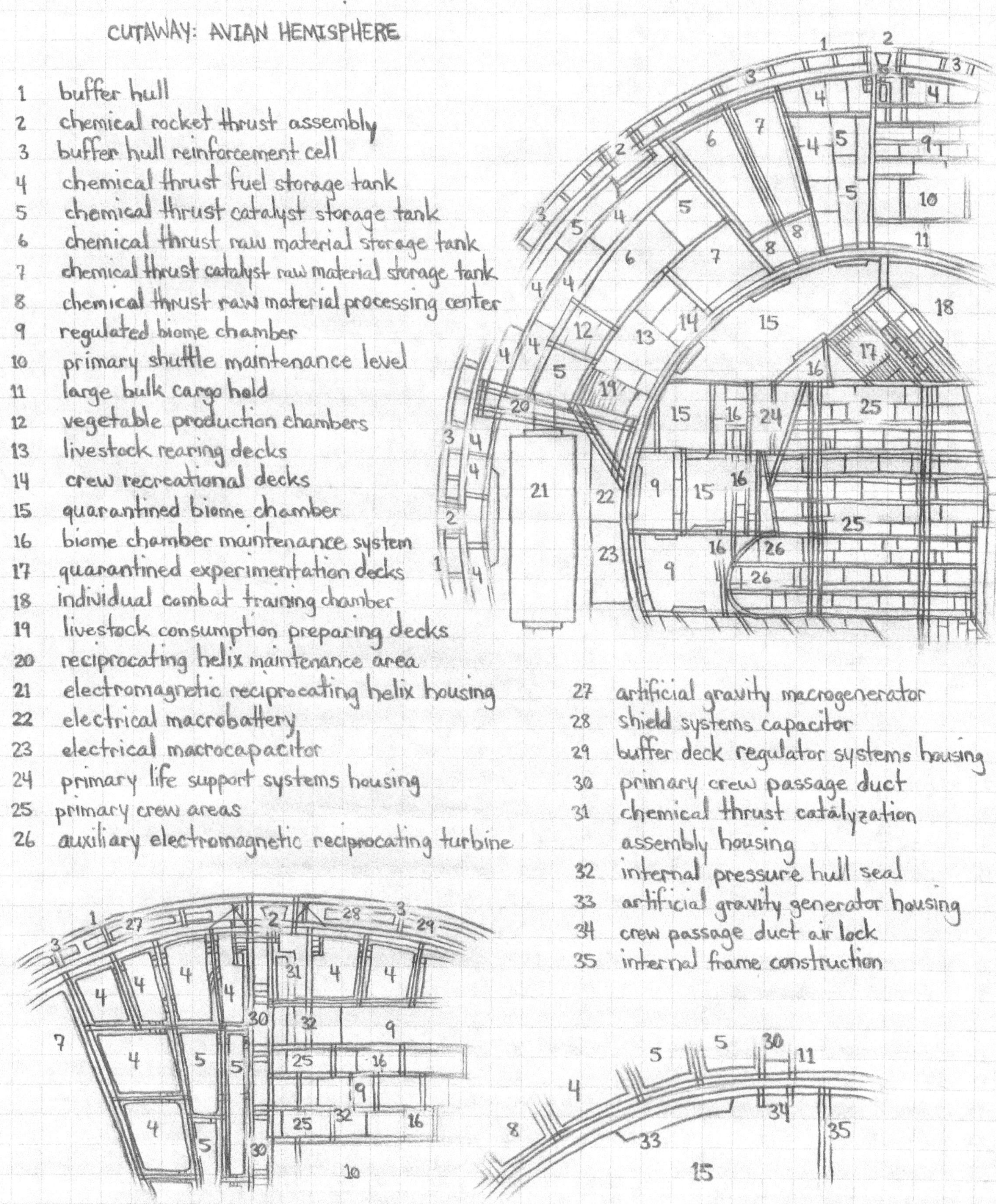

1 buffer hull
2 chemical rocket thrust assembly
3 buffer hull reinforcement cell
4 chemical thrust fuel storage tank
5 chemical thrust catalyst storage tank
6 chemical thrust raw material storage tank
7 chemical thrust catalyst raw material storage tank
8 chemical thrust raw material processing center
9 regulated biome chamber
10 primary shuttle maintenance level
11 large bulk cargo hold
12 vegetable production chambers
13 livestock rearing decks
14 crew recreational decks
15 quarantined biome chamber
16 biome chamber maintenance system
17 quarantined experimentation decks
18 individual combat training chamber
19 livestock consumption preparing decks
20 reciprocating helix maintenance area
21 electromagnetic reciprocating helix housing
22 electrical macrobattery
23 electrical macrocapacitor
24 primary life support systems housing
25 primary crew areas
26 auxiliary electromagnetic reciprocating turbine
27 artificial gravity macrogenerator
28 shield systems capacitor
29 buffer deck regulator systems housing
30 primary crew passage duct
31 chemical thrust catalyzation assembly housing
32 internal pressure hull seal
33 artificial gravity generator housing
34 crew passage duct air lock
35 internal frame construction

Dircens Rirosaw Kthkinpratg

CUTAWAY: EXOTHERMIC HEMISPHERE

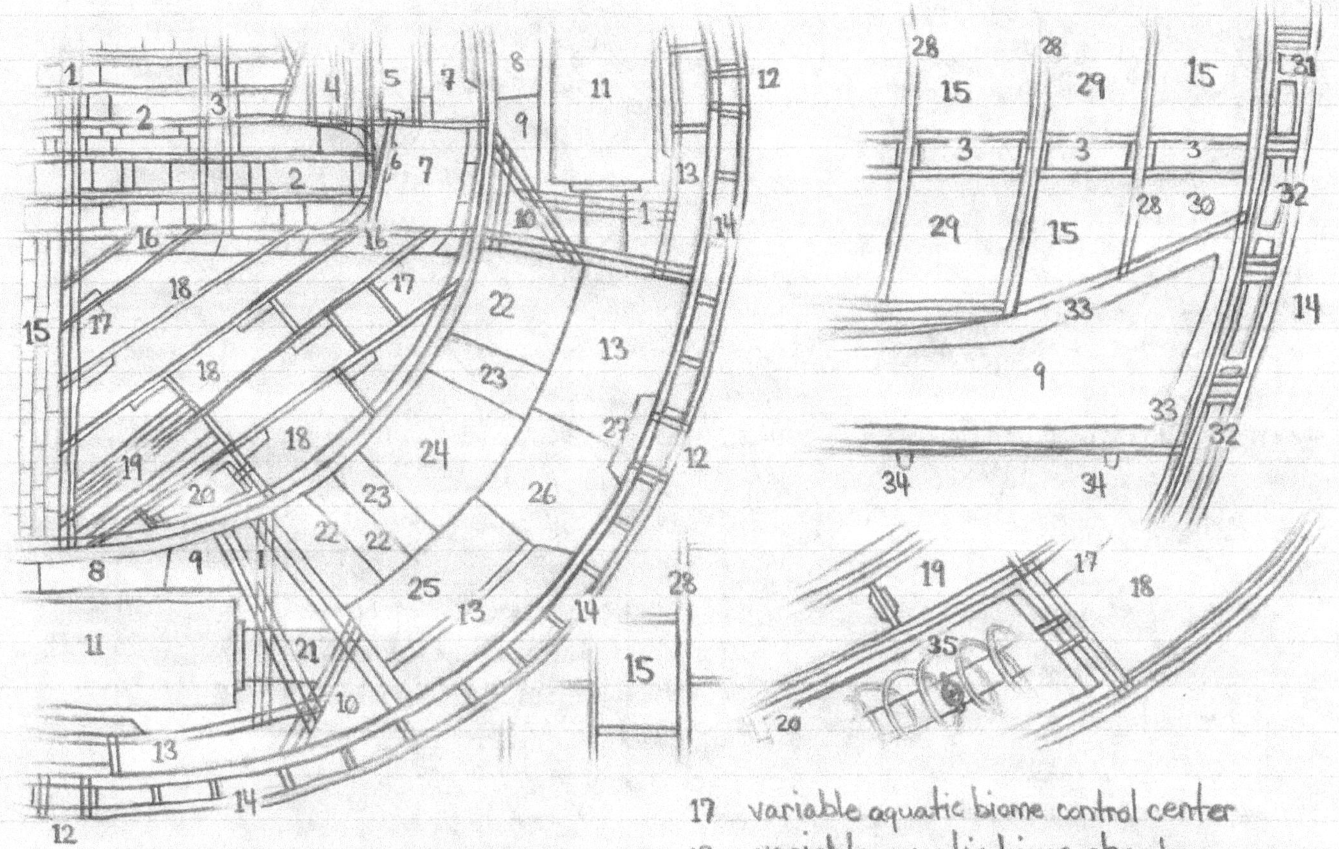

1	internal frame construction	17	variable aquatic biome control center
2	primary crew areas	18	variable aquatic biome chamber
3	primary crew passage duct	19	aquatic biome regulation section
4	biome chamber maintenance system	20	electromagnetic charge generator
5	quarantined biome chamber	21	reciprocating helix housing mounting brace
6	atmospheric recycling induction assembly	22	primary saline water biome
7	regulated biome chamber	23	liquid biome recycling system housing
8	electrical macrocapacitor	24	primary non-saline water biome
9	electrical macrobattery	25	chemical thrust catalyst storage tank
10	reciprocating helix maintenance	26	auxiliary water storage tank
11	electromagnetic reciprocating helix housing	27	chemical rocket regulator housing
12	chemical rocket thrust assembly	28	kinetic-resistant pressure hull
13	chemical thrust fuel storage tank	29	quarantined molecular research chamber
14	buffer hull	30	pressurized atmospheric storage tank
15	microbial research chamber	31	emergency explosive pressure disruptor assembly
16	crew evacuation chamber	32	shield systems capacitor
		33	electrical macrobattery surge buffer
		34	electromagnetic charge generator kinetic buffer
		35	electromagnetic charge dynamo

CUTAWAY: MAMMALIAN HEMISPHERE

1 buffer hull
2 chemical thrust fuel storage tank
3 chemical thrust catalyst raw material storage tank
4 chemical thrust catalyst storage tank
5 chemical rocket thrust assembly
6 regulated mammalian biome chamber
7 primary shuttle maintenance level
8 chemical thrust raw material processing center
9 quarantined avian biome chamber
10 biome chamber maintenance system
11 primary life support systems housing
12 regulated avian biome chamber
13 variable aquatic biome section
14 individual combat training chamber
15 quarantined experimentation decks
16 atmospheric moisture control housing
17 primary crew areas
18 auxiliary electromagnetic reciprocating turbine
19 large silicon-based plant biome chambers
20 minority-base animal biome chambers
21 fungal and protista biome chambers
22 large carbon-based plant biome chambers
23 oxygen atmosphere regulation assembly
24 methane atmosphere regulation assembly
25 communications network support assembly
26 large bulk cargo hold
27 exterior access bay
28 dry silicon-based biome chamber
29 humid carbon-based biome chamber
30 escape pod housing section
31 weapons station support assembly
32 electrical macrobattery
33 shield support assembly
34 electrical macrocapacitor
35 inner hull
36 maintenance and repair storeroom
37 electromagnetic reciprocating helix housing
38 exterior access bay atmospheric storage tank
39 buffer hull pinion rod
40 shield booster node emitter
41 node emitter frequency regulator
42 node emitter transducer housing

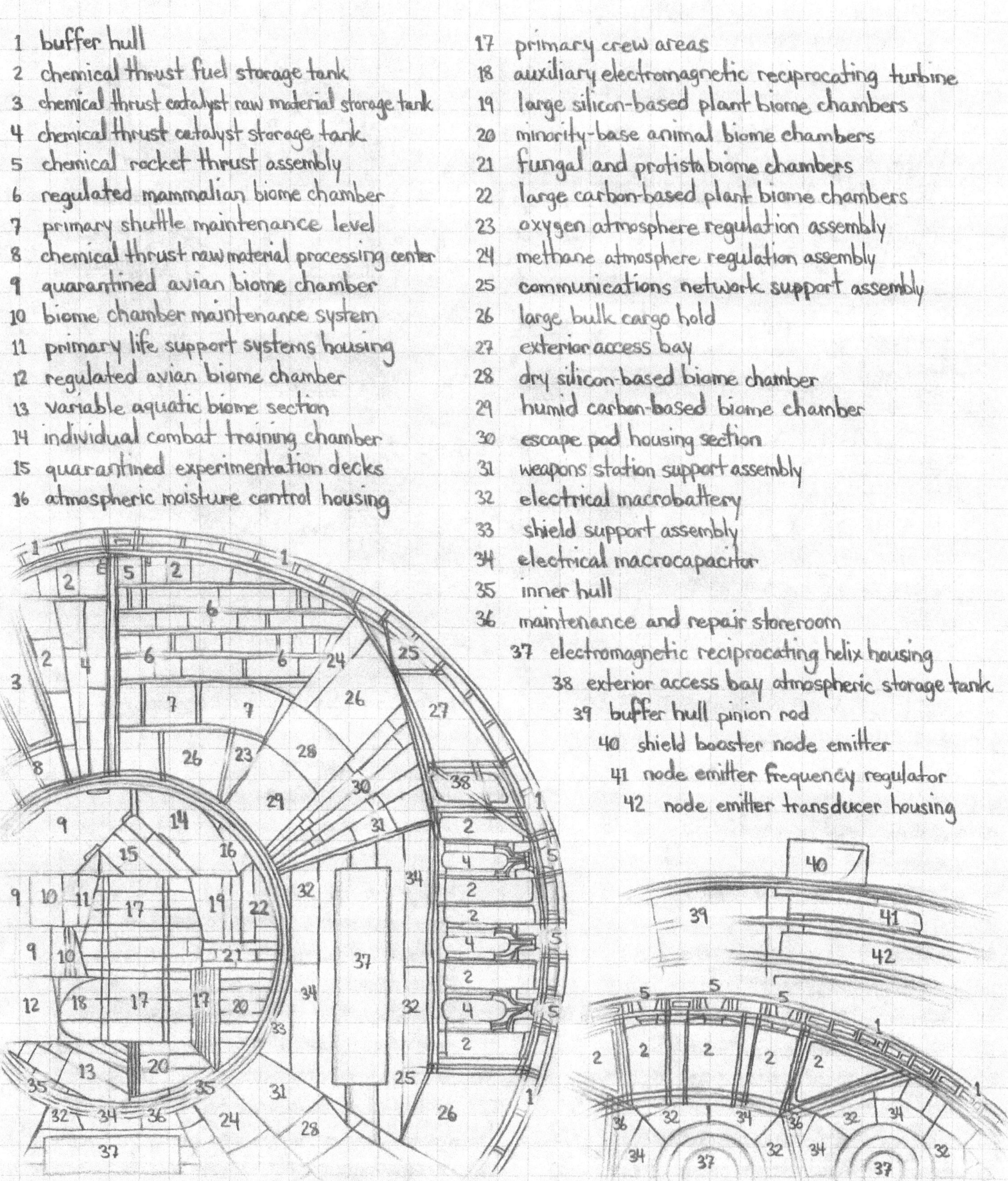

CUTAWAY: CREW DECKS

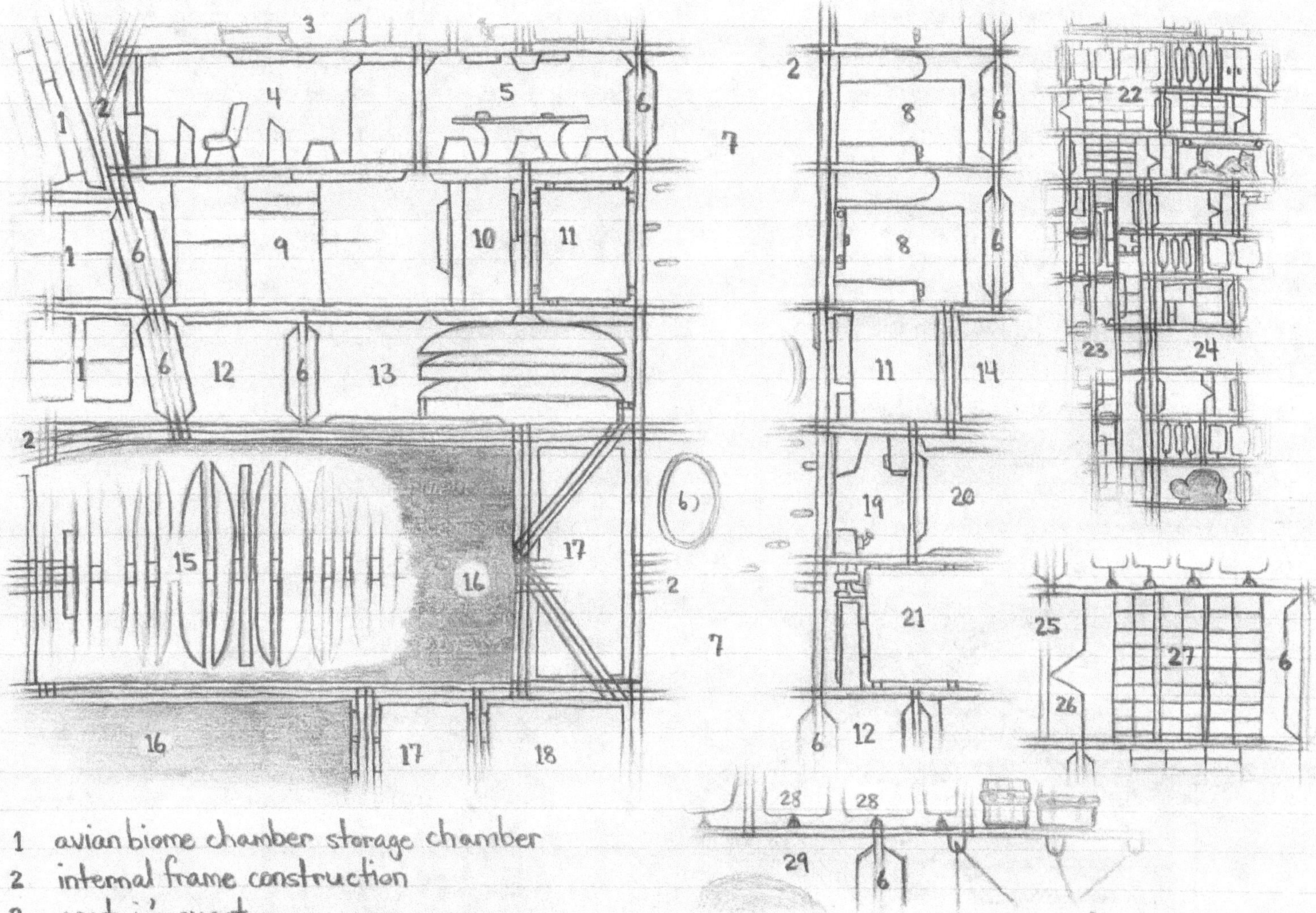

1. avian biome chamber storage chamber
2. internal frame construction
3. captain's quarters
4. auxiliary bridge
5. briefing chamber
6. pressurized hatch
7. primary crew passage duct
8. crew quarters
9. auxiliary bridge computer nexus
10. master memory computer core
11. pressurized atmospheric storage tank
12. airlock chamber
13. spare reciprocating turbine disc storage chamber
14. auxiliary communications nexus
15. auxiliary electromagnetic reciprocating turbine
16. electromagnetic buffer
17. electrical macrobattery
18. electrical macrocapacitor
19. crew refresher unit
20. crew corridor
21. refresher waste processing system
22. fungal and protista research section
23. crew decks
24. minority-based amphibian biome chamber
25. protista research chamber
26. central computer console
27. mold and protozoan storage cells
28. medical suit storage unit
29. zero-gravity nitrogen-based reptile biome chamber

CUTAWAY: WEAPONS STATION

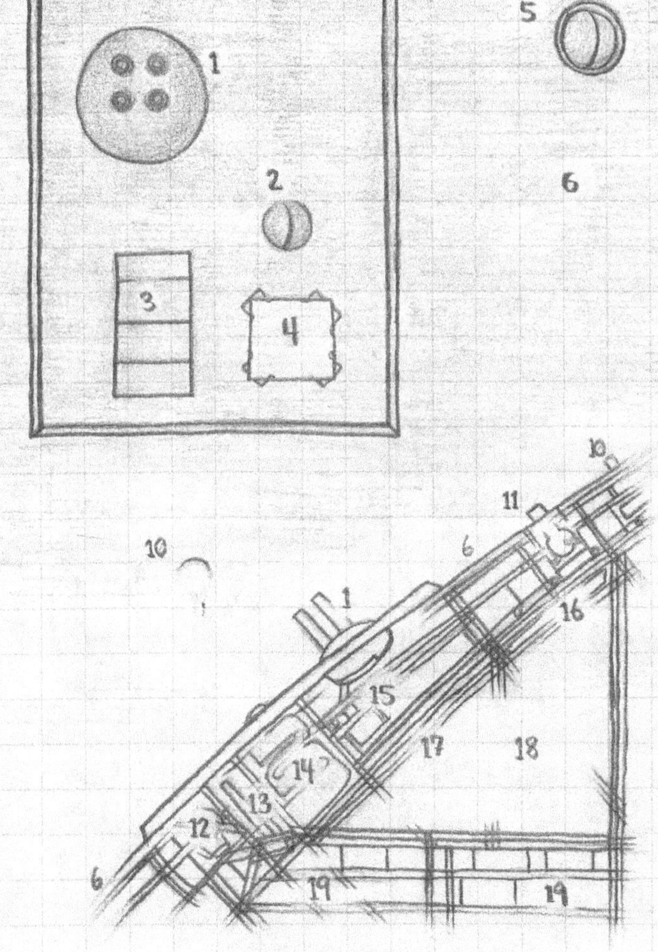

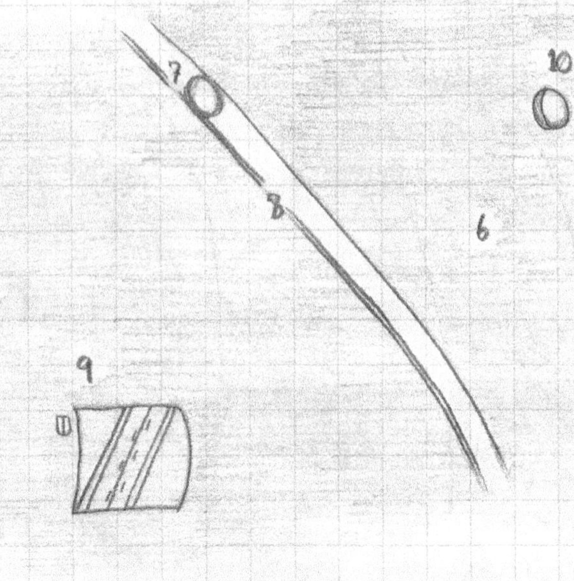

1 quadbarrel laser housing
2 missile chamber hatch
3 kineticannon armor sheath
4 defensive electromagnetic net
5 impulse fuel intake nozzles
6 outer hull
7 external communications emitter
8 external communications reception conduit

9 utility access panel
10 shield booster node emitter
11 ion impulse thrust nozzle
12 kineticannon armor sheath
13 kineticannon assembly
14 kineticannon ammunition belt
15 quadbarrel laser systems chassis
16 exterior access bay reserve battery
17 internal frame construction
18 exterior access bay
19 crew areas
20 guided missile loading chamber

CUTAWAY: ESCAPE POD ASSEMBLY

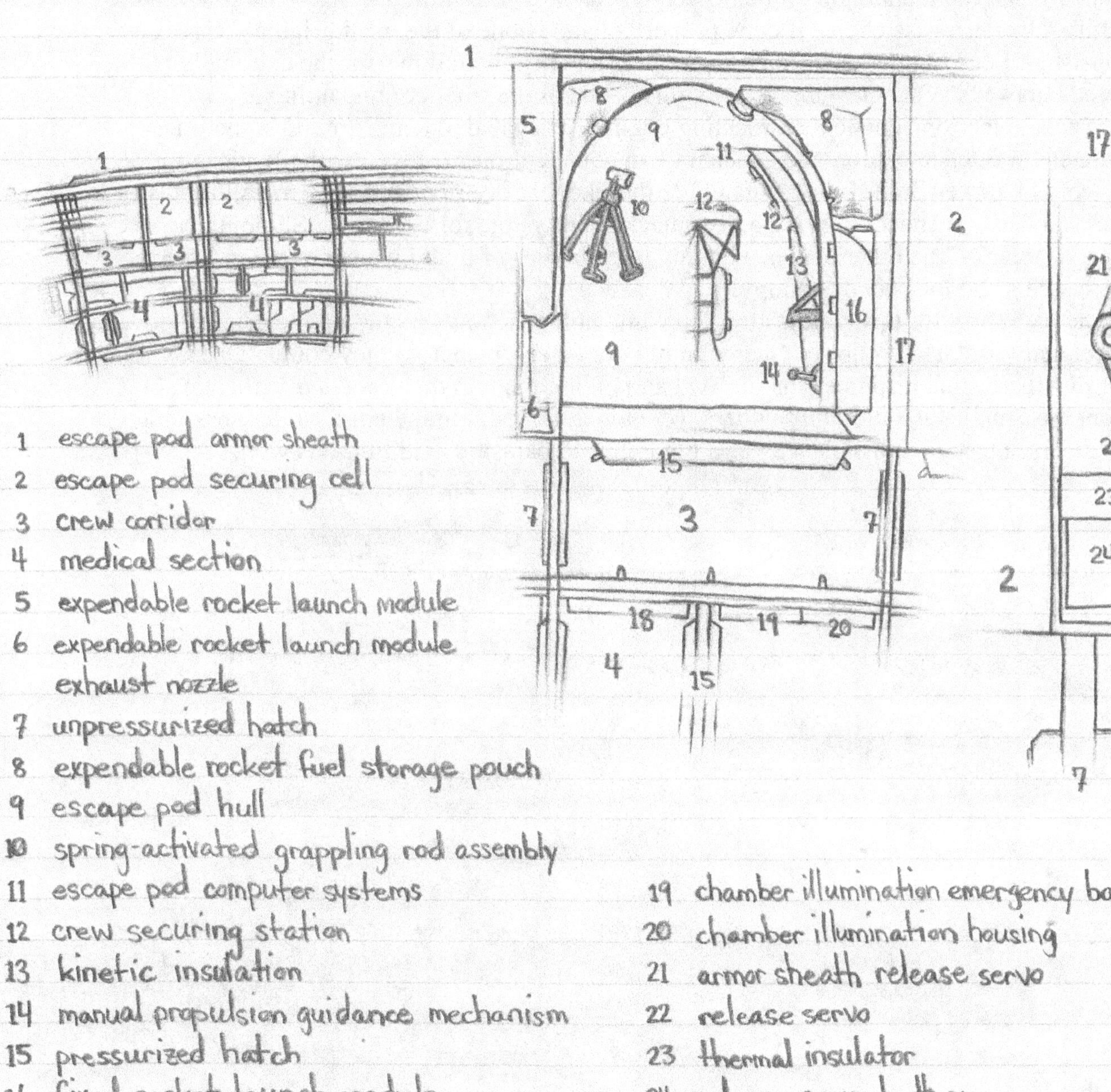

1. escape pod armor sheath
2. escape pod securing cell
3. crew corridor
4. medical section
5. expendable rocket launch module
6. expendable rocket launch module exhaust nozzle
7. unpressurized hatch
8. expendable rocket fuel storage pouch
9. escape pod hull
10. spring-activated grappling rod assembly
11. escape pod computer systems
12. crew securing station
13. kinetic insulation
14. manual propulsion guidance mechanism
15. pressurized hatch
16. fixed rocket launch module
17. escape pod armor sheath control mechanism housing
18. thermal generator
19. chamber illumination emergency battery
20. chamber illumination housing
21. armor sheath release servo
22. release servo
23. thermal insulator
24. release servo battery
25. armor sheath release command computer
26. expendable rocket fuel fail-safe stopper
27. expendable rocket fuel duct

Set 32:
Alliance of Containment armored vessels

The extraplanetary ship here is specifically made for the Alliance of Containment, the interim command structure of forces opposed to the Gaepvihn between the implosion of the White System and the foundation of the Seoreh Ybedäm Confederation. This fighter makes use of the Ojif—always a wise choice if done properly—and is one of the most original designs my most consistent Lego builder devised. The fact it is an Ojif pilot allows for the extremely constricted cutaways. One may notice, also, this is one of the smaller units utilizing an unconventional electromagnetic reciprocating engine. They had to come around sometime.

Later I wanted to explore the concept of an aquatic drone. I toyed with the idea of it being a scout or survey drone into gas giants or the like, but even *Lone Soldier* metallurgy isn't up to that standard. It ended up being a fast-attack submersible for use on the Shipbuilder homeworld, Aroldin, and other bodies with any large bodies of liquid when not too caustic for external systems and the cockpit canopy.

The backstory for this craft is after the white hole reaction concluding the original novella of this arc, many isolated groups of Gaepvihn hid out on any planetoid they could. Oceans were ideal for this (harboring resources for survival and hiding them in the process of collecting them), but the Small Wise and Shipbuilders were too good at finding them for it to work long. Having undersea bases on this planet was a hindrance to parasitic ambitions, as well.

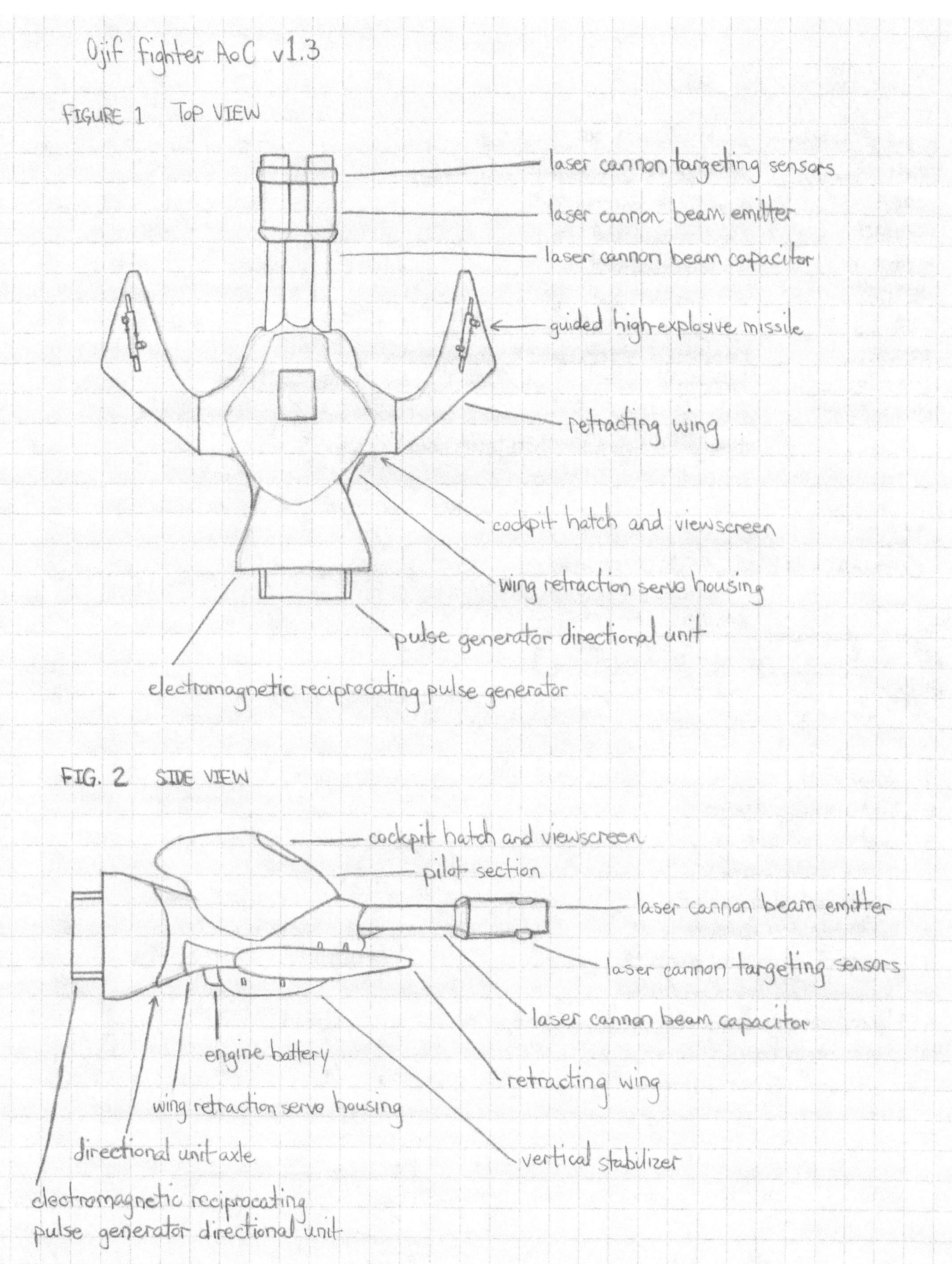

Ojif fighter AoC v1.3
FIGURE 1   TOP VIEW
laser cannon targeting sensors
laser cannon beam emitter
laser cannon beam capacitor
guided high-explosive missile
retracting wing
cockpit hatch and viewscreen
wing retraction servo housing
pulse generator directional unit
electromagnetic reciprocating pulse generator
FIG. 2   SIDE VIEW
cockpit hatch and viewscreen
pilot section
laser cannon beam emitter
laser cannon targeting sensors
laser cannon beam capacitor
retracting wing
engine battery
wing retraction servo housing
directional unit axle
vertical stabilizer
electromagnetic reciprocating
pulse generator directional unit

Ojif fighter Gluk AoC v1.3

CLASSIFICATION: small armored attack vessel
TYPE: Alliance of Containment-class fighter
CREW: one pilot (Species 150)
LENGTH: 30 standard feet
WIDTH: 28 standard feet
HEIGHT: 12 standard feet
MASS: 160 standard mass units
ARMOR: reinforced steetanicarb and pyroceramite hull
ENGINE: high-yield electromagnetic reciprocating pulse generator
ARMAMENT: two offensive laser cannon, four guided high-explosive missile, two defensive laser disruption shield arrays

CUTAWAY: OFFENSIVE LASER CANNON

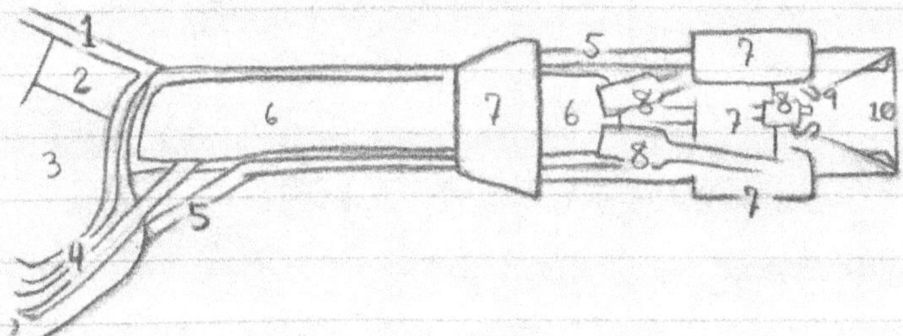

1 outer hull
2 life support computer
3 ejection fuel pod
4 engine power conduit
5 computer relay conduit
6 laser cannon capacitor
7 weapons targeting computer
8 laser cannon beam generator
9 laser beam emitter tube
10 laser beam focus chamber

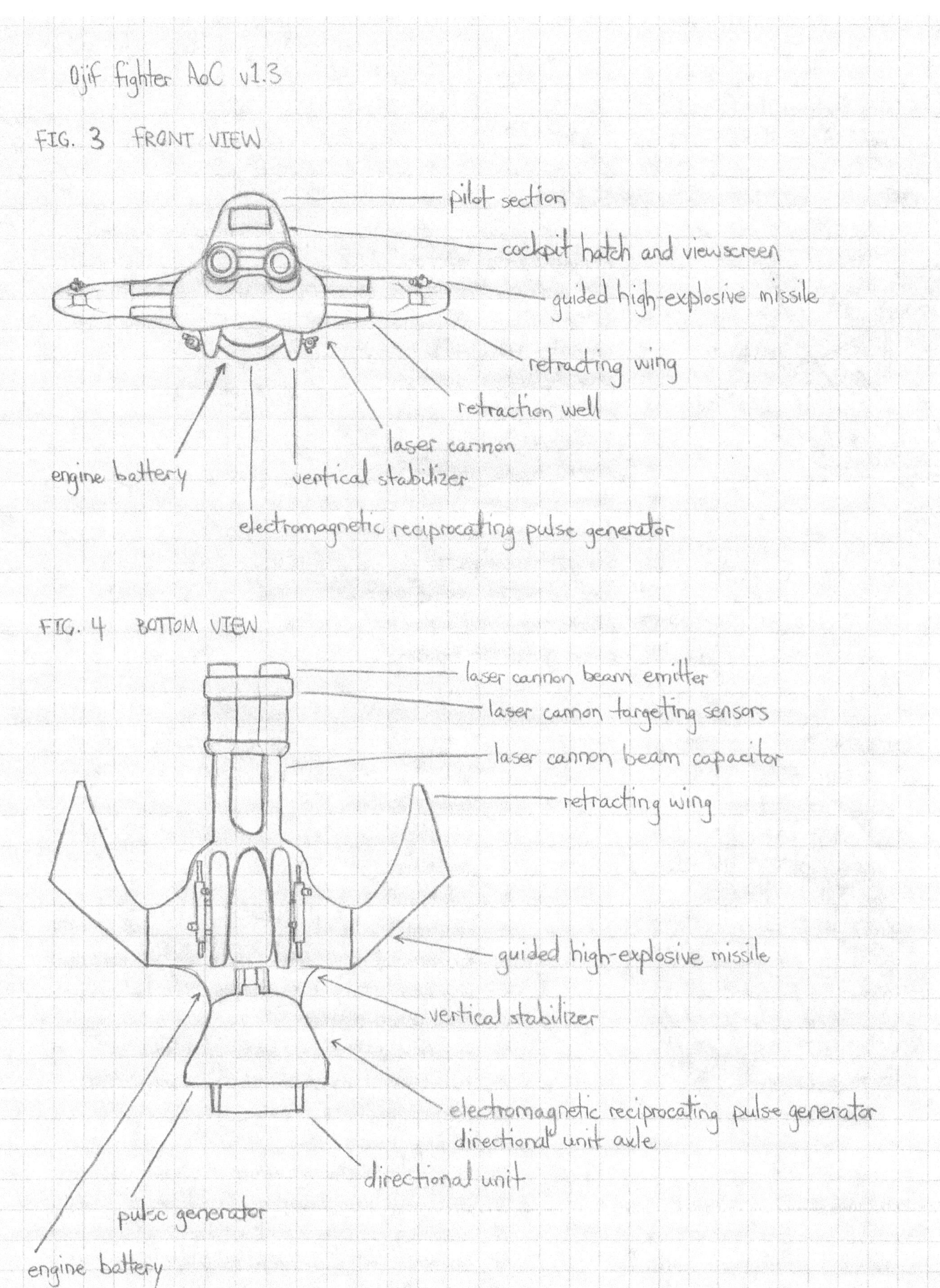

Ojif fighter AoC v1.3
FIG. 3   FRONT VIEW
pilot section
cockpit hatch and viewscreen
guided high-explosive missile
retracting wing
retraction well
laser cannon
engine battery
vertical stabilizer
electromagnetic reciprocating pulse generator
FIG. 4   BOTTOM VIEW
laser cannon beam emitter
laser cannon targeting sensors
laser cannon beam capacitor
retracting wing
guided high-explosive missile
vertical stabilizer
electromagnetic reciprocating pulse generator
directional unit axle
directional unit
pulse generator
engine battery

Ojif fighter AoC v1.3

CUTAWAY: RETRACTING WING SERVO

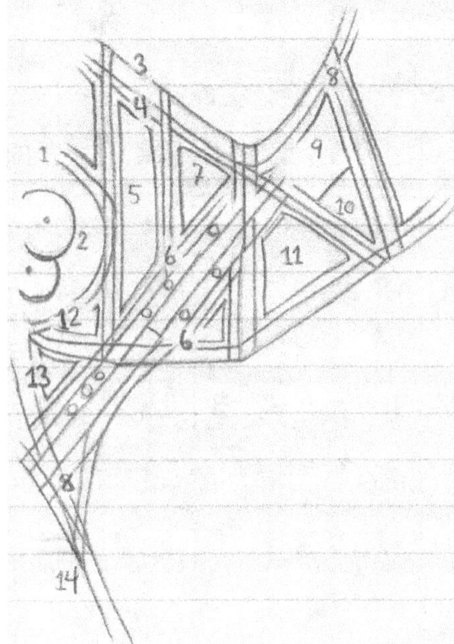

1 electromagnetic buffer
2 high-yield electromagnetic reciprocating pulse generator
3 outer hull
4 computer relay conduit
5 primary engine capacitor
6 retraction servo
7 emergency battery
8 internal frame construction
9 defensive laser disruption array
10 defensive laser disruption emitter
11 navigations computer
12 wing retraction control computer
13 retraction servo capacitor
14 pulse generator housing

CUTAWAY: PILOT SECTION

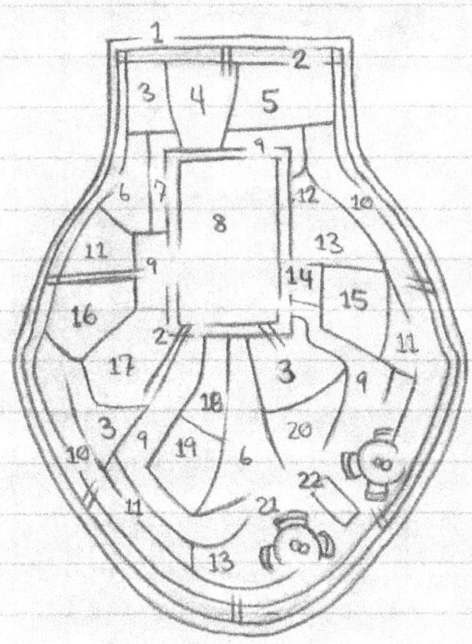

5 life support computer
6 homing beacon
7 atmospheric pressurizer
8 cockpit
9 pilot access duct
10 ejection fuel pod
11 ejection jet directional nozzle control computer
12 ejection jet fuel regulation interface
13 emergency systems
14 communications encoding computer
15 navigational-weapons interface computer
16 communications array
17 sensor array
18 sustenance storage unit
19 defensive laser disruption shield array
20 ejection jet directional nozzle regulating computer
21 ejection jet directional nozzle
22 expendable anti-gravity emitter

1 outer hull
2 internal frame construction
3 pressurized atmospheric tank
4 primary navigational computer

Ojif aquatic attack craft AoC v1.1

FIGURE 1   TOP VIEW

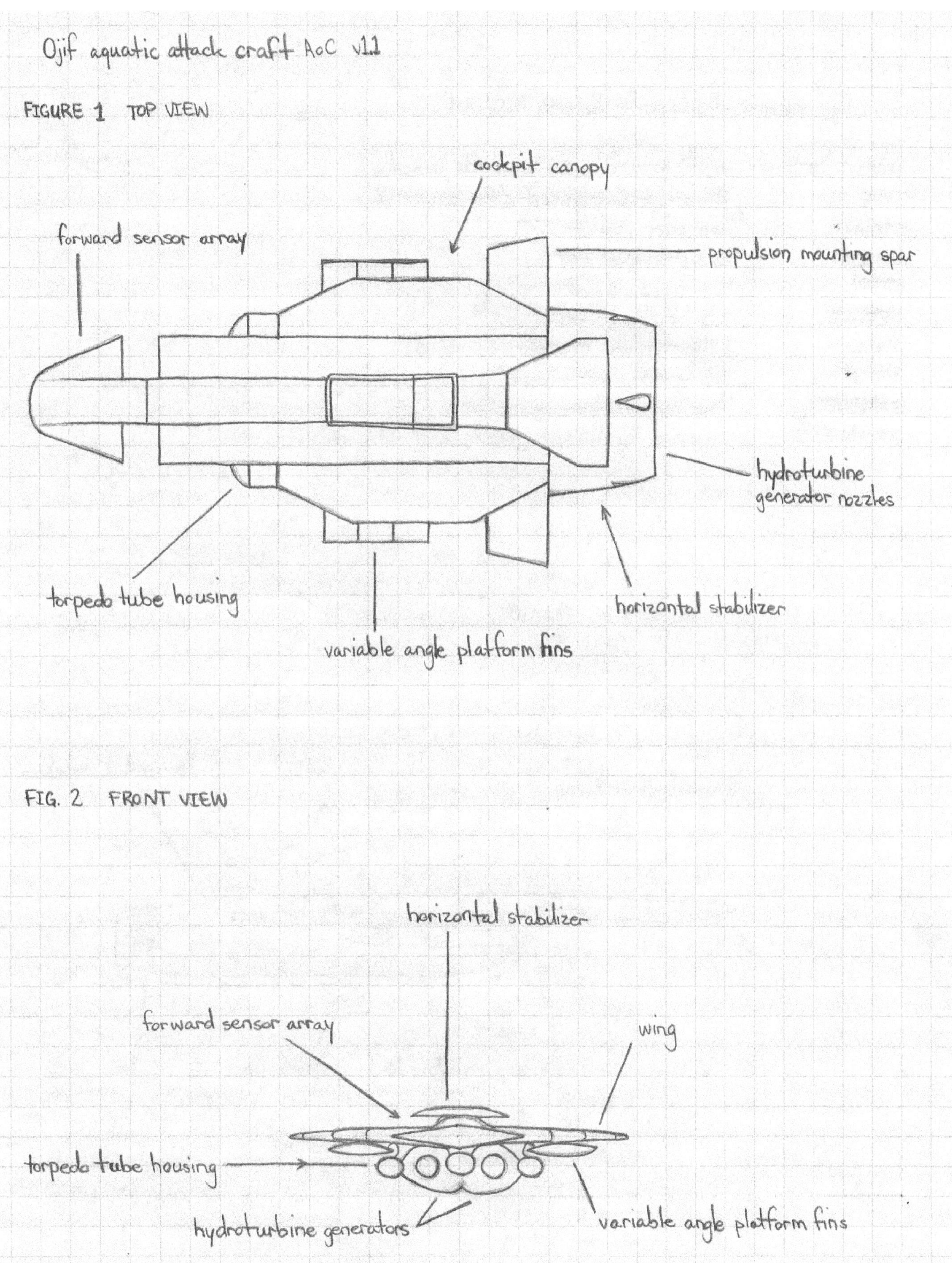

FIG. 2   FRONT VIEW

Ojif aquatic attack craft Hoirwen AoC v1.1

CLASSIFICATION: small armored aquatic attack vessel
TYPE: Alliance of Containment class submersible
CREW: one pilot (Species 150)
LENGTH: 22.2 standard feet
WIDTH: 11.4 standard feet
HEIGHT: 3.5 standard feet
MASS: 1,200 standard mass units (armed)
ARMOR: reinforced steetanicarb
ENGINES: two hydroturbine generators
ARMAMENT: capacity for three torpedoes and electromagnetic pulse

FIG. 3 SIDE VIEW

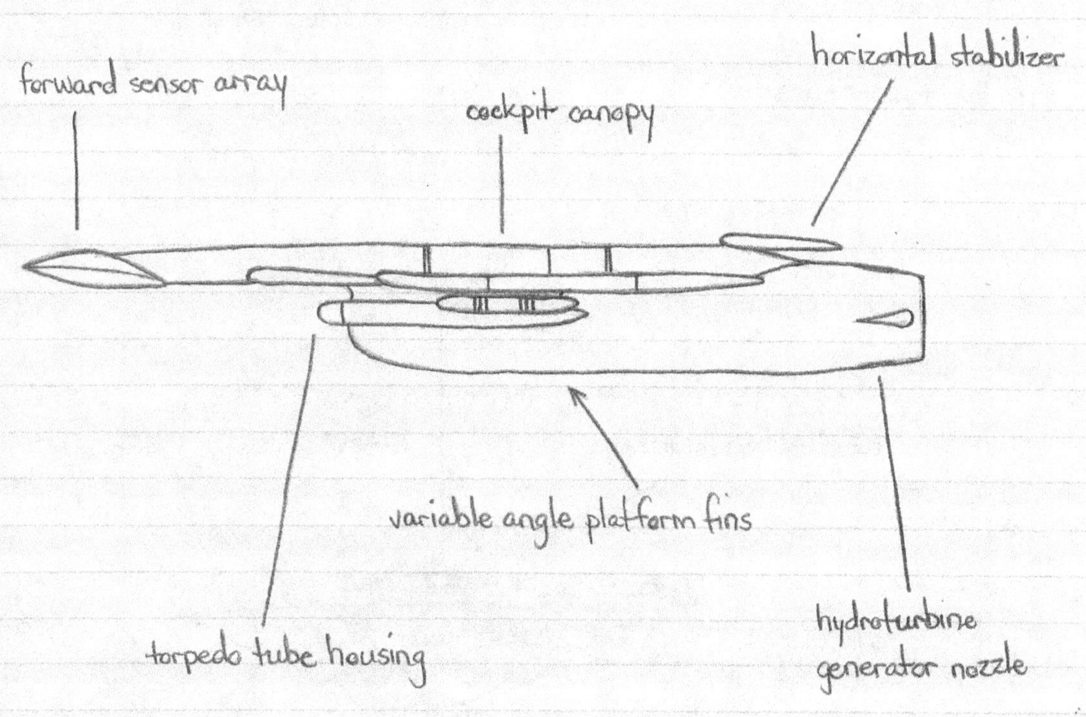

Set 33:
early Confederation ships

Building of Confederation judicial ships started as one of the bonding activities between different cantos, beginning with the SYS-E001. Using a revolutionary design, it was the first large-scale production with a Crimson alloy—and the largest to date with such a dramatic tactical division capability. Unfortunately, it was also one of my first (if not *the* first) *Lone Soldier* ship I designed on graph paper, so it needed extensive revision. Originally, I did nothing with the internal complement of fighters attached to the SYS-E001. They evolved from a flying box fit inside the launch duct (hence the battering ram fore and aft ends), later collapsible with a separable cockpit assembly to save space.

There would need to be at least one enforcement ship per canto. As a weapons platform and delivery system, the *Bennu* is not the prime example of Seoreh Ybedäm Confederation technology and tactics, but that is kind of the point; the second-tier Confederation ships are supposed to support units of the cantos. It is not meant to supersede their authority unless necessary, and if possible, not be made or presented in such a way member states are insulted or outclassed. Showing up others in the club quickly makes it a small club.

Unfortunately, the egalitarian mindset behind the Confederation's procedure is what allows its collapse. Less noble parties use its limitations against the federal level, subverting its presence and undermining the core values it espouses for an individual's or individual group's gain at expense of the system, regardless of the long-term consequences. Welcome to the flaw of representative democracy, scifi fans! … sigh …

Much later I went back and reinvented the shrink-fits, then designed the early classes of medium to large transports, drones, and Confederation fighters not berthed by the judicial enforcement ships ("heavies"). Although the first variants share the class name with the enforcement capital ships, they have their own classes after that time. Confederation leaders anticipated the need for transports, not the need for so many fighters. It is a sign of the dark times approaching, the Nrel-ekians would say.

I decided to work in some first-level politics because it made the logistics of the *Kehsid*-class fighter more practical: the Miltind would have some of the best impulse fuel of this spatial region, and stand a good chance of winning the bid for primary provider of Confederation fighters. They would be the first to reclaim the fighters, also, should the Confederation fail—as the Miltind expect in less than the lifespan of their fighter. When they were disappointed they provided the next "heavy" class, with the same ulterior motives.

The cockpit is the first with a complete canopy heads-up display, and a practical free-floating pilot's station like some ships of the **masterful** science fiction series *Babylon 5*. The sentient itself may choose how it is comfortable and how to anticipate maneuvering, be it in space or atmosphere.

Another advancement involves the life support system. It has a regular artificial scrubber, but that is the auxiliary system. Apart from the fighter's mechanics and select officers, only a few knew genetically modified Ko were added to improve efficiency. (I decide organic technology is usually more efficient.) There is a moral issue here, but it is dealt with much like the Ojif for most sentients who actually care about the treatment of the Ko. This is not a majority of Confederation member races.

Transport drone design one, model four, is meant for hard vacuum and zero gravity. It *can* go between planets, but this is not advisable. I had to keep it small enough to supply the *Bennu* directly, as well as other period Confederation ships.

Seoreh Ybedäm Enforcement Ship SYS-E001 *Bennu*

FIGURE 1   TOP VIEW

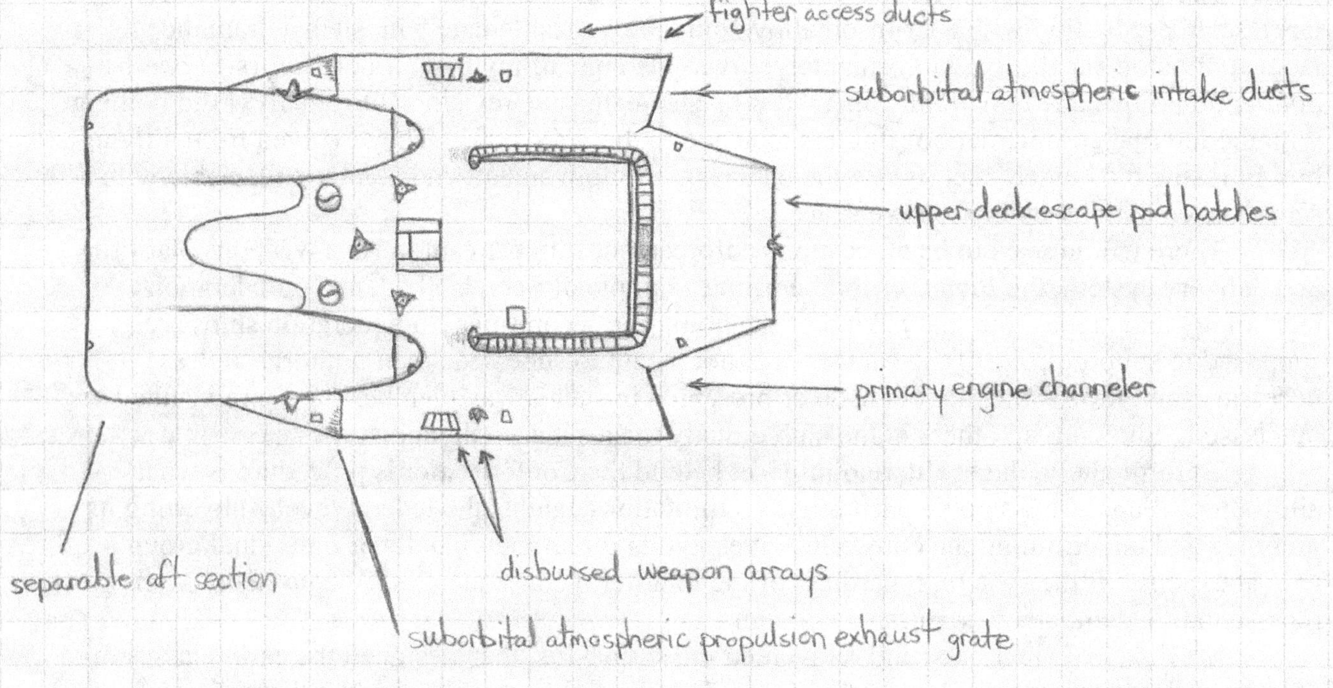

FIG. 2   SIDE VIEW

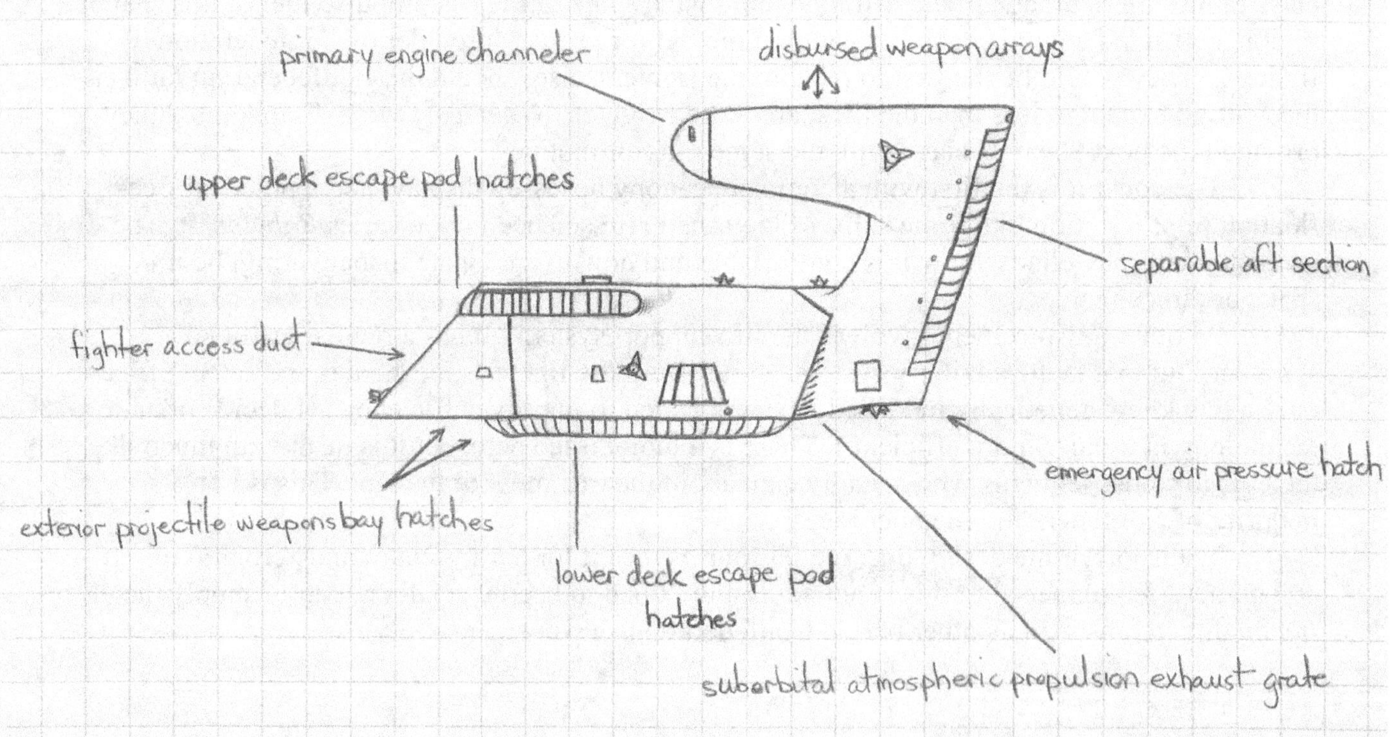

114

Seoreh Ybedäm SYS-E001

CLASSIFICATION: Seoreh Ybedäm ship, *Kehsid*-class
TYPE: judicial armored craft
CREW: ≈ 78 sentients (twenty-five officers, fifty-three enlisted)
LENGTH: 280 standard Confederation feet
WIDTH: 150 standard Confederation feet
HEIGHT: 135 standard Confederation feet
MASS: 420,000 standard mass units
ARMOR: steetanicarb-reinforced steetanicrim alloy
ENGINES: electromagnetic thermogravitic channeler, high-yield electromagnetic reciprocating turbine
ARMAMENT: ten adjustable laser projectors, two anti-ship lasers, five projectile weapons stations,
                complement of four manned fighters

FIG. 3   FRONT VIEW

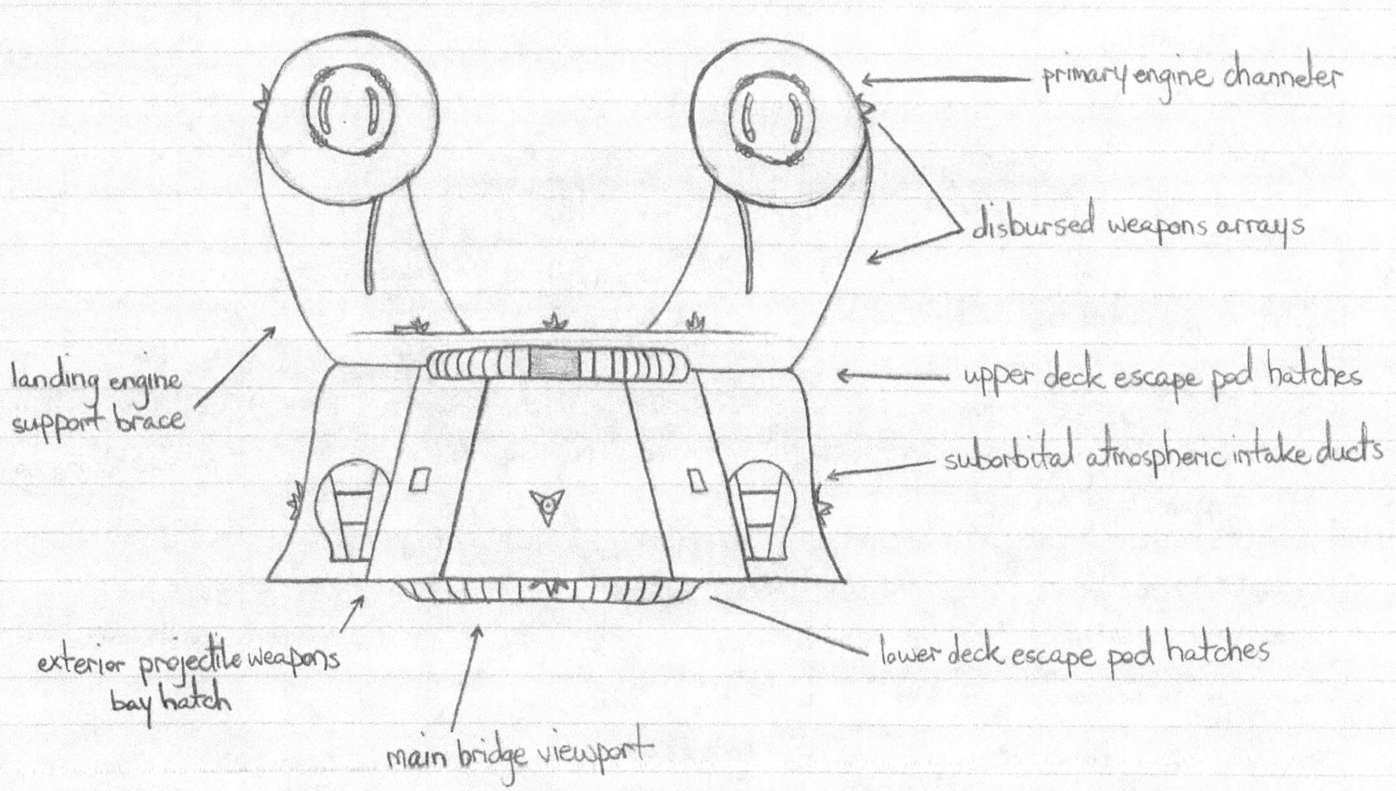

Search Ybedäm Enforcement Ship SYS-E001 *Bennu*

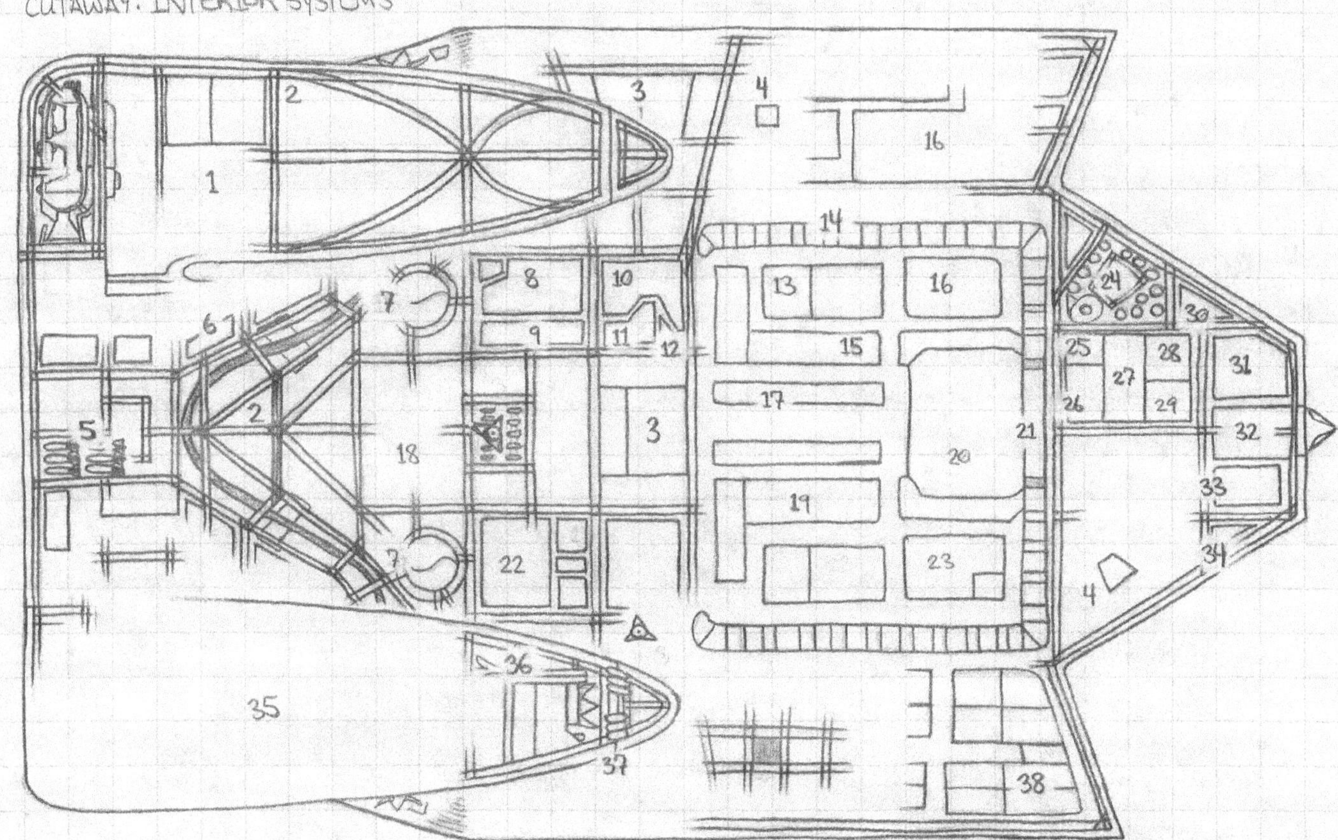

1	port engine maintenance area	20	main bridge
2	internal frame construction	21	main bridge viewscreen
3	fighter access duct retractable hatch	22	atmospheric scrubber
4	exterior projectile weapons bay hatch	23	captain's quarters
5	rear projectile weapons bay	24	port bow weapon projectile bay
6	separation control computer	25	primary life support computers
7	landing/take-off rocket fuel conduit hatch	26	primary propulsion interface
8	rocket fuel storage tank	27	primary communications computer
9	landing/take-off rocket control interface	28	primary navigation computer
10	primary navigational-propulsion interface	29	primary weapons guidance systems
11	auxiliary communications computer system	30	hyperspace generator node
12	fighter access hatch control system	31	forward sensor array
13	vertical transport shaft	32	laser platform capacitor
14	upper deck escape pod hatches	33	forward shield capacitor
15	auxiliary systems console and interface assembly	34	electromagnetic interference generator
16	crew galley	35	electromagnetic thermogravitic generator
17	auxiliary memory bank	36	electromagnetic thermogravitic channeler
18	primary fighter launch area	37	primary anti-ship laser housing unit
19	auxiliary briefing room	38	crew quarters

Search Ybedam Enforcement Ship SYS-E001 *Bennu*

CUTAWAY: DECK PROFILE

1 outer hull
2 internal frame construction
3 primary anti-ship weapon hatch servo
4 spatial targeting sensor
5 adjustable laser projector assembly
6 adjustable laser projector beam generator
7 adjustable laser projector capacitor
8 electrogravitic propulsion channeler insulator
9 thermogravitic initializer electromagnetic catalyzer

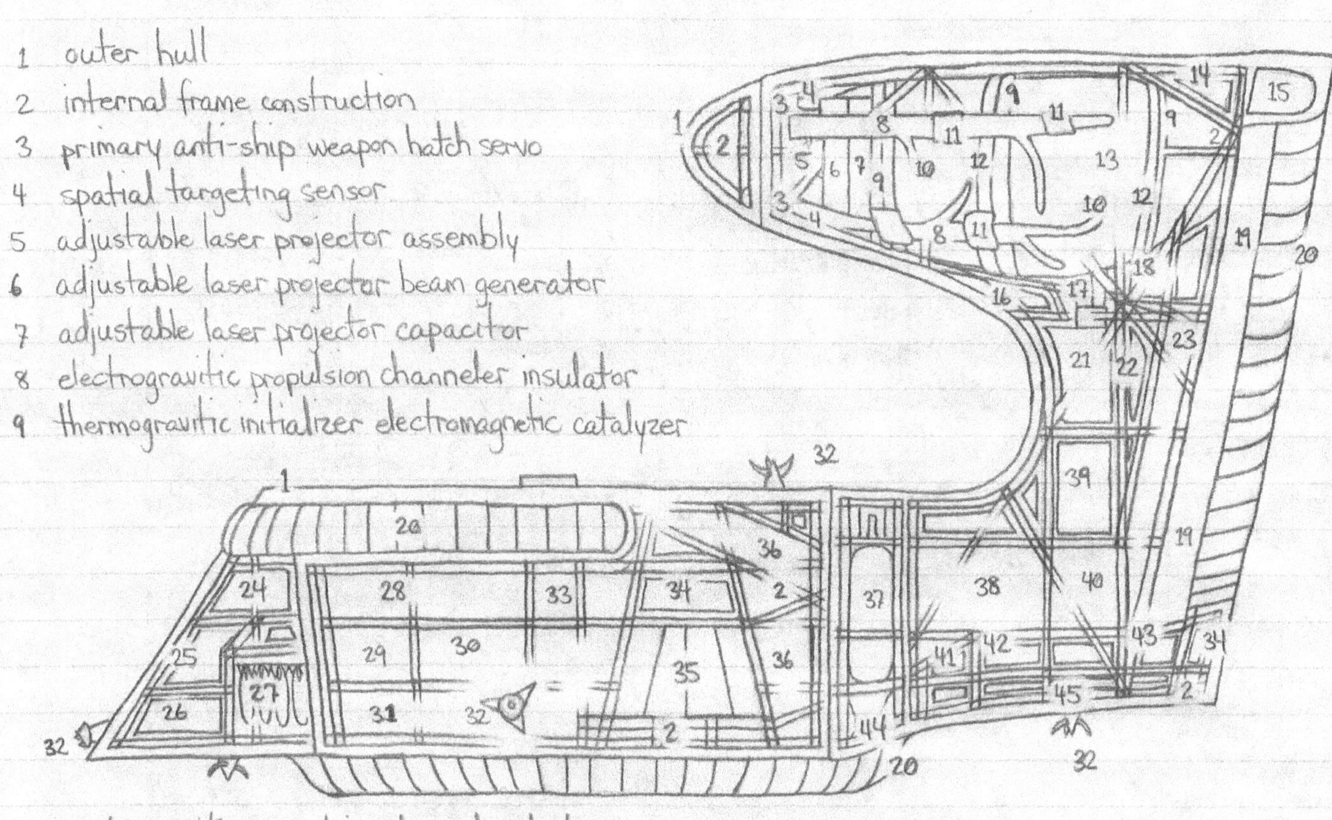

10 electrogravitic propulsion channeler duct
11 electrogravitic propulsion channeler regulator
12 initializer activation unit elastic reinforcement band
13 thermogravitic initializer activation unit
14 emergency thermoelectric countermeasures cell
15 crew escape pod access duct atmospheric pressurizer
16 shield signal amplifier node
17 thermogravitic initializer regulator conduit
18 engineering console
19 crew escape pod access duct
20 escape pod hatches
21 thermogravitic initializer storage cell
22 gravitational sensor and control
23 engineer access duct
24 forward sensor array
25 electromagnetic countermeasures
26 emergency power capacitor
27 projectile weapons bay

28 crew galley
29 auxiliary bridge
30 medical bay
31 detention cells
32 adjustable laser projector
33 crew galley storage facility
34 sensor array
35 auxiliary fighter launch duct retractable hatch
36 fighter launch duct
37 landing/take-off rocket fuel tank
38 fighter maintenance bay and facilities
39 atmospheric tank
40 emergency airlock chamber
41 fighter launch duct maintenance storage unit
42 atmospheric pressurizer
43 escape pod computer control interface
44 landing/take-off rocket nozzle
45 aft keel shield array

117

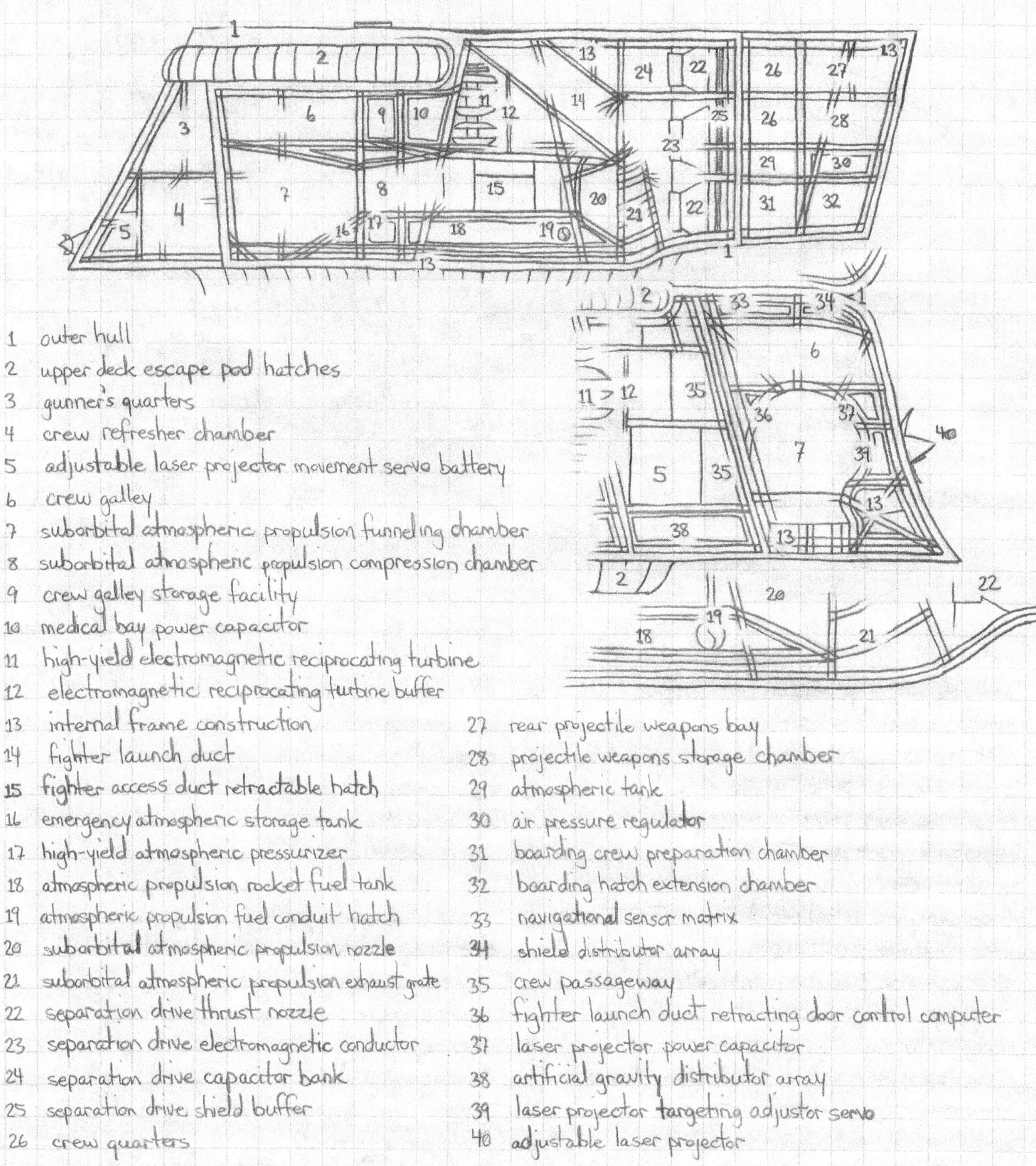

1   outer hull
2   upper deck escape pod hatches
3   gunner's quarters
4   crew refresher chamber
5   adjustable laser projector movement servo battery
6   crew galley
7   suborbital atmospheric propulsion funneling chamber
8   suborbital atmospheric propulsion compression chamber
9   crew galley storage facility
10   medical bay power capacitor
11   high-yield electromagnetic reciprocating turbine
12   electromagnetic reciprocating turbine buffer
13   internal frame construction
14   fighter launch duct
15   fighter access duct retractable hatch
16   emergency atmospheric storage tank
17   high-yield atmospheric pressurizer
18   atmospheric propulsion rocket fuel tank
19   atmospheric propulsion fuel conduit hatch
20   suborbital atmospheric propulsion nozzle
21   suborbital atmospheric propulsion exhaust grate
22   separation drive thrust nozzle
23   separation drive electromagnetic conductor
24   separation drive capacitor bank
25   separation drive shield buffer
26   crew quarters
27   rear projectile weapons bay
28   projectile weapons storage chamber
29   atmospheric tank
30   air pressure regulator
31   boarding crew preparation chamber
32   boarding hatch extension chamber
33   navigational sensor matrix
34   shield distributor array
35   crew passageway
36   fighter launch duct retracting door control computer
37   laser projector power capacitor
38   artificial gravity distributor array
39   laser projector targeting adjustor servo
40   adjustable laser projector

CUTAWAY: ELECTROMAGNETIC THERMOGRAVITIC GENERATOR

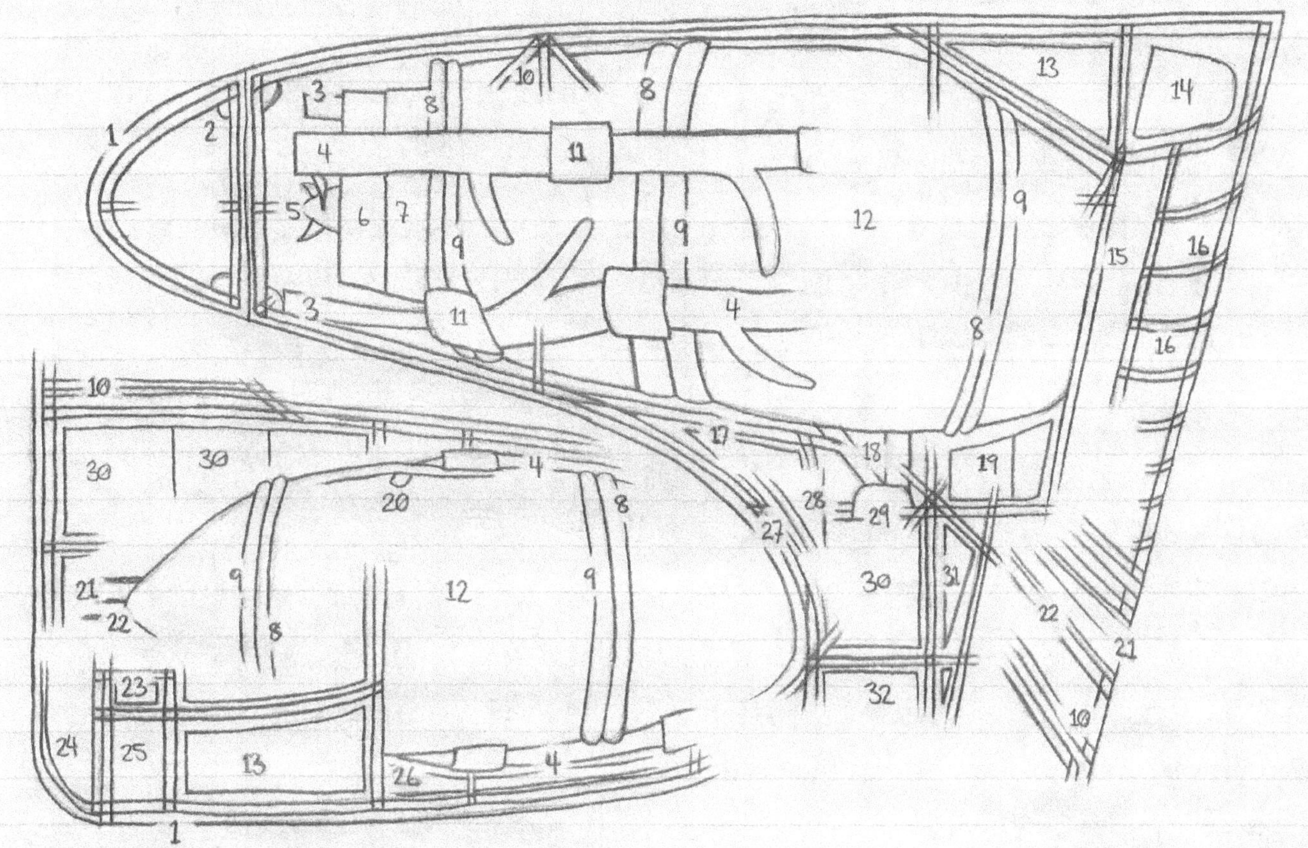

1	outer hull	17	shield signal amplifier node
2	primary anti-ship weapon hatch servo	18	thermogravitic initializer regulator conduit
3	spatial targeting sensor	19	engineering console
4	electrogravitic propulsion channeler insulator	20	thermogravitic generator matter director coil
5	adjustable laser projector assembly	21	electrogravitic propulsion channeler
6	adjustable laser projector beam generator	22	electrogravitic propulsion channeler radiation sheath
7	adjustable laser projector capacitor	23	anti-radiation emitter
8	initializer activation unit elastic reinforcement band	24	crew escape pod
9	thermogravitic initializer electromagnetic catalyzer	25	crew escape pod access duct
10	internal frame construction	26	electromagnetic thermogravitic generator cushion
11	electrogravitic propulsion channeler regulator	27	landing engine support brace
12	thermogravitic generator catalyzing chamber	28	landing engine support brace placement battery
13	emergency thermoelectric countermeasures cell	29	thermogravitic initializer regulator
14	crew escape pod access duct atmospheric pressurizer	30	thermogravitic initializer storage cell
15	crew escape pod access duct	31	gravitational sensor and control
16	crew escape pod securing assembly	32	atmosphere tank

Seroeh Ybedäm Enforcement Ship SYS-E001 *Bennu*

CUTAWAY: ADJUSTABLE LASER PROJECTOR ASSEMBLY

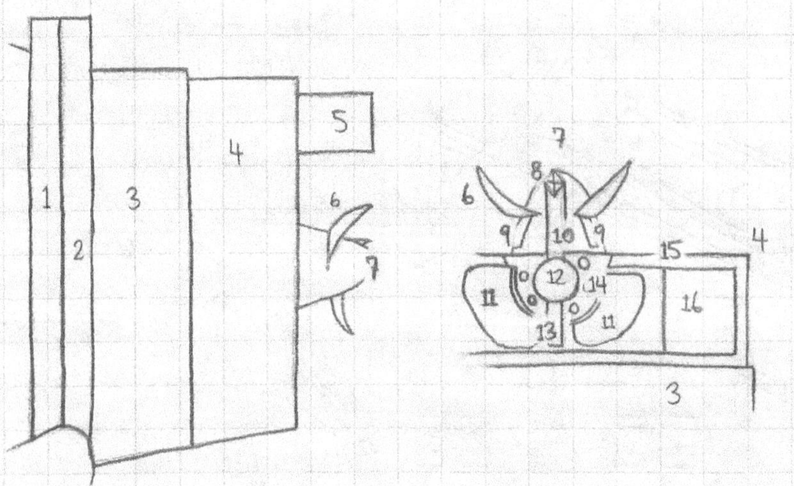

3 adjustable laser projector capacitor
4 adjustable laser projector beam generator
5 spatial targeting sensor
6 stray particle refocus flap
7 laser beam projector dome
8 laser beam focalizer crystal
9 stray particle refocus flap servo
10 laser beam conduit
11 electron amplification capacitance gel
12 electron spherical diamond focalizer matrix
13 diamond focalizer matrix stabilizing rod
14 laser beam conduit targeting servo bearings
15 beam generator housing
16 raw electron generator material

1 thermogravitic initializer electromagnetic catalyzer
2 initializer activation unit elastic reinforcement band

CUTAWAY: ESCAPE POD ASSEMBLY

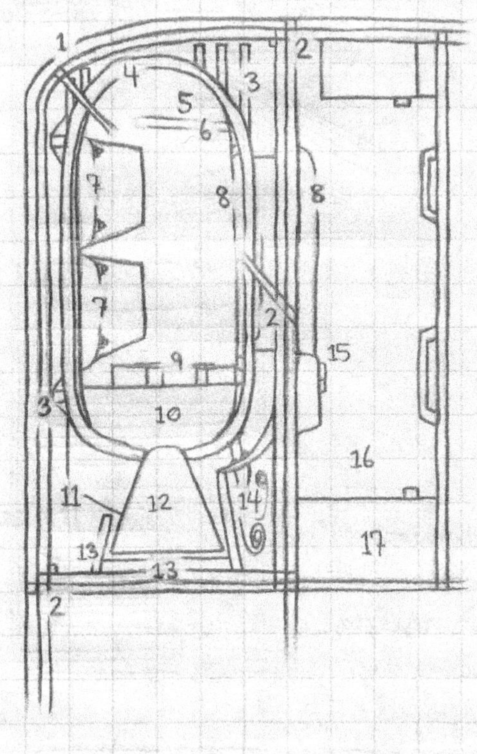

1 outer hull
2 internal frame construction
3 escape pod ramrods
4 escape pod pressurized hull
5 atmospheric tank
6 computer systems and datascreen
7 crew restraint seat
8 pressurized seal door
9 survival gear
10 rocket propulsion fuel tank
11 emergency thrust rocket fuel
12 escape pod rocket propulsion nozzle
13 escape pod rocket propulsion thermal shield
14 escape pod shield generator power relay
15 pressurized seal control console
16 crew escape pod access duct
17 pressurized suit storage bin

Seoreh Ybedäm Enforcement Ship SYS-E001 *Bennu*

CUTAWAY: AFT SEPARATION SECTION

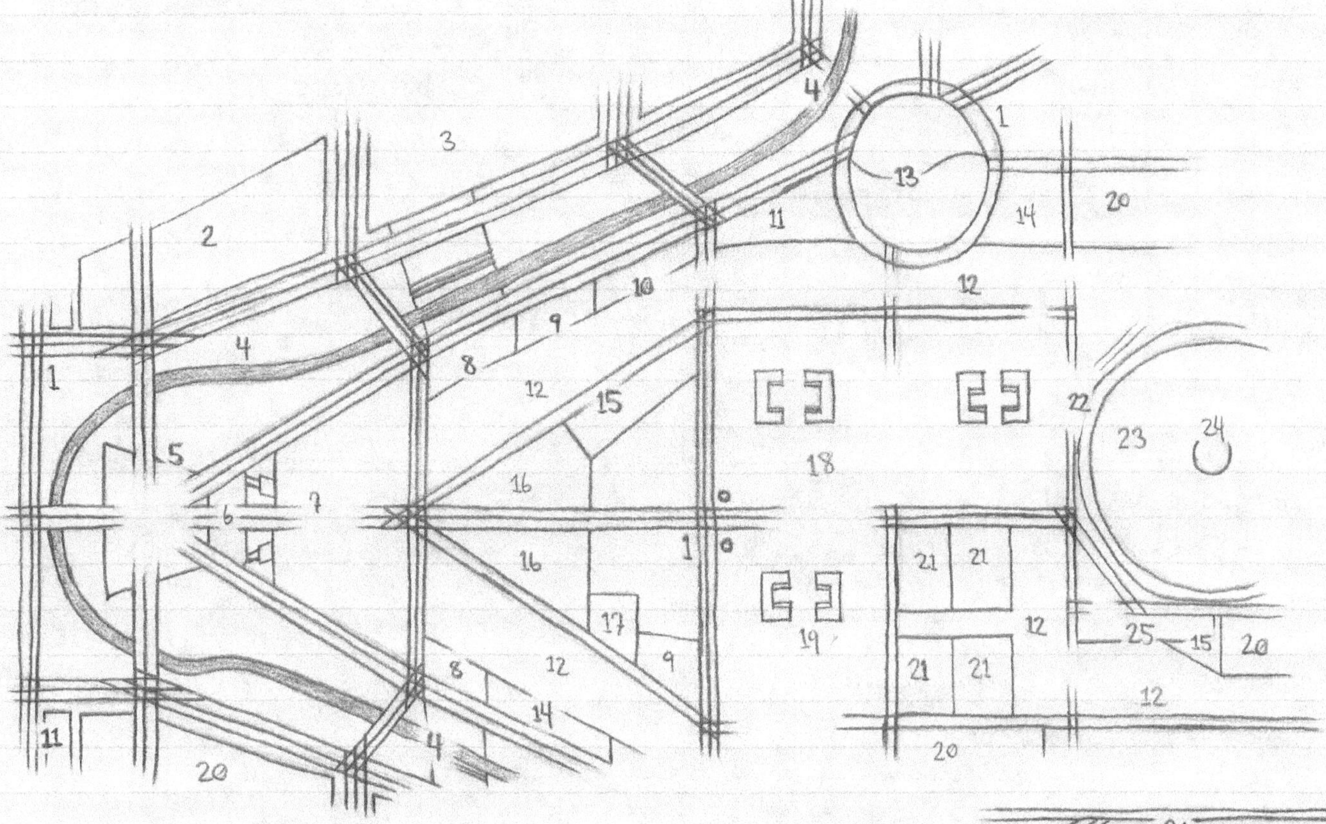

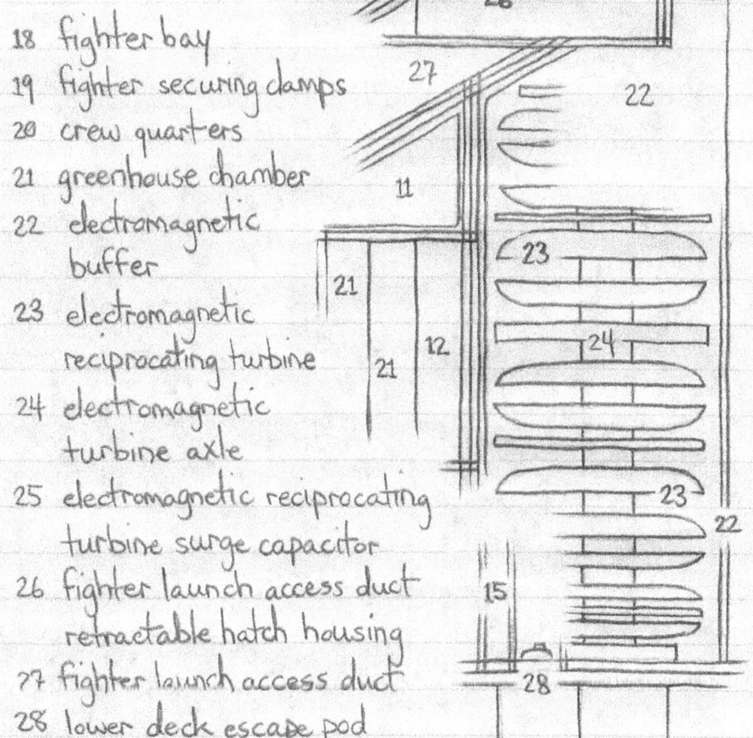

1 internal frame construction
2 separation control computer
3 airlock chamber
4 separation drive shield buffer
5 separation drive thrust nozzle
6 separation drive electromagnetic conductor
7 primary reciprocating turbine power reservoir
8 pressurized separation hull airlock hatch
9 stored water tank
10 water scrubber
11 atmospheric tank
12 crew passageway
13 landing/take-off rocket fuel conduit hatch
14 atmospheric pressurizer control station
15 atmospheric scrubber
16 engineer's quarters
17 power tool replacement parts storage

18 fighter bay
19 fighter securing clamps
20 crew quarters
21 greenhouse chamber
22 electromagnetic buffer
23 electromagnetic reciprocating turbine
24 electromagnetic turbine axle
25 electromagnetic reciprocating turbine surge capacitor
26 fighter launch access duct retractable hatch housing
27 fighter launch access duct
28 lower deck escape pod access chamber and hatch

Search Ybedäm Enforcement Fighter SYS-F3001

FIGURE 1 TOP VIEW

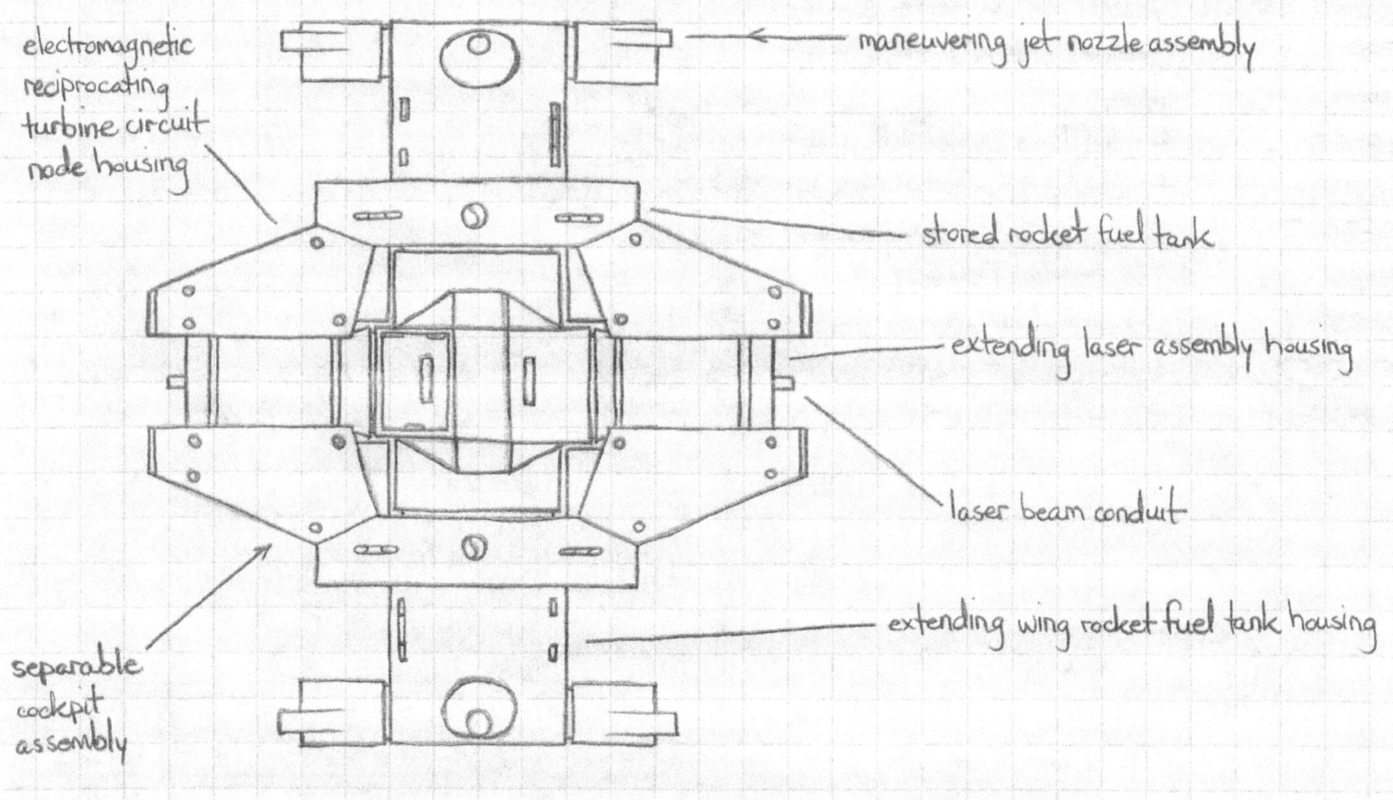

FIG. 2 SIDE VIEW

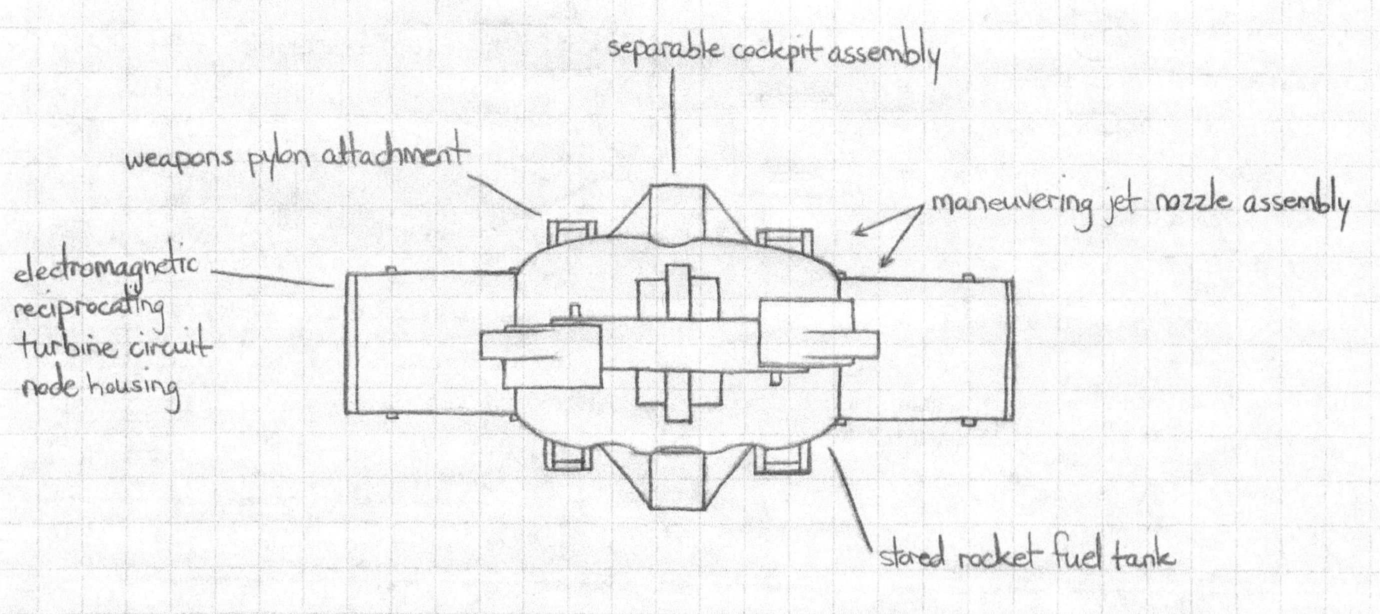

Seoreh Ybedäm SYS-F3001

CLASSIFICATION: Seoreh Ybedäm fighter, Kehsid-class
TYPE: judicial armored small craft
CREW: pilot
LENGTH: 4 standard Confederation feet
WIDTH: 4 standard Confederation feet (extended)
HEIGHT: 1.8 standard Confederation feet (with cockpit)
MASS: 338 standard mass units (with cockpit)
ARMOR: pyroceramite-coated steetanicarb
ENGINES: high-yield electromagnetic reciprocating turbine circuit; maneuvering rocket assembly
ARMAMENT: two offensive laser turrets, capacity for eight missiles and two guided rockets

FIG. 3 FRONT VIEW

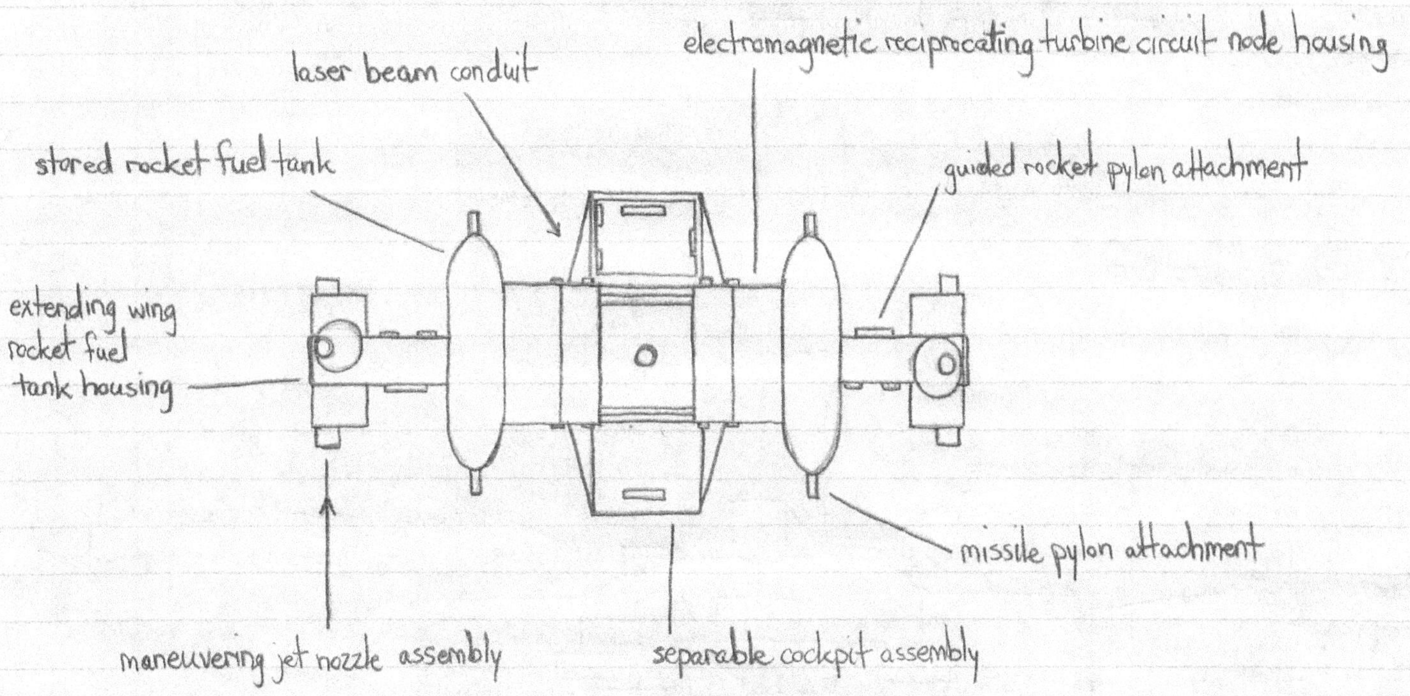

Search Ybedäm Enforcement Fighter SYS-F3001

CUTAWAY: INTERIOR SYSTEMS

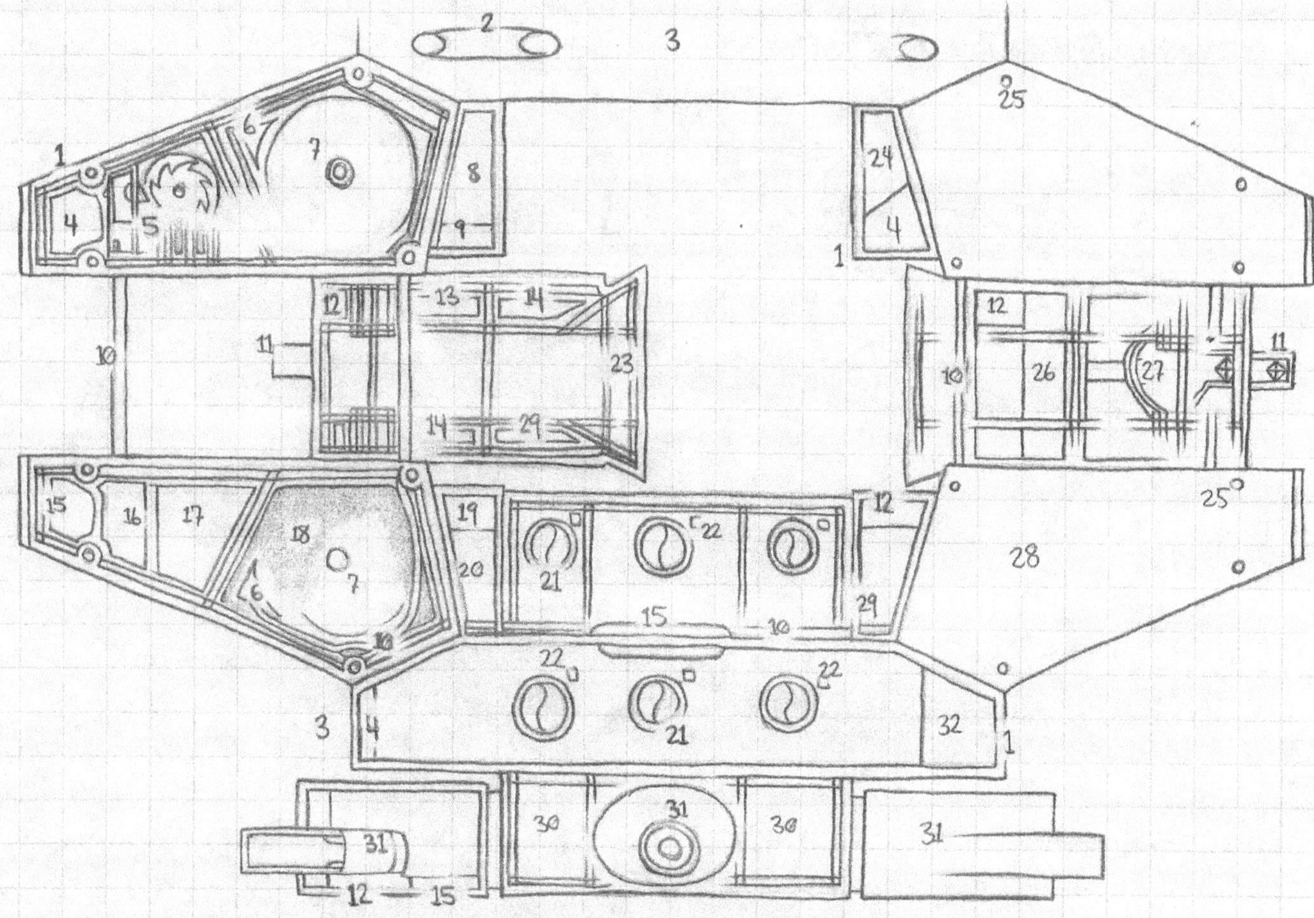

1	pressure hull	17	electromagnetic circuit capacitor
2	weapons pylon attachment	18	electromagnetic buffer
3	stored rocket fuel tank	19	shield ammeter
4	sensor array	20	communications array
5	securing rod assembly	21	rocket fuel transfer valve hatch
6	electromagnetic reciprocating turbine circuit node	22	rocket fuel transfer safety inhibitor
7	electromagnetic reciprocating turbine	23	cockpit assembly technical link-up assembly
8	weapons maintenance computer	24	cockpit assembly synchronizing computer
9	memory computer	25	removeable casing cover securing pinions
10	electromagnetic reciprocating turbine circuit conduit	26	electron generator unit
11	laser conduit	27	electron energizing chamber
12	spatial sensor	28	electromagnetic reciprocating turbine casing cover
13	surge capacitor	29	navigational array
14	homing beacon amplifier	30	maneuvering jet pressurized conduit
15	shield distributor field generator node	31	maneuvering jet nozzle assembly
16	targeting computer	32	stored rocket fuel tank pressurizer

Search Ybedäm Enforcement Fighter SYS-F3001

CUTAWAY: SEPARABLE COCKPIT ASSEMBLY

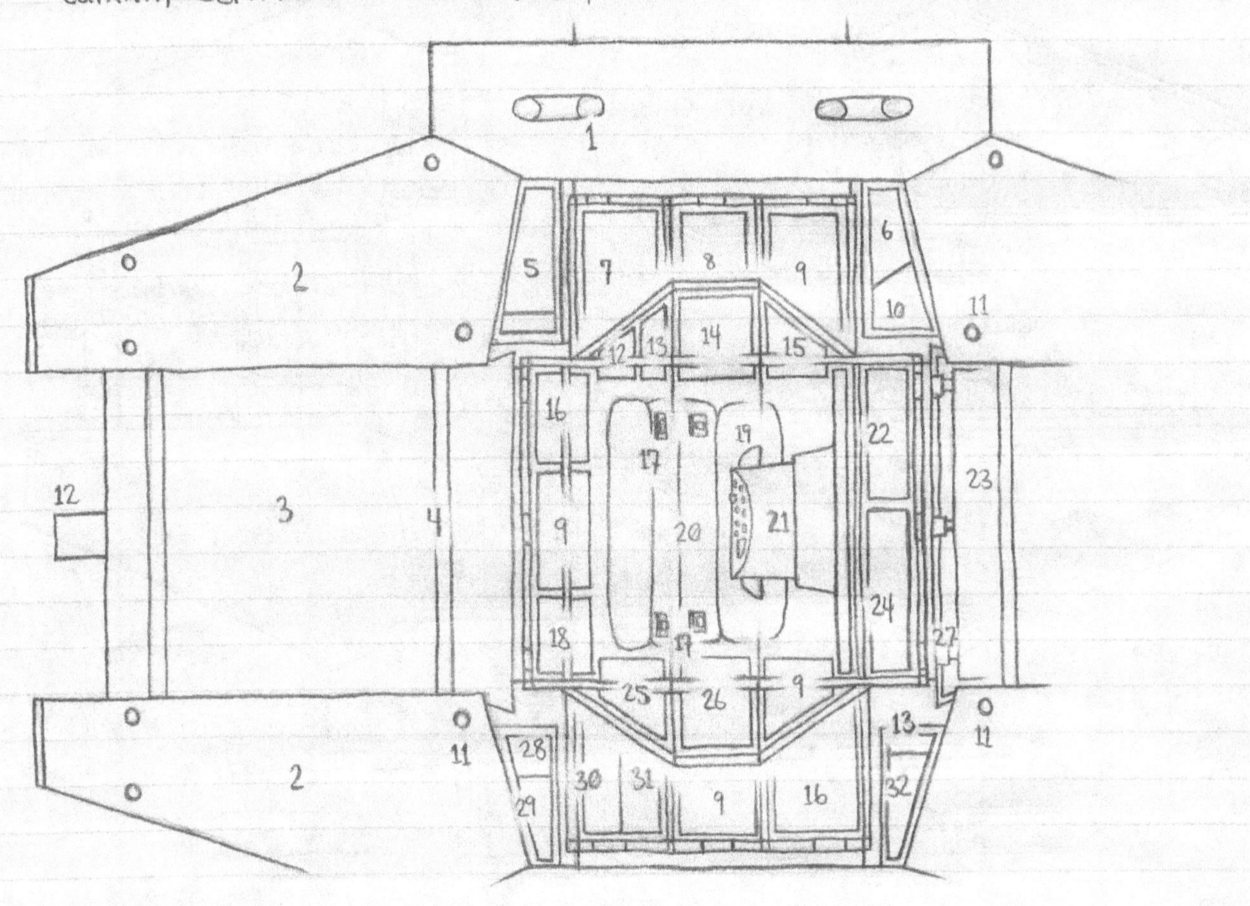

1 weapons pylon attachment
2 electromagnetic reciprocating turbine circuit node housing
3 extending laser assembly housing
4 electromagnetic reciprocating turbine circuit conduit
5 weapons maintenance computer
6 cockpit assembly synchronizing computer
7 communications array
8 systems capacitor
9 atmospheric tank
10 sensor array
11 removeable casing cover securing pinions
12 laser conduit
13 spatial sensor
14 navigational array
15 life support computer
16 shield generator
17 pilot securing straps
18 primary memory computer
19 pilot control interface manual command apparatus
20 pilot seating unit
21 pilot control interface extension sheath
22 emergency equipment
23 cockpit assembly technical link-up assembly
24 shield capacitor
25 atmospheric pressurizer
26 atmospheric scrubber
27 technical link-up assembly adjustment servo
28 shield ammeter
29 communications array
30 cockpit attachment control console
31 propulsional-navigational interface
32 navigational array

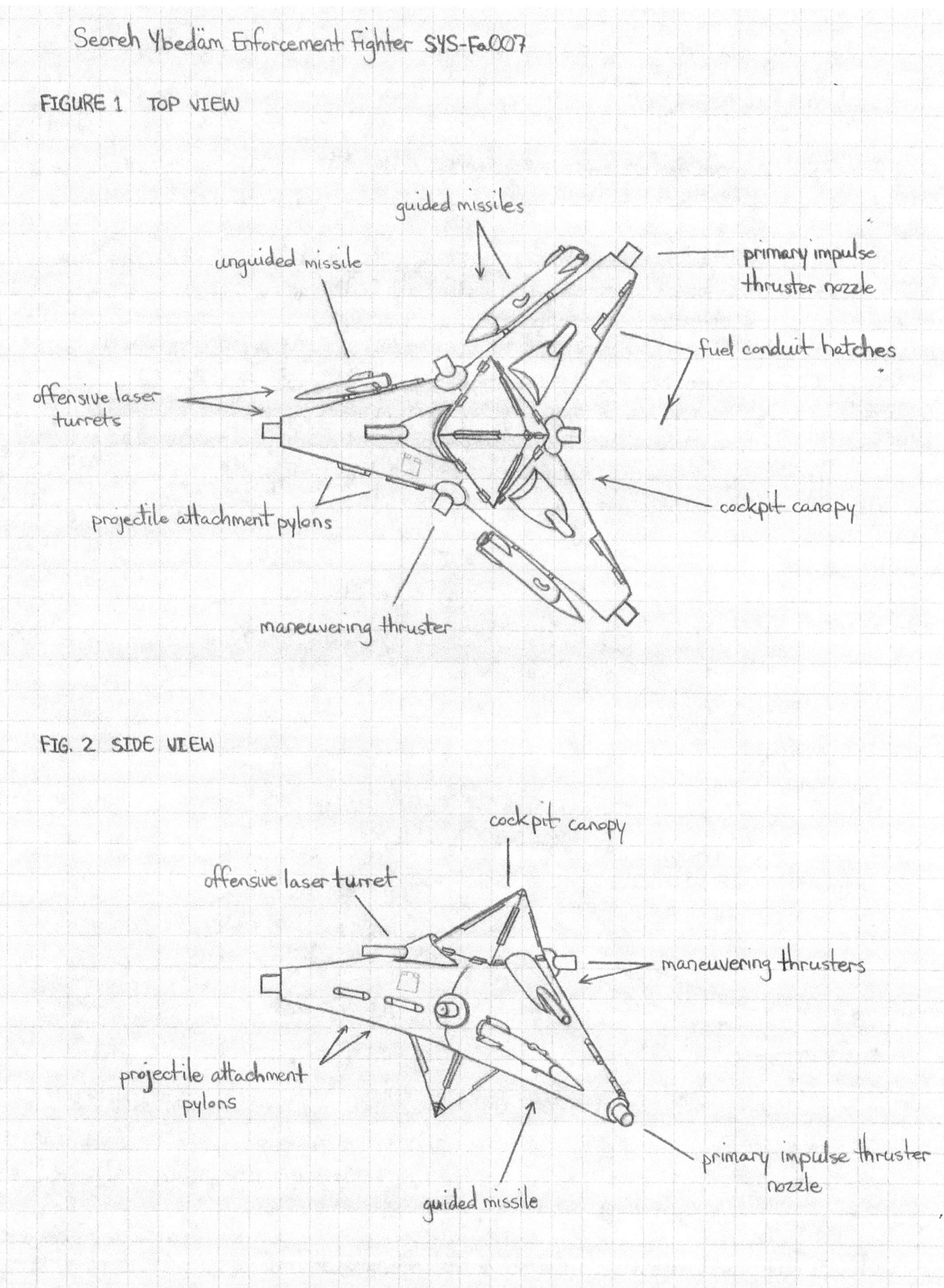

Seoreh Ybedäm Enforcement Fighter SYS-Fa007

FIGURE 1   TOP VIEW

guided missiles
unguided missile
primary impulse thruster nozzle
fuel conduit hatches
offensive laser turrets
cockpit canopy
projectile attachment pylons
maneuvering thruster

FIG. 2 SIDE VIEW

cockpit canopy
offensive laser turret
maneuvering thrusters
projectile attachment pylons
primary impulse thruster nozzle
guided missile

Seoreh Ybedäm SYS-Fa007

CLASSIFICATION: Seoreh Ybedäm autonomous fighter, *Kehsid-class*
TYPE: judicial armored small craft
CREW: pilot
LENGTH: 4.2 standard Confederation feet
WIDTH: 4.1 standard Confederation feet
HEIGHT: 2 standard Confederation feet
MASS: 480 standard mass units (fully equipped)
ARMOR: steetanicarb with steetanicrim gilding
ENGINES: Miltindrive Cor HY-chem assembly V8-26, standard hyperspace capacity
ARMAMENT: three offensive laser turrets, capacity for two guided and two unguided missiles

FIG. 3 FRONT VIEW

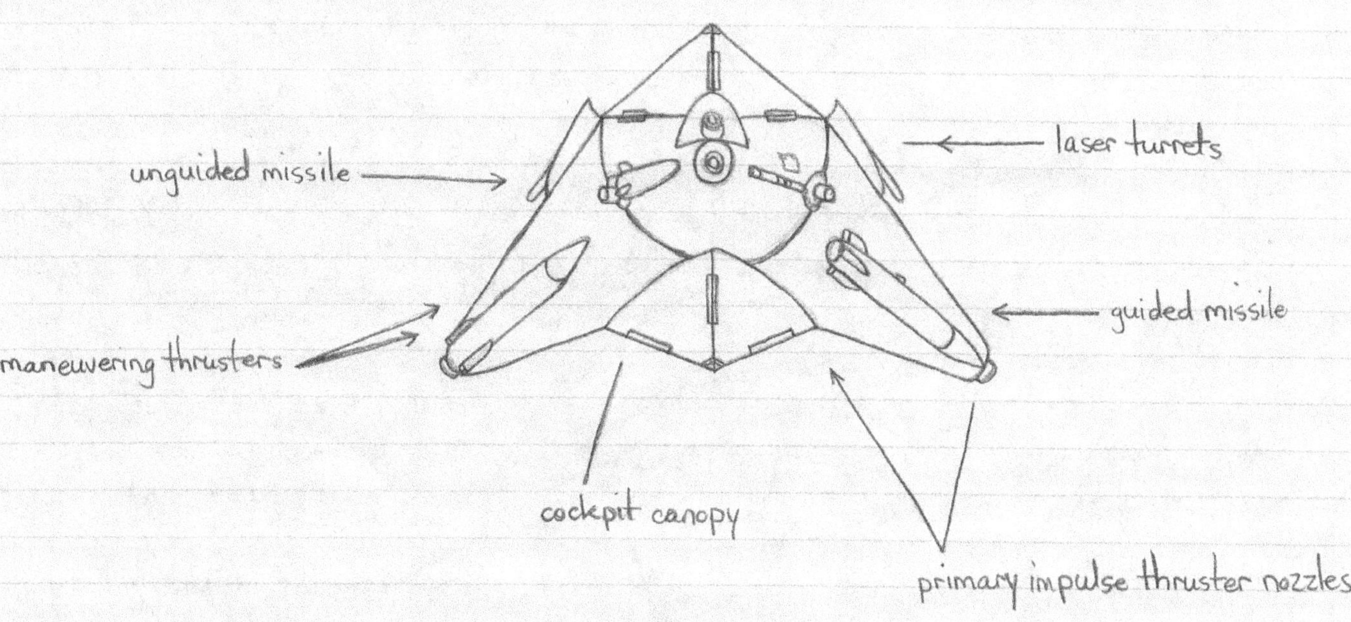

Seoreh Ybedäm Enforcement Fighter SYS-Fa007

CUTAWAY: INTERIOR SYSTEMS

1 projectile attachment pylon
2 weapons control interface
3 primary electrical capacitor
4 navigational sensor array
5 shield generator
6 time equalization field generator
7 maneuvering thruster assembly
8 sensor array
9 hyperspace field generator
10 primary impulse thruster assembly
11 impulse fuel storage tank
12 spatial sensor
13 fuel conduit hatch
14 weapons targeting sensors

15 laser assembly surge capacitor
16 communications assembly
17 cockpit canopy
18 offensive laser turret
19 auxiliary navigational computer
20 anion surge adapter

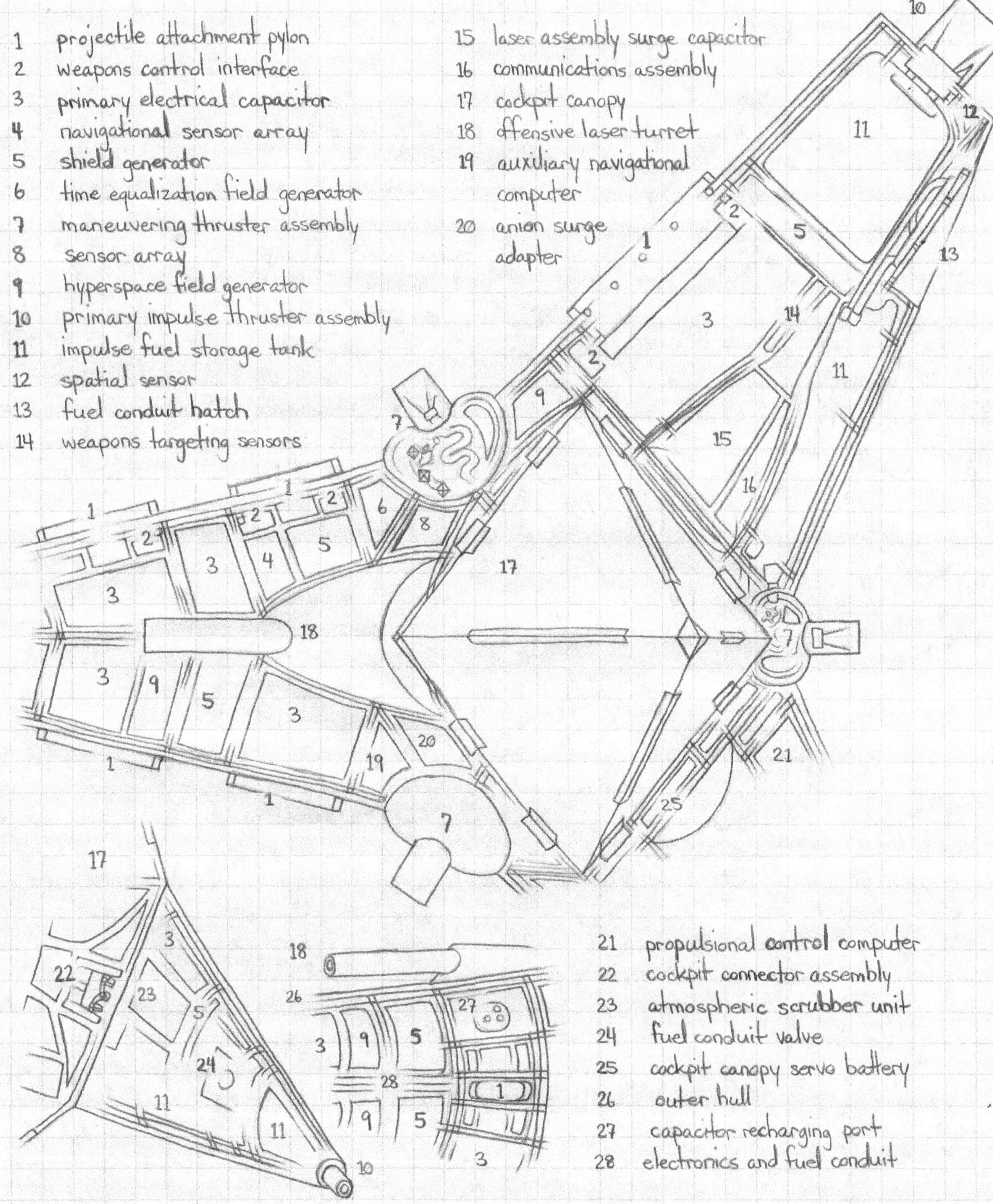

21 propulsional control computer
22 cockpit connector assembly
23 atmospheric scrubber unit
24 fuel conduit valve
25 cockpit canopy servo battery
26 outer hull
27 capacitor recharging port
28 electronics and fuel conduit

Seoreh Ybedäm Enforcement Fighter SYS-Fa007

CUTAWAY: COCKPIT ASSEMBLY

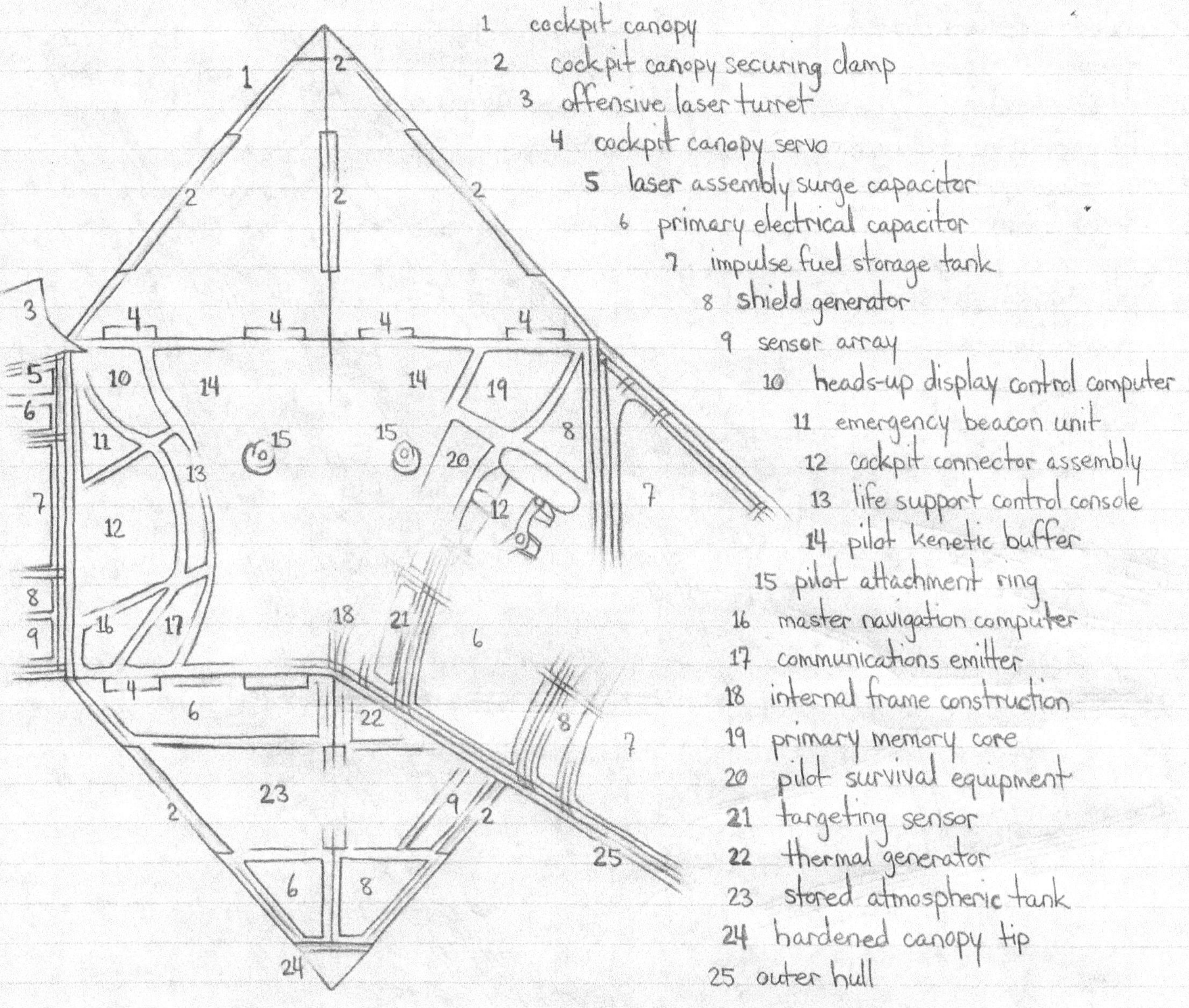

129

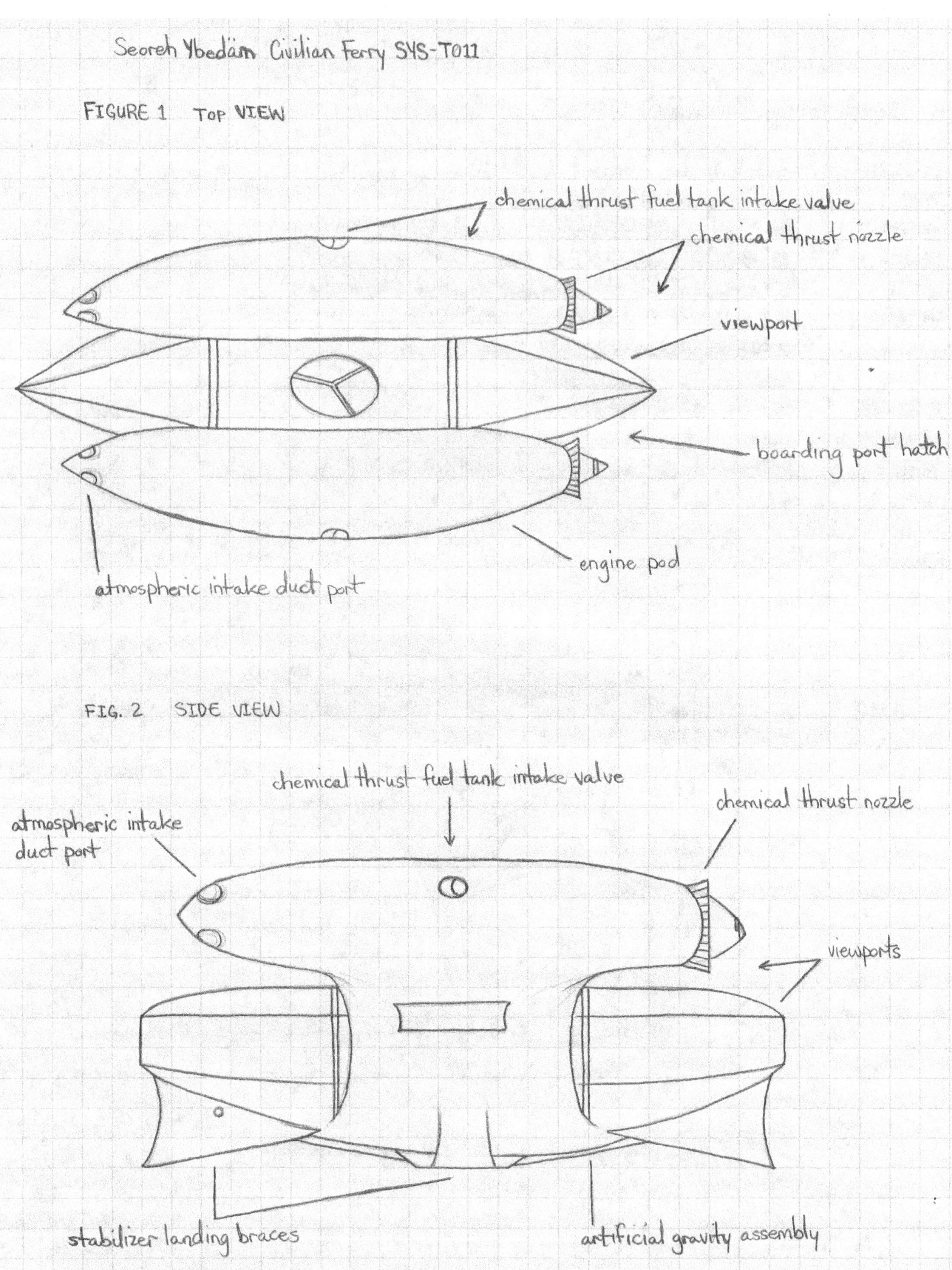

Seoreh Ybedäm Civilian Ferry SYS-T011

FIGURE 1   TOP VIEW

chemical thrust fuel tank intake valve
chemical thrust nozzle
viewport
boarding port hatch
engine pod
atmospheric intake duct port

FIG. 2   SIDE VIEW

chemical thrust fuel tank intake valve
chemical thrust nozzle
atmospheric intake duct port
viewports
stabilizer landing braces
artificial gravity assembly

Seoreh Ybedäm Civilian Ferry SYS-T011

CLASSIFICATION: Seoreh Ybedäm transport, Kehsid-class
TYPE: civilian personnel and cargo ferry
CREW: two (pilot and technician) (capacity for 26 passengers)
LENGTH: 12 standard Confederation feet
WIDTH: 5.9 standard Confederation feet
HEIGHT: 5.9 standard Confederation feet
MASS: 2,100 standard mass units (fully loaded)
ARMOR: laser-resistant steetanicarb
ENGINES: two chemical thrust assembly pods
ARMAMENT: none
RANGE: 450 standard Confederation miles (average)

FIG. 3   FRONT VIEW

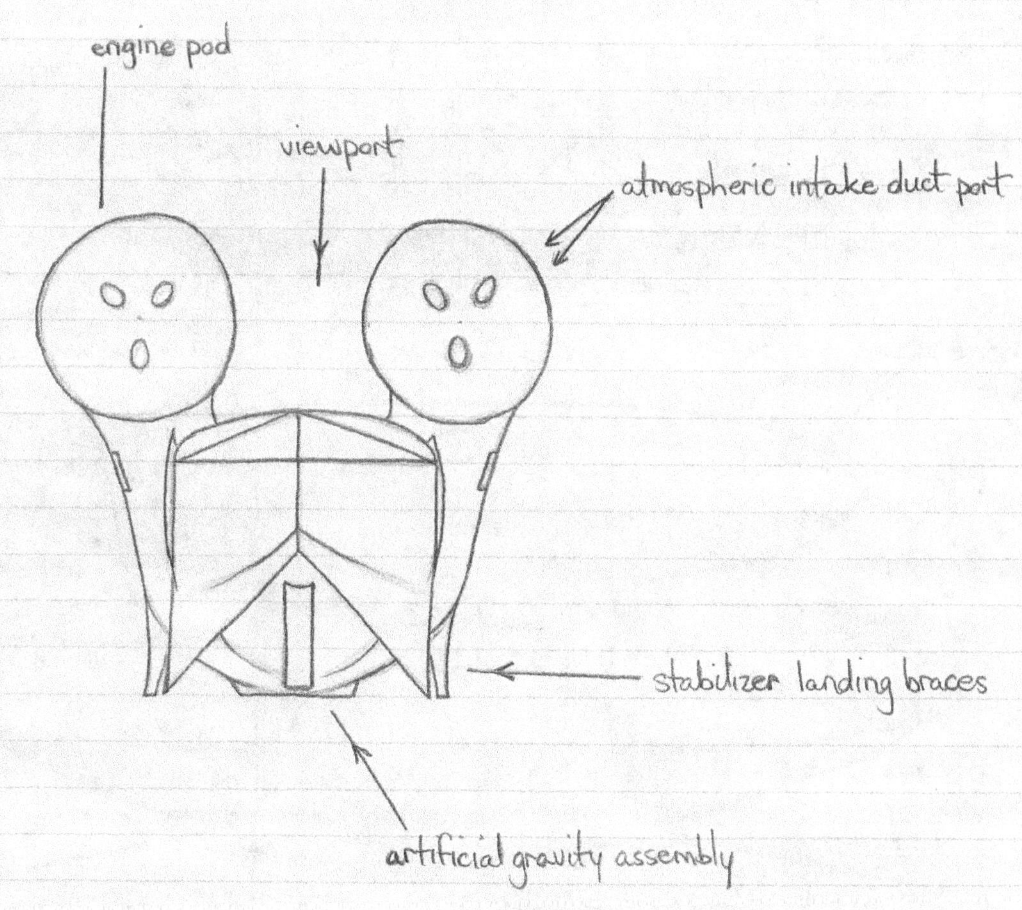

Seoreh Ybedäm Civilian Ferry SYS-T011

CUTAWAY: PASSENGER COMPARTMENT

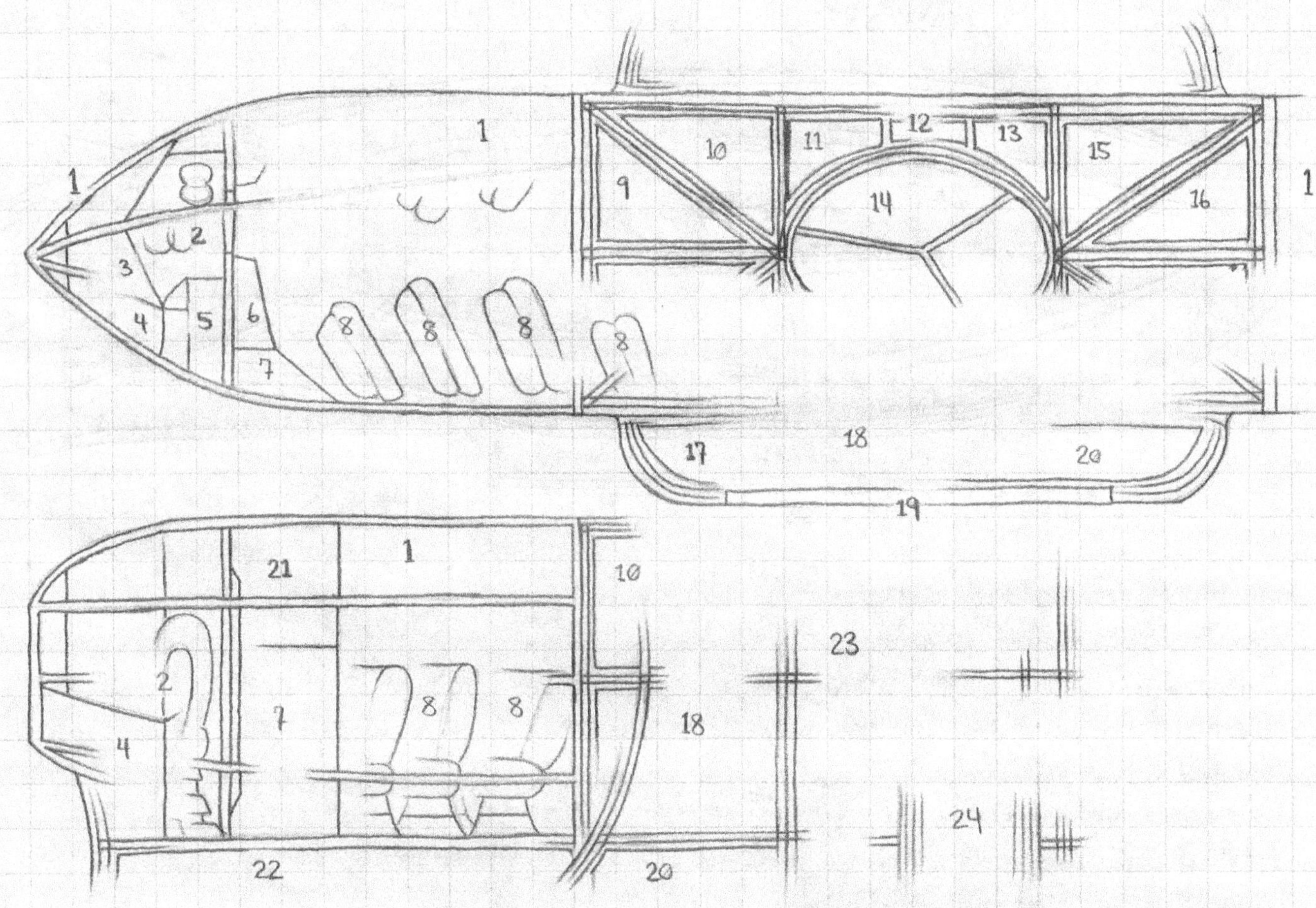

1	observation viewscreen	13	boarding port hatch servo battery
2	pilot seating unit	14	boarding port hatch
3	flight control console	15	atmospheric scrubber
4	communications control computer	16	refresher atmospheric tank
5	memory core	17	sensor array
6	life support control computer	18	passenger area
7	emergency medical storage unit	19	viewport
8	passenger seating unit	20	cargo space
9	thermal generator electrical alternator	21	passenger entertainment console
10	electric capacitor	22	primary battery
11	boarding port hatch servo housing	23	boarding passageway
12	boarding port hatch servo control computer	24	navigational array

Scorch Ybedäm Civilian Ferry SYS-T011

CUTAWAY: ENGINE POD

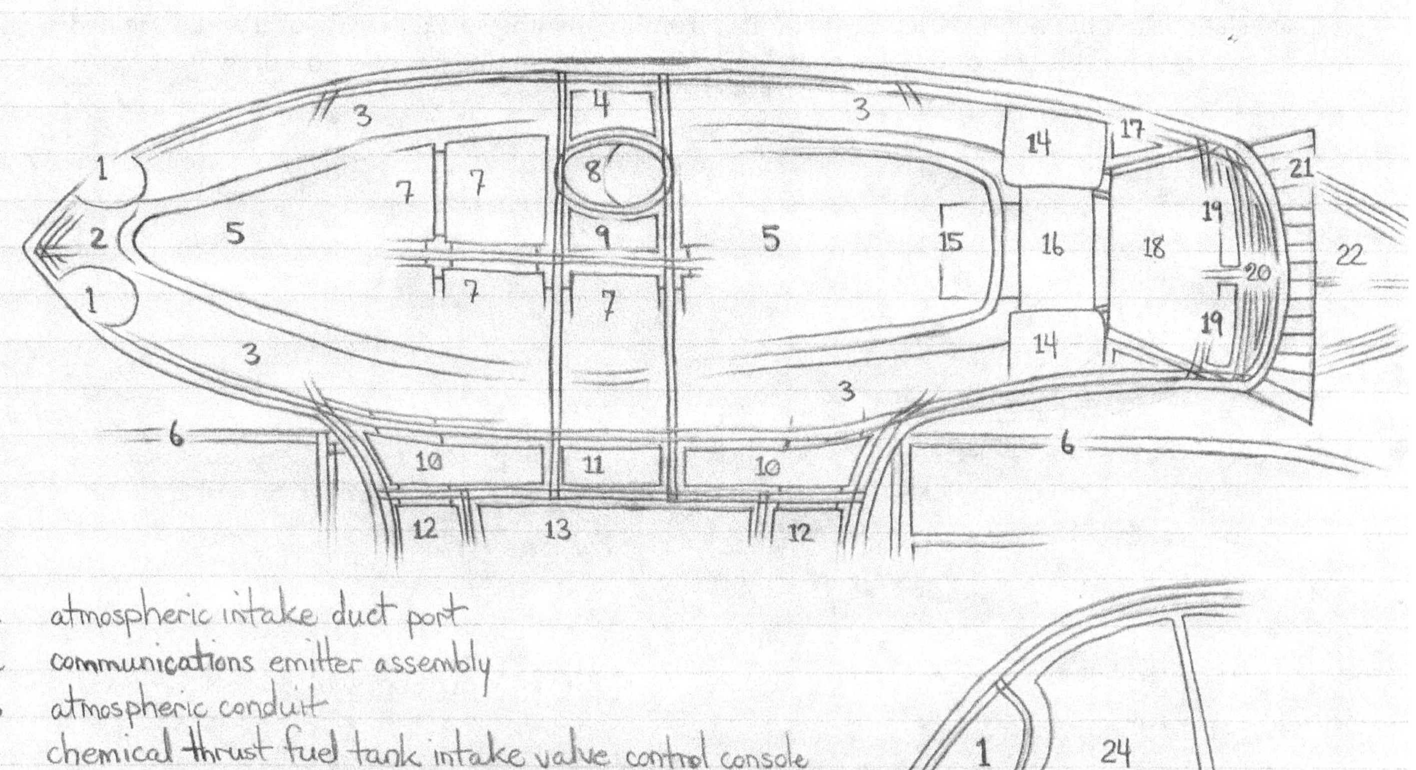

1   atmospheric intake duct port
2   communications emitter assembly
3   atmospheric conduit
4   chemical thrust fuel tank intake valve control console
5   chemical thrust fuel tank
6   observation viewscreen
7   electrical capacitor
8   chemical thrust fuel tank intake valve
9   intake valve pressure regulator
10 sensor array
11 electrical ammeter
12 radiation countermeasures
13 viewport
14 atmospheric conduit pressure regulator
15 chemical thrust ignition regulator
16 combustion chamber
17 propulsion control computer
18 chemical thrust nozzle chamber
19 chemical thrust nozzle output adjuster servo

20 output adjuster control computer
21 chemical thrust nozzle output adjuster
22 primary battery
23 electrical conduit
24 communications receiver

Set 34:

Gôlsniv

      This I fondly dub the astronomical moped, because it is a civilian in-system transport. It can't sustain a hyperspace drive and has limited capability. It is best this craft be used between space stations, really, but my friend who built it from Legos was so excited about it and there had to be a market for this sort of thing at some point during the Confederation. So I drew it.

Gôlsniv short-range Interworld skiff v47

FIGURE 1   TOP VIEW

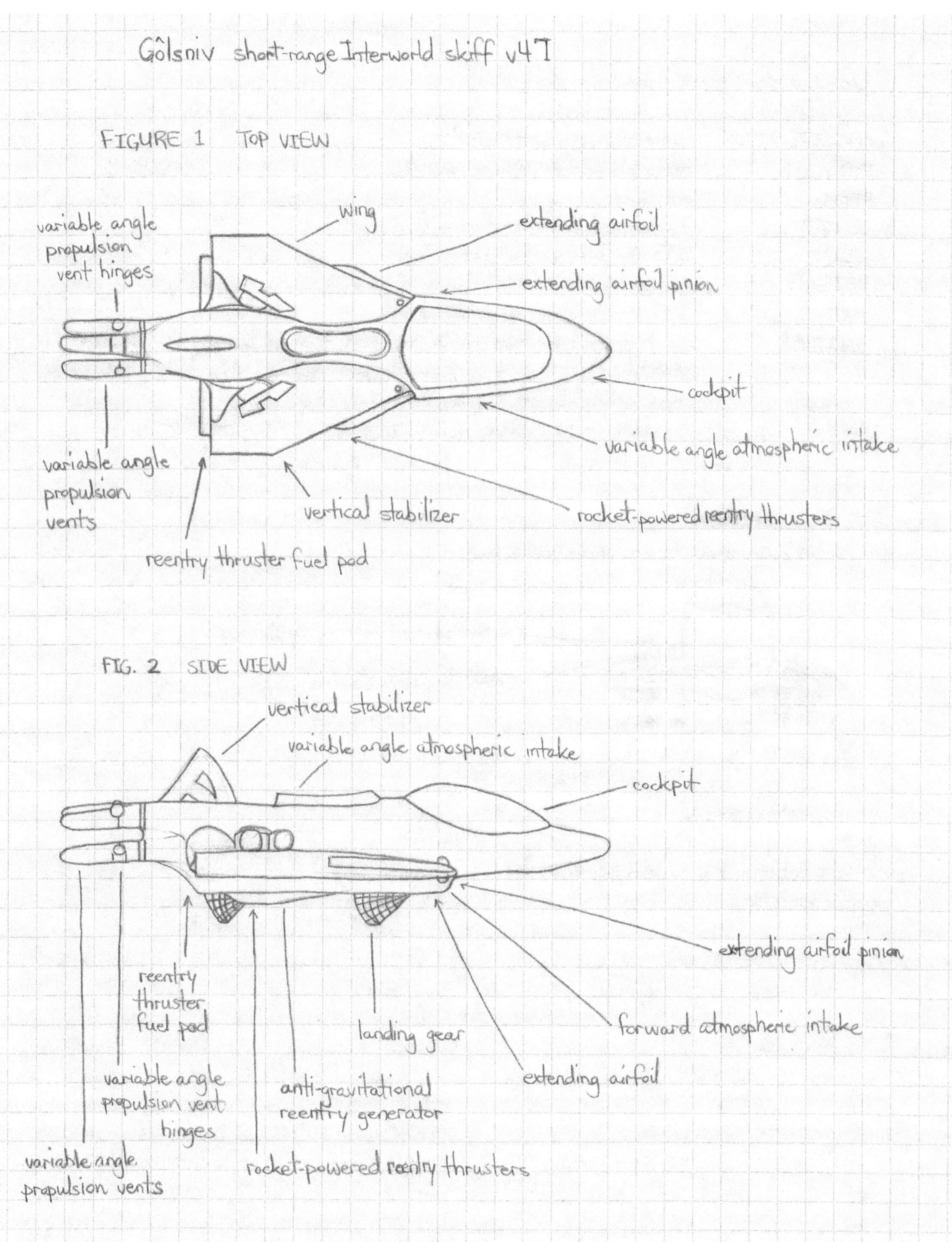

Gôlsniv short-range Interworld skiff v47

CLASSIFICATION:	civilian in-system transport
TYPE:	trans-planetoid impulse vessel
CREW:	one pilot
LENGTH:	7 standard Confederation feet
WIDTH:	3.15 standard Confederation feet
HEIGHT:	1.7 standard Confederation feet
MASS:	375 standard mass units
ENGINE:	one high-yield electromagnetic reciprocating disc engine, three primary variable angle rocket propulsion vents, two reentry rocket thrusters, two anti-gravitational reentry generators
RANGE:	0.0006831024 light-years (6,462,628,013 km/4,015,682,842 miles)

FIG. 3   FRONT VIEW

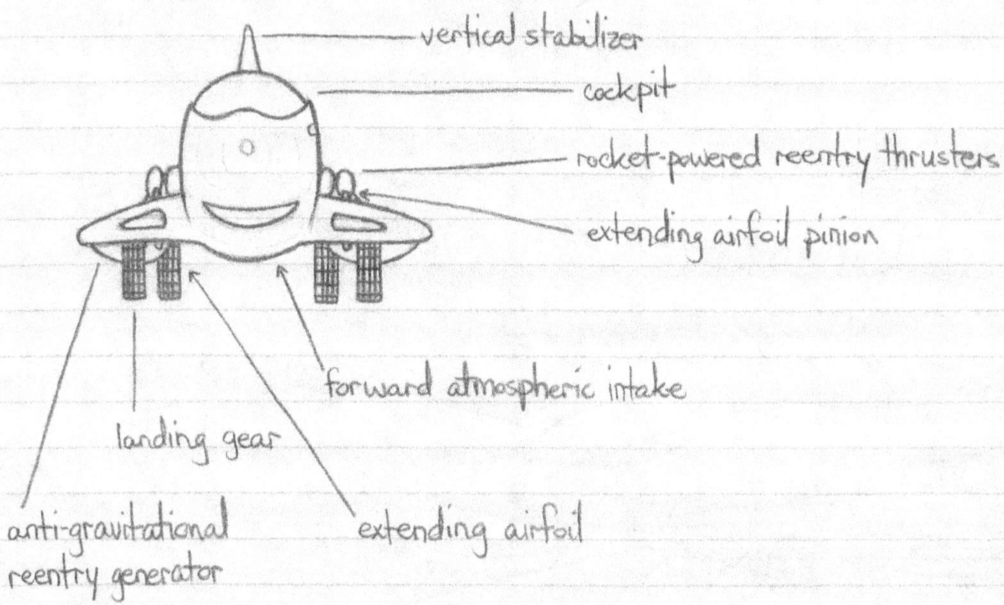

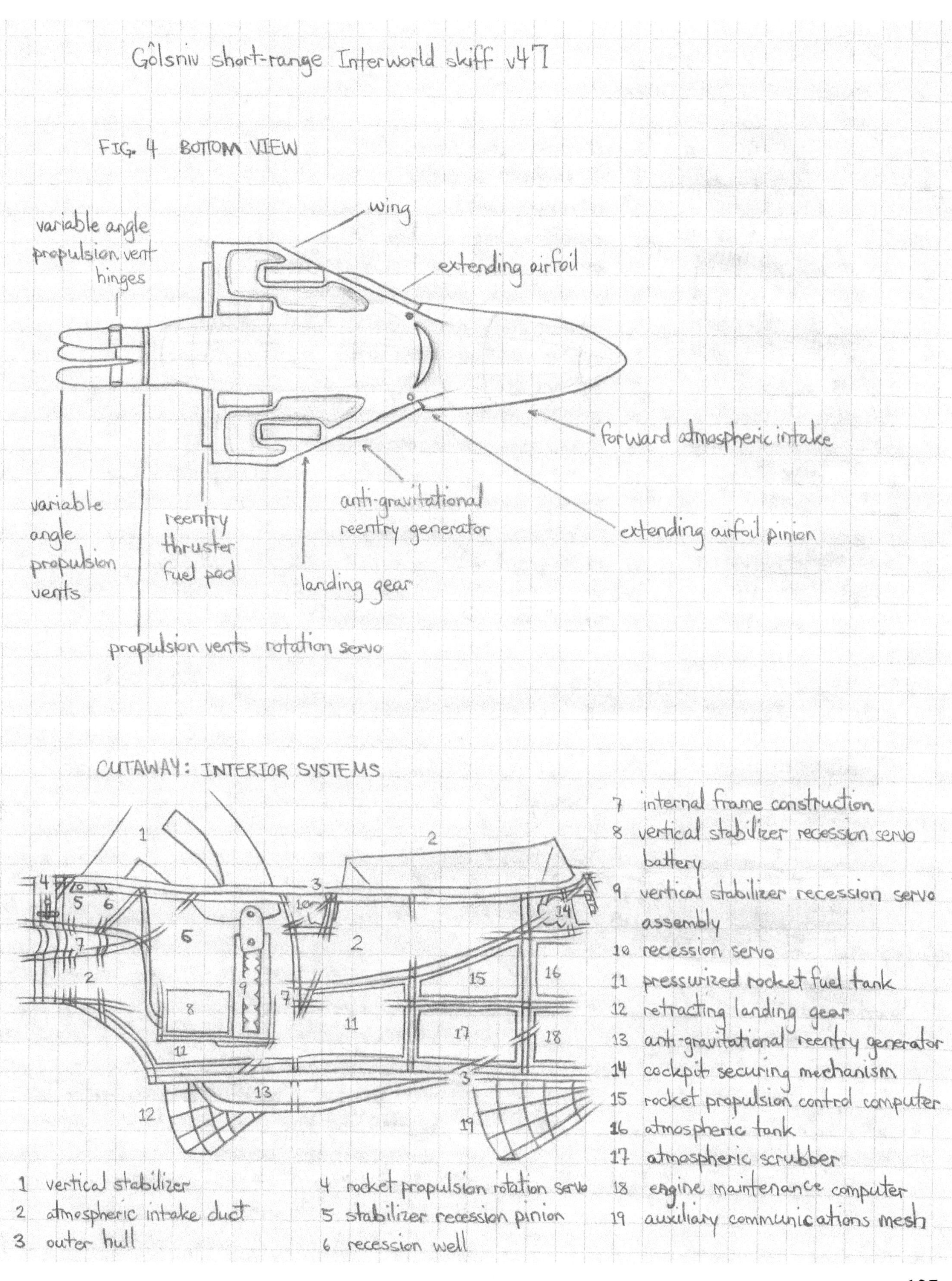

137

CUTAWAY: WING STRUCTURE

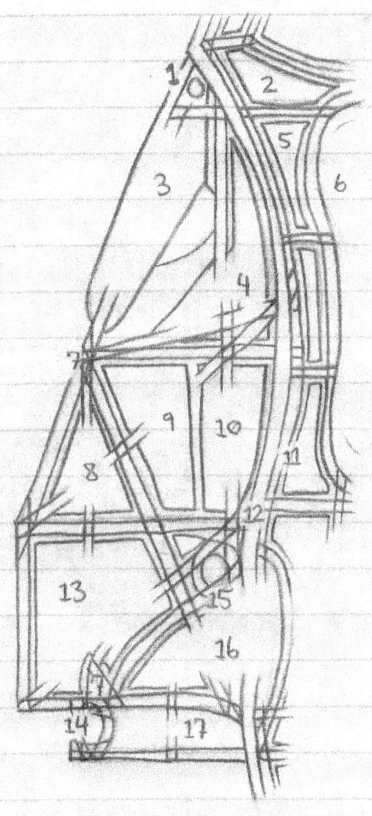

1 extending airfoil pinion
2 life support computer
3 extending airfoil
4 emergency engine capacitor
5 extending airfoil control computer
6 variable angle atmospheric intake
7 interior frame construction
8 master communications array
9 primary sensor array
10 primary navigational array
11 atmospheric intake recession computer
12 outer hull
13 primary sensor array
14 rocket fuel intake nozzle
15 rocket fuel duct
16 reentry thruster fuel pod
17 propulsional interface computer

CUTAWAY: FORWARD ELECTROMAGNETIC RECIPROCATING DISC ENGINE

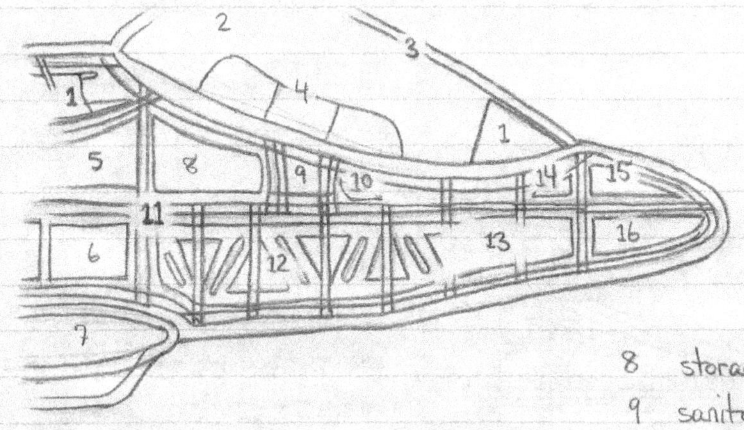

1 control computer
2 cockpit
3 cockpit viewscreen
4 pilot reclining mat
5 atmosphere tank
6 electromagnetic reciprocating engine battery
7 wing
8 storage compartment
9 sanitary ejection vent
10 pressure control assembly
11 reciprocating disc engine buffer
12 electromagnetic reciprocating disc engine
13 booster battery
14 emergency homing beacon
15 sensor array
16 defensive shield array

Set 35:

Scoutship 26

This is a Tundais scout ship made and used early after the Confederation formed, when Detalernu races began to feel the need to settle their neighboring stars and become a daunting power in themselves. The Tundais were, in fact, slow and unwilling to settle new worlds in comparison to the Jenapse or the Vookro, but they didn't want to be left out completely.

I didn't feel like drawing this, but the intra-system ion drive for this vehicle is located on the outside of the chemical launch rocket section. Ion drives need little room if their material is directed properly and I didn't see anything else to fill the inevitable other side of an additional page with. I just would hate to be assigned to this ship, since it means weeks of cramped living and monotony. But the weapons are nifty…

Hālkraft Scoutship 26

FIGURE 1 TOP VIEW

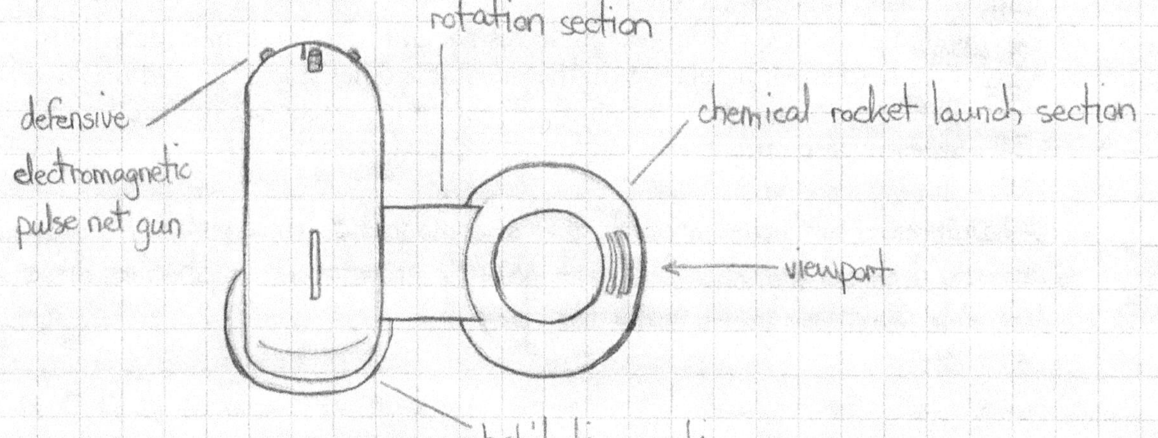

FIG. 2 FRONT VIEW

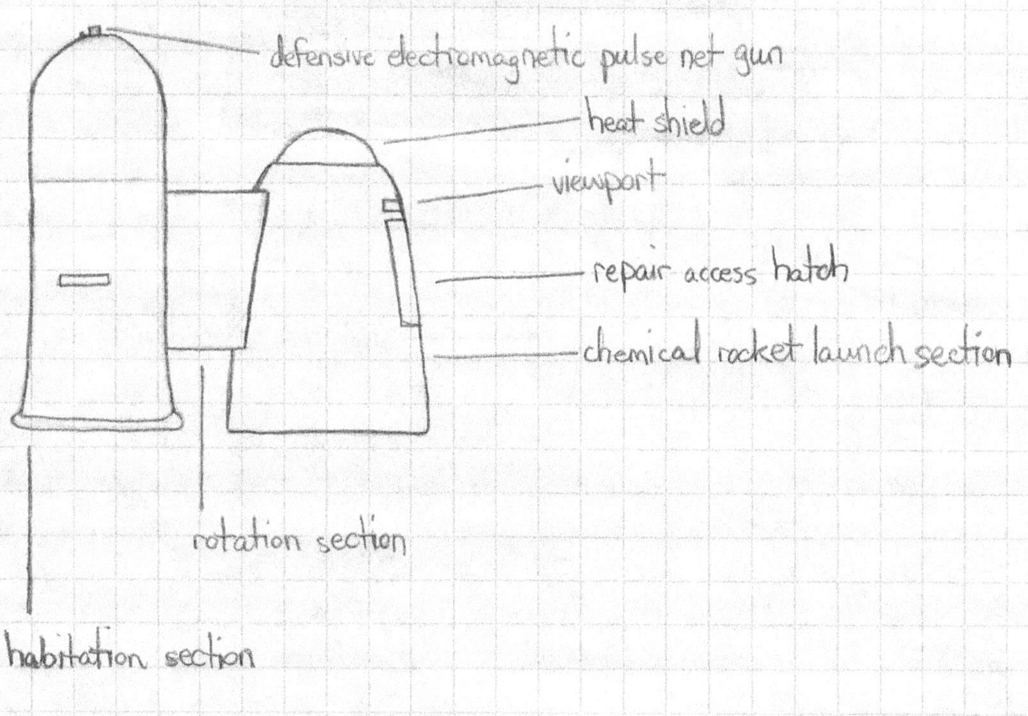

Hālkraft *Scoutship 26*

CLASSIFICATION: Hālkraft deep-space scout ship
TYPE: advanced colonization research vessel
CREW: two
LENGTH: 3 sicles
WIDTH: 3.5 sicles
HEIGHT: 3.8 sicles
MASS: 3,842 Tundais mass units
ARMOR: steealumicarb with pyroceramite resin and magnetic armor plating
ENGINES: primary chemical launch rocket, anti-gravity generator, intra-system ion drive
ARMAMENT: defensive electromagnetic pulse net guns

FIG. 3   SIDE VIEW

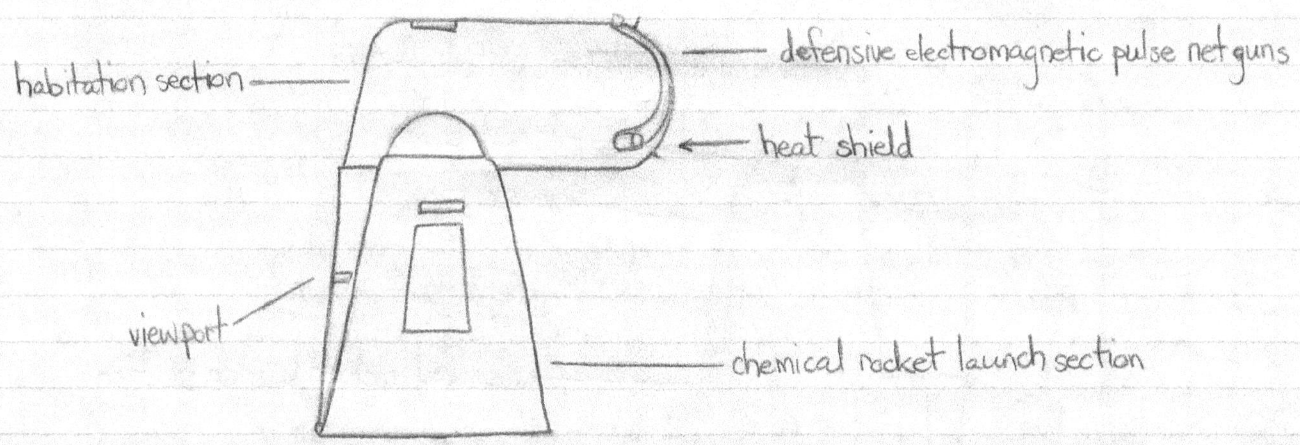

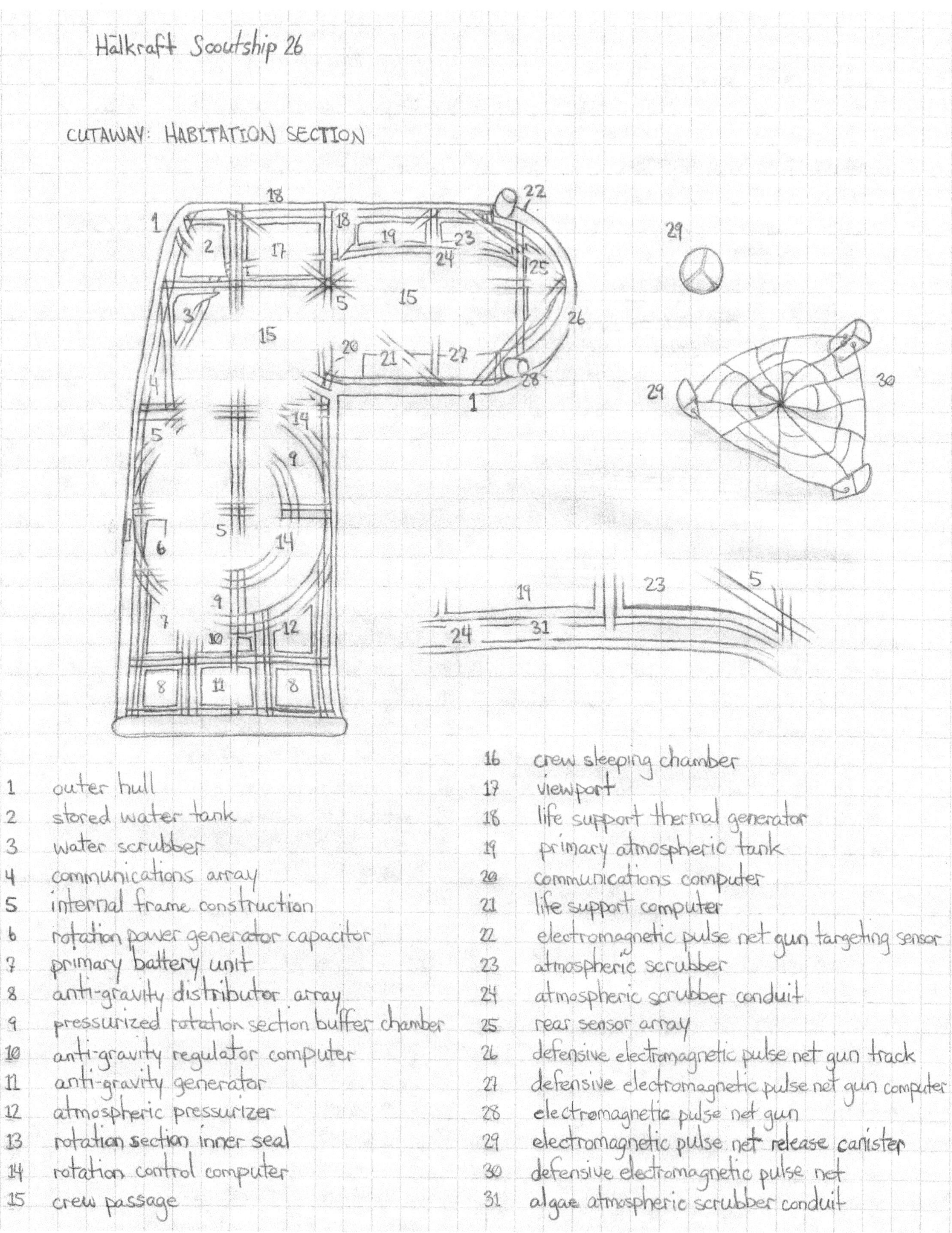

1   outer hull
2   stored water tank
3   water scrubber
4   communications array
5   internal frame construction
6   rotation power generator capacitor
7   primary battery unit
8   anti-gravity distributor array
9   pressurized rotation section buffer chamber
10 anti-gravity regulator computer
11 anti-gravity generator
12 atmospheric pressurizer
13 rotation section inner seal
14 rotation control computer
15 crew passage

16 crew sleeping chamber
17 viewport
18 life support thermal generator
19 primary atmospheric tank
20 communications computer
21 life support computer
22 electromagnetic pulse net gun targeting sensor
23 atmospheric scrubber
24 atmospheric scrubber conduit
25 rear sensor array
26 defensive electromagnetic pulse net gun track
27 defensive electromagnetic pulse net gun computer
28 electromagnetic pulse net gun
29 electromagnetic pulse net release canister
30 defensive electromagnetic pulse net
31 algae atmospheric scrubber conduit

142

CUTAWAY: ROTATION SECTION

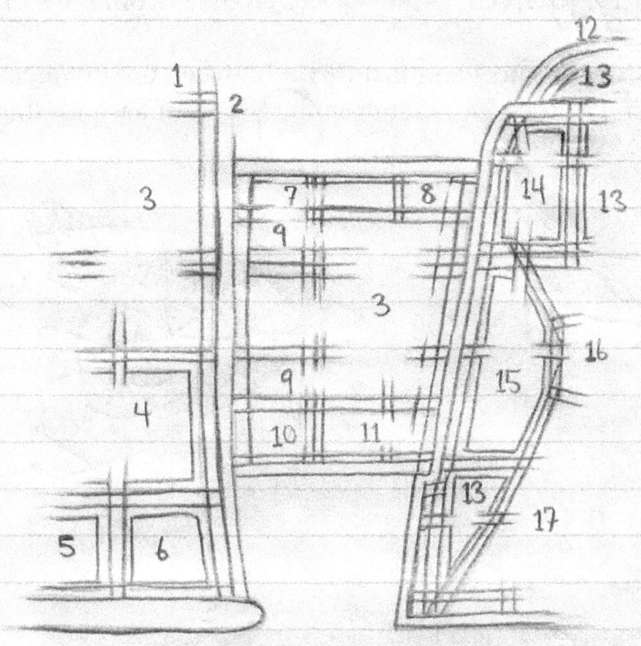

1. internal frame construction
2. outer hull
3. crew passage
4. primary battery unit
5. anti-gravity generator
6. anti-gravity distributor array
7. navigational array
8. manual rocket control station
9. pressurized buffer chamber
10. heat energy converter
11. rotation servo battery
12. escape velocity heat shield
13. chemical rocket fuel tank
14. chemical rocket initializer
15. rotation servo housing
16. chemical rocket combustion chamber
17. chemical rocket nozzle

Set 36:

Wavewalker

This ship is a civilian cruise vessel for the Shipbuilder homeworld, but most often used on Aroldin between sea cities. Its pontoons use an actual proposed aquatic generator I saw in *Popular Mechanics* called the Gorlov turbine. It is derived, somewhat obviously, from a water spider.

This type of craft would be used often for transport and fast travel between underwater and hovering habitations on Aroldin. By the end of the Confederation the Shipbuilder and Small Wise populations must be in the thousands. They love watery worlds.

Aroldin courier surface *Trade Weaver*-class ship *Wavewalker*

FIGURE 1   TOP VIEW

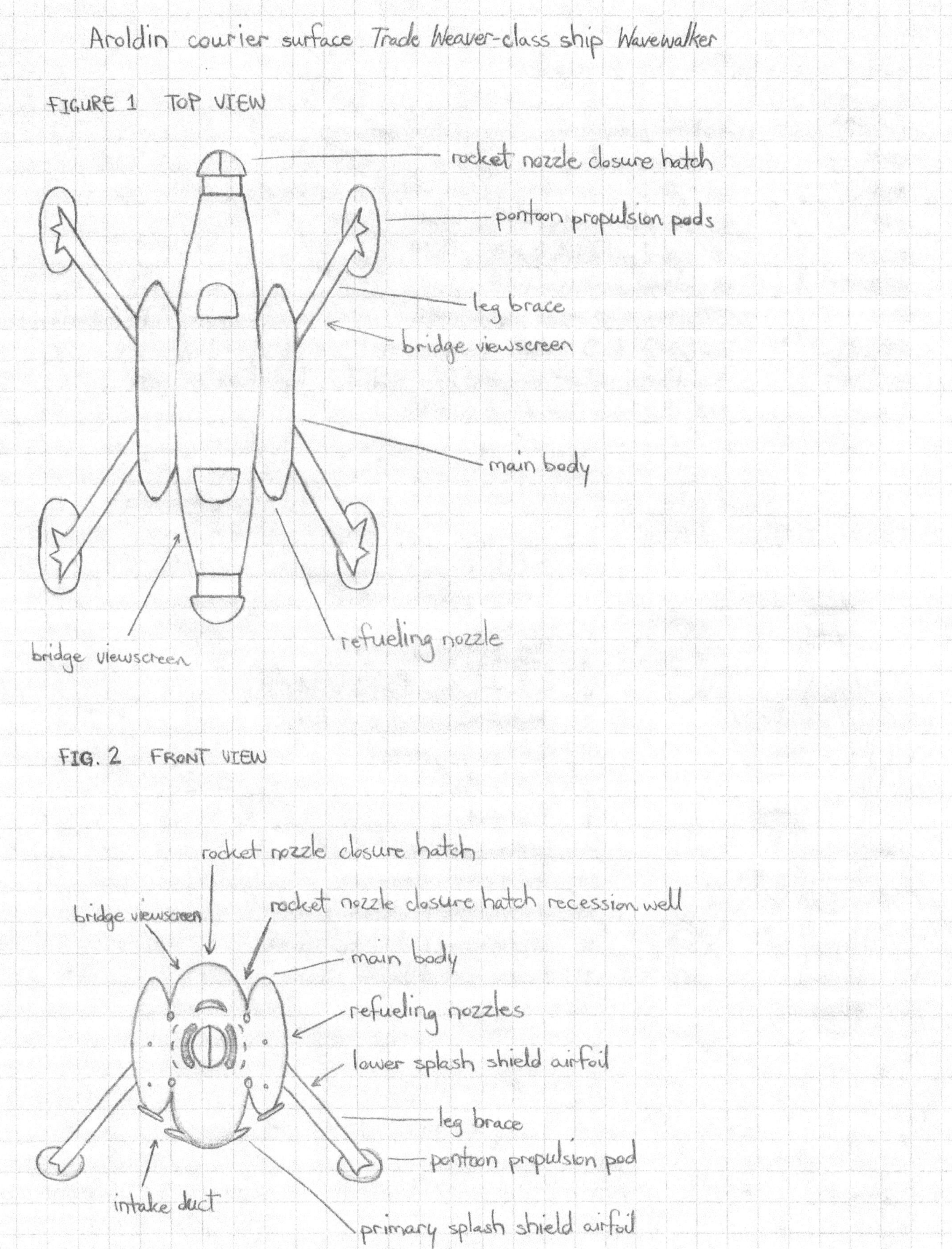

FIG. 2   FRONT VIEW

Aroldin courier surface ship *Wavewalker*

CLASSIFICATION: medium ocean-borne cargo/passenger ship
TYPE: Trade Weaver-class
CREW: four officers, as many as six Ehtadhh passengers
LENGTH: 40 standard Confederation feet
WIDTH: 30 standard Confederation feet
HEIGHT: 18 standard Confederation feet
MASS: 1,528 standard mass units (empty), 7,308 standard mass units (fueled and loaded)
ARMOR: Dex Hox grade 3 civilian steetanicarb
ENGINES: two heavy rocket engines, four hydrofoil hydroturbine pods
RANGE: 170+ standard Confederation miles

CUTAWAY: INTERIOR SYSTEMS

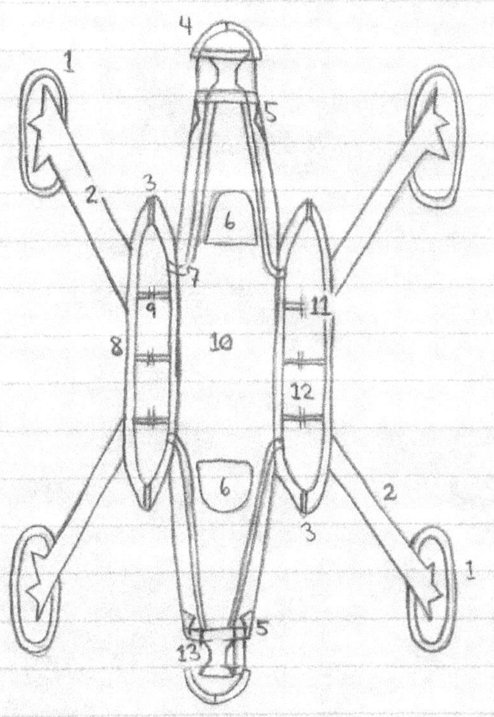

1   pontoon propulsion pod
2   leg brace
3   refueling nozzle
4   rocket nozzle closure hatch
5   rocket nozzle closure hatch well
6   bridge viewscreen
7   fuel cable
8   fuel pod
9   pressurized tank valve
10 main crew area
11 pressurized tank wall
12 pressurized rocket fuel tank
13 heavy rocket engine nozzle

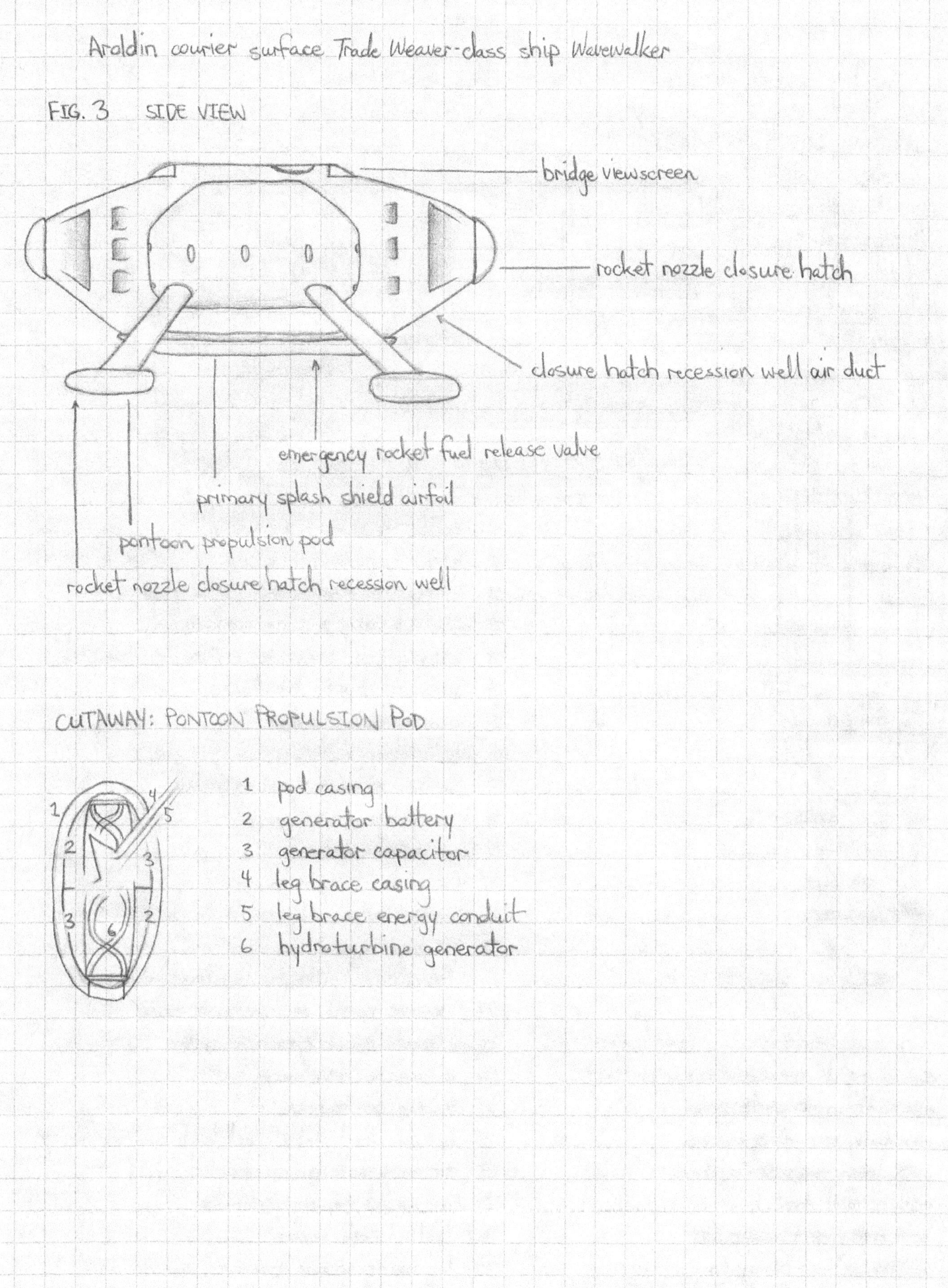

Araldin courier surface Trade Weaver-class ship Wavewalker
FIG. 3   SIDE VIEW
bridge viewscreen
rocket nozzle closure hatch
closure hatch recession well air duct
emergency rocket fuel release valve
primary splash shield airfoil
pontoon propulsion pod
rocket nozzle closure hatch recession well
CUTAWAY: PONTOON PROPULSION POD
1
2
3
4
5
6
1   pod casing
2   generator battery
3   generator capacitor
4   leg brace casing
5   leg brace energy conduit
6   hydroturbine generator

Aroldin courier surface Trade Weaver-class ship *Wavewalker*

CUTAWAY: INTERIOR SYSTEMS

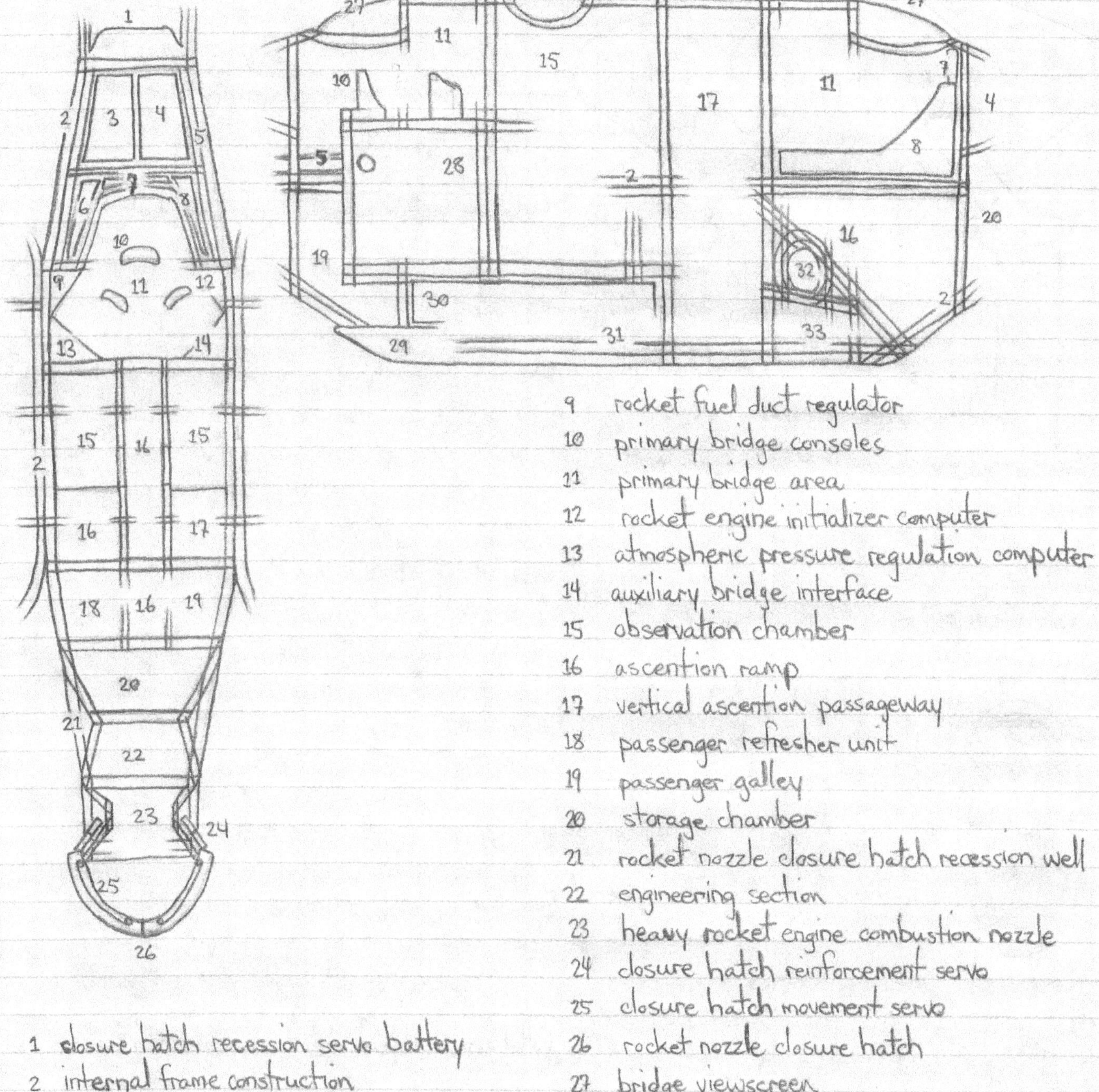

1   closure hatch recession servo battery
2   internal frame construction
3   sanitary recycling system
4   propulsion computer systems
5   rocket fuel duct
6   primary memory computer
7   master control computer
8   navigational-propulsional interface
9   rocket fuel duct regulator
10   primary bridge consoles
11   primary bridge area
12   rocket engine initializer computer
13   atmospheric pressure regulation computer
14   auxiliary bridge interface
15   observation chamber
16   ascention ramp
17   vertical ascention passageway
18   passenger refresher unit
19   passenger galley
20   storage chamber
21   rocket nozzle closure hatch recession well
22   engineering section
23   heavy rocket engine combustion nozzle
24   closure hatch reinforcement servo
25   closure hatch movement servo
26   rocket nozzle closure hatch
27   bridge viewscreen
28   pressurized rocket fuel tank anchor frame
29   primary splash shield airfoil
30   artificial gravity generator
31   bathylscape room
32   leg brace anchor frame
33   primary hydroturbine capacitor

Lynop civilian orbital station P2-S16

CLASSIFICATION: civilian orbital station
TYPE: geosynchronous residential platform
CREW: four (capacity for 23 passengers)
LENGTH: 45 standard Confederation feet
WIDTH: 51 standard Confederation feet
HEIGHT: 19.2 standard Confederation feet
MASS: 43,505 standard mass units
ARMOR: pyroceramite-coated steetanicarb

FIG. 2   FRONT VIEW

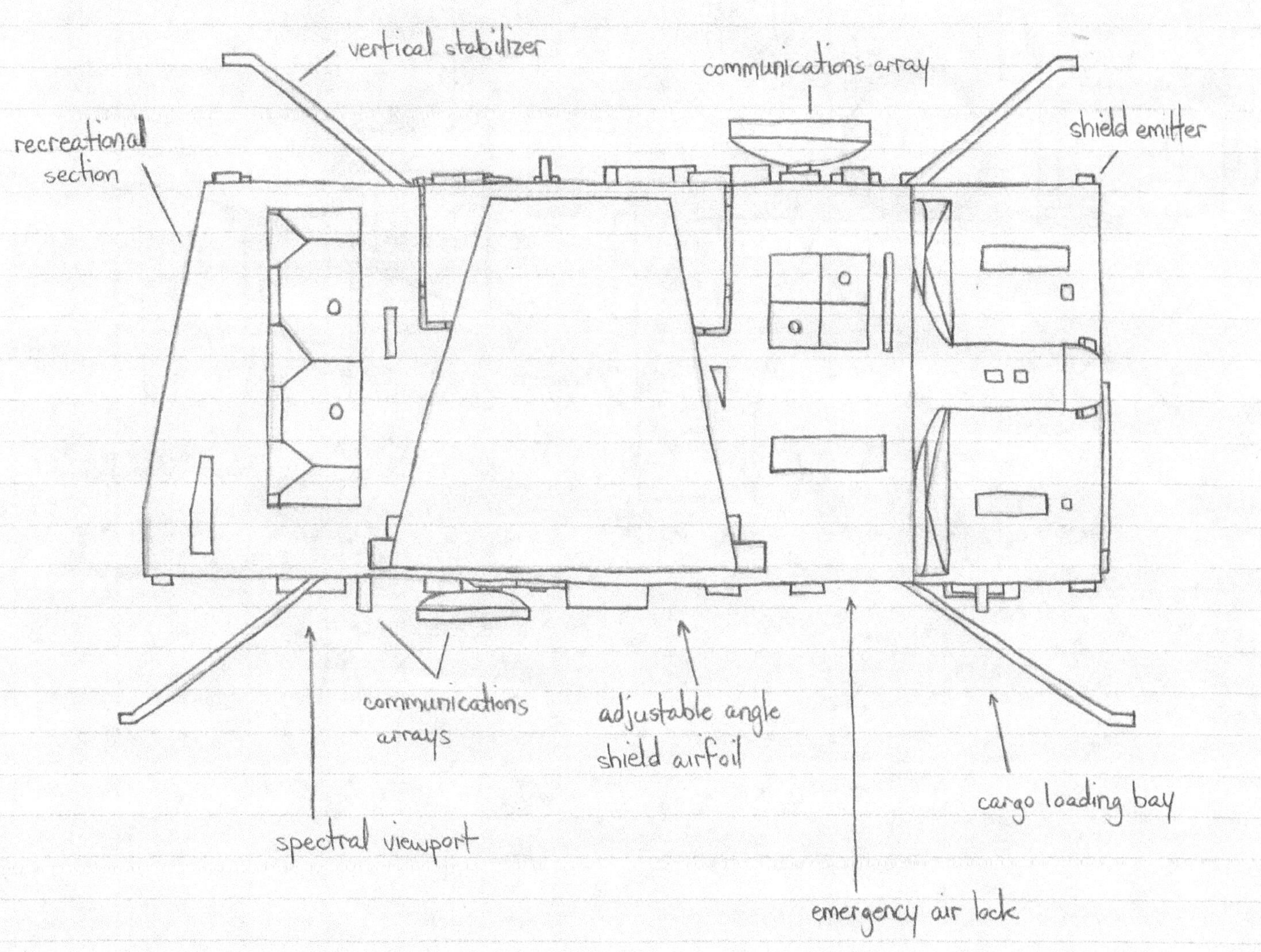

151

Lynop civilian orbital station P2-S16

FIG. 3 SIDE VIEW

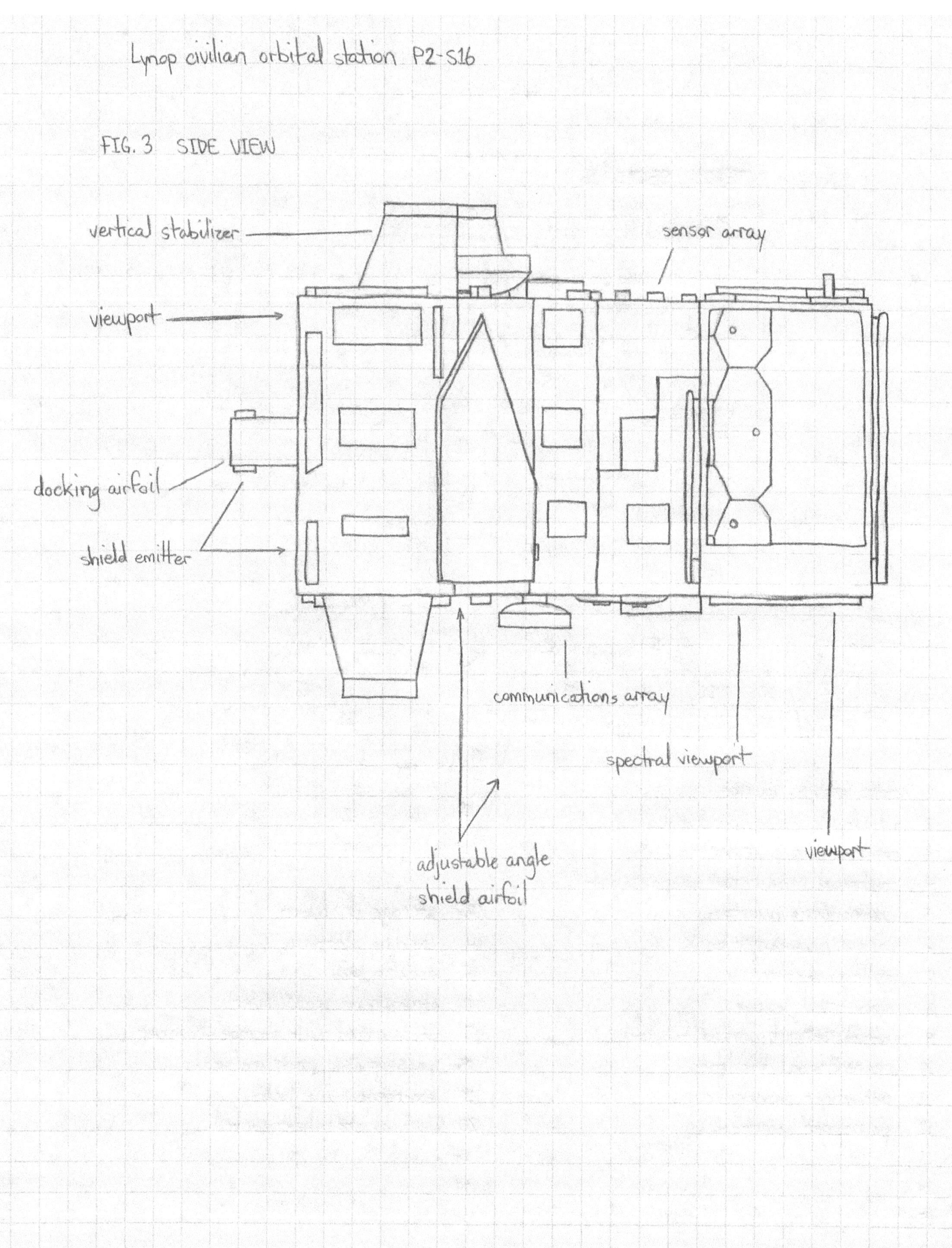

152

Lynap civilian orbital station P2-S16

CUTAWAY: INTERIOR SECTIONS

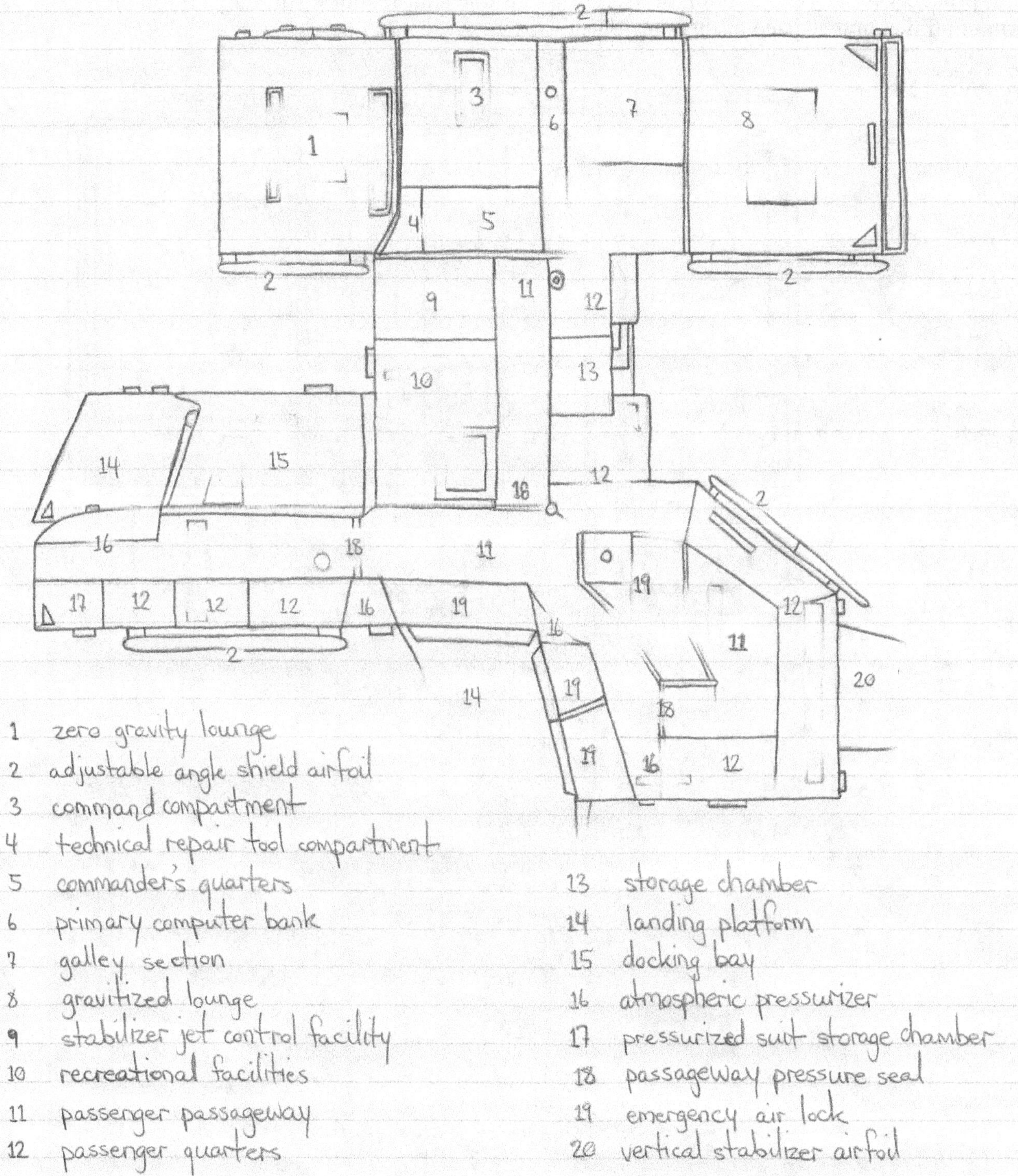

1 zero gravity lounge
2 adjustable angle shield airfoil
3 command compartment
4 technical repair tool compartment
5 commander's quarters
6 primary computer bank
7 galley section
8 gravitized lounge
9 stabilizer jet control facility
10 recreational facilities
11 passenger passageway
12 passenger quarters
13 storage chamber
14 landing platform
15 docking bay
16 atmospheric pressurizer
17 pressurized suit storage chamber
18 passageway pressure seal
19 emergency air lock
20 vertical stabilizer airfoil

153

# Set 38:
P2-SH32

There isn't much to say about this transport. It is meant to ferry people and supplies between stations and the planetary surface for a single, large string of vacation facilities in near orbit of Lynop Prime. Each station in this company's control has two shuttles (hence SH-31 and SH-32). It probably has a long duration of use, for a reusable shuttle, but it still burns through this maximum travel in the space of three or four local years, I would guess.

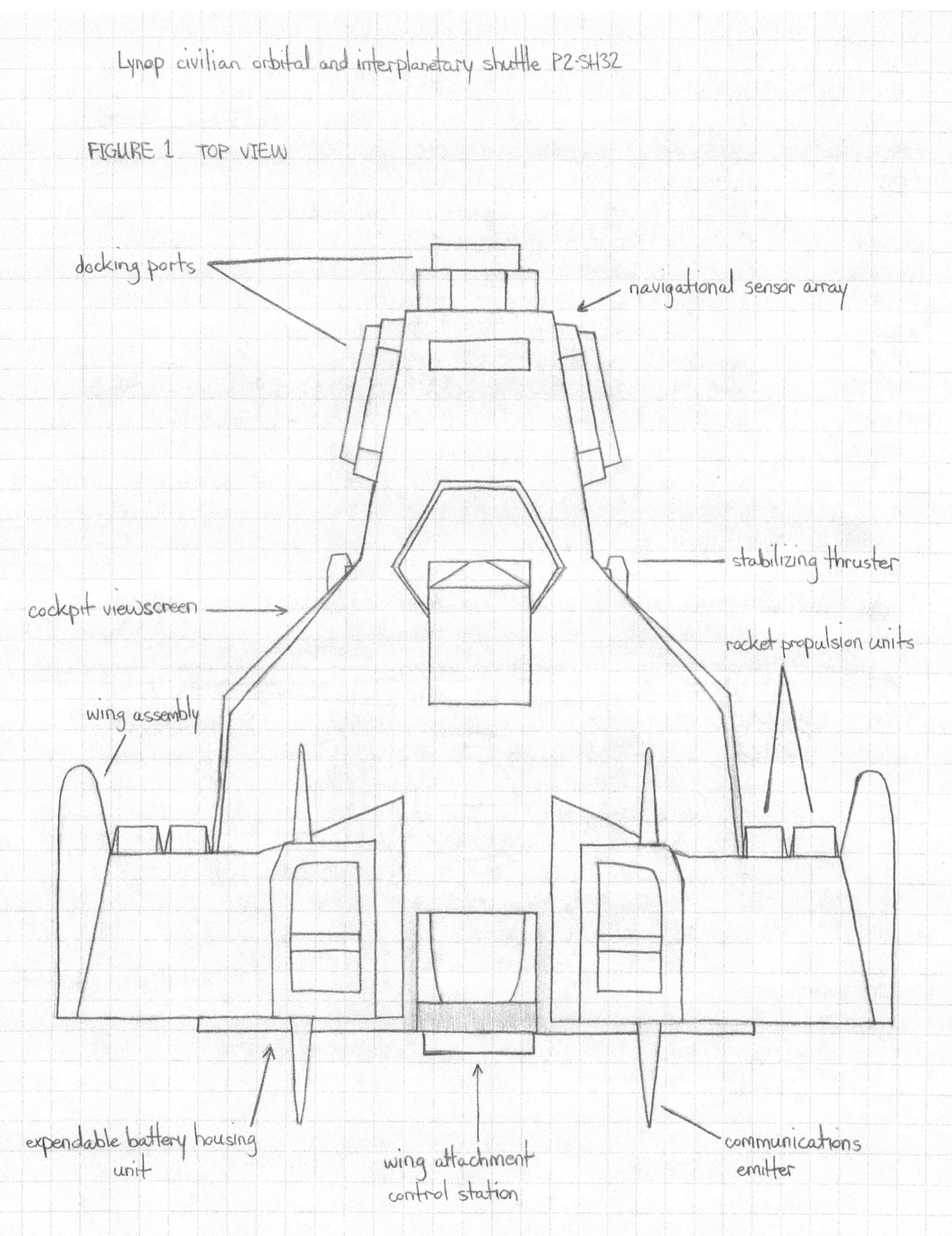

Lynop civilian orbital and interplanetary shuttle P2-SH32
FIGURE 1   TOP VIEW
docking ports
navigational sensor array
stabilizing thruster
cockpit viewscreen
rocket propulsion units
wing assembly
expendable battery housing unit
wing attachment control station
communications emitter

155

Lynop civilian orbital and interplanetary shuttle P2-SH32

CLASSIFICATION: Lynopte medium-range shuttle
TYPE: station/system civilian transport, special
CREW: two (pilot and copilot) (with capacity for 8 passengers)
LENGTH: 29 standard Confederation feet
WIDTH: 27 standard Confederation feet
HEIGHT: 8 standard Confederation feet
MASS: 21,764 standard mass units (wings attached)
ARMOR: pyroceramite-coated steetanicarb
ENGINE: three rechargeable high-capacitance batteries and four detachable rocket engines
RANGE: 0.00004 9019 light-years (463,753,399 km / 288,162,426 miles) maximum

FIG. 2   FRONT VIEW

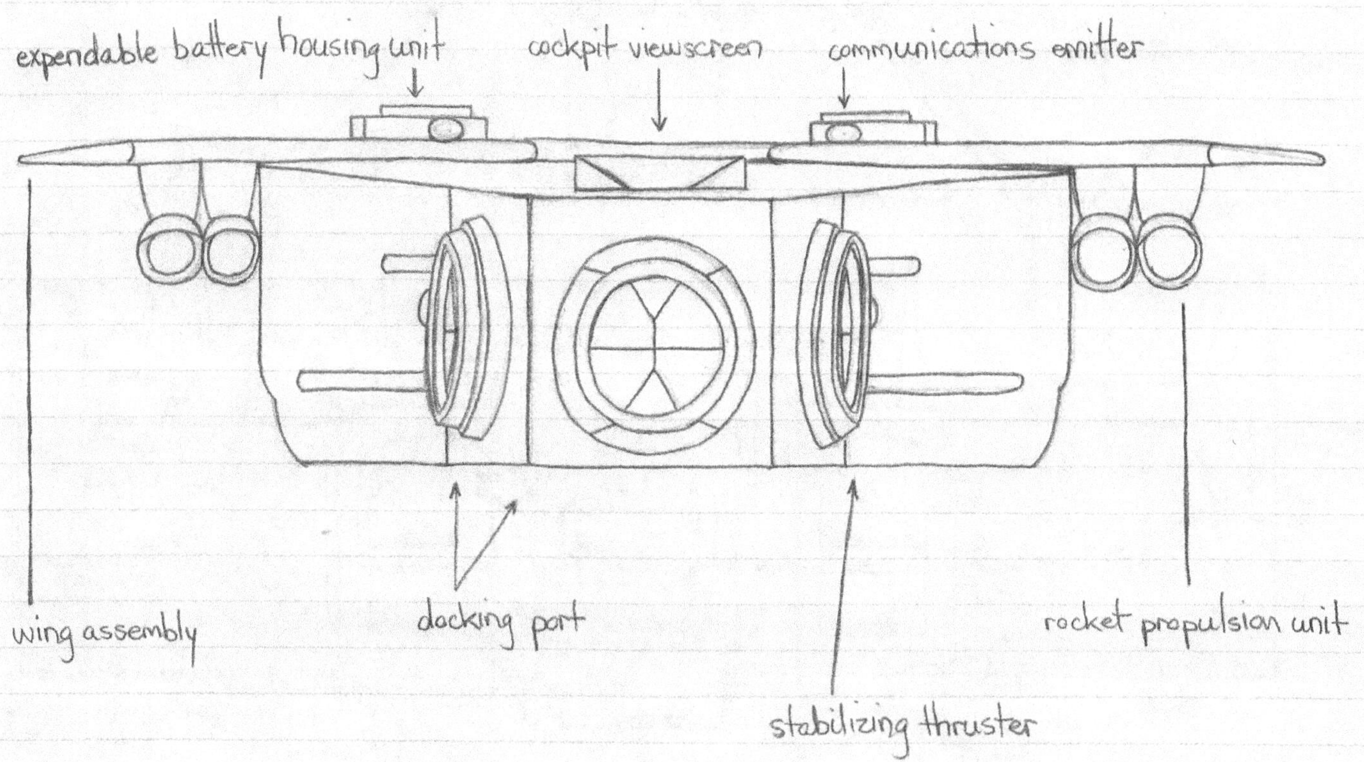

Lynop civilian orbital and interplanetary shuttle P2-SH32

FIG. 3   SIDE VIEW

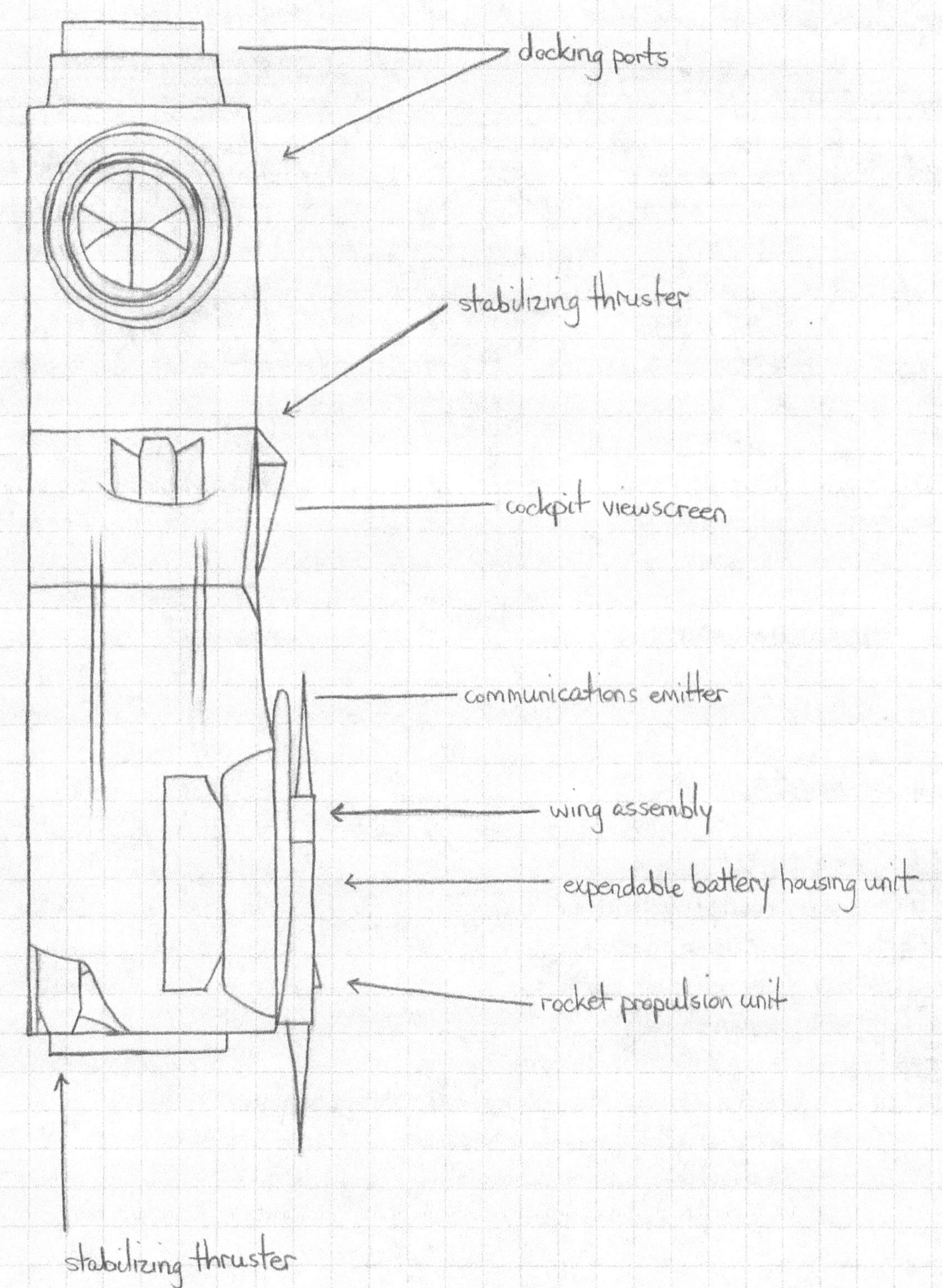

Lynop civilian orbital and interplanetary shuttle P2-SH32

FIG. 4 REAR VIEW

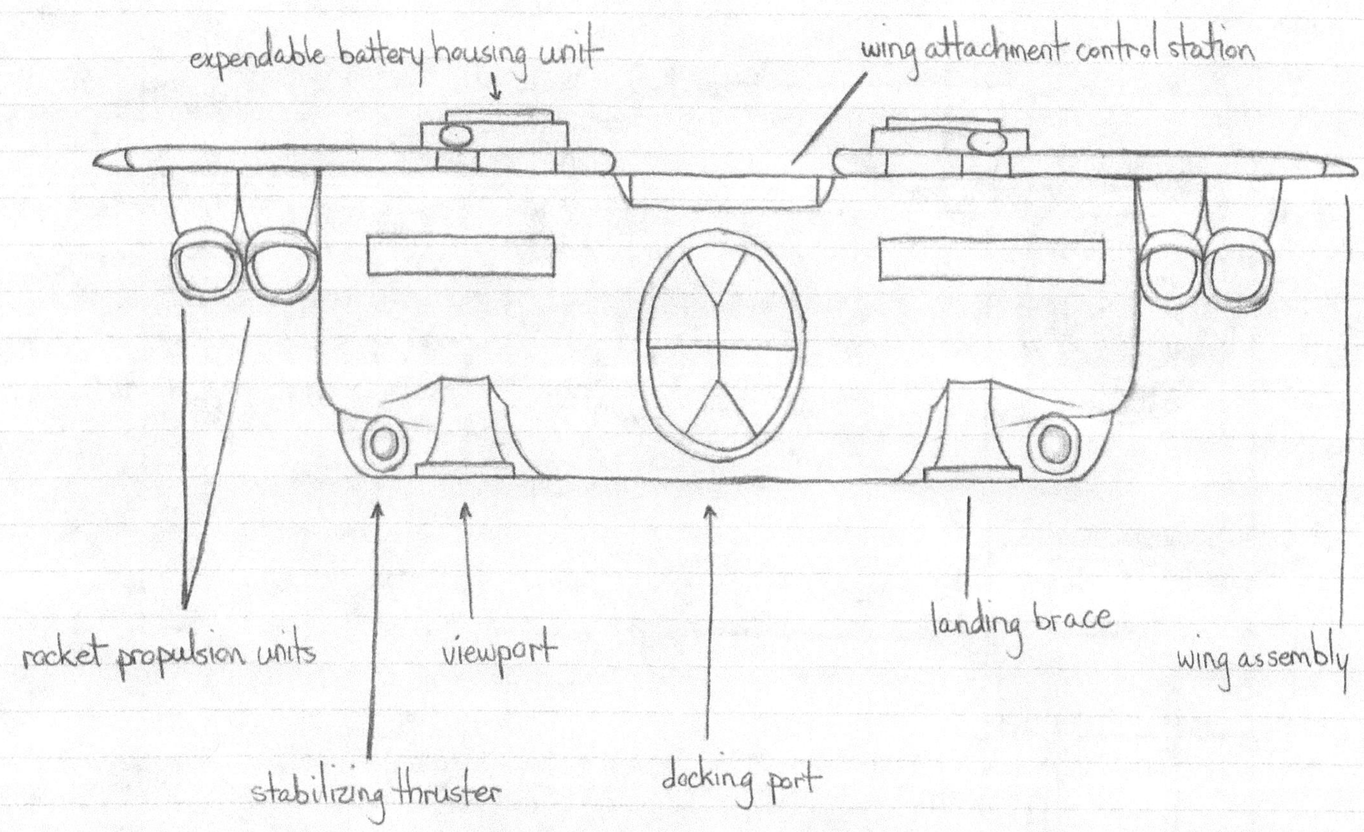

CUTAWAY: PASSENGER CHAMBER

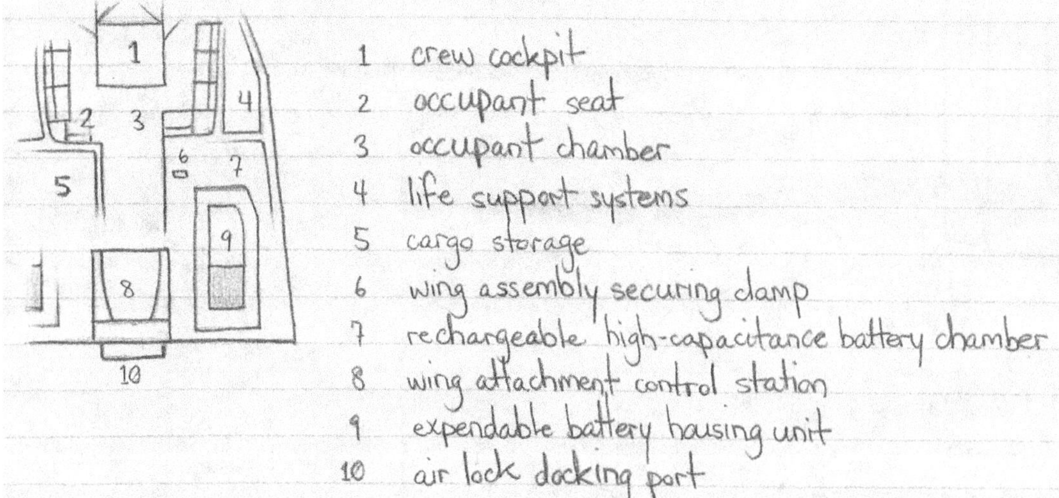

1   crew cockpit
2   occupant seat
3   occupant chamber
4   life support systems
5   cargo storage
6   wing assembly securing clamp
7   rechargeable high-capacitance battery chamber
8   wing attachment control station
9   expendable battery housing unit
10 air lock docking port

158

This craft's designer expected it to be smaller. *Lone Soldier* physics, however, made it the present size and internal configuration. It serves well as a military messenger vessel on several worlds, but it fares badly outside them. It is built with some of the highest-grade Dex Hox hull plating, so even unarmed it can get where it needs to go against most enemies. Other models are nearly capable of electromagnetic stealth while active and are the premier *Dircens Rirosaw* reconnaissance vessels. This ship features one of the varieties of propulsion developed after the Parasite War. Such an engine system is uncommon, but how many nearly-indestructible ships of such a small size would a person need?

This is one of the most distinctive examples of how I had to modify the basic design of the electromagnetic reciprocating turbines. This ship can't run long on electrical batteries, so it needs a generator compact enough to carry but with capacity to run the whole thing effectively. Short of a new energy source, the electromagnetic reciprocating turbines and variants thereof will remain the principal EM propulsion system of *Lone Soldier* craft. Another is a double helix, probably destined to become the standard design for large engines if sentients making it can develop a helix strand capable of withstanding the EM stresses of the reciprocating field and specialized enough to conduct a controllable current to outside capacity storage units. I haven't decided if they will or not, yet.

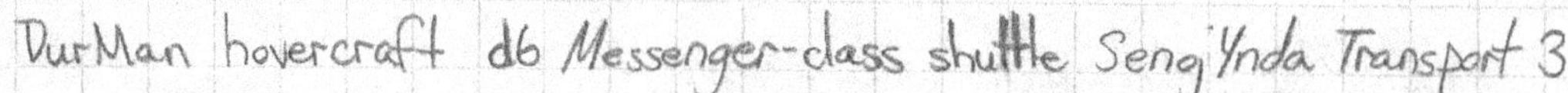

FIGURE 1   TOP VIEW

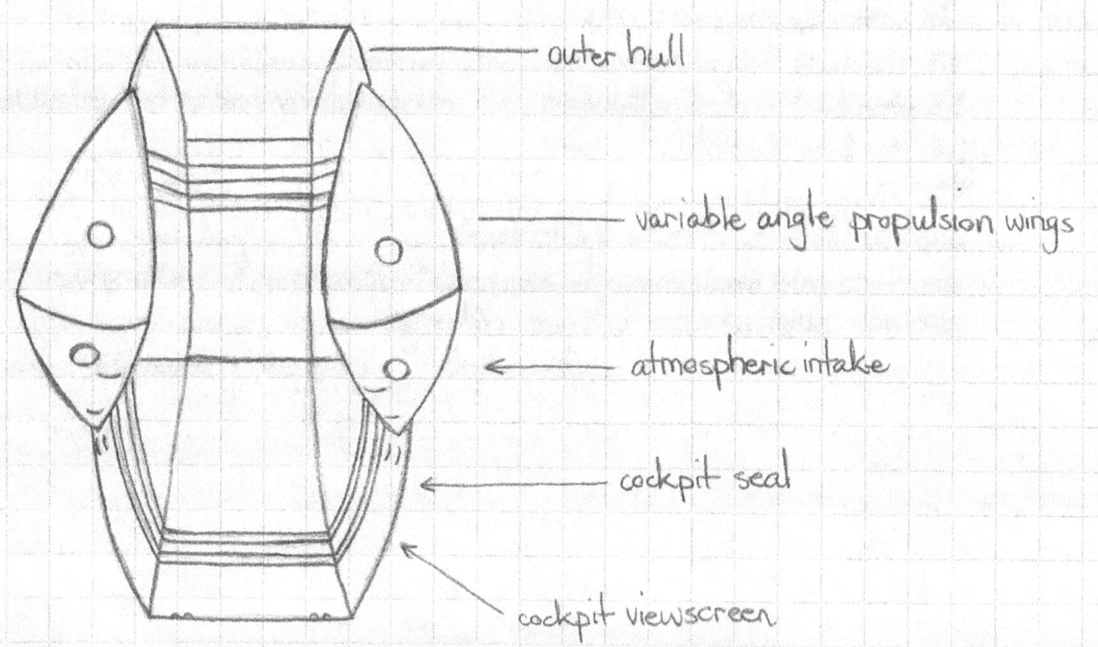

FIG. 2   FRONT VIEW

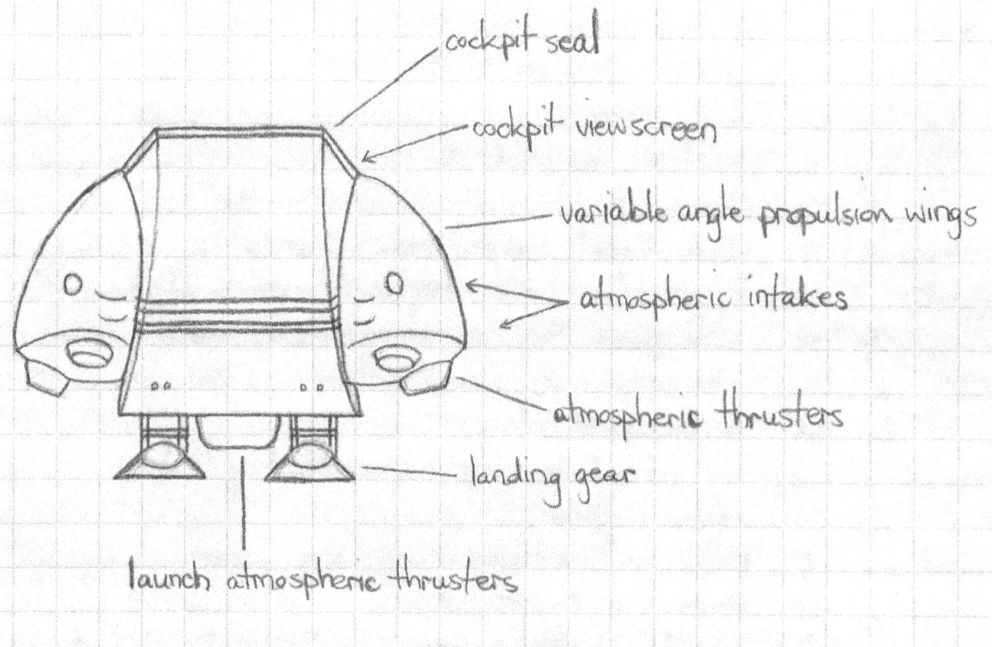

DurMan hovercraft shuttle *Senoj Ydna Transport 3*

CLASSIFICATION: Messenger-class hovercraft
TYPE: d6 DurMan Industries shuttle
CREW: pilot (possibly one passenger)
LENGTH: 3.5 standard Confederation feet
WIDTH: 1.3 standard Confederation feet (4.3 standard Confederation feet extended)
HEIGHT: 1.6 standard Confederation feet
MASS: 3,250 standard mass units
ARMOR: Dex Hox grade 6 military steetanicarb
ENGINES: one high-yield electromagnetic reciprocating turbine, four atmospheric thrusters
RANGE: 350,000 standard miles without recharging

CUTAWAY: VARIABLE ANGLE PROPULSION WING

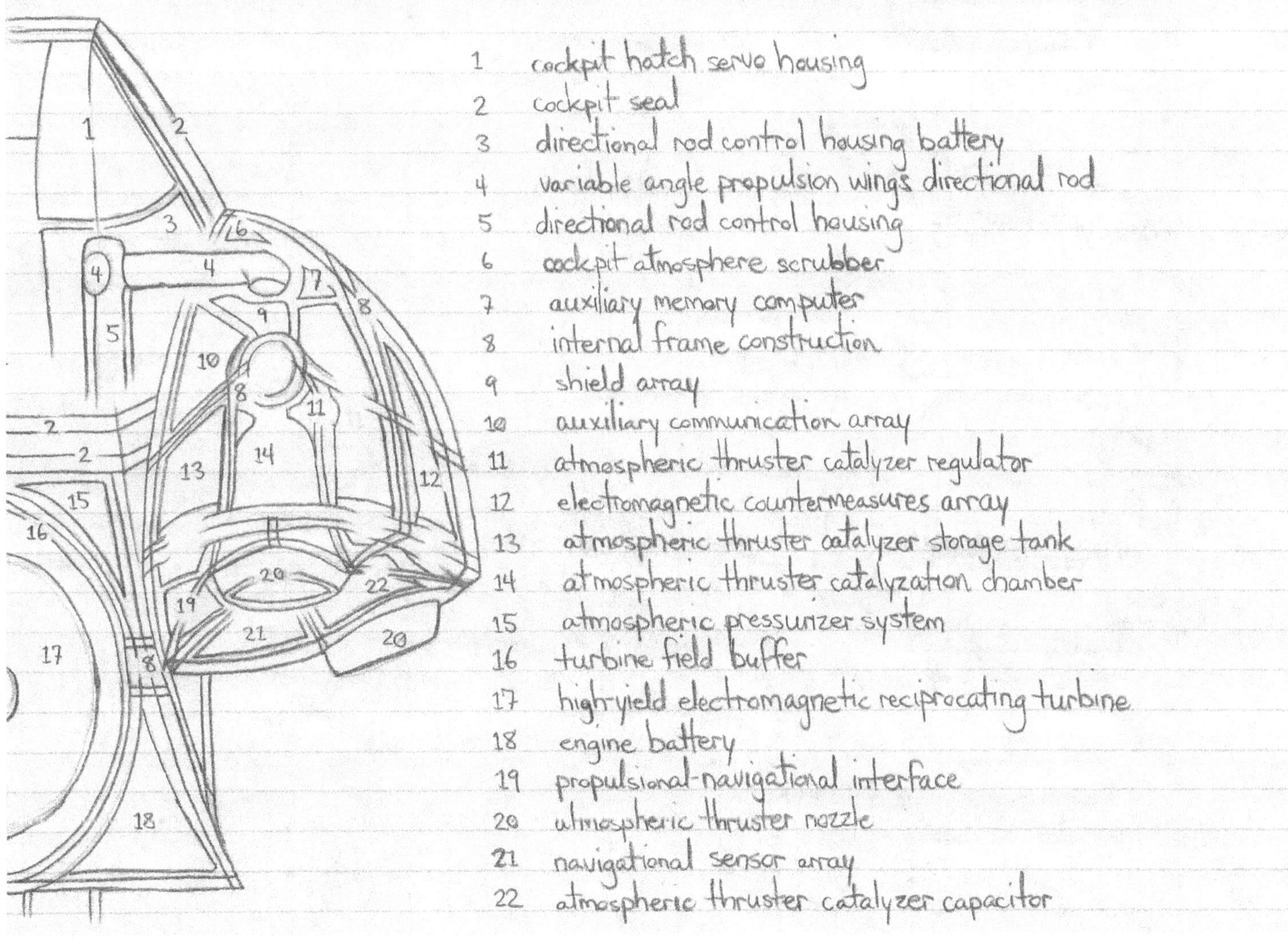

1	cockpit hatch servo housing
2	cockpit seal
3	directional rod control housing battery
4	variable angle propulsion wings directional rod
5	directional rod control housing
6	cockpit atmosphere scrubber
7	auxiliary memory computer
8	internal frame construction
9	shield array
10	auxiliary communication array
11	atmospheric thruster catalyzer regulator
12	electromagnetic countermeasures array
13	atmospheric thruster catalyzer storage tank
14	atmospheric thruster catalyzation chamber
15	atmospheric pressurizer system
16	turbine field buffer
17	high-yield electromagnetic reciprocating turbine
18	engine battery
19	propulsional-navigational interface
20	atmospheric thruster nozzle
21	navigational sensor array
22	atmospheric thruster catalyzer capacitor

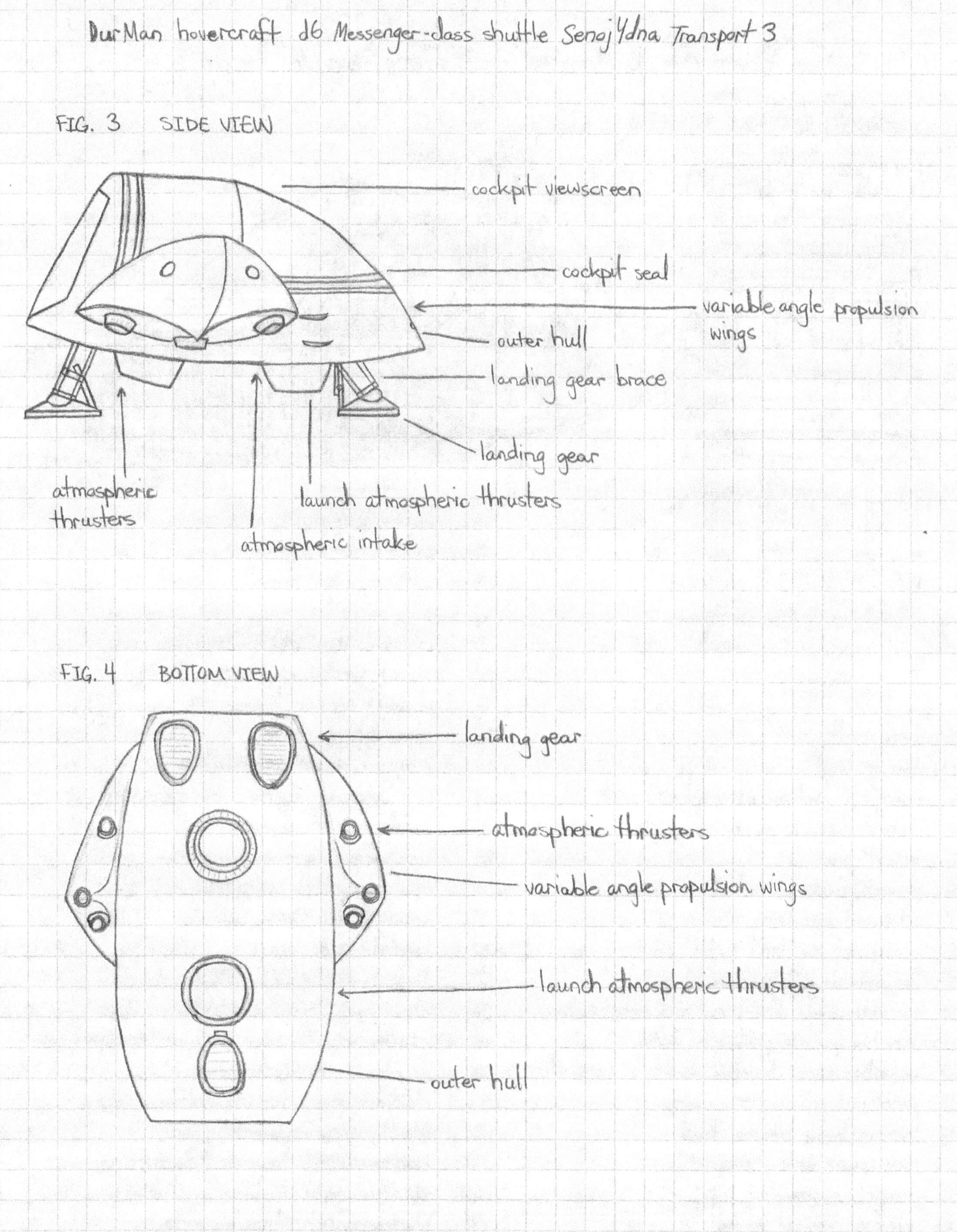

DurMan hovercraft d6 Messenger-class shuttle Senoj Ydna Transport 3

FIG. 3   SIDE VIEW

cockpit viewscreen
cockpit seal
variable angle propulsion wings
outer hull
landing gear brace
landing gear
atmospheric thrusters
launch atmospheric thrusters
atmospheric intake

FIG. 4   BOTTOM VIEW

landing gear
atmospheric thrusters
variable angle propulsion wings
launch atmospheric thrusters
outer hull

162

CUTAWAY: INTERIOR SYSTEMS

1	outer hull	18	engine battery
2	storage unit	19	pilot control panel displays
3	emergency cockpit atmospheric tank	20	cockpit viewscreen
4	fluid storage tank	21	pilot control device
5	cockpit seal	22	flight control panel computer bank
6	primary communication array	23	shield array
7	occupant securing straps	24	primary memory computer
8	occupant seating unit	25	atmospheric tank
9	variable angle directional rod	26	internal frame construction
10	variable angle directional rod crossbeam	27	self-destruct engine surge generator
11	variable angle propulsion wing	28	landing gear recession well
12	variable angle direction rod servo generator	29	cockpit seal control computer
13	artificial gravity regulator	30	ejection control computer
14	atmospheric intake duct	31	landing gear servo battery
15	occupant entry steps	32	landing gear brace
16	engine capacitor	33	launch atmospheric thruster nozzle
17	ejection control panel	34	atmospheric thruster catalyzer regulator
		35	atmospheric thruster catalyzer storage tank
		36	anti-gravity generator
		37	electromagnetic turbine buffer
		38	electromagnetic deionizing disc
		39	electromagnetic reciprocating turbine
		40	electromagnetic turbine anchor casing
		41	electromagnetic turbine axle

163

As a model for the Ehtadhh's Nosyd Disc, I thought it prudent to make a sketch of the standard solar collection power generator. The Confederation profits from manufacture, sale, and regulation of chemical fuels, nuclear material and rights, and recharge stations. Satellites like this orbit any medium-sized yellow star 0.4 to 0.6 AUs, and are made of much magnesium.

Electromagnetic reciprocating turbines are the region's core powerplant, equating to a perpetual motion machine. They harness energy by generating an EM storm. They require intermittent recharge to keep them from being rendered electromagnetically inert, or else it requires a hard jump-start likely to destroy the electronics of the whole ship. Recharge cables are attached via long conduits led into the engineering section.

I envision an extensive network of these around a few yellow stars, heavily guarded and probably without many or any orbiting bodies. The notable exception for this would be the Idermta System itself. Even after the Confederation falls, these solar recharge systems will probably remain in the same hands and organize themselves. Thus they can better try to avoid being seized or destroyed by the new factions.

Since I lapsed in making energy ships, I came up with a ship to sell electricity. There were ten of each Confederation energy ship in a line (*Charger 1*, *Static Spark 6*, et cetera), and when the ship could no longer be practically maintained it was replaced. Often this involved cannibalizing the previous namesake. This specific ship is the third craft bearing the name *Charger 3*. The dimpled surface is to improve atmospheric reentry, slightly.

Though there were several lines of energy ships during the Confederation energizing network… not that I can think of witty names for many… each ship broke down and was replaced at its own rate. The *Charger 3* could conceivably be the third generation of the name as the *Farad 8* is in its fourth. Odds are these energy ships travel between systems in groups while guarded by Confederation warships. They utilize a new concept evolving in the turbine's design, involving periodic acmes of electromagnetism. When the engineer harvests the energy and converts it for various usages, the output falls again. High-yield capacitors are essential, but not yet developed well enough for the attempts at punctuated double-helical reciprocating turbines. Theoretically they could be as productive with significantly less mass and maintenance.

Seoreh Ybedäm Photovoltaic Satellite SYS-S480

FIGURE 1   PROFILE VIEW

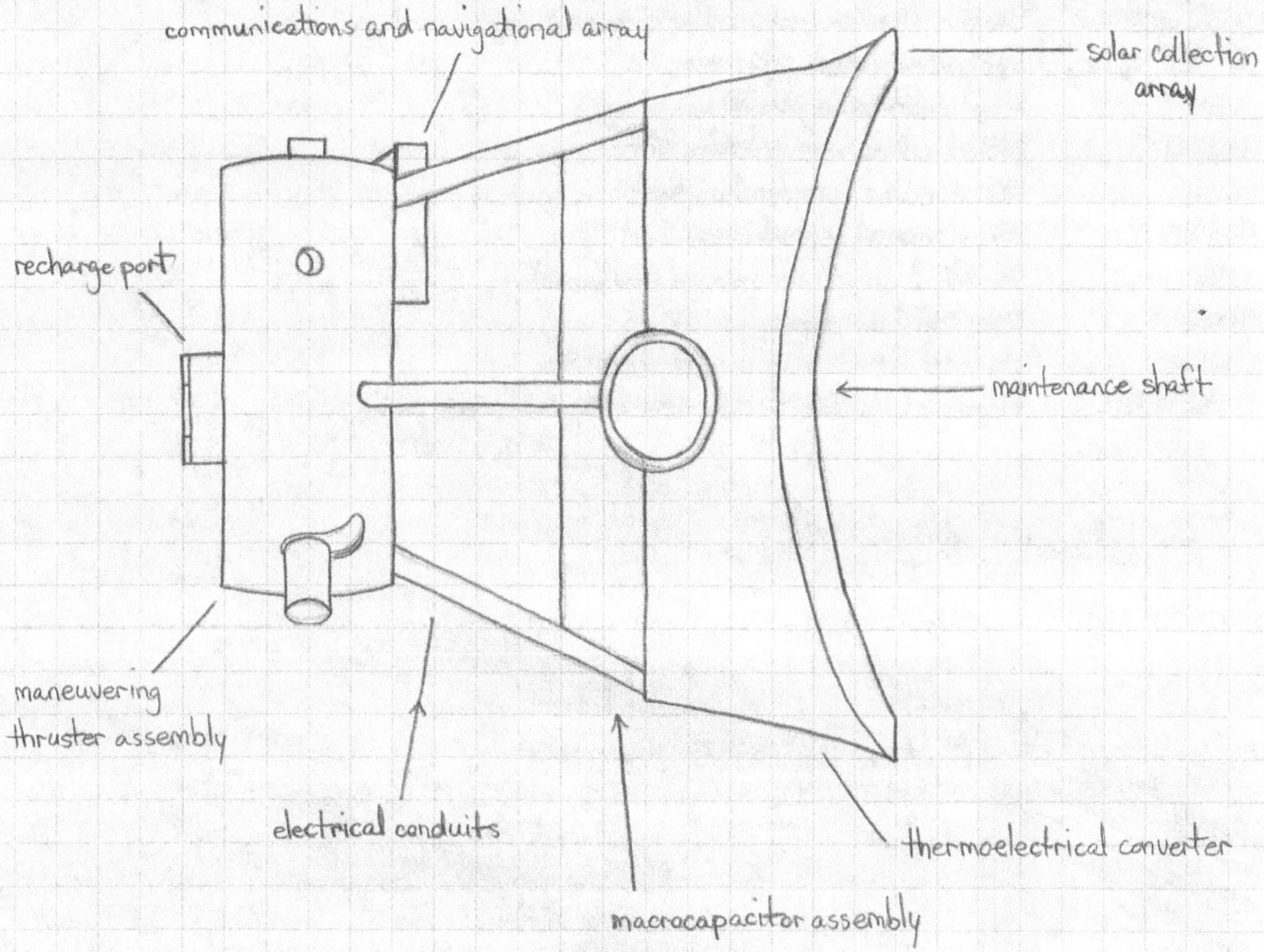

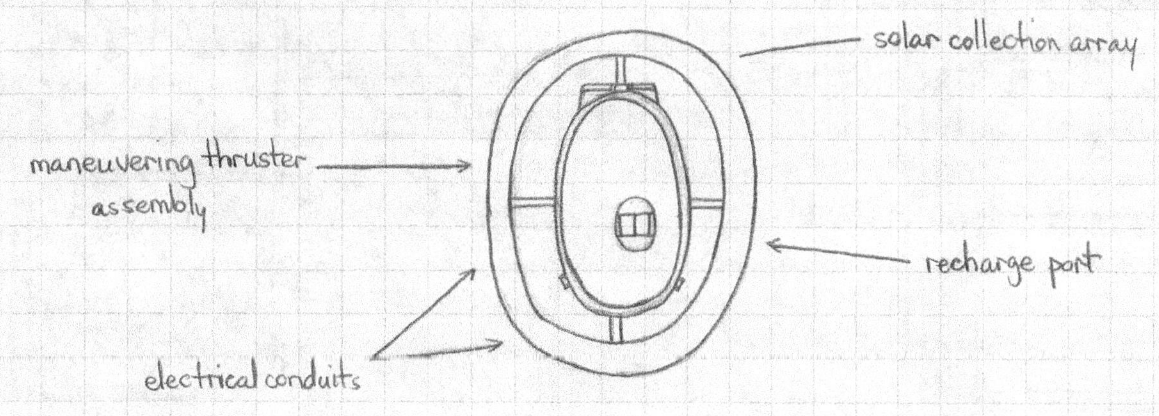

FIG. 2   APPROACH VECTOR

Seoreh Ybedam Photovoltaic Satellite SYS-S480

CLASSIFICATION: Seoreh Ybedam solar collection drone, Graslnh le-class
TYPE: automated power generator
CREW: three maintenance staff
LENGTH: 205 standard Confederation feet
WIDTH: 170 standard Confederation feet
HEIGHT: 200 standard Confederation feet
MASS: 78,500 standard mass units (fully fueled)
ARMOR: laser-resistant steetanicarb
ENGINE: chemical maneuvering thruster assembly
IMPLEMENTS: electrical macrocapacitor assembly, recharge port

CUTAWAY: INTERIOR SYSTEMS

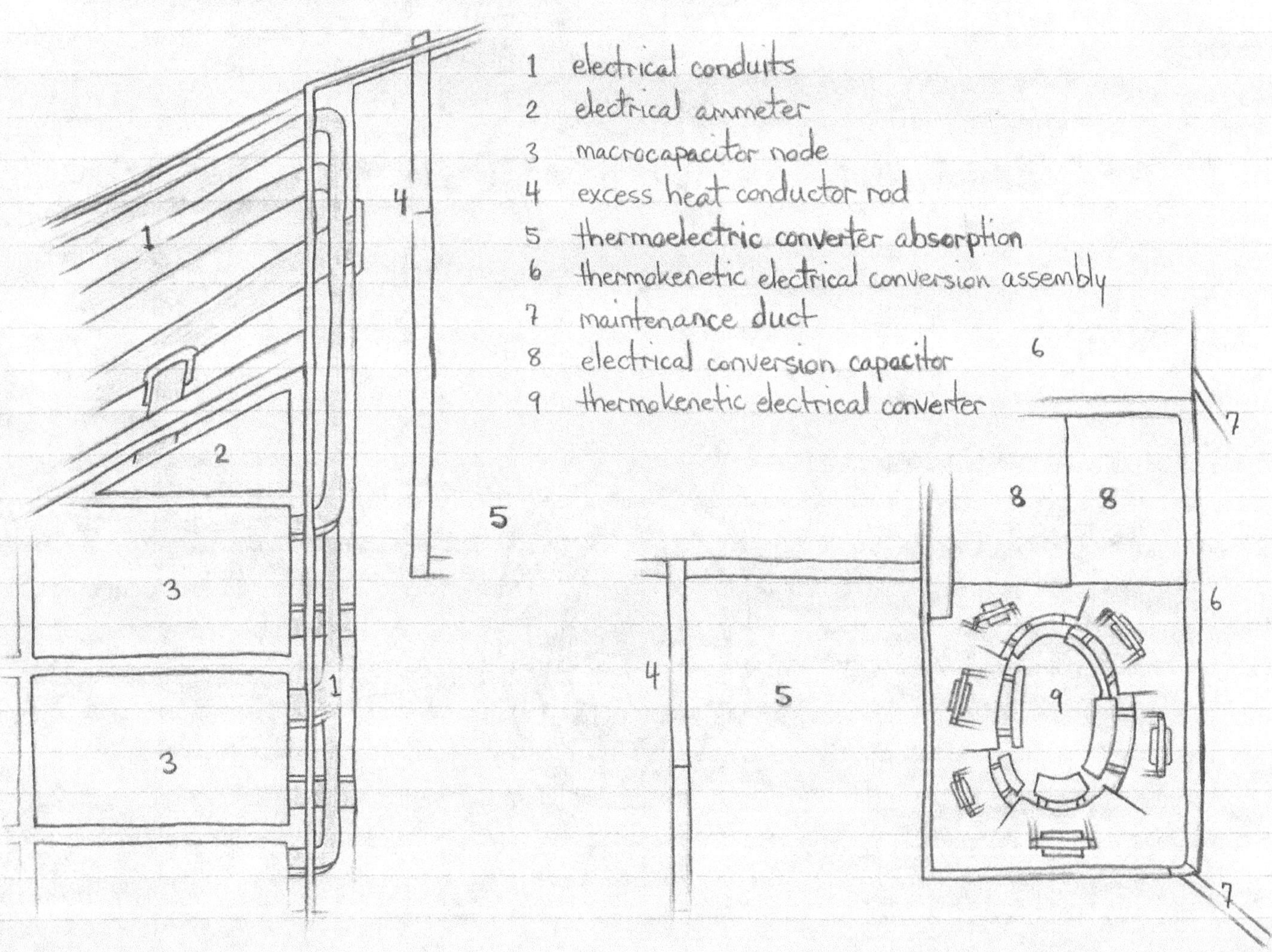

Seoreh Ybedäm Photovoltaic Satellite SYS-S480

CUTAWAY: MANEUVERING THRUSTER ASSEMBLY

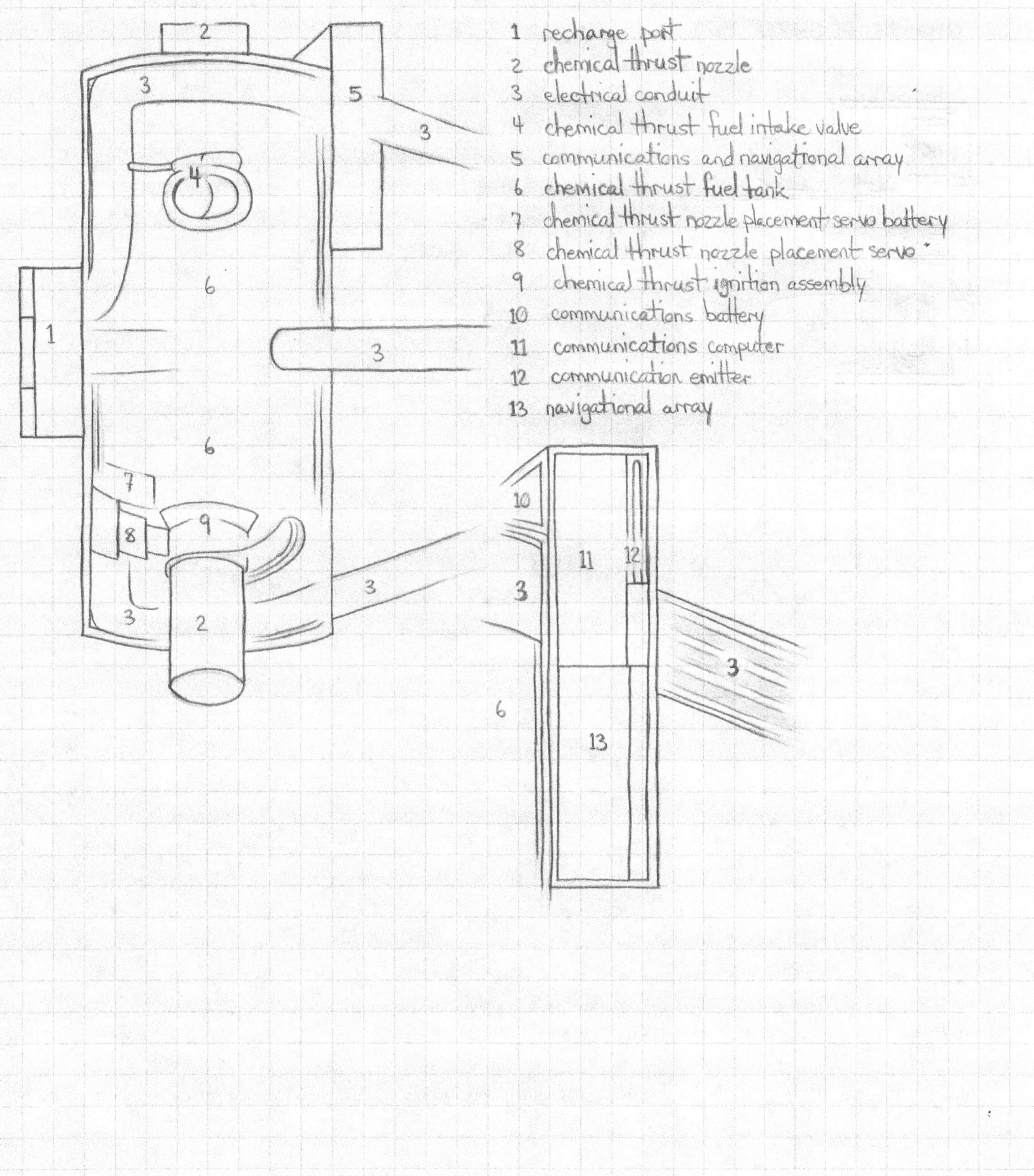

Seoreh Ybedäm Photovoltaic Satallite SYS-S480

CUTAWAY: RECHARGE PORT

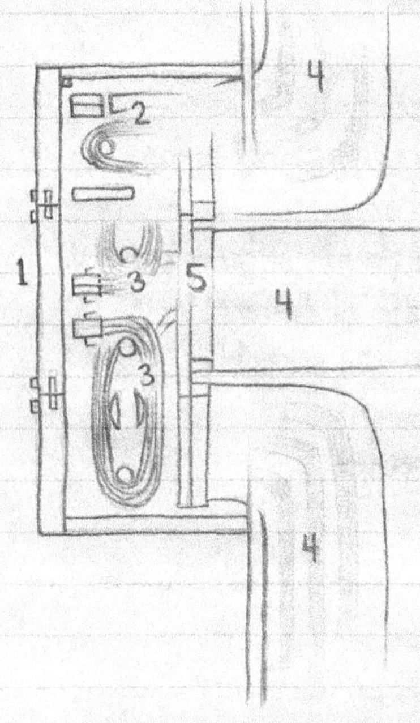

1 electrical outlet hatch cover
2 heavy voltage outlet assembly
3 mild voltage outlet assembly
4 electrical conduits
5 electrical adapter plates

Seoreh Ybedäm Energy Ship SYS-V128 Charger 3

FIGURE 1 SIDE VIEW

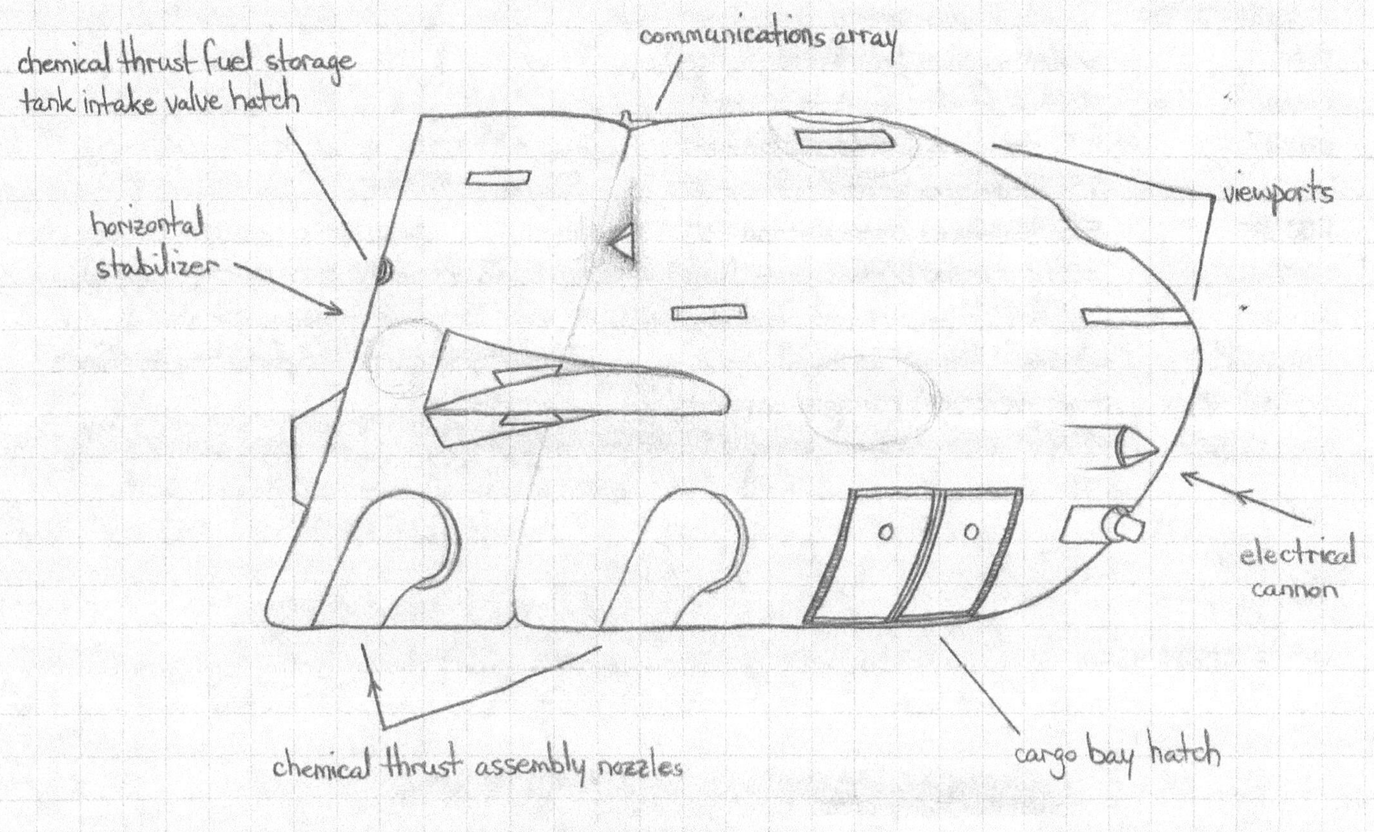

FIG. 2 FRONT VIEW

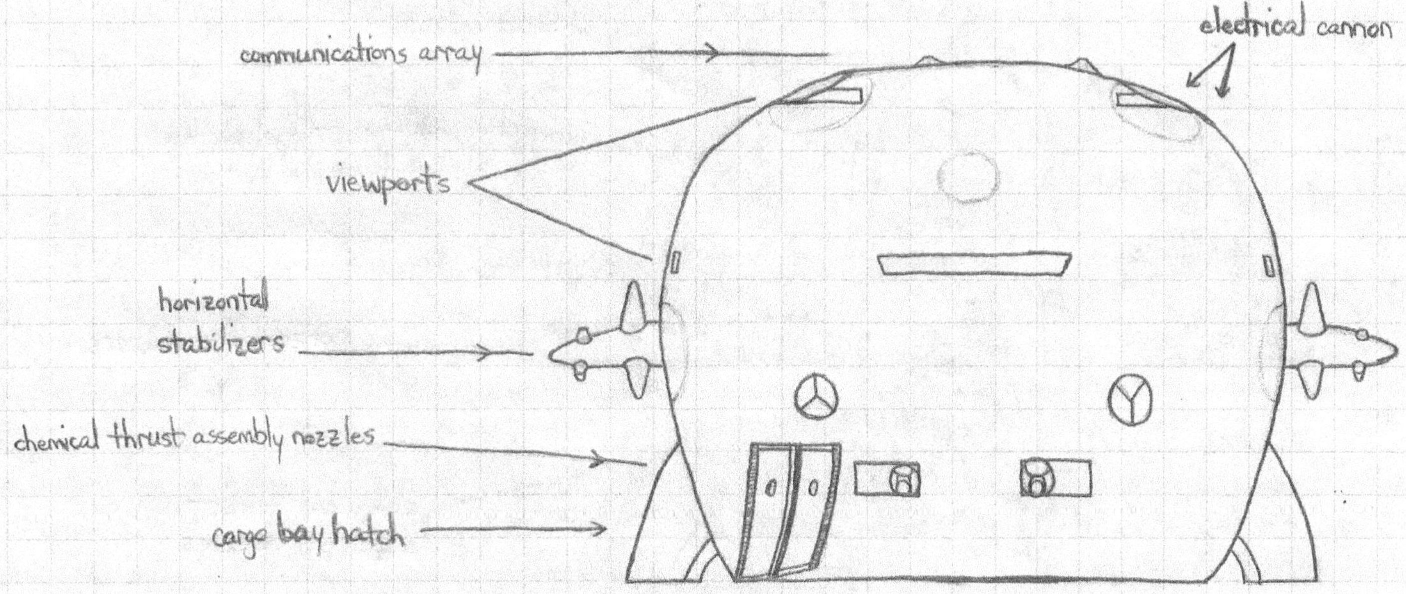

Seoreh Ybedäm SYS-V128

CLASSIFICATION: Seoreh Ybedäm energy ship, *Epjia-class*
TYPE: power regeneration vessel
CREW: 8 (two officers, four technicians)
LENGTH: 9.8 standard Confederation feet
WIDTH: 7.9 standard Confederation feet
HEIGHT: 5.5 standard Confederation feet
MASS: 33,372 standard mass units (unequipped), 16,172 standard mass units (equipped)
ARMOR: steetanicarb-reinforced steetanicrim alloy with 13-gen electromagnetic shields
ENGINES: chemical thrust assembly, two large-yield electromagnetic reciprocating turbines
ARMAMENT: four electrical cannon, capacity for twelve missiles
AMPLITUDE: 205,000,000 electrical units (683,806 statvolts) maximum electrical cannon yield,
                   381 macrocurrent units per minute (24 kilocoulombs) maximum recharge capacity

FIG. 3   REAR VIEW

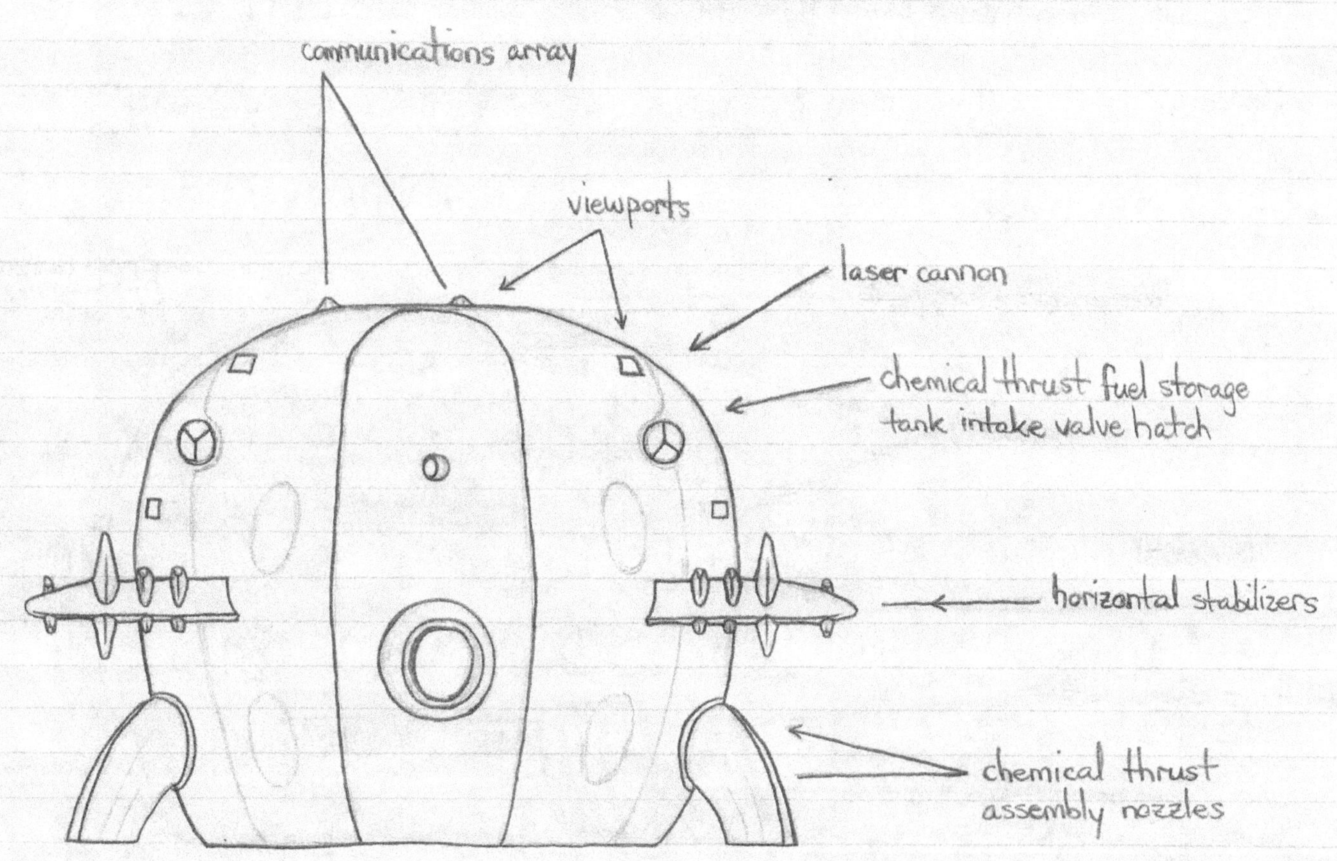

Seoreh Ybedäm Energy Ship SYS-V128 Charger 3

FIG. 4   TOP VIEW

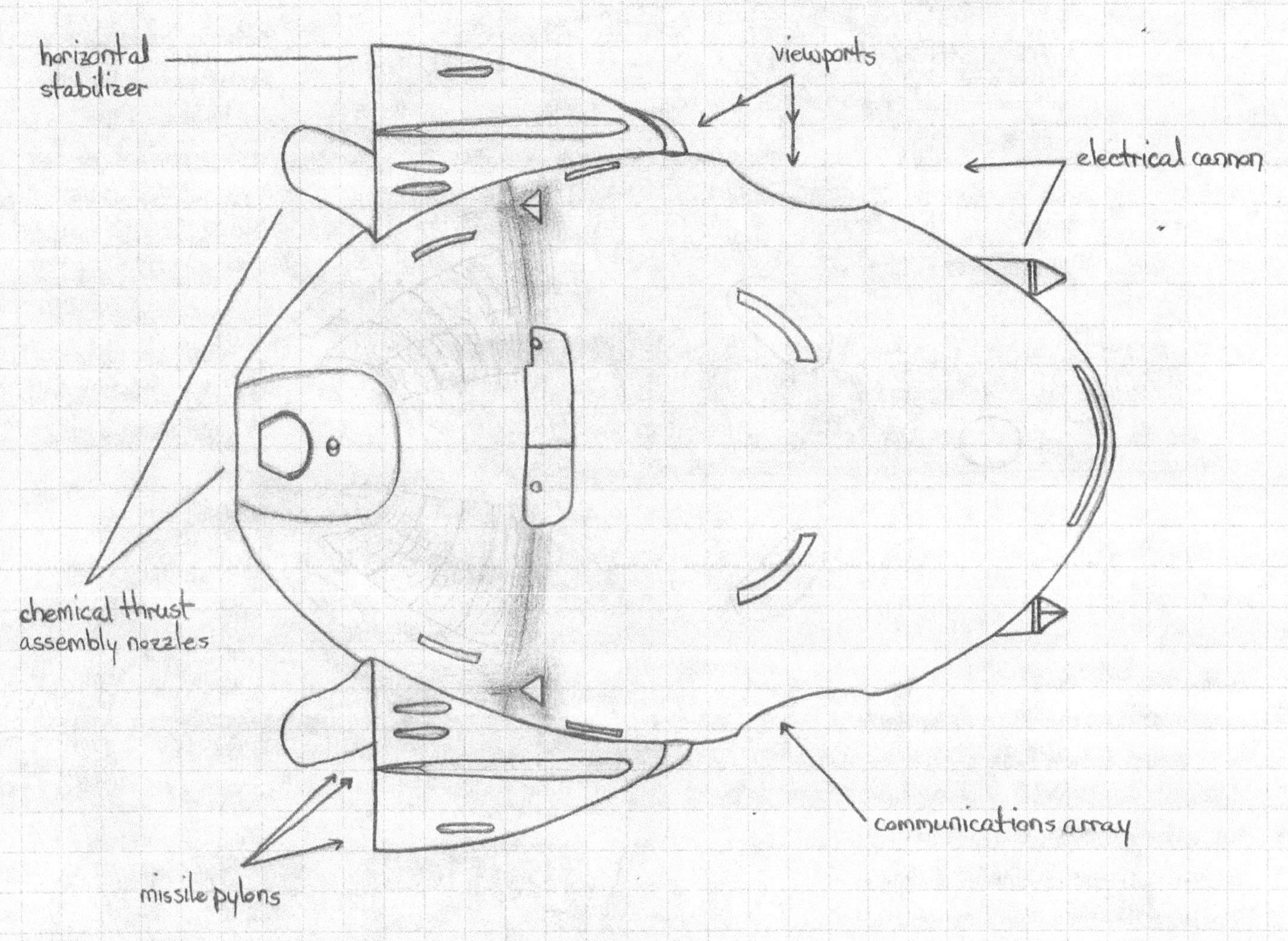

Seoreh Ybedäm Energy Ship SYS-V128 Charger 3

CUTAWAY: INTERIOR SECTIONS

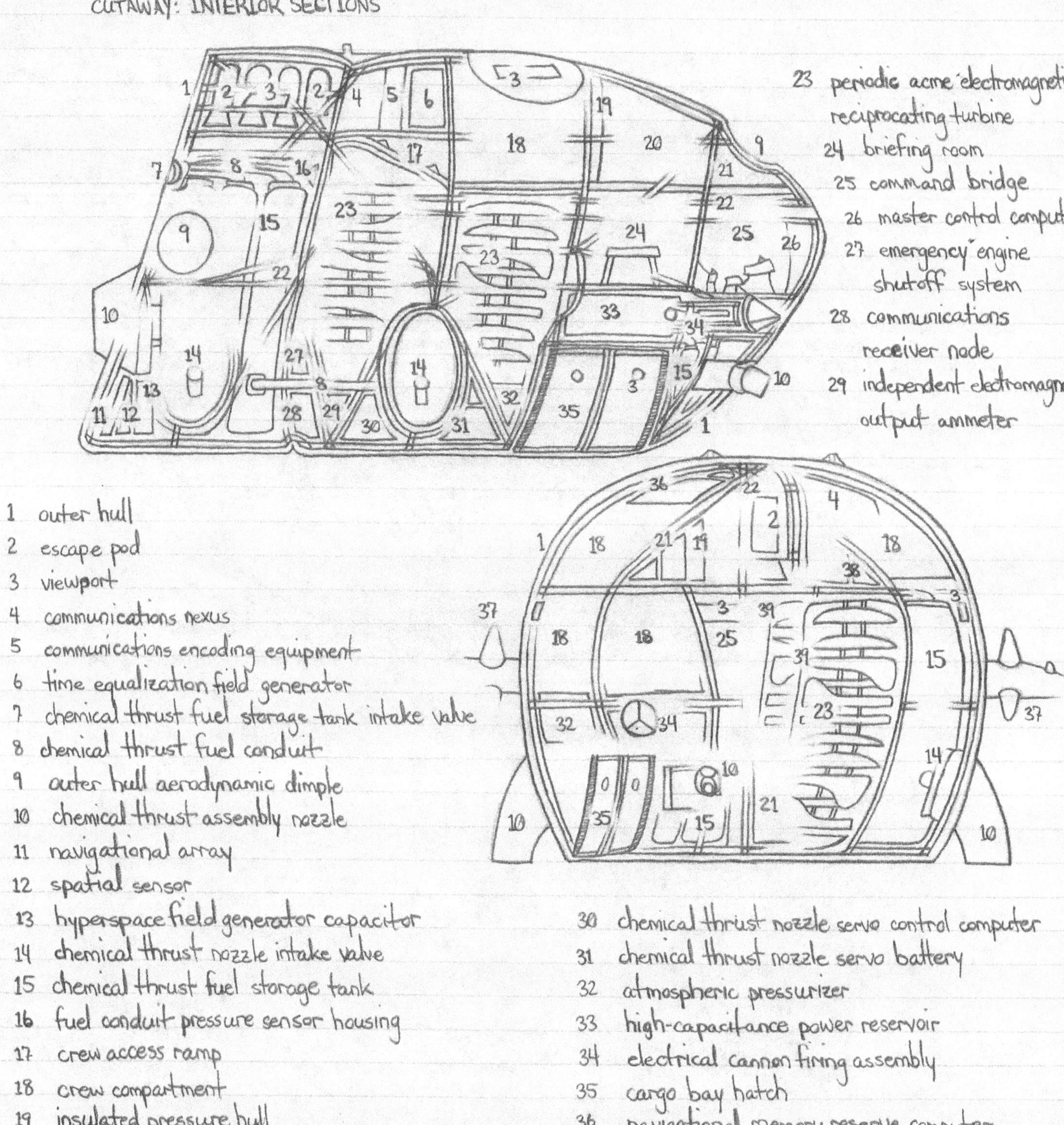

1 outer hull
2 escape pod
3 viewport
4 communications nexus
5 communications encoding equipment
6 time equalization field generator
7 chemical thrust fuel storage tank intake valve
8 chemical thrust fuel conduit
9 outer hull aerodynamic dimple
10 chemical thrust assembly nozzle
11 navigational array
12 spatial sensor
13 hyperspace field generator capacitor
14 chemical thrust nozzle intake valve
15 chemical thrust fuel storage tank
16 fuel conduit pressure sensor housing
17 crew access ramp
18 crew compartment
19 insulated pressure hull
20 power regulation chamber
21 electrical capacitor
22 internal frame construction

23 periodic acme electromagnetic reciprocating turbine
24 briefing room
25 command bridge
26 master control computer
27 emergency engine shutoff system
28 communications receiver node
29 independent electromagnetic output ammeter

30 chemical thrust nozzle servo control computer
31 chemical thrust nozzle servo battery
32 atmospheric pressurizer
33 high-capacitance power reservoir
34 electrical cannon firing assembly
35 cargo bay hatch
36 navigational memory reserve computer
37 horizontal stabilizer
38 atmospheric scrubber sensor array
39 electromagnetic buffer

172

<h1 style="text-align:center">Set 41:</h1>

Wealtrayd

There have to be interstellar RVs in the Confederation, so I made one like the Winnebago from *Spaceballs*. It is likely owned by a wealthy family and makes its hyperspace travel from commercial jump points. It is best suited for an intra-system tour, though.

I can imagine how the family arguments would go. One child wants to open a window. Both parents give the appropriate negative response. The child is perturbed but moves on. Later it says, "I have to use the bathroom."

When informed his sibling is in it, the child asks, "Can I flush it from here so he will be done sooner?"

"If you do, he will be VERY cold. Don't." The child laughs, remarking it would be funny. One of the parents replies, "Do you want to lose your allowance for the next four years?"

And for the parents, after the children: wouldn't you hate to find that crooked mechanic stuck out there in the Omzo System with this thing? "How much does a navigation sensor array cost these days, really?"

"How badly you want to get home there, rich boy?"

Hence the vacation from hell, as found in one of my short stories.

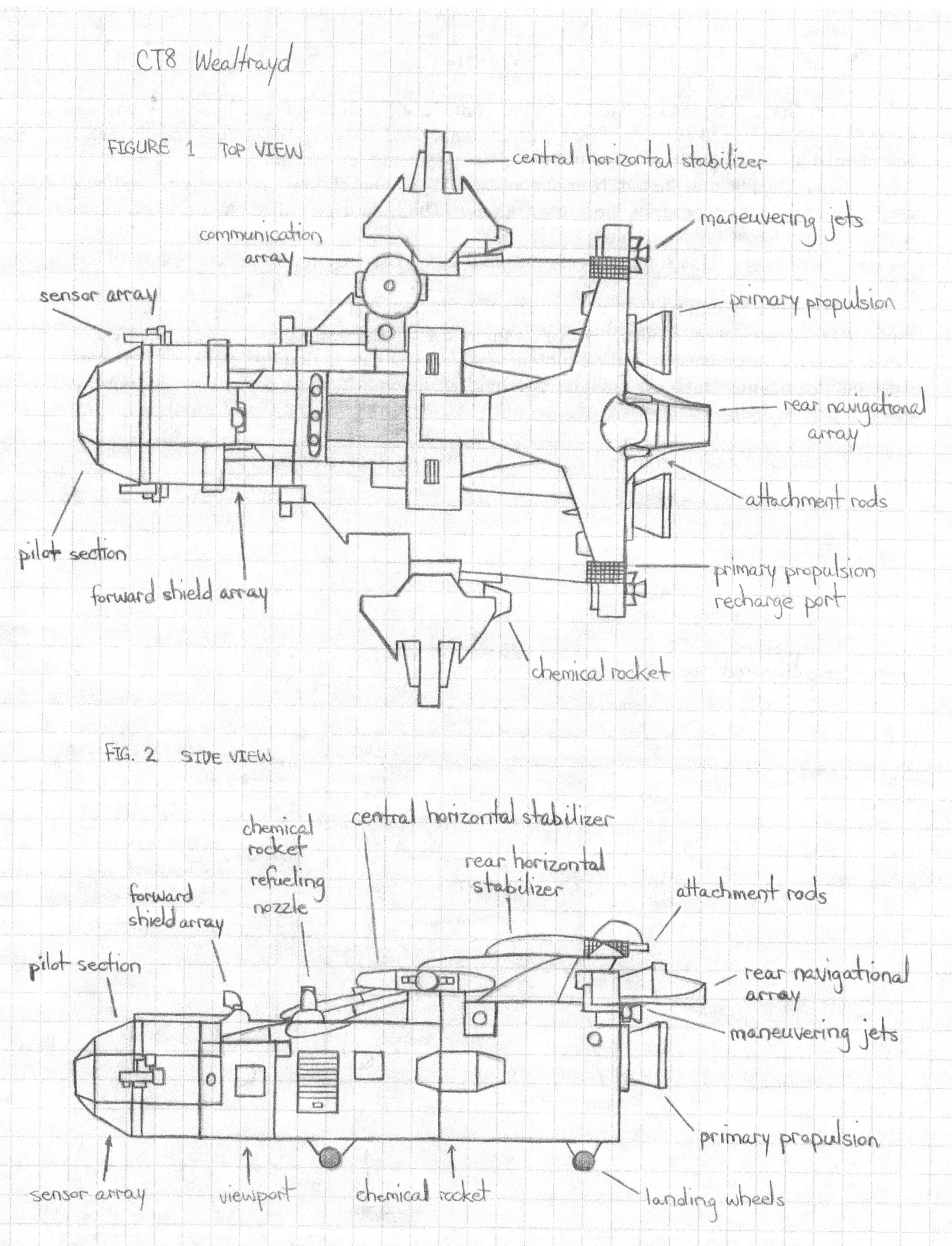

CT8 Wealtrayd

FIGURE 1   TOP VIEW

central horizontal stabilizer
maneuvering jets
communication array
primary propulsion
sensor array
rear navigational array
pilot section
attachment rods
forward shield array
primary propulsion recharge port
chemical rocket

FIG. 2   SIDE VIEW

chemical rocket refueling nozzle
central horizontal stabilizer
rear horizontal stabilizer
attachment rods
forward shield array
pilot section
rear navigational array
maneuvering jets
primary propulsion
sensor array
viewport
chemical rocket
landing wheels

174

CT8 Wealfrayd

CLASSIFICATION: small civilian transport
TYPE: privately-owned recreational courier
CREW: pilot (capacity for 4 Lynopte passengers)
LENGTH: 15.3 standard Confederation feet
WIDTH: 14.3 standard Confederation feet
HEIGHT: 6.8 standard Confederation feet
MASS: 21,387.5 standard mass units
ARMOR: pyroceramite-coated steetanicarb
ENGINES: two chemical rockets, high-yield ion generator
RANGE: 0.00073 5554 light-years (6,958,878,142 km/4,324,037,759 miles)

FIG. 3 FRONT VIEW

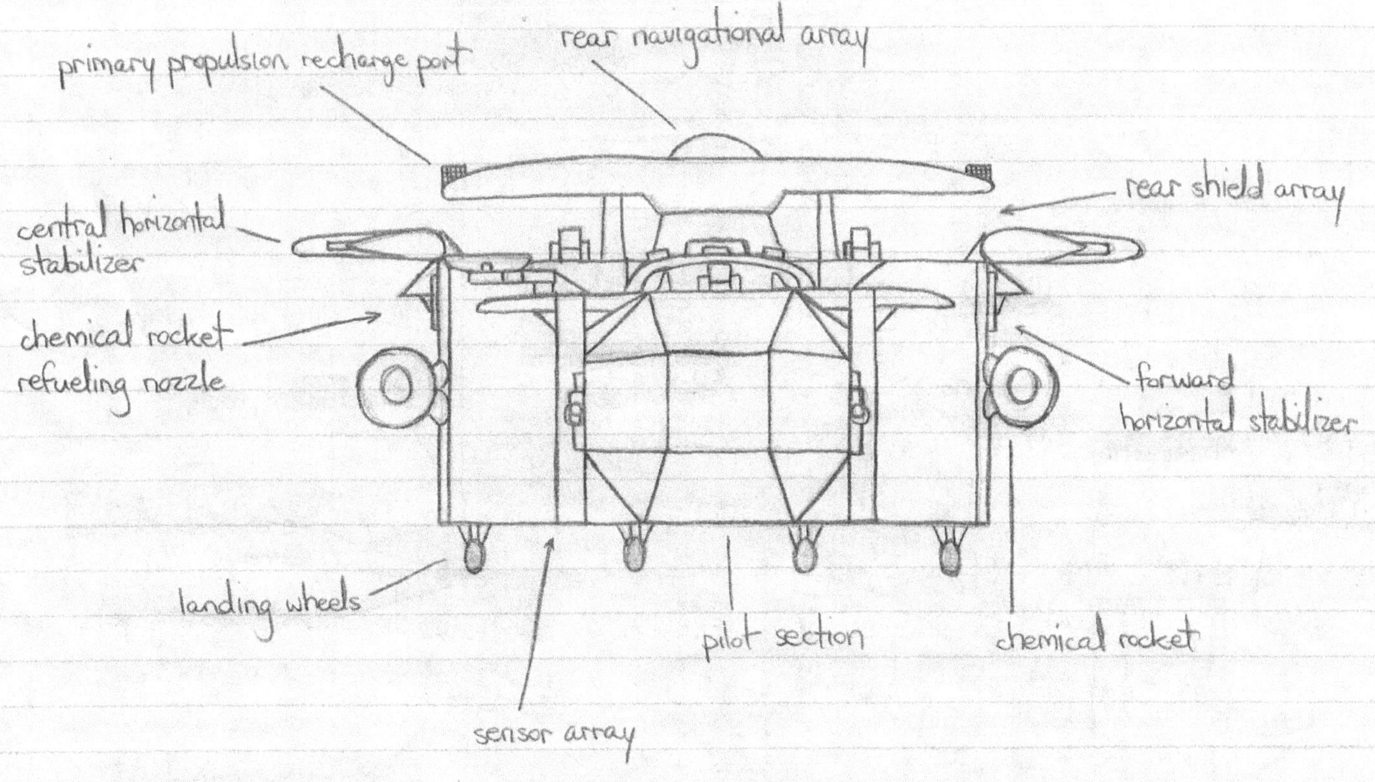

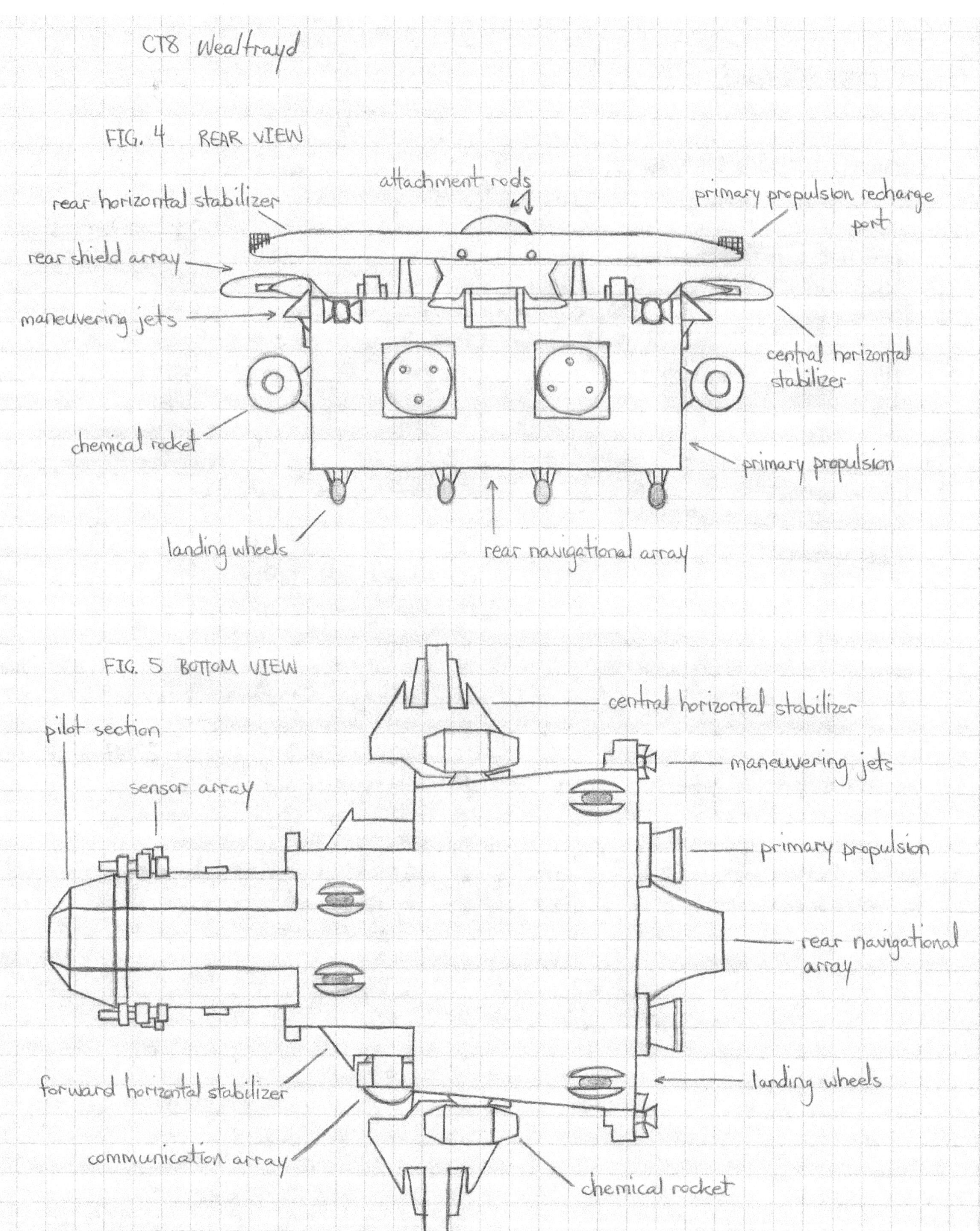

CT8 Wealfrayd
FIG. 4   REAR VIEW
rear horizontal stabilizer
attachment rods
primary propulsion recharge port
rear shield array
maneuvering jets
central horizontal stabilizer
chemical rocket
primary propulsion
landing wheels
rear navigational array
FIG. 5 BOTTOM VIEW
central horizontal stabilizer
pilot section
sensor array
maneuvering jets
primary propulsion
rear navigational array
forward horizontal stabilizer
landing wheels
communication array
chemical rocket

CT8 Wealfrayd

CUTAWAY: INTERIOR SYSTEMS

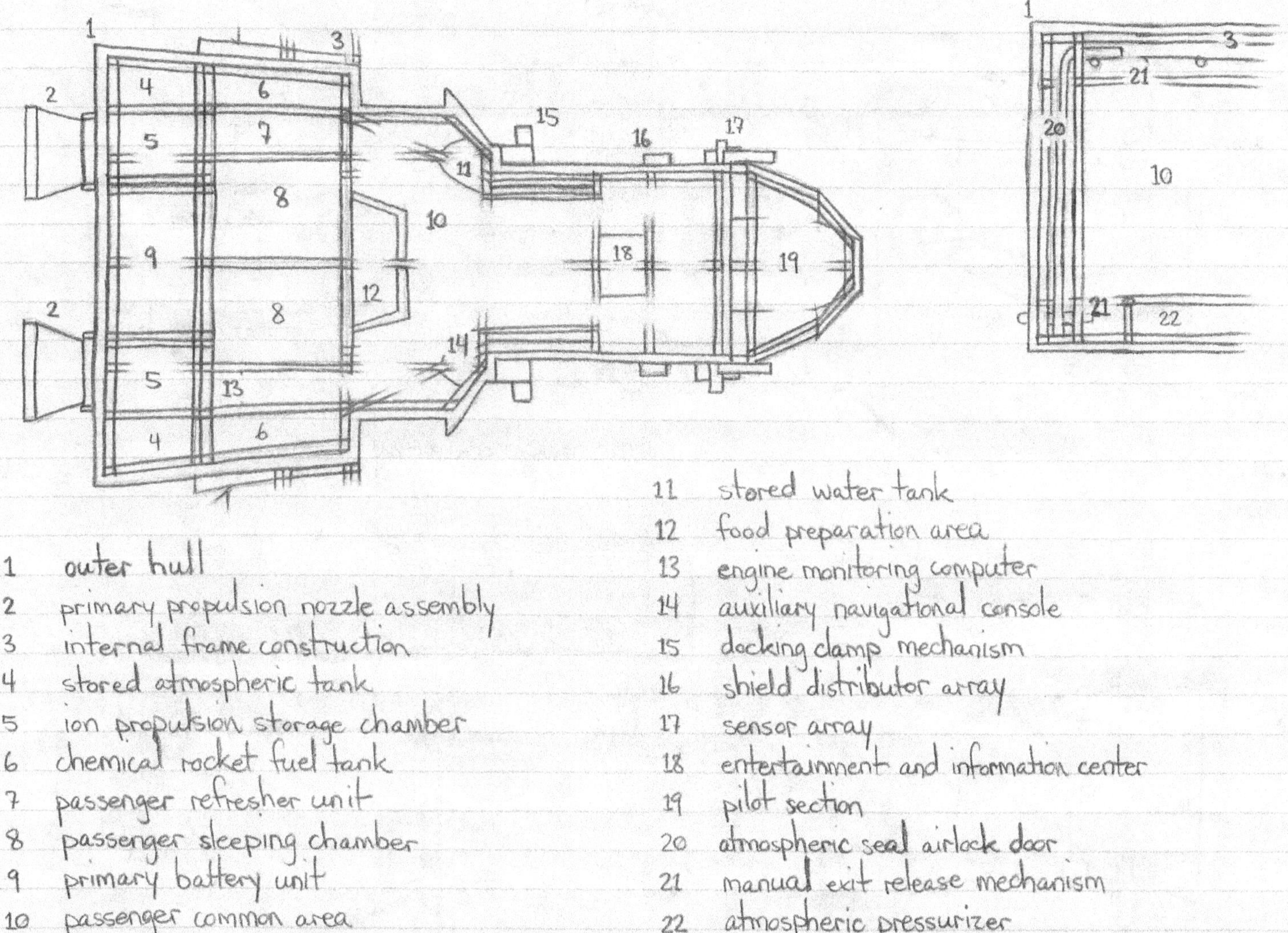

1   outer hull
2   primary propulsion nozzle assembly
3   internal frame construction
4   stored atmospheric tank
5   ion propulsion storage chamber
6   chemical rocket fuel tank
7   passenger refresher unit
8   passenger sleeping chamber
9   primary battery unit
10 passenger common area

11 stored water tank
12 food preparation area
13 engine monitoring computer
14 auxiliary navigational console
15 docking clamp mechanism
16 shield distributor array
17 sensor array
18 entertainment and information center
19 pilot section
20 atmospheric seal airlock door
21 manual exit release mechanism
22 atmospheric pressurizer

177

More Schematics

Find these other books of schematics by Reliĉ Kimah:

VOLUME I:
INTO PARASITIC RIVALRIES

VOLUME III:
THE STABILITY TO THE DISSOLUTION

www.ingramcontent.com/pod-product-compliance
Lightning Source LLC
Chambersburg PA
CBHW081515250726

48659CB00009B/2819